CHRISTIAN IDENTITY CRISIS

DO WE HAVE IT ALL WRONG?

J. William Smith

ISBN: 978-1-7333001-4-8
LCCN: 2025911626

KITSON BOOKS, LLC
P.O. Box 2886
East Liverpool, OH 43920
https://jwkitson.com
info@jwkitson.com

Book design by Forest City Publications

DEDICATION

To all those who seek the truth of God's revelation to us in His Word, which is Jesus Christ (Hebrews 1:1-2). I also dedicate this to those saints who seek to "make all men see what *is* the fellowship of the mystery, which from the beginning of the world hath been hid in God, who created all things by Jesus Christ" (Ephesians 3:9). May we all strive to "study to show ourselves approved unto God, a workman that needs not to be ashamed, rightly dividing the word of truth" (2 Timothy 2:15). Let us magnify the name of Jesus Christ as we present ourselves a "living sacrifice" for His use in this world.

TABLE OF CONTENTS

Acknowledgements — i

Why Is There So Much Confusion? — 1

A Blunder Often Overlooked — 47

An Overview of the Book of Acts and Why It Matters — 87

A Brief Journey Through Acts — 121

Unscriptural Assumptions — 185

"Know Ye Not..." — 215

God's Eternal Purpose — 245

The "One New Man" — 289

The Body or the Bride? — 343

Water Baptism: Should We or Should We Not? — 401

Rightly Dividing the End Times: Part One — 439

Rightly Dividing the End Times: Part Two — 485

Final "Thots" — 533

About the Author — 545

ACKNOWLEDGEMENTS

This book started over forty years ago when I first heard about the "revelation of the mystery" and "rightly dividing the word of truth." I had no clue that I would be spending numerous years compiling a book to help explain these simple, yet vital biblical concepts. They have changed my whole understanding of what God's will is for my life, and I've seen these same biblical principles conform others into "the image of Jesus Christ."

The book is lengthy because I wanted to directly quote as many Scripture references as possible into the text itself to help my readers grasp the doctrines being taught. In the thousands of hours I have researched and studied, there have been times when my thoughts were interrupted because I had to pause to look up a Bible reference, so I wanted to write a book that would provide ample evidence, in context, to help my readers grasp vital doctrines needed for a victorious Christian life.

The material will be very uncomfortable at times, especially for those who cling to the traditions they have always known. However, if all believers would allow the Holy Spirit to guide them, the Church could truly help transform the world, as it did in the first century under the apostles themselves. Thanks to the "traditions of men," we've drifted from the truth, and this book is dedicated to the purpose of rebuilding what has been lost. My desire is that we may "endeavor to keep the unity of the Spirit in the bond of peace," and by writing this book in "layman's terms," it is my desire that all readers can use the material in this book as a guide and reference for those times when "traditions attempt to rob us of truth."

CHAPTER 1

Why Is There So Much Confusion?

*I am crucified with Christ: nevertheless I live;
yet not I, but Christ liveth in me: and the life
which I now live in the flesh I live by the faith
of the Son of God, who loved me, and gave
himself for me. Galatians 2:20*

What is *Our* Identity in Christ?

We are "fearfully and wonderfully made," and God declared that He knew us "before the foundation of the world." Eventually, as Psalm 139 states, there came a time when He knit us together in our mothers' wombs and established the number of days we would have on Earth. Even with such wonderful truths about God's knowledge of us, we often find ourselves lacking in our knowledge of Him, leaving us wondering who we are, and what purpose God has for our lives. Yes, each of us has a specific reason for our existence, but Christian traditions have often stolen the wisdom we need to "walk worthy of the calling we have received" (Eph.4:1). When believers ignore essential doctrines associated with who we are "in Christ," we often find ourselves drifting throughout a vast ocean of uncertainty, often mired in secular ideologies.

This book was written to assist believers with their knowledge of basic biblical truths, because the sad reality is this: Believers have an identity crisis, and we have tens of thousands of denominations to prove this. Thankfully, there is a profound solution to this crisis, and it is my sincere prayer that the Holy Spirit, who is our true Teacher, will reveal it to you throughout the biblical passages found within this book. Remember, you are, after all, "fearfully and wonderfully made," so let us investigate our identity and purpose in Jesus Christ—the One who died and rose again for the entire world. After all, God knows what He is doing in and through us.

> *28 And we know that all things work together*
> *for good to them that love God, to them who*
> *are the called according to his purpose.*
> *Romans 8:28*

In Genesis 1:26, God said, "Let us make man in our *image*, after our *likeness*," and from "the dust of the earth," God made Adam (man), and so, the *human* experience began. Some doubt the existence of this historical Adam, but if he wasn't a real person, we are left to ponder why he appears in the genealogy of Jesus Christ (Luke 3), as well as the numerous references in the New Testament where all human beings are associated with Adam in the flesh (our Adamic nature). Even the typology used by the Apostle Paul (between Adam and Christ) is quite significant for understanding this identity all humans possess in the sight of God, who miraculously breathed *the breath of life* into Adam, and "he [Adam] became a living soul" (Gen. 2:7). We aren't just flesh; we are all a trinity: body, soul, and spirit, which means we, too, are eternal beings from the moment of our conception. That is when human development begins, regardless of our ideological persuasions.

Since Adam, every human ever conceived in this world has inherited his nature, and subsequently, we are under the curse of "the law of sin and death," regardless of our age. After all, we have cemeteries that proves this "law of sin and death," and each human will one day face the reality of this inevitable conclusion to our existence. There is, however, a merciful and gracious way to change the eternal outcome of this reality, and Paul reminds us of this truth in Romans.

> *23 For the wages of sin is death; but the gift of*
> *God is eternal life through Jesus Christ our*
> *Lord. Romans 6:23*

In our human nature, we are *spiritually* dead (Eph. 2:1; Col. 2:13), and if it were possible for us to live a righteous life in the flesh, Christ would have never needed to die in our place (Gal. 2:21). When we hear and respond in faith to the gospel, the Holy Spirit quickens us (makes us spiritually alive), and it is by personal faith in the redemption that is made available in Christ that we are fully saved from the eternal penalty of our sins. This is *now* given by grace, through faith, apart from any works we might perform. Grace is, after all, "the unmerited (unearned) favor of God."

> *8 For by grace are ye saved through faith; and*
> *that not of yourselves: it is the gift of God:*
> *9 Not of works, lest any man should boast.*
> *Ephesians 2:8-9*

The Greatest News

Thanks to God's amazing and gracious gift of eternal life, we *do not* have to be trapped within this Adamic nature (unless we choose to embrace it as our own identity). Adam was made in the image of God, and we are the offspring of Adam (after he sinned), and unfortunately, we were born with his fallen, sinful nature, which we, too, choose to consciously act upon. God did not *cause* sin; Adam *chose* it. Adam was once free to serve righteousness, but instead, he chose to serve sin, and it is no different for us. The Apostle Paul warns us about choosing to become slaves to sin.

> *16 Know ye not, that to whom ye yield*
> *yourselves servants to obey, his servants ye are*
> *to whom ye obey; whether of sin unto death, or*
> *of obedience unto righteousness? 17 But God*
> *be thanked, that ye were the servants of sin,*
> *but ye have obeyed from the heart that form of*
> *doctrine which was delivered you. 18 Being*
> *then made free from sin, ye became the*
> *servants of righteousness. Romans 6:16-18*

Had Adam remained sinless, as God made him, we would have been born with a sinless nature as well (Gen. 1:28). However, the "law of sin and death" became known to Adam once he had "fallen from grace," but thankfully this led to a miraculous promise in Genesis 3 regarding Christ's future triumph over death. After the serpent beguiled Eve in the Garden of Eden, God stated:

> *15 And I will put enmity between thee and the woman, and between thy seed and her seed; it shall bruise thy head, and thou shalt bruise his heel. Genesis 3:15*

God's Redemptive Plan to Restore Humanity

Thankfully, all our sins were eventually imputed (credited) to Christ on the cross, and once we *personally* place our faith (trust) in His shed blood as payment for our *own* sins, God imputes (credits) His righteousness to us (2 Corinthians 5:21). When Christ was raised from the dead, this proved to us that God was satisfied with the sacrifice Christ did on our behalf (Rom. 4:25). This is God's complete work of redemption for us (John 19:30). To many, this plan of redemption is "foolishness" (I Cor. 1:18), even though it comes at no cost to all (Rom. 3:24). God, due to His holiness, does not simply pardon sinners; He fully pays the penalty Himself, declaring us "not guilty" in His sight. If this still offends you, then I suspect you would rather embrace your own standard of wisdom and righteousness rather than embrace God's. This is our choice, of course.

We are all born "in Adam," but thankfully, God's grace is given freely to us through faith in Christ's death and resurrection on our behalf, and we can be baptized *by* one Spirit and placed "into Christ, wherein we stand" (Romans

5:1-2; I Cor. 12:13). It is the "quickening of the Spirit" that takes us from death to life because the "law of sin and death" has now been replaced with "the law of the Spirit of life [that is] in Christ Jesus" (Rom. 8:1-2). Thankfully, God loves us, and because Christ died for us, we have the opportunity to have a new identity *in Him*, which is eternally secure in *heavenly places in Christ* (Eph. 1:3; 2:6). Remember, life is a miracle—*you* are a miracle—and God's love and redemptive plan through Jesus Christ for humanity is the greatest gift we could ever possess. Graciously, it is offered *at no cost* to anyone who *personally* places their faith in the redemption (freedom by payment of a price) available through Jesus Christ. He finished all that was necessary to save us, even though many believers feel they must add to this already completed, redemptive plan. Remember, salvation is offered at no cost to us.

> *[24] Being justified freely by his grace through*
> *the redemption that is in Christ Jesus:*
> *Romans 3:24*

This redemptive plan was necessary because humanity is totally incapable of immortality through our own efforts. Yes, there are also many people who are convinced they have done "too many bad things" for God to forgive them; however, sin is not as powerful as God's grace.

> *Therefore being justified by faith, we have*
> *peace with God through our Lord Jesus*
> *Christ: [2] By whom also we have access by faith*

> *into this grace wherein we stand, and rejoice*
> *in hope of the glory of God... [19] For as by one*
> *man's disobedience many were made sinners,*
> *so by the obedience of one shall many be made*
> *righteous. [20] Moreover the law entered, that*
> *the offence might abound. But where sin*
> *abounded, grace did much more abound:*
> *[21] That as sin hath reigned unto death, even so*
> *might grace reign through righteousness unto*
> *eternal life by Jesus Christ our Lord. Romans*
> *5:1-2 and 19-21*

Justified Freely by His Grace

The *greatest* news is this: The world's sins were paid for already, and *through faith* in Christ's redemption (freedom by payment of a price), we are not only forgiven, but we *can now be* justified (declared righteous) in Christ "by grace, *through faith*" (Eph. 2:8-9) in His death and resurrection, which was done on our behalf. Today, *religion* demands works (by us) to receive salvation, but "the gift of God is eternal life through Jesus Christ our Lord" (Rom. 6:23), and any payment needed for this gift was already paid for on the cross. You can't earn salvation today—just accept it as a gift through faith in the work of redemption done already by Jesus.

Regrettably, many won't place their faith in Jesus Christ because of pride and ignorance of this blessed truth, and as a result, they are not *justified* (declared righteous) in the sight of God. Many seek to find some other means to bring about their own righteousness, but they will always fall short of

God's holiness and glory (Rom. 3:23) because they have not placed their faith in the only redemption made available for the entire world, which was the death of Jesus Christ.

Our Savior was "raised for our justification" (Rom. 4:25), and this means that God was completely satisfied with the sacrifice (atonement) Jesus completed for us (Rom. 3:24-26). The resurrection was God's receipt, which guarantees that our sins were "paid in full." God reconciled Himself to the world, but individuals in this world must reconcile themselves to Him *through faith* in the death and resurrection of Jesus Christ. Yes, the sins of the *entire* world have been fully paid, but humanity must be justified *through faith* in the redemption made available through Christ Jesus. You can choose to either place your faith in what has already been done on your behalf, or you are left to trust in yourself to satisfy a debt for which you can never fully pay on your own.

Paul clearly taught these truths in the following passages:

> *19 To wit, that God was in Christ, reconciling the world unto himself, not imputing their trespasses unto them; and hath committed unto us the word of reconciliation [restored to fellowship]. 20 Now then we are ambassadors for Christ, as though God did beseech you by us: we pray you in Christ's stead, be ye reconciled to God. 21 For he [God] hath made him [Jesus] to be sin for us, who knew no sin; that we might be made the righteousness of God in him. 2 Corinthians 5:19-21*

*3 For this is good and acceptable in the sight
of God our Saviour; 4 Who will have all men to
be saved, and to come unto the knowledge of
the truth. I Timothy 2:3-4*

One of Two Choices

As I previously mentioned, there are two *eternal* natures (identities) humans can have in the sight of God today, and both Romans 5 and I Corinthians 15 offer insight into each of them.

*12 Wherefore, as <u>by one man</u> sin entered into
the world, and death by sin; and so death
passed upon all men, for that all have sinned:
Romans 5:12*

*21 For since by man [Adam] came death, by
man [Christ] came also the resurrection of the
dead. 22 For as <u>in Adam</u> all die, even so <u>in
Christ</u> shall all be made alive.
I Corinthians 15:21-22 (brackets by author)*

There are many identities we might personally choose to embrace in this life, but again, God will either declare us to be "in Adam" or "in Christ" when He righteously judges the world "in the ages to come." Adam was made to live forever, but his sin brought death to himself, as well as all those who are descendants of him, which is the entire human race. According to Psalm 51:5, like David, we are also "…shapen in iniquity; and in sin did my mother conceive me."

The result of Adam's sin is what has led all humans to be at enmity (in opposition) to God. The "first Adam" brought the "law of sin and death" upon all, but the "Second Adam" brought life and immortality through His faithfulness, along with our faith in what He has done for us. Again, we now have a new law: "the law of the Spirit of life in Christ Jesus," which has "made me (us) free from the law of sin and death" (Rom. 8:2). Thanks to this gospel of the grace of God, we now know God has offered salvation to the human race, especially to those who believe Christ died for them and was raised again for their justification (Rom. 4:25; I Tim. 4:10). The simplicity of the gospel for today is summed up in the following verses:

> *Moreover, brethren, <u>I declare unto you the gospel which I preached unto you</u>, which also ye have received, and <u>wherein ye stand;</u> 2 By which also ye are saved, if ye keep in memory what I preached unto you, unless ye have believed in vain. 3 <u>For I delivered unto you first of all that which I also received, how that Christ died for our sins according to the scriptures; 4 And that he was buried, and that he rose again the third day according to the scriptures</u>:*
> *I Corinthians 15:1-4*

By God's grace (a divine favor we cannot earn), we have been provided *the way* to be restored to fellowship (reconciled) to God, and through Christ, we are no longer at enmity with God. He has removed this hostility between Himself and humanity through faith in the shed blood of Christ.

> *13 <u>But now</u> in Christ Jesus ye who sometimes*
> *were far off are made nigh <u>by the blood of</u>*
> *<u>Christ</u>. 14 For he is our peace, who hath made*
> *both one, <u>and hath broken down the middle</u>*
> *<u>wall of partition between us</u>; 15 <u>Having</u>*
> *<u>abolished in his flesh the enmity, even the law</u>*
> *<u>of commandments contained in ordinances</u>; for*
> *to make in himself of twain one new man, so*
> *making peace; 16 And that he might reconcile*
> *both unto God in one body <u>by the cross</u>,*
> *<u>having slain the enmity thereby</u>: Eph. 2:13-16*

> *21 For he [God] hath made him [Christ] to be*
> *sin for us, who knew no sin; that we might be*
> *made the righteousness of God in him.*
> *2 Corinthians 5:21 (brackets by author)*
> *22 And almost all things are by the law purged*
> *with blood; and without shedding of blood is*
> *no remission. Hebrews 9:22*

As glorious as these passages are, we must admit that a holy, righteous God is not obligated to redeem us from our old nature "in Adam," especially since we freely and willingly exercise the "deeds of the flesh" every day, even celebrating these deeds at times (Rom. 1:32). Romans 3:23 is clear: "For all have sinned and come short [continually] of the glory [goodness] of God." We often ignore God's love, mercy, and grace because we choose to cleave to the things we love in this world, especially the choice to sin, which is falling short of God's righteous standard. As I stated, God knows that sin leads to death, but He offers the gift of eternal life to us (through Jesus Christ).

The Mystery Regarding Salvation for Today

Salvation has, in essence, always been by grace, through faith; however, has God *always* proclaimed that faith in the shed blood and resurrection of Jesus Christ was the means of salvation? Did the Old and New Testament saints (Abraham, Moses, David, etc.) know this means of salvation prior to Jesus Christ revealing it to the Apostle Paul *beginning* with his conversion in Acts 9? Many believers assume there has only been one salvation gospel preached throughout the entire Bible, so are we not forced to wonder what the Apostle Paul meant by "the preaching of Jesus Christ, according to the revelation of the mystery, *which was kept secret since the world began*." This revelation of "the mystery" was first given, by Jesus Christ, to the Apostle Paul, so it couldn't have been known "in times past." This fact alone undermines many things taught by most denominations throughout the history of the Church. Paul declared to the Romans:

> *25 Now to him that is of power to stablish you according to my gospel, and the preaching of Jesus Christ, according to the revelation of the mystery, which was kept secret since the world began, 26 But now is made manifest, and by the*

scriptures of the prophets [prophetic writings],
according to the commandment of the
everlasting God, <u>made known to all nations for</u>
<u>the obedience of faith</u>: [27] *To God only wise, be*
glory through Jesus Christ for ever. Amen.
Romans 16:25-27

Most believers are completely oblivious to this passage, which was finally "made known to all nations for the obedience of faith." Is this "mystery" being preached in *all* churches and denominations today? The Apostle Paul even declared in Ephesians 3:9 that we are "to make all men see what is *the fellowship of the mystery*, which from the beginning of the world *hath been hid in God*." Sadly, the traditions of men continue to rob us of this vital truth, specifically "the revelation of the mystery." Since this "mystery…was kept secret since the world began," we can confidently affirm that it couldn't have been made known to or by the apostles and prophets prior to Acts 9 (when Paul was converted). If the Body of Christ would understand and accept this truth concerning "the mystery," there would be greater unity in Christianity, not the divisions we see today. I will certainly explain this special revelation to Paul throughout this book, but even though many pastors do preach elements of "the mystery" (that Jesus revealed to Paul), they often do not explain why it was given to another apostle (not the Twelve), at a specific time, and for a specific purpose. In essence, "the mystery" still remains a mystery because of various traditions.

Thousands of denominations still attempt to "establish their own righteousness," mostly ignoring this special revelation to Paul, through whom God had chosen to reveal the ultimate means by which humanity could be justified (declared righteous) in His sight. It is through *this* gospel, which Paul called "my gospel," that salvation has been offered to the world, apart from Israel and the Law of Moses. The twelve apostles were yet ignorant of "the mystery" until Paul taught it to them (as explained in detail in Galatians 2). Remember, it was "kept secret since the world began but now is made manifest (known)...."

We know today that we are justified (declared righteous) through faith in the blood of Jesus Christ; however, prior to this "mystery," many saints often wondered how God could justify them.

Psalm 8 contains this question: "What is man, that thou [God] art mindful of him?"

Job 9:2 poses this question: "How shall man be just with God?"

In Psalm 143:2, King David prayed, "Do not bring your servant into judgment, for no one living is righteous before you [God]." Remember, in the Old Testament, sin did bring divine judgment, so *mercy* was needed for the Israelites who'd violated the Law they agreed to obey (Joshua 24:24).

Isaiah (64:6) lamented, "...all our righteousness is as filthy rags...."

Romans 11:34-35 also asked, "... who hath known the mind of the Lord? Or who hath been His counsellor? Or who hath first given to him, and it shall be recompensed [paid back] to him again?"

It only takes one sin to make us sinners, but it only took one death (of Jesus) to pay for it all.

17 For if by one man's offence death reigned by one; much more they which receive abundance of grace and of the gift of righteousness shall reign in life by one, Jesus Christ.)
Romans 5:17

11 And every priest standeth daily ministering and offering oftentimes the same sacrifices, which can never take away sins: 12 But this man, after he had offered one sacrifice for sins for ever, sat down on the right hand of God; 13 From henceforth expecting till his enemies be made his footstool.
Hebrews 10:11-13 (to the Jews)

Eventually, throughout many of the writings of the Apostle Paul, God provided the answer for these saints who wondered how God could make humanity righteous before Him. In Paul's first sermon in Acts 13, and later in Romans 3 and 4, Paul revealed:

38 Be it known unto you therefore, men and brethren, that through this man is preached unto you the forgiveness of sins: 39 And by him all that believe are justified from all things, from which ye could not be justified by the law of Moses. Acts 13:38-39

> *28 Therefore we conclude that a man is <u>justified</u>*
> *<u>by faith</u> without the deeds of the law.*
> *Romans 3:28*

> *4 Now to him that worketh is the reward not*
> *reckoned of grace, but of debt. 5 But to him*
> *that worketh not, but believeth on him that*
> *justifieth the ungodly, his faith is counted for*
> *righteousness. Romans 4:4-5*

The only identity that offers eternal life with God our Savior is the one identity He offers to us through Christ (John 14:6). Paul uses the phrase "in Christ" over 70 times in his epistles, so this is how important it is for those who believe. We are then *immersed* "into Christ" *by* one Spirit when we believe the gospel that Jesus died, was buried, and rose again for us (I Cor. 12:13; 15:3-4). God takes us out of being "in Adam," and He places us "in (into) Christ," giving us "all spiritual blessings in heavenly places in Christ Jesus" (Eph. 1:3; 2:6).

The Alternatives to God

When others claim little to no association with God, perhaps their identity is somehow connected mainly through some cultural construct, identity politics, or maybe some social or financial status. Are they prominent in their community, or are they just an average citizen? Perhaps their identity rests upon the academic laurels they have gained through scholarly achievements, their association with certain people, or maybe their identity is recognized by a special skill or talent they have that others lack. Whatever it is that defines them, their identity matters because it is deeply associated with their character, politics, relationships, morals, the decisions they make, and the actions and consequences that follow. We are also learning how our identities can be rooted in the validations we receive from others. Regardless of whatever secular identities we choose in our lives, let us not forget that such identities are only temporary, not eternal. Whether our identity is "in Adam" or "in Christ," God loves us, and Christ died for us! I hope you trust in Christ, for He is our Hope and our eternal salvation, apart from works of righteousness we might perform to earn His favor.

> *8 Be not thou therefore ashamed of the*
> *testimony of our Lord, nor of me his prisoner:*
> *but be thou partaker of the afflictions of the*
> *gospel according to the power of God; 9 Who*
> *hath saved us, and called us with an holy*
> *calling, not according to our works, but*
> *according to his own purpose and grace,*
> *which was given us in Christ Jesus before the*
> *world began,*
> *2 Timothy 1:8-9*

What a glorious truth it is to know my personal sins (and yours) were imputed (placed upon) Christ on a hill called Calvary, and upon the moment of personal faith in His completed work of redemption for us, His righteousness is then put to the believer's account (2 Cor. 5:21). God makes this available *to all*, especially those who believe the gospel of Christ (I Tim. 2:4; 4:10). Why would *anyone* reject such a glorious offer, especially when it is given at no cost to us (Rom. 3:24)?

Most people do not realize that God's love and moral standards are also for the benefit and protection of humanity; however, it is the exercise of our free will that has the potential to bring chaos and harm to our lives, especially when we choose not to "retain God in our knowledge." Jesus declared that the Law is summed up in this: "Love your neighbor as yourself"; however, look at the contempt raging within homes, communities, and governing bodies. Our world seems to be on a perpetual, steady stream of vile information that attempts to demonize and divide even those within the Body of Christ. As previously mentioned, had Adam chosen to obey God, we would not have inherited a sinful nature, which has brought so much suffering and sorrow throughout this world. Sadly, Adam "fell short" of God's goodness (glory), and we have inherited his sinful nature, which we willingly serve, even though it has brought so much destruction to our world. If you have personally rejected what God has so graciously offered to you, then you are still "in Adam," but you can change that identity through faith in the completed work of Christ on your behalf. If you do, you are placed "into Christ," and your life will always be safely "hid with Christ." This is further explained in the following verses:

> *<u>If ye then be risen with Christ, seek those things which are above</u>, where Christ sitteth on the right hand of God. ² Set your affection on things above, not on things on the earth. ³ For*

*ye are dead, <u>and your life is hid with Christ in</u>
<u>God</u>. ⁴ When Christ, who is our life, shall
appear, then shall ye also appear with him in
glory. Colossians 3:1-4*

*¹³ And you, being dead in your sins and the
uncircumcision of your flesh, hath he
quickened together with him, <u>having forgiven</u>
<u>you all trespasses</u>; ¹⁴ Blotting out the
handwriting of ordinances that was against us,
which was contrary to us, and took it out of the
way, nailing it to his cross;
Colossians 2:13-14*

Man's Attempts Through Religion

To believers at Corinth, the Apostle Paul wrote:

*Therefore seeing we have this ministry, as we
have received mercy, we faint not; ² But have
renounced the hidden things of dishonesty, not
walking in craftiness, nor handling the word of
God deceitfully; but by manifestation of the
truth commending ourselves to every man's
conscience in the sight of God. ³ <u>But if our</u>
<u>gospel be hid, it is hid to them that are lost:</u>
⁴ <u>In whom the god of this world hath blinded</u>
<u>the minds of them which believe not, lest the</u>
<u>light of the glorious gospel of Christ, who is</u>
<u>the image of God, should shine unto them.</u>
2 Corinthians 4:1-4*

The "god of this world" is none other than Satan himself, and there isn't a religion he doesn't use or manipulate to keep humanity's identity "in Adam." By allowing people to believe they might be "good enough" someday to make it to Heaven, usually through some religious works instituted by a denomination, Satan is able to undermine our need (and the security) for the cleansing power of the blood of Christ. Satan does everything he can to "make the cross of Christ of none effect" (I Cor. 1:17), and yes, he is capable of using any "form of godliness" (often promoted through a works-based religion). Salvation *today* is by grace, through faith…apart from works, but "in times past," there were different works that accompanied faith, but with Jesus Christ came "grace and truth," and we must be careful to remember "to whom" various biblical passages were written, and "at what time" were they to be applied.

Eventually, Jesus Christ revealed to the Apostle Paul that salvation is "not by works of righteousness," but "through faith in His blood" (Rom. 3:25). "In times past," salvation was given to those who obeyed God's specific commands *at that time*. Did God tell Abraham to place his faith in the shed blood and resurrection of Jesus for salvation? Did God tell Noah that salvation was "by grace, though faith, apart from works"? Did God tell Moses that Jesus was the fulfillment of the Law? Of course not, because the means of salvation we have today is now through "the preaching of Jesus Christ, according to the revelation of the mystery, *which was kept secret since the world began*." Abraham, Noah, Moses, David, and even the twelve apostles did not know this revelation until Jesus Christ revealed it to Paul shortly after his conversion in Acts 9.

We must also recognize how Satan's greatest achievements of deception are not only found in his ability to convince humanity that he doesn't exist, but his ability to also "transform himself into an angel of light" (2 Cor. 11:14). As mentioned, Satan also promotes a "form of godliness," which leads to many divisions within the Body of Christ. After all, his handiwork is also seen within the thousands of so-called Christian denominations around the world. How many of these denominations base their "righteousness" upon their ongoing works they perform before God, while forgetting that God's righteousness is imputed by and through faith, specifically when we trust in the work that has already been done for us (the cross and resurrection of Christ)? Paul mentioned this specifically in the following verse:

> *21 I do not frustrate the grace of God: for if righteousness come by the law, then Christ is dead in vain. Galatians 2:21*

The Mystery Gospel Often Ignored…Thanks to Tradition
If you ask numerous believers what we must do to be saved, you will hear various *suggestions* offered through their denominational upbringings. You might hear them explain how you must "repent and be baptized for the remission of sins," or maybe you will be told to simply love Jesus (and others), or maybe you should just "keep His commandments." Yes, some of these are scriptural, but do these believers ever explain "to whom" such commands were given, and "at what

time"? Still, others (like me) will share with you that salvation is "by grace, through faith, apart from works"; however, many are not likely to connect such a message with "…the preaching of Jesus Christ, according to the revelation of the mystery, *which was kept secret since the world began*" (Rom. 16:25).

If you have never heard of this "revelation of the mystery," you are not alone. This "mystery" was revealed *after* Acts 9, and it was given, as I stated, by "revelation of Jesus Christ" (Gal. 1:11-12) to and through the Apostle Paul. Tragically, because of ignorance, this "revelation of the mystery" is still "kept secret" from millions of people. It is Satan who is winning the battle for the souls of millions, and it is being done through a "form of godliness" in the name of religion, which is notorious for robbing us of vital truths. If pastors and priests ignore the "revelation of the mystery" in their peaching, it can greatly impede someone from truly knowing Christ as their Savior. It can also lead to a diminished walk (or faithful obedience) for the believer. Paul warns us of this in his letter to the Galatians.

8 But though we, or an angel from heaven,
preach any other gospel unto you than that
which we have preached unto you, let him be
accursed. 9 As we said before, so say I now
again, if any man preach any other gospel
unto you than that ye have received, let him be
accursed. Galatians 1:8-9

If your denomination isn't striving "to make all men see what is the fellowship of the mystery, which from the beginning of the world has been hid in God…" (Eph. 3:9), then you should question why your pastors and priests are not fully preaching about the "revelation of the mystery" to Paul by Jesus Christ (after Acts 9). If your pastor or priest is still insisting that you "follow in the footsteps of Jesus" (found in the so-called "gospels"), then you might ask them to explain what Paul meant by his gospel being "kept secret" at the time of the earthly ministry of Jesus described in Matthew, Mark, Luke, and John. If a pastor or priest proclaims salvation to be by grace, but they also insist on some sort of cooperation with God by works and sacraments, then is salvation really the "*unmerited* favor of God" as they promote, and do they truly know the differences between the justification and sanctification of the believer? Sure, many will provide some sort of answer, but do they still insist that the gospel preached by Jesus in the "gospels" is the exact same gospel He "kept secret" until Paul? Did the "gospels" ever teach Jews and Gentiles that salvation was through faith in the blood and resurrection of Jesus, apart from works? After forty years, I haven't read of such a gospel in Matthew, Mark, Luke, and John—as well as the early chapters in Acts.

As I have mentioned, many pastors (whether they realize it or not) do promote some portions of "the mystery," which centers on faith in the shed blood of Jesus Christ and His resurrection for salvation; however, *when* they insist that Acts 2 (Pentecost) is the beginning of the Church, the Body of Christ, they have obviously failed to realize that Acts 2 says nothing about salvation being "by grace, through faith…apart from works," nor does it teach anything about Jews and Gentiles being baptized *by* one Spirit into *one body* through "the preaching of the cross" (I Cor. 1:17). After all, the cross was a place of national shame to Israel (Acts 2:36-37), not a means by which both Jews and Gentiles could be saved into "one body" by it. Peter *never* proclaimed (in Acts 2) anything about Gentiles being "justified from all things from which you could not be justified by the Law of Moses" (as Paul did in Acts 13:38-39). Also, none of the twelve apostles ever mentioned such a group of believers called *the Body of Christ*, let alone this Body being "seated in heavenly places in Christ." In fact, they never taught "all the house of Israel" (Acts 2:36) that they had "a citizenship in heaven" (Phil. 3:20). The twelve apostles were still expecting the Kingdom and "the new heavens and the new earth" (2 Pet. 3:13) where they would be "seated on twelve thrones, judging the twelve tribes of Israel" (Matt. 19:28).

Let us remember, there was no such gospel preached in Acts 2 about salvation being "by grace, through faith, apart from works." Salvation "apart from works" was not proclaimed until Acts 13 (some 12-15 years after Pentecost). In fact, Peter never departed from his Acts 2 gospel message of repentance and water baptism, even when he visited (by special revelation) the home of a Gentile named Cornelius in Acts 10. Once again, the twelve apostles never told the Jews and proselytes (Gentiles) at Pentecost (or the Gentiles in Acts 10) how they could be saved by grace, *through faith* in the shed blood of Christ and His resurrection. What they *did* teach at Pentecost was "repent and be (water) baptized for the remission of sins," which is a phrase Paul *never* commands in his thirteen epistles to members of the Body of Christ. In fact, the Body of Christ (the Church) was *not* taught until Paul *first* mentioned it to the Corinthians (I Cor. 3:10; 12:12-27). *Should this not cause us to question why this is so?* Let us never forget that it is *tradition*, not the word of God, that teaches that the Body of Christ, the Church, began at Pentecost.

Since Paul declared the gospel he preached to be "the mystery, kept secret since the world began," how is it possible that any past apostle or prophet knew of this revelation prior to Paul's conversion in Acts 9? From Genesis 12 to Acts 7, God's focus was on fulfilling the "promises made unto the fathers," which is why Jesus Christ was "a minister of the circumcision" (Rom. 15:8). Jesus said nothing about this "mystery" for a specific reason, which I'll quote soon from I Corinthians 2:6-8. Paul *did not* receive the gospel of the grace of God from any man because, again, no one knew of the "gospel of the grace of God" prior to Paul's conversion.

> *10 For do I now persuade men, or God? or do I*
> *seek to please men? for if I yet pleased men, I*
> *should not be the servant of Christ. 11 But I*
> *certify you, brethren, that the gospel which*
> *was preached of me is not after man. 12 For I*
> *neither received it of man, neither was I taught*
> *it, but by the revelation of Jesus Christ.*
> *Galatians 1:10-12*

According to many traditionalists, if there is only one people of God, one Church, one gospel, and one destiny of believers found from Genesis to Revelation, how could Paul make the claim that his gospel was "the revelation of the mystery, *which was kept secret since the world began*"? In fact, a disciple named Stephen (in Acts 7:38) mentioned the "Church in the wilderness," and we know this Church was given the Law by Moses, so how could this Church be the same Church that was told (by Paul) "…for you are not under the law, but under grace" (Rom. 6:14)? So, if there was only one people of God, one Church, and one gospel throughout the Bible, we must wonder what Paul meant by the following verses:

> *7 But contrariwise, when they saw that <u>the gospel of the uncircumcision was committed unto me, as the gospel of the circumcision was unto Peter</u>; 8 (For he that wrought effectually in Peter to the apostleship of the circumcision, the same was mighty in me toward the Gentiles:) 9 And when James, Cephas, and John, who seemed to be pillars, perceived the grace that was given unto me, they gave to me and Barnabas the right hands of fellowship; <u>that we should go unto the heathen, and they unto the circumcision</u>. Galatians 2:7-9*

If Paul simply became "the thirteenth apostle," and he taught the same gospel as the twelve apostles, how could he make the following claims?

> *3 How that <u>by revelation</u> he made known <u>unto me the mystery</u>; (as I wrote afore in few words,*

4 Whereby, when ye read, ye may understand my knowledge in the mystery of Christ)
5 Which in other ages was not made known unto the sons of men, as it is now revealed unto his holy apostles and prophets by the Spirit; Ephesians 3:3-5

23 If ye continue in the faith grounded and settled, and be not moved away from the hope of the gospel, which ye have heard, and which was preached to every creature which is under heaven; whereof I Paul am made a minister; 24 Who now rejoice in my sufferings for you, and fill up that which is behind of the afflictions of Christ in my flesh for his body's sake, which is the church: 25 Whereof I am made a minister, according to the dispensation of God which is given to me for you, to fulfil the word of God; 26 Even the mystery which hath been hid from ages and from generations, but now is made manifest to his saints: 27 To whom God would make known what is the riches of the glory of this mystery among the Gentiles; which is Christ in you, the hope of glory: 28 Whom we preach, warning every man, and teaching every man in all wisdom; that we may present every man perfect in Christ Jesus: 29 Whereunto I also labour, striving according to his working, which worketh in me mightily. Colossians 1:23-29

> *15 This is a faithful saying, and worthy of all acceptation, that Christ Jesus came into the world to save sinners; of whom I am chief.*
> *16 Howbeit for this cause <u>I obtained mercy, that in me first</u> Jesus Christ might shew forth all longsuffering, <u>for a pattern to them which should hereafter believe on him to life</u> everlasting. I Timothy 1:15-16*

Since this gospel of grace was *first* revealed to Paul, how can we say it was already proclaimed by anyone prior to his conversion in Acts 9? The gospel preached at Pentecost (in Acts 2) certainly happened before the conversion of Paul. That stated, is the gospel of the grace of God (Acts 20:24) the pattern your pastor or priest is following, or is your church still enforcing the principles of the so-called Great Commission ("repent and be baptized" and "keep the commandments"), which is often mixed with a little grace, through faith, without works? Is your denomination sharing "the preaching of Jesus Christ, according to the revelation of the mystery, which was kept secret since the world began," or is your denomination insisting on strict obedience to what Jesus taught in to "the lost sheep of the house of Israel" in the so-called "gospels" (Matt. 15:24; Rom. 15:8)? Many believers completely omit the fact that Jesus proclaimed to have come "...to none other than to the lost sheep of the house of Israel," and this was stated in the presence of a Gentile woman who was pleading for her daughter to be healed.

Thankfully, many theologians do preach that Jesus Christ died for us, and that He was raised from the dead; however, was this gospel message the same one that was preached by John the Baptist, Jesus, and His disciples during Christ's earthly ministry? I don't recall anywhere in the "gospels," or early Acts, where faith in the death and resurrection of Jesus Christ was taught for salvation, nor do I recall such a gospel being taught within the so-called Great Commission, which specifically insisted that believers "be baptized in the name of the Father, the Son, and the Holy Ghost…and to observe all that I have commanded"? After all, didn't Jesus instruct the "lost sheep of the house of Israel" (in "the gospels") to "keep the commandments" (John 14:15; Matt. 28:16-20)? If this is "our commission" for today, shouldn't we still adhere to its instructions and demand water baptism and the keeping of the Law of Moses for our obedience? The so-called Great Commission was certainly known prior to Paul's conversion, so what gospel was Paul referencing when he taught, "…*my gospel*, and the preaching of Jesus Christ, according to the revelation of the mystery, *which was kept secret since the world began*"?

After forty years of studying, I haven't found anyone, *prior to Paul*, who preached salvation by grace, through faith in the shed blood and resurrection of Jesus Christ, apart from works. Keep in mind that Abraham, Moses, the prophets, and the twelve apostles knew nothing about such a gospel because it was "kept secret since the world began." Secondly, I have never found one passage, prior to Paul's conversion, that taught that Gentiles could become "fellow heirs" with Christ, *apart* from Israel (Rom.11:11). Yes, the Old and New

Testaments do *prophesy* about Gentile salvation, but it is always in the context of "the promises made unto the fathers," which brings blessings to all nations *through* Abraham's seed (Isaac and Jacob (Israel)). There is nothing in prophecy about "the mystery"; otherwise, Paul could not have claimed his gospel to be "the mystery, which was kept secret since the world began."

Many believers assume Jesus taught (on the earth) that salvation was through faith in His death and resurrection; however, if this were correct, we should consider the following passages:

21 From that time forth began Jesus to shew unto his disciples, <u>how that he must go unto Jerusalem, and suffer many things of the elders and chief priests and scribes, and be killed, and be raised again the third day.</u> 22 <u>Then Peter took him, and began to rebuke him, saying, Be it far from thee, Lord: this shall not be unto thee.</u> 23 But he turned, and said unto Peter, <u>Get thee behind me, Satan: thou art an offence unto me</u>: for thou savourest not the things that be of God, but those that be of men. 24 Then said Jesus unto his disciples, If any man will come after me, let him deny himself, and take up his cross, and follow me.
Matthew 16:21-24

31 Then he took unto him the twelve, and said unto them, Behold, we go up to Jerusalem, and *all things that are written by the prophets concerning the Son of man shall be accomplished. ³² For he shall be delivered unto the Gentiles, and shall be mocked, and spitefully entreated, and spitted on: ³³ And they shall scourge him, <u>and put him to death: and the third day he shall rise again. ³⁴ And they understood none of these things: and this saying was hid from them, neither knew they the things which were spoken.</u> Luke 18:31-34*

Just one chapter before Jesus entered Jerusalem on "Palm Sunday" (Luke 19), Jesus revealed to the twelve apostles the events that would take place regarding His death and resurrection in Jerusalem. However, in Matthew 16, Peter rebuked Jesus for such a statement, and in Luke 18, "they understood none of these things." If Jesus and the twelve apostles proclaimed salvation through faith in His shed blood and resurrection throughout the so-called "gospels" (and early Acts), why would the passages in both Matthew and Luke claim such ignorance on the part of the disciples, especially when Jesus Christ was just days away from the crucifixion and resurrection? Again, the prophets (through John the Baptist), and the twelve apostles, knew nothing about salvation by grace, through faith in the shed blood and resurrection of Jesus Christ. Paul was chosen *first* to reveal this "revelation of the mystery," which declared salvation to both Jews and Gentiles through Israel's fall (Rom. 11:11), leading to the "preaching of the cross" by Paul.

Again, it is quite apparent that they were *not* already proclaiming salvation by grace, through faith in the blood and resurrection of Jesus Christ, especially when Luke 18:34 explains how "this saying (revelation) was hid from them." However, why was the gospel of salvation (through faith in the death and resurrection of Christ) hidden from them, especially so close to the actual events taking place in Jerusalem? The Apostle Paul provides the answer in his letter to the Corinthians.

> *⁶ Howbeit we speak wisdom among them that are perfect: yet not the wisdom of this world, nor of the princes of this world, that come to nought: ⁷ But we speak the wisdom of God in a mystery, <u>even the hidden wisdom, which God ordained before the world unto our glory</u>: ⁸ Which none of the princes of this world knew: <u>for had they known it, they would not have crucified the Lord of glory</u>.*
> *I Corinthians 2:6-8*

Had anyone known that salvation would be available to the entire world (both Jews and Gentiles) through faith in the death, burial, and resurrection of Jesus Christ, "they would not have crucified the Lord of glory," especially Satan. This is why the gospel of the grace of God (Act 20:24) was declared to be "the preaching of Jesus Christ, according to the revelation of the mystery, which was kept secret since the world began" (Rom. 16:25). So *no*, John the Baptist, Jesus, and the twelve apostles *did not* preach (during the earthly ministry of Jesus) the same means of salvation as the Apostle Paul did much later. Remember, it was Jesus Christ, by direct revelation to Paul, that the "revelation of the mystery" was first made known to him after his conversion in Acts 9 (I Tim. 1:16).

So, What Did Jesus Teach During His Earthly Ministry?
Since "the revelation of the mystery" was still "kept secret" until Paul's conversion, what did Jesus command His disciples to preach to "the lost sheep of the house of Israel"? They certainly did not understand the significance of what the death and resurrection would accomplish for the world, so what were they instructed to teach?

> *5 These twelve Jesus sent forth, and commanded them, saying, <u>Go not into the way of the Gentiles, and into any city of the Samaritans enter ye not</u>: 6 But go rather <u>to the lost sheep of the house of Israel.</u> 7 And as ye go, preach, saying, <u>The kingdom of heaven is at hand</u>.*
> *Matthew 10:5-7*

What did Jesus later tell Paul to preach to Jews and Gentiles?

> *Moreover, brethren, <u>I declare unto you the gospel which I preached unto you</u>, which also ye have received, and wherein ye stand; 2 <u>By which also ye are saved</u>, if ye keep in memory*

> *what I preached unto you, unless ye have*
> *believed in vain.* ³ *For I delivered unto you*
> *first of all that which I also received, how that*
> *Christ died for our sins according to the*
> *scriptures;* ⁴ *And that he was buried, and that*
> *he rose again the third day according to the*
> *scriptures:*
> *I Corinthians 15:1-4*

Again, when Jesus proclaimed in Matthew 16 and Luke 18 that He must go to Jerusalem to suffer and die (and be raised again on the third day), the apostles "understood none of these things." So, how can any pastor or priest insist that Jesus and His disciples (in "the gospels") were preaching any kind of gospel about salvation being by grace, *through faith* in the death and resurrection of Christ (apart from works), especially when Peter took the time to rebuke Jesus (Matthew 16) for making such a claim about His death and resurrection? This glorious gospel (by grace, through faith in the blood and resurrection) was still "hid in God" (I Cor. 2:7-8; Eph. 3:9) at the time of Christ's earthly ministry, as well as Pentecost in Acts 2, and now we know why.

Our Identity Crisis

I pose many of these questions because I believe there is a tragic identity crisis within Christianity. It stems from a lack of knowledge about the very fundamental reasons why Paul was called (by God) to reveal the "gospel of the grace of God" (Acts 20:24) to the entire world. This calling occurred not long after Israel blasphemed the Holy Ghost in Acts 7, which I will explain in subsequent chapters, along with the differences between *the gospel of the kingdom* and *the gospel of the grace of God.*

Israel's rejection led to "the revelation of the mystery, which was kept secret since the world began," but many believers never seem to wonder why this "mystery" was revealed in the first place? Paul emphasized part of the reason in the following passage:

> *11 I say then, Have they [Israel] stumbled that*
> *they should fall? God forbid: but rather*
> *through their fall salvation is come unto the*
> *Gentiles, for to provoke them to jealousy.*
> *Romans 11:11 (brackets by author)*

Is this passage insinuating that God is "done with Israel"? If so, why did Paul later reveal in that same chapter that Israel (as a nation) was yet to be saved (Rom. 11:25-29)? Paul even stated, "God forbid" at the notion that Israel had stumbled beyond recovery. Romans 11:29 does state that "the gifts and calling of God are without repentance (irrevocable)," so no, God is not done with His promises to Israel. His promises to that nation do not depend upon their faithfulness, nor do His promises to the Body of Christ depend upon ours.

According to this passage (Rom. 11:11), did salvation come to the Gentiles in the form of the so-called Great Commission? If the Great Commission is the Church's calling today, why aren't most pastors and priests adhering strictly to its teachings? Are all pastors and priests commanding "repent and be baptized for the remission of sins"? Are all of them commanding strict obedience to the Law of Moses? Are they commanding their congregations to "sell all that they have, and to have all things common" (Acts 2:44)? What about the "sign gifts" of tongues, healings, etc.? Why aren't all believers capable of such "gifts"?

Let us look specifically at what the *Great Commission* taught:

> *16 Then the eleven disciples went away into Galilee, into a mountain where Jesus had appointed them. 17 And when they saw him, they worshipped him: but some doubted. 18 And Jesus came and spake unto them, saying, All power is given unto me in heaven and in earth. 19 Go ye therefore, and teach all nations, baptizing them in the name of the Father, and of the Son, and of the Holy Ghost: 20 Teaching them to observe all things whatsoever I have commanded you: and, lo, I am with you always, even unto the end of the world. Amen. Matthew 28:16-20*

According to the "gospels," we know the Great Commission (the gospel of the kingdom) commanded obedience to everything Jesus taught during His earthly ministry, so why aren't all pastors and priests insisting on water baptizing, keeping the commandments, and preaching that "the kingdom of heaven is at hand"? Shouldn't we also obey the command to "heal the sick, cleanse the lepers, raise the dead, cast out devils, freely ye have received, freely give"? After all, this is what Jesus declared when He told His disciples to "go *not* into the way of the Gentiles…but go rather to the lost sheep of the house of Israel" (Matt. 10:5-7). If we are to adhere to all that Jesus taught, we must wonder how any denomination could read Matthew 10 and still preach that the Church, the Body of Christ, has now replaced Israel (Matt. 15:24), especially since the Body of Christ did not exist until *after* Christ's earthly ministry was completed. Again, where in "the gospels" did Jesus proclaim that salvation was "by grace, through faith (in the death and resurrection), apart from works"? It seems apparent that what many churches have adopted as their doctrines aren't necessarily aligned to what we are commanded to do today, especially after "the revelation of the mystery" was "made known" to and through Paul by Jesus Christ.

Just because the Church (throughout history) adopted various doctrines and traditions, this does not make those doctrines and traditions "worthy of all acceptance," especially when they are in opposition to "the revelation of the mystery." Paul's gospel existed before the Roman Catholic, Orthodox, and Protestant denominations came into existence, so the Body of Christ is not a denomination; it is, however, made up of true believers currently found within various denominations! Again, I must ask: If the Body of Christ began in Acts 2, as tradition insists, why was there a need for "the revelation of the mystery, kept secret since the world began"? Remember, no such revelation was made known until *after* Acts 9?

Do Believers Know What It Means to "Rightly Divide" the Scriptures?

This is a challenging question, but most well-known theologians never address the reason for the confusion gripping Christianity, especially considering "the mystery" Jesus revealed to Paul. Catholics, Orthodox, and Protestant believers battle fiercely to defend their understanding of the Bible, as well as their denomination's traditions, but how many of them ever pause to examine the one command that would resolve the majority of differences we have within our Christian faith? This command is found in the following verse:

> *15 Study to shew thyself approved unto God, a*
> *workman that needeth not to be ashamed,*
> *rightly dividing the word of truth.*
> *2 Timothy 2:15*

Paul also commanded Timothy:

> *Paul, an apostle of Jesus Christ by the*
> *commandment of God our Saviour, and Lord*
> *Jesus Christ, which is our hope; 2 Unto*
> *Timothy, my own son in the faith: Grace,*
> *mercy, and peace, from God our Father and*
> *Jesus Christ our Lord. 3 As I besought thee to*
> *abide still at Ephesus, when I went into*
> *Macedonia, that thou mightest charge some*
> *that they teach no other doctrine, 4 Neither*
> *give heed to fables and endless genealogies,*

which minister questions, rather than godly
edifying which is in faith: so do.
I Timothy 1:1-4

In the same chapter as 2 Timothy 2:15, Paul even told Timothy to entrust the gospel he taught him to "faithful men," not denominations or any magisterium of a religion organization.

Thou therefore, my son, be strong in the grace
that is in Christ Jesus. 2 And the things that
thou hast heard of me among many witnesses,
the same commit thou to faithful men, who
shall be able to teach others also.
2 Timothy 2:1-2

Why *didn't* Paul command Timothy to follow what Jesus taught during His earthly ministry under the "gospel of the kingdom"? The following verse explains:

16 Wherefore henceforth know we no man after
the flesh: yea, though we have known Christ
after the flesh, yet now henceforth know we
him no more. 17 Therefore if any man be in
Christ, he is a new creature: old things are
passed away: behold, all things are become
new. 2 Corinthians 5:16

The *New* Creature is the Body of Christ, not the Messianic Kingdom Church already proclaimed at Pentecost (to which

3,000 souls were added to the "little flock" already there (Luke 12:32; Acts 1:15)). I will explain more on this subject, but for now, the "little flock" were the Jewish remnant who had accepted Jesus as the Messiah of Israel, having "believed on His name" (John 3:16).

The gospel Paul proclaimed is the most misunderstood gospel in all Scripture, not because it is impossible to understand, but rather it is often buried by religious traditions, which seem to supersede Paul's message given by Jesus Christ. Many believers attempt to bypass 2 Timothy 2:15 for the sake of their traditions as well, often clinging to the belief that "all denominations lead down the same path." In obedience to 2 Timothy 2:15, we are to "cut straight" what Jesus intended for various believers at specific times (such as His instructions to the nation of Israel under the gospel of the kingdom, and His instructions to the Body of Christ under the gospel of the grace of God). If we do not "rightly divide the word of truth," we will not understand "to whom" Jesus was instructing, "at what time," and for "what intent."

So, what are we to "rightly divide"? We are to "cut straight" the truth. What is the truth?

> *13 In whom ye also trusted, <u>after that ye heard</u>*
> *<u>the word of truth, the gospel of your salvation</u>:*
> *in whom also after that ye believed, ye were*
> *sealed with that holy Spirit of promise,*
> *14 Which is the earnest of our inheritance until*
> *the redemption of the purchased possession,*
> *unto the praise of his glory. Ephesians 1:13-14*

You are to "rightly divide" the truth, "the gospel of your salvation," but sadly, millions of believers aren't completely sure about their salvation at all. Keep in mind, if there was only one "gospel of your salvation" in Scripture, there would be no need to divide anything associated with it. The command of 2 Timothy 2:15 proves that the means of salvation has indeed changed, and we must "rightly divide" what all believers were told to place their faith in throughout the ages. This is the root cause of our identity crisis in Christianity.

In the last days, we know perilous times will come, and many will *not* "endure sound doctrine" (2 Tim. 4:3). In fact, some will simply "depart from the faith, giving heed to seducing spirits, and doctrines of devils" (I Tim. 4:1). This was already occurring while the apostles were still alive. After examining many of the writings and contradictory statements of the "Patristic Church Fathers" (after the first century), I maintain that this departure of the gospel accelerated shortly after Paul's and Peter's deaths.

From the time of Adam and Eve, Satan's goals have oftentimes been very subtle, especially as seen in many churches today. He continues to entice humanity with self-improvement, rather than following God; slap a label of morality and "godliness" on whatever feels good in their own eyes; combine as many religious works as necessary to undermine the sufficiency of the "blood of Christ" for salvation; and then use as many pulpits as possible to sell the *traditions of men* to the masses. This deception dates to the time of the apostles themselves, especially when the Judaizers insisted that Gentiles obey the Law of Moses (Acts 15;

Gal.2). Again, errors and divisions already existed in the earliest churches, to which the apostles had to correct through their letters (Acts 15:6-12; Rom. 16:17; I Cor. 3:3; I Cor. 11:18). Thankfully, we are still able to use these letters to "correct" some of the same errors today (2 Tim. 3:16-17).

Perhaps the best human understanding of 2 Timothy 2:15 comes from the man who completed the first English translation of the Bible. His name was Myles (Miles) Coverdale, and he was a Catholic before converting to the Anglican faith. He wisely stated:

It shall greatly help you to understand Scriptures
If thou mark not only what is spoken or written,
But of whom, and to whom, with what words, at what time.
Where, to what intent, with what circumstances,
Considering what goeth before and what followeth after.

So, Do Believers *Really* Have It All Wrong?

I'm certain the question posed on the cover of this book has caused some confusion, or perhaps outright anger for even daring to ask whether believers do, in fact, have it all wrong. Honestly, can we name *one* doctrine that believers do not argue and divide over, especially between the countless denominations claiming the name of Jesus Christ? Paul made his gospel of grace *very clear* before there were ever any Roman Catholic, Orthodox, or Protestant churches. Regardless, many of these churches still combine (into one gospel) what Jesus declared to "the lost sheep of the house of Israel," and what He later declared to the Body of Christ. We must "rightly divide" between them.

Even though most pastors and priests claim that salvation is by grace, through faith in the finished work of Christ, they still insist that Acts 2 is where such a gospel of their salvation began. What is still taught in Acts 2 (repentance and water baptism) did not include anything about faith in the shed blood of Jesus Christ and His resurrection, nor did it teach how Gentiles can be *fellow heirs* with Christ, apart from Israel. Acts 2 was still under the Law, and it wasn't until Acts 13 (well over a decade later) that "justification" was preached as being *apart from* "the Law of Moses." Those who refute these differences often do so by ignoring the command to "rightly divide the word of truth" in 2 Timothy 2:15. Regrettably, many theologians take the liberty to "spiritualize" various passages from the Bible to fit any narrative they choose to follow.

Failing to "rightly divide the word of truth" is the very reason why believers argue over the means of salvation, baptism, application of the Ten Commandments, works verses faith, the operation of the Holy Spirit today, eternal security, how believers are to walk in this present evil age, the so-called rapture of the Church and the Second Coming, and which church is the *one true Church* for today. Believers also argue over the so-called sacraments and how they are to be practiced, a literal interpretation verses an allegorical approach to the Bible, who will occupy the prophesied Millennial Kingdom, the various judgments of "the just and the unjust," and whether the sign gifts are still in operation today by the Spirit.

Do you get the point I am making? Look at the confusion we've caused for nonbelievers as well. Whether Catholic,

Orthodox, or Protestant, there are often many churches that still argue over their doctrines within their own denominations. In truth, there doesn't seem to be any "sound doctrine" that isn't ridiculed, argued, or outright denied today.

Sadly, almost every church, in some way, has obviously suppressed "the preaching of Jesus Christ, according to the revelation of the mystery, which was kept secret since the world began"; otherwise, this gospel of the grace of God would be well known by *all* believers. Instead of preaching what Paul taught to us, by revelation of Jesus Christ, most denominations have retreated to the earthly ministry of Jesus for their "marching orders," even though He clearly taught, "I am not sent but unto the lost sheep of the house of Israel," and this was to confirm the promises God made to the "seed of Abraham" (Matt. 15:24; Rom. 15:8).

After Israel's national rejection of Jesus and the Holy Ghost in Acts 7, this left Gentiles with "no hope, and without God in the world" (Eph. 2:11-12). *But now*, through the "preaching of Jesus Christ, according to the revelation of the mystery," Gentiles have been "brought nigh to God by the blood of Jesus Christ" (Eph. 2:13). *Prophecy* declared Gentiles would be brought nigh unto God *through Israel*, but God chose the Apostle Paul to declare a specific gospel message (The Mystery: the "hidden wisdom"), which was not made known until *after* the conversion of Paul in Acts 9. In Isaiah, we are taught that Gentiles will be saved through Israel, but "the mystery" revealed that Gentiles can now be saved "apart from Israel." We must "rightly divide" the differences between the Gentiles mentioned in prophecy and believers mentioned in "the mystery."

⁵ And now, saith the LORD that formed me from the womb to be his servant, to bring Jacob again to him, Though Israel be not gathered, yet shall I be glorious in the eyes of the LORD, and my God shall be my strength. ⁶ And he said, It is a light thing that thou shouldest be my servant to <u>raise up the tribes of Jacob, and to restore the preserved of Israel: I will also give thee for a light to the Gentiles, that thou mayest be my salvation unto the end of the</u> earth. Isaiah 49:5-6 (taught through prophecy, not the Mystery)

Since the time of the Apostle Paul, instead of Israel being the "light to the Gentiles," and Israel being the source of God's "salvation unto the end of the earth," God is now using the gospel of the grace of God (Acts 20:24) as the means of salvation, "which was preached to every creature which is under heaven; whereof I Paul am made a minister…" (Col. 1:23). The resulting chaos that believers and theologians have created by ignoring 2 Timothy 2:15 has led to utter confusion, and the destruction of many people (and their faith), as well as some diabolical anti-Semitic beliefs within the Church itself. No, God is not fulfilling His promises to Israel through the Church (the Body of Christ), rather He is blessing the "new creature" (the Church) so we might "provoke Israel to jealousy." God is proving to Israel that they, too, can be "blessed with all spiritual blessings," which God has unconditionally promised to do for Israel "in the ages to come." God is not dealing with nations today; He is saving individual Jews and Gentiles into the "new creature," the Body of Christ. The "gospel of your salvation" must be "rightly divided"; otherwise, you will forever struggle to fully grasp the "hope of your calling" as a member of the Body of Christ.

As we begin the following chapters, I must ask: *Do believers have it all wrong, and if so, what can we do to fix this?*

CHAPTER 2

A Blunder Often Overlooked

¹⁵ Study to shew thyself approved unto God, a
workman that needeth not to be ashamed,
rightly dividing the word of truth.
2 Timothy 2:15

A Brief Review

In the first chapter, we examined the differences between being "in Adam" or "in Christ," and I also introduced the importance of "rightly dividing the word of truth," which is the focus of much of the material in this book. When believers fail to obey 2 Timothy 2:15, they end up with religious practices that have "a form of godliness but denies the power thereof" in various ways (2 Tim. 3:5). Those who say they are "following the words of Jesus," are often the same people who pay no attention "to whom" Jesus was speaking, "at what time," and "for what purpose or intent" He taught (while on Earth). Remember, He was "sent to none other than to the lost sheep of the house of Israel" (Matt. 15:24) to "fulfill the promises made unto the fathers" (Gen. 12:1-3; Rom. 15:8).

Jesus only interacted with two Gentiles in the "gospels," even stating to one that "it is not meet (right) to take the children's bread (Israel) and to cast it to dogs (Gentiles)." How can theologians insist that Jesus was sent to the Gentiles, or even to the Body of Christ at the time of His earthly ministry, especially when the Body of Christ had not yet been revealed until after Israel had blasphemed the Holy Ghost in Acts 7?

In the context of Jesus "confirming the promises made unto the fathers," it is important to note that this *spiritual fall* of Israel did not void God's promises to Abraham, as some suppose. The Gentile *nations* will indeed be blessed *through* Abraham's seed (Isaac and Jacob) "in the ages to come," but for now, God is blessing *individual* Jews and Gentiles, and He is placing them into the Body of Christ, which is *not* "spiritual Israel." Unless you "rightly divide the word of truth," you will not understand the fulfillment of God's unconditional promises to Abraham, nor will you fully understand what God is accomplishing *now* through the "new creature" (the Body of Christ).

Paul later revealed the glorious truth that "...in Him (Christ) should all fullness dwell" (Col. 1:19), so this simply means that when Israel is finally redeemed and "born again" (as a nation), it will be through their realization of the Seed, which is Christ (Gal. 3:16) that "all the nations will be blessed" at that time (Gen. 12:1-3; Isa. 60:1-3; Zech. 8:13; 10:1-12; Rom. 11:26). Just because God added the Law many years after His unconditional promises were made to Abraham, this does not "make void" what God promised to Abraham and his seed. Galatians 3:17 confirms this. The "promises made unto the fathers" were also the specific reason why Jesus declared to the woman at the well that "salvation is of the Jews" (John 4:22). It wasn't until Israel's "fall" in Acts 7 that Jesus gave to Paul "the revelation of the mystery, which was kept secret since the world began." This is why we must "rightly divide the word of truth"; otherwise, theologians will continue to invent ways to explain away "the revelation of the mystery."

By Grace, Through Faith in What?
As I briefly mentioned in the first chapter, we know that salvation has always been by God's grace, through faith in what He declared at specific times, but the question I must ask is this: What did humanity (from Adam to Paul) place their faith in to be saved from the penalty of sin? Faith is often defined as taking God at His word, regardless of our opinions, and we are to trust in His faithfulness, no matter the consequences. So, did those from Adam to the time of Paul's conversion, place their faith in the death and resurrection of Jesus Christ to save them? Of course not, because this gospel was not proclaimed until Paul revealed it "by revelation of Jesus Christ" (Gal. 1:11-12) sometime after Acts 9. From Adam to the time of "the revelation of the mystery," salvation was by faith, plus obedience to what God declared (said), such as "do not eat from the tree," "bring the proper sacrifice," "build an ark," "you shall be a father of many nations," and "obey my commandments," or whatever commands God also gave to these saints prior to "the revelation of the mystery, kept secret since the world began." Under the Law, the Jews offered the blood of "bulls and

goats" to *cover* their sins, but it wasn't until Jesus revealed to Paul "the mystery" that we fully learned that "faith in His blood" could fully provide "the remission of sins" (Rom. 3:24-26).

The glorious *gospel of the grace of God* (Acts 20:24), which teaches that salvation is by grace, through faith in the shed blood and resurrection, was not proclaimed until Jesus Christ saved the Apostle Paul in Acts 9. Through prophecy, we know that it was *not* a mystery that the Messiah would suffer and die and be raised again (Job 19:25-27; Psalm 49:13-15; Isa. 53); however, the world had no idea that through faith in His blood and resurrection, both Jews and Gentiles could be saved into one Body "by the cross." This was a mystery, which is "unsearchable" in Scripture until Paul's epistles (Eph. 3:8). We should also remember that I Corinthians 2:7-8 also reveals why this means of salvation was "kept secret since the world began." Remember, "they would not have crucified the Lord of glory."

Chapter 1 of John's gospel stated the following about Jesus:

> *In the beginning was the Word, and the Word*
> *was with God, and the Word was God. 2 The*
> *same was in the beginning with God. 3 All*
> *things were made by him; and without him was*
> *not any thing made that was made. 4 In him*
> *was life; and the life was the light of men.*
> *5 And the light shineth in darkness; and the*
> *darkness comprehended it not…17 For the law*

> *was given by Moses, <u>but grace and truth came
> by Jesus Christ</u>. John 1:1-5 and 17*

This passage does not explain *when* the "grace and truth" of Jesus Christ would be revealed to the entire world, but we know *now* that it was through the gospel of the grace of God (revealed to Paul) that this grace was made fully known and available to all (Acts 20:24; Col. 1:25; I Tim. 2:4).

What Gospel Was Revealed from Adam Until the Time of Moses?

If we recall, after Adam sinned, God said unto the serpent (Satan):

> *15 And I will put enmity between thee and the
> woman, and <u>between thy seed and her seed</u>; it
> shall bruise thy head, and thou shalt <u>bruise his
> heel</u>. Genesis 3:15*

Did Adam, Eve, and Satan understand what God was saying in this passage? Not at all, but we *now* have the benefit of understanding the gospel that God was presenting to them (Christ's defeat over Satan); however, had Satan known the significance of this passage—at that time—he would have made sure that Christ would not have been crucified (I Cor. 2:8). We understand Genesis 3:15 now through "the revelation of the mystery, which was kept secret since the world began."

Even John the Baptist did not know anything about salvation being by grace, through faith, apart from works.

Instead, he preached "the baptism of repentance for the remission of sins" (Mark 1:4). Yes, Jesus spoke of His death and resurrection in Matthew and Luke, as I mentioned in the first chapter, but that didn't mean they understood the full extent of what Christ's sacrifice would mean to both Jews and Gentiles in the Body of Christ. Peter, in Acts 2, also mentioned the death and resurrection of Jesus, but he never told the Jews and proselytes at Pentecost to place their faith in the blood and resurrection for salvation, especially "apart from works." He told them to "repent and be baptized for the remission of sins."

For Adam's obedience, he was required *not* to eat from the Tree of the Knowledge and Good and Evil in order to maintain his glorified state of being. He was disciplined for his sin by being removed from the garden and having to toil all the days of his life. In fact, the first religious act, after the fall, was when Adam and Eve attempted to cover their nakedness by their own means (fig leaves). However, God covered them in garments of skin, which came through sacrifice of something else *outside* of humanity. Adam and Eve certainly did not understand Hebrews 9:22, which stated, "without the shedding of blood, there is no remission (of sins)." We must be careful when attempting to insert current knowledge about something into a time when it was *not yet* revealed. This only brings more confusion.

Throughout the time of Adam to Moses, faith came with various requirements for obedience, and had those works not been carried out, it was considered a sin against God. In the case of Noah, had he refused to act upon his faith (and build the ark), he would have died in the flood. So, from Adam to

Moses, salvation was by *faith and obedience* in what God commanded them to do at that time. We know Adam was told *not* to eat from a certain tree, Cain and Abel were told to bring the proper sacrifice, Noah was told to build the ark, and Abraham left his home to travel to the land God promised him and his seed. Remember, the Law was not yet known to Israel until Moses.

A Special Case Involving Abraham

Abraham was told by God the following:

> *Now the LORD had said unto Abram, <u>Get thee</u>*
> *<u>out of thy country</u>, and from thy kindred, and*
> *from thy father's house, <u>unto a land that I will</u>*
> *<u>shew thee</u>: 2 <u>And I will make of thee a great</u>*
> *<u>nation</u>, and I will bless thee, and make thy*
> *name great; and thou shalt be a blessing:*
> *3 And I will bless them that bless thee, and*
> *curse him that curseth thee: <u>and in thee shall</u>*
> *<u>all families of the earth be blessed</u>. 4 <u>So Abram</u>*
> *<u>departed, as the LORD had spoken unto him</u>;*
> *and Lot went with him: and Abram was*
> *seventy and five years old when he departed*
> *out of Haran. Genesis 12:1-4*

> *4 And, behold, <u>the word of the LORD came unto</u>*
> *<u>him</u>, saying, This [steward of his house*
> *(Eliezer)] shall not be thine heir; but <u>he that</u>*
> *<u>shall come forth out of thine own bowels shall</u>*
> *<u>be thine heir [Isaac]</u>. 5 And he brought him*

> *forth abroad, and said, Look now toward*
> *heaven, and tell the stars, if thou be able to*
> *number them: and he said unto him, So shall*
> *thy seed be. ⁶ And he [Abraham] believed in*
> *the LORD; and he counted it*
> *to him for righteousness.*
> *Genesis 15:4-6 (brackets by author)*

Paul used Abraham (in Galatians) to prove a point regarding the gospel of grace. Paul used Abraham to prove the truth that justification (to declare one righteous) can indeed come by faith *without works of the Law*, especially before Abraham (a Gentile) was circumcised. However, James uses Abraham differently in his epistle, of course, because he was writing to the "twelve tribes scattered abroad," not the Body of Christ.

> *⁶ Even as Abraham believed God, and it was*
> *accounted to him for righteousness. ⁷ Know ye*
> *therefore that they which are of faith, the same*
> *are the children of Abraham. ⁸ And the*
> *scripture, foreseeing that God would justify the*
> *heathen through faith, preached before the*
> *gospel unto Abraham, saying, In thee shall all*
> *nations be blessed. ⁹ So then they which be of*
> *faith are blessed with faithful Abraham.*
> *Galatians 3:6-9*

Did Abraham know the gospel of the grace of God, or that Gentiles would be saved by faith alone in the sacrifice of

Jesus Christ? Not at all, because we are told that the gospel preached to Abraham was "...*in thee* shall all nations be blessed." All nations were to be blessed through both his seed (Israel) and The Seed (Christ), but the only gospel Abraham had faith in *at that time* was how all the nations would be blessed *through him*. Paul only mentioned Abraham to the Galatians to prove the point that Abraham was declared righteous *before* he was circumcised, proving to the Gentiles (in the Body of Christ) that "the gospel of the uncircumcision" Paul preached was, in fact, to them (Gal. 2:7-9). Circumcision was given as a seal for a righteousness Abraham *already had* years earlier. Today, the Holy Spirit is our seal (Eph. 1:13; 4:30), and our justification is the work of God—not us. This is all accomplished by the faithfulness of Jesus Christ, especially to those who *believe* the gospel Jesus gave to Paul.

I will address Abraham in the context of the Body of Christ later, but again, did God reveal to Abraham that faith in the death and resurrection of Jesus Christ would save him? Of course not, because the gospel of Christ was "not made known unto the sons of men" at that time (Eph. 3:5). Jesus Christ came to "fulfill the promises made unto the fathers" (Rom. 15:8), and it was this promise to Abraham (through his promised seed (Isaac)) that all the nations (families) of the earth would be blessed. Abraham believed God, and he believed salvation would come through his seed (Israel), but he had no idea that God would save Gentiles (from those nations) *apart* from Israel, through a different gospel (Rom. 11:11). This gospel of the grace of God was for "our glory," and it was known in God "before the world began" (I Cor.

2:7; Eph. 1:4). Abraham was called out "since the world began," so he did not know the gospel of the grace of God. As I explained at the beginning of this chapter, Paul revealed to us that Christ was The Seed (of Abraham) for salvation to the ends of the earth (Gal. 3:16), but this did not void the *unconditional* promises God made with Abraham in Genesis. Paul often brings clarity to what God kept secret millennia before he (Paul) was saved by grace. This is why we must also "rightly divide the word of truth," even in the Old Testament Scriptures.

What Gospel was Preached from Moses to Early Acts?
Now, from Moses until Christ (about 1500 years), and into the early chapters of Acts, faith *and* following the Law was given for Israel's obedience. During that time, Gentiles could only be saved by converting to Judaism and following the requirements of the Law, including circumcision (Ex. 12:48; Neh. 10:28; Acts 2:10). Is this the means of salvation today for Gentiles? Not at all!

Now, regarding the Law, "to whom" was it given for obedience?

> *6 And Moses took half of the blood, and put it*
> *in basons; and half of the blood he sprinkled*
> *on the altar. 7 And he took the book of the*
> *covenant, and read in the audience of the*
> *people: and they said, All that the LORD hath*
> *said will we do, and be obedient. 8 And Moses*
> *took the blood, and sprinkled it on the people,*
> *and said, Behold the blood of the covenant,*

which the LORD hath made with you concerning all these words…¹² And the LORD said unto Moses, Come up to me into the mount, and be there: <u>and I will give thee tables of stone, and a law, and commandments which I have written; that thou mayest teach them</u>. ¹³ And Moses rose up, and his minister Joshua: and Moses went up into the mount of God. Exodus 24:6-8 and 12-13

I say the truth in Christ, I lie not, my conscience also bearing me witness in the Holy Ghost, ² That I have great heaviness and continual sorrow in my heart. ³ For I could wish that myself were accursed from Christ for my brethren, <u>my kinsmen according to the flesh</u>: ⁴ <u>Who are Israelites; to whom pertaineth the adoption, and the glory, and the covenants, and the giving of the law, and the service of God, and the promises;</u> ⁵ <u>Whose are the fathers, and of whom as concerning the flesh Christ came</u>, who is over all, God blessed for ever. Romans 9:1-5

After 1500 years of failing to obey the Law, and "going about to establish their own righteousness" (Rom. 10:3), Israel (Jews) soon found themselves also at enmity with God, having fallen into the same condition as the Gentiles, which Paul described in Romans 1.

> *28 <u>And even as they did not like to retain God in their knowledge, God gave them over to a reprobate mind, to do those things which are not convenient;</u> 29 Being filled with all unrighteousness, fornication, wickedness, covetousness, maliciousness; full of envy, murder, debate, deceit, malignity; whisperers, 30 Backbiters, haters of God, despiteful, proud, boasters, inventors of evil things, disobedient to parents, 31 Without understanding, covenantbreakers, without natural affection, implacable, unmerciful: 32 <u>Who knowing the judgment of God, that they which commit such things are worthy of death, not only do the same, but have pleasure in them that do them.</u>*
> *Romans 1:28-32*

Because Israel stumbled at the cross, and fell spiritually in Acts 7 (at the stoning of Stephen), God could eventually declare the following:

> *9 What then? are we better than they? No, in no wise: <u>for we have before proved both Jews and Gentiles, that they are all under sin</u>...*
> *19 Now we know that what things soever the law saith, <u>it saith to them who are under the law: that every mouth may be stopped, and all the world may become guilty before God</u>.*
> *Romans 3:9 and 19*

God had chosen Israel to be a "kingdom of priests," and it was obedience to what God said, especially the Law of Moses to Israel, that He could make them "a peculiar treasure… above all people"; however, we know Israel had "not submitted themselves unto the righteousness of God," and this caused them to fall under God's judgment, often leading to captivity by their enemies, as well as God "divorcing" them due to their "spiritual" adultery, which was when they turned from God and worshipped other gods (a violation of the Law they agreed to obey).

> *5 Now therefore, <u>if ye will obey my voice indeed</u>, <u>and keep my covenant</u>, then ye shall be a peculiar treasure unto me <u>above all people</u>: for all the earth is mine: 6 And ye shall be unto me <u>a kingdom of priests</u>, and <u>an holy nation</u>. These are the words which thou [Moses] shalt speak unto <u>the children of Israel</u>.*
> *Exodus 19:5-6 (brackets by author)*

> *7 <u>Unto you</u> therefore which believe he is precious: but unto them which <u>be disobedient, the stone which the builders disallowed, the same is made the head of the corner,</u> 8 And a <u>stone of stumbling, and a rock of offence</u>, even to them which stumble at the word, <u>being disobedient</u>: whereunto also they were appointed. 9 <u>But ye are a chosen generation, a royal priesthood, an holy nation, a peculiar people;</u> that ye should shew forth the praises*

of him who hath called you out of darkness into his marvellous light; ¹⁰ *Which in time past were not a people, but are now the people of God: which had not obtained mercy, but now have obtained mercy. I Peter 2:8-10 (Jews scattered abroad)*

And Moses with the elders of Israel commanded the people, saying, <u>Keep all the commandments which I command you this day.</u> Deuteronomy 27:1

In the following passages, we will see how God was also a Husband to Israel, which obviously makes Israel "the Bride," but He "divorced" Israel, as I previously stated, when the nation committed "spiritual adultery" (by worshipping other gods):

¹⁹ *And <u>I will betroth thee unto me for ever</u>; yea, I will betroth thee unto me in righteousness, and in judgment, and in lovingkindness, and in mercies.* ²⁰ <u>*I will even betroth thee unto me in faithfulness*</u>*: and thou shalt know the* LORD. *Hosea 2:19-20*

⁵ <u>*For thy Maker is thine husband*</u>*; the* LORD *of hosts is his name; <u>and thy Redeemer the Holy One of Israel</u>; The God of the whole earth shall he be called.* ⁶ *For the* LORD *hath called thee as a woman forsaken and grieved in*

spirit, and a wife of youth, when thou wast refused, saith thy God. 7 <u>For a small moment have I forsaken thee; but with great mercies will I gather thee</u>. 8 In a little wrath I hid my face from thee for a moment; <u>but with everlasting kindness will I have mercy on thee, saith the LORD thy Redeemer</u>. Isaiah 54:5-8

8 And I saw, when for all the causes whereby backsliding Israel <u>committed adultery I had put her away, and given her a bill of divorce; yet her treacherous sister Judah feared not, but went and played the harlot also</u>…12 Go and proclaim these words toward the north, and say, <u>Return, thou backsliding Israel, saith the LORD; and I will not cause mine anger to fall upon you: for I am merciful, saith the LORD, and I will not keep anger for ever.</u> 13 Only acknowledge thine iniquity, that thou hast transgressed against the LORD thy God, <u>and hast scattered thy ways to the strangers</u> under every green tree, and ye have not obeyed my voice, saith the LORD. 14 <u>Turn, O backsliding children</u>, saith the LORD; <u>for I am married unto you</u>: and I will take you one of a city, and two of a family, <u>and I will bring you to Zion:</u>
Jeremiah 3:8 and 12-14

> *31 Behold, the days come, saith the LORD, <u>that I</u>*
> *<u>will make a new covenant with the house of</u>*
> *<u>Israel, and with the house of Judah</u>: 32 <u>Not</u>*
> *<u>according to the covenant that I made with</u>*
> *<u>their fathers in the day that I took them by the</u>*
> *<u>hand to bring them out of the land of Egypt</u>;*
> *<u>which my covenant they brake</u>, although <u>I was</u>*
> *<u>an husband unto them</u>, saith the LORD:*
> *Jeremiah 31:31-32*

From Adam to Moses, faith *and* obedience to what God commanded was necessary for salvation, and even in Israel's unfaithfulness (at times), God was still faithful to bring Israel back to Himself. Their salvation, however, did *not* include "faith in the death and resurrection of Jesus Christ," which had not yet been "made known." Regardless, from Moses until the time of Jesus Christ (and early Acts), Israel was still under faith *and* obedience to the Law, but did Jesus immediately remove the Law of Moses when He came "to His own" (Israel) "and His own received Him not" (John 1:11)? Did Israel know anything about salvation being "by grace, through faith...apart from the deeds of the Law" at the time Jesus Christ was on Earth? Didn't Jesus command people to "keep the commandments" (Matt. 19:17; John 14:15 and 21)?

Again, do you recall what Jesus taught His disciples about His death and resurrection in Matthew 16:21-24 and Luke 18:31-34? Remember, in Matthew 16, Peter rebuked Him, and in Luke, "they understood none of these things" when Jesus revealed what would occur in Jerusalem (His death and resurrection). Faith is believing God's word, no matter the time in Scripture, but it wasn't until "the revelation of the mystery" given to Paul that God declared justification to be by faith in the finished work of Jesus, apart from works, especially works of the Law. This was "not made known" until after Acts 9. Again, we must "rightly divide the word of truth."

What Did Jesus Command During His Earthly Ministry?
For those believers who insist on "following the words of Jesus" in "the gospels," would it not be prudent for them to recognize "to whom" Jesus was speaking, and for "what purpose" during the so-called "gospels"? Was He not "a minister of the circumcision, to confirm the promises made unto the fathers" at that time (Rom. 15:8)? If you recall, God promised that "the nations" were to be blessed through Abraham's seed (Israel), so can we at last understand why Jesus would say, "I am not sent but unto the lost sheep of the house of Israel," and "salvation is of the Jews"?

Let us briefly examine what Jesus taught during His earthly ministry and see if believers today are capable of such obedience. Keep in mind that many believers also assume Jesus abolished the Law when He ascended and gave the so-called "Great Commission." They also continue to believe He taught salvation through faith in His blood and the resurrection during His earthly ministry; however, it wasn't until Acts 13:38-39 (through Paul's preaching some 12-15 years later) that justification (apart from the Law of Moses) was first revealed to the Jews and proselytes at Antioch. Yes, the Law was fulfilled at the time of the death of Jesus; which was the shedding of "the blood of the new testament" (covenant) of Jeremiah 31; however, this does not mean the Law of Moses was immediately removed by Jesus (or by the twelve apostles). Where in Acts 2 did the apostles declare salvation to be by grace, through faith, apart from the deeds of the Law? It is nowhere to be found! There is simply no evidence that the gospel of the grace of God was proclaimed at Pentecost.

So, what did Jesus specifically command to "the lost sheep of the house of Israel"?

> *17 Think not that I am come to destroy the law, or the prophets: <u>I am not come to destroy, but to fulfil.</u> 18 For verily I say unto you, <u>Till heaven and earth pass</u>, one jot or one tittle shall in no wise pass from the law, till all be fulfilled. 19 <u>Whosoever therefore shall break one of these least commandments, and shall teach men so, he shall be called the least in the kingdom of heaven: but whosoever shall do and teach them, the same shall be called great in the kingdom of heaven.</u> 20 For I say unto you, <u>That except your righteousness shall exceed the righteousness of the scribes and Pharisees, ye shall in no case enter into the kingdom of</u> heaven. Matthew 5:17-20*

Jesus Christ came to fulfill the Law, as well as what the prophets foretold about Him, but again, does this mean Jesus taught His apostles (or anyone) to remove the Law of Moses for obedience? If you claim to be following "the words of Jesus," does your "righteousness exceed the righteousness of the scribes and Pharisees," who knew and studied the Law? If not, you have no place in "the kingdom of heaven."

On the other hand, did Paul teach the Gentiles that they were to maintain obedience under the Law of Moses? Many believers still insist that we are to obey all that Jesus commanded under His earthly ministry, but do they stop to consider "to whom" Jesus came? Did He not teach that He came "to none other than to the lost sheep of the house of Israel"? Did Jesus command Paul to place Gentiles under the Law of Moses? If so, then Paul was outside the will of Jesus Christ when he wrote the following passages to the Romans:

> *24 <u>Being justified freely by his grace through the redemption that is in Christ Jesus</u>: 25 Whom God hath set forth to be <u>a propitiation through faith in his blood</u>, to declare his righteousness for the remission of sins that are past, through the forbearance of God; 26 To declare, I say, at this time his righteousness: that he might be just, and the justifier of him which believeth in Jesus. 27 <u>Where is boasting then?</u> It is excluded. By what law? of works? Nay: but by the law of faith. 28 <u>Therefore we conclude that a man is justified by faith without the deeds of the</u> law. Romans 3:24-28*

> *4 Now to him that worketh is the reward not reckoned of grace, but of debt. 5 But to him*

that worketh not, but believeth on him that
justifieth the ungodly, his faith is counted for
righteousness. Romans 4:4-5

14 For sin shall not have dominion over you:
for ye are not under the law, but under grace.
Romans 6:14

4 For Christ is the end of the law for
righteousness to every one that believeth.
Romans 10:4

During the earthly ministry of Jesus Christ, and the early chapters of Acts, we find *no such gospel* where salvation came by way of grace, through faith (in the death and resurrection of Christ) without works. John the Baptist, Jesus, and the twelve disciples all preached repentance and water baptism for the remission of sins. Jesus Christ kept the Law because He was "born under the Law," but Gentiles were not given the Law; therefore, we are not under it (Rom. 6:14; Gal. 4:4-5). You need not struggle to reconcile Peter's and Paul's messages (taught to them by Jesus) if you simply "rightly divide" to whom each were sent, with what words, and at what time.

So "to whom" did Jesus send His disciples with the gospel of the kingdom?

5 These twelve Jesus sent forth, and
commanded them, saying, Go not into the way
of the Gentiles, and into any city of the

*Samaritans enter ye not: 6 But go rather to the
lost sheep of the house of Israel. 7 And as ye
go, preach, saying, The kingdom of heaven is
at hand. 8 Heal the sick, cleanse the lepers,
raise the dead, cast out devils: freely ye have
received, freely give. Matthew 10:5-8*

*22 And, behold, a woman of Canaan came out
of the same coasts, and cried unto him, saying,
Have mercy on me, O Lord, thou son of David;
my daughter is grievously vexed with a devil.
23 But he answered her not a word. And his
disciples came and besought him, saying, Send
her away; for she crieth after us. 24 <u>But he
answered and said, I am not sent but unto the
lost sheep of the house of Israel.</u> 25 Then came
she and worshipped him, saying, Lord, help
me. 26 But he answered and said, It is not meet
to take the children's bread, and to cast it to
dogs. Matthew 15:22-26*

*8 Now I say that Jesus Christ was a minister of
the circumcision for the truth of God, to
confirm the promises made unto the fathers:
Romans 15:8*

What Jesus taught to "the lost sheep of the house of Israel"
during His earthly ministry *does not* contradict what He
spoke to Paul for the Body of Christ (the new creature).
Again, we need to simply recognize that the twelve apostles

(before Acts 7), and the Apostle Paul (after Acts 7) were sent by Jesus to specific people at a specific time. They each had a specific purpose as well.

> *36 Therefore <u>let all the house of Israel</u> know assuredly, that God hath made the same Jesus, <u>whom ye have crucified</u>, both Lord and Christ [Messiah]. 37 Now when they heard this, they were <u>pricked in their heart</u>, and said unto Peter and to the rest of the apostles, <u>Men and brethren, what shall we do?</u> 38 Then Peter said unto them, <u>Repent, and be baptized every one of you in the name of Jesus Christ for the remission of sins, and ye shall receive the gift of the Holy Ghost.</u>*
> *Acts 2:36-38 (brackets by author)*

Nearly 8-10 years later, Peter was then sent to the home of a Gentile, but their salvation appeared in a different order than Pentecost, and their salvation was still predicated on the only gospel Peter knew at the time: the gospel of the kingdom.

> *44 While Peter yet spake these words, <u>the Holy Ghost fell on all them which heard the word</u>. 45 And <u>they of the circumcision which believed were astonished</u>, as many as came with Peter, because that <u>on the Gentiles also was poured out the gift of the Holy Ghost</u>. 46 For they heard them <u>speak with tongues</u>, and magnify*

God. Then answered Peter, 47 <u>Can any man</u>
<u>forbid water, that these should not be baptized,</u>
which have received the Holy Ghost as well as
we? 48 <u>And he commanded them to be baptized</u>
<u>in the name of the Lord...</u> Acts 10:44-48

On the other hand, Paul's first recorded sermon to the Jews and proselytes at Antioch was quite different.

38 Be it known unto you therefore, men and
brethren, that <u>through this man is preached</u>
<u>unto you the forgiveness of sins</u>: 39 And by him
<u>all that believe are justified from all things,</u>
<u>from which ye could not be justified by the law</u>
<u>of Moses</u>. Acts 13:38-39

17 For Christ sent me not to baptize, but to
preach the gospel: not with wisdom of words,
lest the cross of Christ should be made of none
effect. 18 <u>For the preaching of the cross</u> is to
them that perish foolishness; but unto us which
are saved it is the power of God.
I Corinthians 1:17-18

8 For by grace are ye saved through faith; and
that not of yourselves: it is the gift of God:
9 <u>Not of works</u>, lest any man should boast.
Ephesians 2:8-9

Peter shamed the "house of Israel" over their participation in the crucifixion of Jesus; however, Paul used the crucifixion as the basis for "the preaching of the cross." In fact, he stated:

> *15 So, as much as in me is, I am ready to preach the gospel to you that are at Rome also. 16 For I am not ashamed of the gospel of Christ: <u>for it is the power of God unto salvation to every one that believeth</u>; to the Jew first, and also to the Greek. 17 For therein is the righteousness of God revealed from faith to faith: as it is written, <u>The just shall live by faith</u>. Romans 1:15-17*

That stated (from the time of Jesus Christ's earthly ministry to the conversion of the Apostle Paul), Jesus commanded obedience to the Law of Moses. After all, He was born under the Law to "redeem them that were under the Law."

> *4 But when the fulness of the time was come, God sent forth his Son, made of a woman [Genesis 3:15], made under the law, 5 To redeem them [Israel] that were under the law, that we [Gentiles] might receive the adoption of sons [placing as a full-grown son]. Galatians 4:4-5 (brackets by author)*

Our identity "in Christ," places us as "full-grown" sons, which is the Greek meaning of "adoption," and when Jesus

Christ *was raised from the dead*, He was placed "far above all principality, and power, and might, and dominion…and hath put all things under His feet, and gave Him to be Head over all things to the church, which is His body, the fulness of Him that filleth all in all" (Ephesians 1:18-23). This is *our* identity in Jesus Christ as joint heirs, but again, this does not mean that this message was taught during the earthly ministry of Jesus Christ!

No Catholic, Orthodox, or Protestant church should claim any human as the "head" of their religious organization because it violates the clear teaching of an apostle of Jesus Christ. Christ is the only Head of the Church, The Body of Christ, no matter what *religion* teaches! Christ, as the Head of the Body (a new title), was not preached until Paul's letters. Prior to Paul's conversion, Christ was the Lord and Messiah of Israel, and He is still entitled to sit on "David's Throne" in the Kingdom promised to Israel through God's *unconditional* covenants with both Abraham and David. As for the Body of Christ, Jesus is our Savior, and He is the Head of the Church.

At His ascension, Jesus continued to declared water baptism for the remission of sins, and He also instructed the disciples to "teach them to observe all that I have commanded." Again, what did Jesus command during His earthly ministry to "the lost sheep of the house of Israel"?

> *16 And, behold, one came and said unto him,*
> *Good Master, what good thing shall I do, that I*
> *may have eternal life? 17 And he said unto him,*
> *Why callest thou me good? there is none good*
> *but one, that is, God: <u>but if thou wilt enter into</u>*

life, keep the commandments. 18 He saith unto him, Which? Jesus said, Thou shalt do no murder, Thou shalt not commit adultery, Thou shalt not steal, Thou shalt not bear false witness, 19 Honour thy father and thy mother: and, Thou shalt love thy neighbour as thyself. 20 The young man saith unto him, All these things have I kept from my youth up: what lack I yet? 21 Jesus said unto him, If thou wilt be perfect, go and sell that thou hast, and give to the poor, and thou shalt have treasure in heaven: and come and follow me.
Matthew 19:16-21

The twelve apostles continued this message into Acts 2.

41 Then they that gladly received his word were baptized: and the same day there were added unto them about three thousand souls. 42 And they continued stedfastly in the apostles' doctrine and fellowship, and in breaking of bread, and in prayers. 43 And fear came upon every soul: and many wonders and signs were done by the apostles. 44 And all that believed were together, and had all things common; 45 And sold their possessions and goods, and parted them to all men, as every man had need. Acts 2:41-45

If you believe we are still under the so-called Great Commission (the gospel of the kingdom), then water baptism, signs and wonders, and selling of possessions is expected. As for following the commandments, we have the following instructions to "the lost sheep of the house of Israel":

> *12 Verily, verily, I say unto you, He that believeth on me, the works that I do shall he do also; and greater works than these shall he do; because I go unto my Father. 13 And whatsoever ye shall ask in my name, that will I do, that the Father may be glorified in the Son. 14 If ye shall ask any thing in my name, I will do it. 15 If ye love me, keep my commandments.*
> *John 14:12-15*

> *Whosoever believeth that Jesus is the Christ is born of God: and every one that loveth him that begat loveth him also that is begotten of him. 2 By this we know that we love the children of God, when we love God, and keep his commandments. 3 For this is the love of God, that we keep his commandments: and his commandments are not grievous. I John 5:1-3*

From the time of Jesus (and His earthly ministry) to the preaching of "grace, through faith" by Paul, Jesus did not remove the commandments from His teaching, and even as late as Acts 10, when Peter went by "revelation of Jesus" to the home of Cornelius, a Gentile, he entered the home and declared (some 8-10 years *after* Pentecost):

> *25 And as Peter was coming in, Cornelius met him, and fell down at his feet, and worshipped him. 26 But Peter took him up, saying, <u>Stand up; I myself also am a man</u>. 27 And as he talked with him, he went in, and found many that were come together. 28 And he said unto them, <u>Ye know how that it is an unlawful thing for a man that is a Jew to keep company, or come unto one of another nation</u>; but God hath shewed me that I should not call any man common or unclean. Acts 10:25-28*

Even as late as a decade after Pentecost, Peter was still operating under the Law. Again, during the earthly ministry of Jesus Christ, and even early into the Book of Acts, the Law was still in effect for Jews and proselytes. Most pastors and priests fail to see this.

Was Israel Offered the Kingdom that Jesus Said Was "At Hand"?

Beginning in Acts 2 and 3, the apostles told the Jews (and proselytes) to "repent and be baptized," and many did obey this for they anticipated the kingdom that Jesus declared to be "at hand" during His earthly ministry (Matt. 3:2; 4:17; 10:7; Mark 1:15; Luke 21:31). This Messianic Kingdom was offered again in Acts 3 (before their full rejection in fall in Acts 7).

> *19 Repent ye therefore, and be converted, that your sins may be blotted out, when the times of refreshing shall come from the presence of the Lord. 20 And he shall send Jesus Christ, which before was preached unto you: 21 Whom the heaven must receive until the times of restitution of all things, which God hath spoken by the mouth of all his holy prophets since the world began. Acts 3:19-21*

The twelve apostles were offering the Messianic Kingdom in the early chapters of Acts, which had been promised, and was known "*since* the world began"; however, the gospel of salvation "by grace, through faith…apart from works" was still "*kept secret* since the world began" at the time the apostle offered the kingdom to Israel. It was after the stoning of Stephen in Acts 7 that God finally introduced how salvation was by grace, through faith…apart from works (through the gospel Jesus gave to Paul). (I will explain Acts 7 in subsequent chapters.)

From Adam to Acts 7, no one knew about the "gospel of the grace of God," so the only gospel they had known (and preached) was "the gospel of the kingdom" (Matt. 4:23; 9:35; 24:14; Mark 1:14-15). It wasn't until after Acts 9 that the gospel of the grace of God was made known (Eph. 3:1-5), so no such gospel message about faith in the shed blood and resurrection, or any revelation about the Body of Christ (Jews and Gentiles) having a heavenly citizenship, was ever revealed. It was "unsearchable" (not traceable (Eph. 3:8)). This is why Paul referred to this gospel as "my gospel, and the preaching of Jesus Christ, according to the revelation of the mystery, which was kept secret since the world began, but is now made manifest…" (Rom. 16:25-26).

This is one of several reasons why we must "rightly divide the word of truth"; otherwise, we end up with religious dogmas that force their unnecessary hermeneutics (interpretation) upon Scripture. If we recognize "the mystery," we need not change the earthly ministry of Jesus to "the lost sheep of the house of Israel" in any way, as some theologians must do to support their man-made theologies and covenants. This is how we ended up with theologians somehow making the Body of Christ "spiritual Israel." It is also the reason why people struggle to "follow the words of Jesus" regarding water baptism and obedience to the Commandments, which were not given to the Body of Christ, but rather they were preached to "the house of Israel" during the time Jesus preached on this earth.

Are We Still Under the Law, As Some Insist, or Are We Under Grace?

There are several biblical principles we must acknowledge before we can discover our true identity in Christ: (1) Where in the Bible, prior to Paul's "revelation of the mystery" from Jesus, was it ever made known that salvation was "by grace, through faith in the shed blood of Christ and His resurrection…apart from works (or the Law)? (2) Since Paul explained that the gospel he preached was "not after man… for I neither received it of man, neither was I taught it, but by revelation of Jesus Christ" (Gal. 1:11-12), how can we claim that Paul was just another apostle teaching the same gospel as the twelve apostles? (3) We need to know the differences between the revelation of God through prophecy, and His revelation under the Mystery, and how vital it is to "rightly divide the word of truth" to know these differences.

Paul revealed, through the gospel of the grace of God, the following:

> *16 Knowing that a man is not justified by the works of the law, but by the faith of Jesus Christ, even we have believed in Jesus Christ, that we might be justified by the faith of Christ, and not by the works of the law: for by the works of the law shall no flesh be justified...21 I do not frustrate the grace of God: for if righteousness come by the law, then Christ is dead in vain. Galatians 2:16 and 21*

> *11 But that no man is justified by the law in the sight of God, it is evident: for, The just shall live by faith. 12 And the law is not of faith: but, The man that doeth them shall live in them. 13 Christ hath redeemed us from the curse of the law, being made a curse for us: for it is written, Cursed is every one that hangeth on a tree: 14 That the blessing of Abraham might come on the Gentiles through Jesus Christ; that we might receive the promise of the Spirit through faith. Galatians 3:11-14*

> *15 Having abolished in his flesh the enmity,*
> *even the law of commandments contained in*
> *ordinances; for to make in himself of twain*
> *one new man, so making peace; 16 And that he*
> *might reconcile both unto God in one body by*
> *the cross, having slain the enmity thereby:*
> *Ephesians 2:15-16*

> *13 And you, being dead in your sins and the*
> *uncircumcision of your flesh, hath he*
> *quickened together with him, having forgiven*
> *you all trespasses; 14 Blotting out the*
> *handwriting of ordinances that was against us,*
> *which was contrary to us, and took it out of the*
> *way, nailing it to his cross; 15 And having*
> *spoiled principalities and powers, he made a*
> *shew of them openly, triumphing over them in*
> *it. Colossians 2:13-15*

These instructions were from Jesus Christ to Paul, and yes, they are for our understanding and obedience since the time Paul taught them. Rather than trying to "explain away," or "spiritualize" these passages, why can't we just acknowledge that God changed "the house rules" (dispensation) when it came to the means of salvation for individual Jews and Gentiles, which Paul stated was "by grace, through faith (in Christ's redeeming work), apart from our own works? This was not the gospel of the kingdom preached during the earthly ministry of Jesus, and in early Acts!

Many pastors already believe in salvation by grace, through faith, apart from works, but do they understand why such a gospel was introduced after it had been "hidden from ages past" (Eph. 3:5)? Do they truly realize which apostle was *first* given this revelation, and why it was revealed after Acts 7 (I Tim. 1:16; Eph. 3:6-9)? Is it correct to combine this gospel of grace with the gospel of the kingdom, which commanded "repent and be baptized for the remission of sins"? Wouldn't it be easier to "rightly divide," rather than develop so many theologies that leave much of the understanding of the New Testament into the hands of theologians who "spiritualize" what they obviously refuse to "rightly divide"?

Most believers insist they are "following the words of Jesus" from the "gospels" (Matthew, Mark, Luke, and John), and they do so by not realizing Jesus came only "to the lost sheep of the house of Israel...to confirm the promises made unto the fathers." It wasn't until Paul that we understand the universal nature of His death and resurrection for both Jews and Gentiles. These same theologians also fail to recognize that the Church, the Body of Christ, was still a "hidden wisdom," which no one knew until Jesus revealed it to Paul after Acts 9. Sadly, they pay little to no attention to the fact that Paul was separated (Acts 13:1-2) for a special purpose to the Gentiles, and he is the only apostle in the Scripture to hold the office of "the apostle to the Gentiles" (Rom. 11:13). In fact, ignoring these truths does not make us "spiritually mature."

> *33 For God is not the author of confusion, but of peace, as in all churches of the saints… 37 If any man think himself to be a prophet, or spiritual, <u>let him acknowledge that the things that I write unto you are the commandments of the Lord.</u> 38 But if any man be ignorant, let him be ignorant. I Corinthians 14:33 and 37-38*

Paul's gospel message, "by revelation of Jesus Christ," was the introduction of "the mystery, which was kept secret since the world began," and as such, he was, and still is *the pattern* for those who believe, for they are now "justified from all things, from which (they) could not be justified by the Law of Moses" (Acts 13:38-39). Paul presents this pattern in the following passages:

> *15 This is a faithful saying, and worthy of all acceptation, that Christ Jesus came into the world to save sinners; of whom I am chief. 16 Howbeit for this cause I obtained mercy, that in me <u>first</u> Jesus Christ might shew forth all longsuffering, <u>for a pattern</u> to them which should hereafter believe on him to life everlasting. I Timothy 1:15-16*

> *15 For though ye have ten thousand instructers in Christ, yet have ye not many fathers: for in Christ Jesus I have begotten you through the gospel. 16 Wherefore I beseech you, <u>be ye followers of me</u>. I Corinthians 4:15-16*

Be ye followers of me, even as I also am of Christ. *2 Now I praise you, brethren, that ye remember me in all things, and keep the ordinances, as I delivered them to you.*
I Corinthians 11:1-2

16 Nevertheless, whereto we have already attained, let us walk by the same rule, let us mind the same thing. 17 Brethren, be followers together of me, and mark them which walk so as ye have us for an ensample.
Philippians 3:16-17

3 As I besought thee to abide still at Ephesus, when I went into Macedonia, that thou mightest charge some that they teach no other doctrine, 4 Neither give heed to fables and endless genealogies, which minister questions, rather than godly edifying which is in faith: so do. I Timothy 1:3-4

8 But though we, or an angel from heaven, preach any other gospel unto you than that which we have preached unto you, let him be accursed. 9 As we said before, so say I now again, if any man preach any other gospel unto you than that ye have received, let him be accursed. Galatians 1:8-9

Paul did not say to worship him; he simply declared to "follow me, even as I follow Christ," and yet many believers insist on following Jesus and the twelve apostles' teachings in "the gospels" and early Acts, knowing that Paul was the only "apostle to the Gentiles" given to the Body of Christ. Following Paul's gospel *is* following "the words of Jesus Christ," but thanks to "the traditions of men," many are still attempting to "follow in the footsteps of Jesus," when in fact, His death proved that it was impossible for us to do so (Rom. 8:1-4). This is why Paul is so adamant about proclaiming the gospel of the grace of God, which is still the only gospel we are to be proclaiming for salvation today, not "repent and be baptized for the remission of sins," or "keep the commandments," as an act of obedience to be saved. Many people believe they are saved by grace, but they see it as the initiation into salvation, which must then be accompanied by works (through sacraments) to obtain full justification in the sight of God. Paul is clear when he taught, "But to him that worketh not, but believes on Him that justifies the ungodly, his faith is counted as righteousness" (Rom. 4:5). Again, this is exactly what he taught to the Ephesians.

> *8 For <u>by grace are ye saved through faith</u>; and*
> *that not of yourselves: it is the gift of God:*
> *9 <u>Not of works</u>, lest any man should boast.*
> *Ephesians 2:8-9*

Many believers refuse to acknowledge this change in the administration of God's salvation plans between the earthly ministry of Jesus and what He taught later to Paul through the "revelation of the mystery." The words *stewardship, fellowship, and dispensation* are words Paul uses in his epistles to describe this change in the administration of God's plan for salvation. Note the following passages:

> *² If ye have heard of <u>the dispensation of the grace of God</u> which is given me to you-ward:*
> *Ephesians 3:2*

> *⁹ <u>And to make all men see what is the fellowship of the mystery,</u> which from the beginning of the world hath been hid in God, who created all things by Jesus Christ:*
> *Ephesians 3:9*

> *²⁵ Whereof I am made a minister, <u>according to the dispensation of God which is given to me for you, to fulfil the word of God</u>;*
> *Colossians 1:25*

If this "mystery" is not being proclaimed in your church, you need to ask why. Many priests and pastors will boast how the Bible is "filled with mysteries," but I am talking directly about "The Mystery," which was *first* revealed to Paul "as a pattern" for the "new creature," the Body of Christ. As stated earlier, many clergy will attempt to combine the gospel of the kingdom (Great Commission) with the gospel of the grace of God, and this is why we have so many denominations today. We just need to "rightly divide the word of truth" to avoid much of the confusion. I certainly believe in every word Jesus said, but I also ascribe to how important it is to know "to whom" Jesus spoke, and "at what time" He proclaimed His "good news" messages.

Tragically, many clergy often overlook the fact that there was an even *Greater* Commission given to Paul in 2 Corinthians.

> *17 Therefore if any man be in Christ, <u>he is a new creature</u>: old things are passed away; behold, all things are become new. 18 And all things are of God, who hath reconciled us to himself by Jesus Christ, <u>and hath given to us the ministry of reconciliation</u>; 19 To wit, that God was in Christ, reconciling the world unto himself, not imputing their trespasses unto them; <u>and hath committed unto us the word of reconciliation</u>. 20 Now then we are ambassadors for Christ, as though God did beseech you by us: we pray you in Christ's stead, be ye reconciled to God. 21 <u>For he hath made him to be sin for us, who knew no sin; that we might be made the righteousness of God in him.</u> 2 Corinthians 5:17-21*

The only means of reconciliation with God, which has been made available since Paul received it, is for us to place our faith in the shed blood and resurrection of Christ for the "remission of sins." It is "faith in His blood" that brings this forgiveness.

24 Being justified freely by his grace through the redemption that is in Christ Jesus: 25 Whom God hath set forth to be a propitiation through faith in his blood, to declare his righteousness for the remission of sins that are past, through the forbearance of God; 26 To declare, I say, at this time his righteousness: that he might be just, and the justifier of him which believeth in Jesus. Romans 3:24-26

We must "rightly divide" between the words of Paul and the other apostles. By combining their gospels, and failing to obey 2 Timothy 2:15, we have created many denominations that always argue over the doctrines of Law and Grace, water baptism, and our walk as believers. This need not be the case.

Chapter Conclusion

This is just the "tip of the iceberg" when studying why the Bible appears to have contradictions between the teachings of the prophets and the twelve apostles, and that of Paul's ministry, primarily to the Gentiles. "Rightly dividing" has been put into place to help believers differentiate the Scriptures that have been written *to* them, *about* them, and *for* them. There are no contradictions in the Bible; just a failure to "rightly dividing" it!

In the next two chapters, we will examine an overview of the Book of Acts, and how it reveals the transition between God's dealings with Israel, and how He has diverted His plan of salvation for Israel and the nations over to individual Jews and Gentiles in the Body of Christ, which was "kept secret since the world began." We will also see why God made this drastic change from the promises of an earthly kingdom to Israel to the heavenly citizenship for the Body of Christ.

CHAPTER 3

An Overview of the Book of Acts and Why It Matters

28 Be it known therefore unto you, that the salvation of God is sent unto the Gentiles, and that they will hear it. 29 And when he had said these words, the Jews departed, and had great reasoning among themselves. Acts 28:28-29

Why the Book of Acts Needs "Rightly Divided"

May we never forget the transitional nature of this important narrative written by Luke. The transition in Acts (change from one *known* program to something *new*) was initiated around the time of the events involving the stoning of Stephen (Acts 7) and the conversion of Paul in Acts 9 (circa AD 34). Prior to these events, "salvation was of the Jews" (John 4:22), and God's focus on Israel was the fulfillment of "the promises made unto the fathers," which the twelve apostles officially began to offer to Israel in the early chapters of Acts.

This offer came on the heels of the gospel *they* preached with Jesus ("the kingdom of heaven is *at hand*"), which was to the "lost sheep of the house of Israel" (Matt. 10:5-7;15:24). They were told to begin in Jerusalem (Luke 24:47) before venturing out into the whole world. Interestingly, it was Paul (prior to his conversion) who had thwarted much of their efforts in Jerusalem. As a result, James, Peter, and John had to write to the "twelve tribes scattered abroad" in their letters to the "circumcision" (Jews), and after the fall of Jerusalem in AD 70, it was the gospel of the grace of God that was able to provide the only means of salvation to the world, regardless of what religious traditions may boast. Can a person be saved today without faith in the death and resurrection of Jesus Christ? Of course not, but many theologians fail to realize that no one can be saved today under the so-called Great Commission because this commission says nothing about salvation being by grace, through faith, without works. It teaches nothing about the Body of Christ, the "new creature" with a heavenly citizenship. This was all revealed under "the revelation of the mystery, which was kept secret since the world began." You cannot be saved today through "repent and be baptized for the remission of sins." It is now "through faith in His blood" (Rom. 3:25). This is the main reason why we need to understand the Book of Acts, "rightly divided."

John the Baptist initiated the gospel of the kingdom when he declared to Israel: "Repent, for the kingdom of heaven is at hand." Those who heard and responded were saved through the "baptism of repentance for the remission of sins" (Matt. 3:1-2; Lk. 3:3; Mk. 1:1-4; John 1:19-34; Acts 2:38-39). This was the only gospel available for salvation at the time of the earthly ministry of Jesus Christ, which instructed believers to "believe on His name" (as *the* Christ, the Messiah). As I have written, there had not yet been a gospel that preached salvation by grace, through faith in the shed blood and resurrection of Jesus (apart from works). It was yet "unsearchable," and kept "hid in God" (Eph. 3:8-9) for a specific purpose. Israel had to reject God, the Son, and the Holy Ghost (as well as the Messianic Kingdom) before this "revelation of the mystery" could be revealed to the whole world. This rejection occurred in Acts 7 at the stoning of Stephen. Instead of judgement (Acts 7:54-56), God thankfully poured out His grace (instead of wrath) when He saved Paul on the road to Damascus and sent him with the gospel of the grace of God (Acts 20:24).

May we never forget that during the earthly ministry of Jesus Christ, it had *not yet* been preached that any Jew, let alone a Gentile, could be "justified from all things, from which you could *not* be justified by the Law of Moses" (John 14:15; Acts 13:38-39). This gospel was yet a "hidden wisdom" ordained by God for us (the Body of Christ) "before the world began" (2 Tim. 1:9). Our identity crisis has been created by those who attempt to combine the salvation proclaimed during the earthly ministry of Jesus Christ, and the further revelation Jesus had given to Paul for Gentiles, apart from any conversion to Judaism first. This is why it is called "the mystery."

At the stoning of Stephen in Acts 7:51-60, Israel's leaders (the Sanhedrin) had blasphemed the Holy Ghost, and they continued their hostility against those who had accepted Jesus as *the* Christ (the Messiah). This led to national Israel's spiritual fall, just like Gentiles who'd already been given over to a "reprobate mind" millennia before Israel's rejection of

Christ (Rom.1:28; 9:30-32). It wasn't until Israel had "fallen" in Acts 7 that "both Jews and Gentiles" were declared to be "under sin" (Rom. 3:9). Thankfully, this was declared so that God could have mercy on us all (Rom. 11:32). This mercy was then provided through Jesus under "the revelation of the mystery."

Interestingly, while Stephen was being stoned to death, he gazed up into heaven and "saw the Son of man *standing* at the right hand of God" (Acts 7:55-56). The next prophetic event that should have occurred would have been the Tribulation (Matthew 24), but something prevented this from taking place. It was obviously "the revelation of the mystery" that Jesus revealed to Paul, beginning in Acts 9. God was finally revealing something He had "kept secret since the world began." Since Israel had "received Him not," this meant that the Gentiles could not be blessed without that nation, as God had promised through the prophets. A different means of salvation was about to be announced for the first time, and it was to become the "pattern" to all who believe.

Again, prior to Paul's conversion, where in the Scriptures did anyone reveal that salvation was by grace, through faith in the blood and resurrection of Jesus, apart from works? Where had it been preached that Gentiles could be "joint heirs" with Jesus Christ, apart from Israel? Where did Gentiles, prior to Paul's conversion, even know about having a "citizenship in heaven" (Phil. 3:20)? God will still fulfill His earthly kingdom promises to Israel, but for now, He is working on restoring Heaven through the Body of Christ. I will explain this two-fold purpose of God soon.

Acts 7 is a pivotal chapter because it showed how Israel had both "stumbled at the cross" and officially fell spiritually when they refused the Holy Ghost and had Stephen put to death. Those who killed Stephen laid their clothes at the feet of a zealous Pharisee named Saul (Acts 7:58), and thus, an important transition period in Acts began to unfold. Romans 11 helps reveal this.

> *11 I say then, Have they stumbled that they should fall? God forbid: but rather <u>through their fall salvation is come unto the Gentiles</u>, for to provoke them to jealousy. 12 Now if the fall of them be the riches of the world, and the diminishing of them the riches of the Gentiles; how much more their fulness? 13 For I speak to you Gentiles, <u>inasmuch as I am the apostle of the Gentiles, I magnify mine office</u>: 14 If by any means I may provoke to emulation them which are my flesh, and might save some of them. 15 For <u>if the casting away</u> of them be the reconciling of the world, <u>what shall the receiving of them be</u>, but life from the dead?*
> *Romans 11:11-15*

The transition in Acts (from the gospel of the kingdom to the gospel of the grace of God) occurred for nearly three decades, ending about AD 62 when Paul declared to the Jews: "Be in known therefore unto you, that the salvation of God is sent unto the Gentiles, and that they will hear it" (Acts 28:28). Not long after this, in AD 70, the Temple was destroyed in Jerusalem, and Israel was officially cut off from the possibility of being the means through which salvation could be taken to the "ends of the earth" (Isa. 49:6), which was God's plan throughout prophecy (and still is). Remember, Jesus came "to fulfill the promises made unto the fathers" (Rom. 15:8).

Thankfully, God did not leave the world without a plan for salvation. We are *now* able to be reconciled (restored to fellowship) with God through the good news that Paul referred to as "my gospel, and the preaching of Jesus Christ, according to the revelation of the mystery, which was kept secret since the world began, but now is made manifest…" (Rom. 16:25-26). This is what Paul referred to as the "gospel of the grace of God" (Acts 20:24), and it was revealed *after* his conversion in Acts 9. Again, there is no biblical evidence of this gospel in Scripture prior to Paul's conversion. If there were, it wouldn't be called "the mystery." Even the believers in Acts 2 knew absolutely nothing about Paul's gospel message to Gentiles, apart from Israel. After all, Israel had not yet "fallen" at the time of Pentecost. How far reaching was this this gospel of God's grace?

> *24 But none of these things move me, neither*
> *count I my life dear unto myself, <u>so that I</u>*
> *<u>might finish my course with joy, and the</u>*
> *<u>ministry, which I have received of the Lord</u>*
> *<u>Jesus, to testify the gospel of the grace of God.</u>*
> *Acts 20:24*

*23 If ye continue in the faith grounded and
settled, and be not moved away from <u>the hope
of the gospel</u>, which ye have heard, and <u>which
was preached to every creature which is under
heaven; whereof I Paul am made a minister;</u>
Colossians 1:23*

Before this gospel was revealed, Gentiles were "given over to a reprobate mind" long before God revealed this "hidden wisdom" to Paul, which was "kept secret since the world began" (Rom. 1:28; 16:25; I Tim. 1:8-9). Gentiles had no favor with God, apart from converting to Judaism; however, faith in the blood of Jesus changed this, and now, Gentiles can be fellow heirs with Christ (Rom. 8:17; Eph. 3:6), having been brought "nigh unto God" by Christ's blood (Eph. 2:13).

*11 Wherefore remember, that ye being in time
past Gentiles in the flesh, who are called
<u>Uncircumcision</u> by that which is called the
<u>Circumcision</u> in the flesh made by hands;
12 <u>That at that time ye were without Christ,</u>
being <u>aliens from the commonwealth of Israel,</u>
and <u>strangers from the covenants of promise,</u>
<u>having no hope,</u> and <u>without God in the world</u>:
13 <u>But now in Christ Jesus ye who sometimes
were far off are made nigh by the blood of
Christ.</u> Ephesians 2:11-13*

A Disastrous Omission in Doctrine

Most believers simply dismiss the "revelation of the mystery" as being nothing more than Paul's continuation of the Great Commission—something he was *supposedly* sent by the other apostles to preach to the Gentiles (Galatians 1:11-12). Remember, Gentiles were "strangers from Israel" and "without God in the world" prior to Paul's conversion. If we do not "rightly divide" between the events at Pentecost, Israel's "spiritual fall" in Acts 7, Paul's calling in Acts 9, his first recorded sermon in Acts 13 (differing from Peter's in Acts 2), and his final declaration that "the salvation of God is sent unto the Gentiles" in Acts 28, we will not understand most of the Book of Acts. We will also struggle to figure out why Paul continued to preach about Jesus in synagogues (while also establishing Gentile churches), declared that justification was apart from the Law of Moses, how he became the only apostle to be called "the apostle to the Gentiles," why he circumcised Timothy and water baptized *some* people, and why he eventually stopped preaching "to the Jew first." Again, the Book of Acts shows the transition between the gospel of the kingdom and the gospel of the grace of God, even though many believers omit this distinction altogether.

From the passage I quoted previously from Ephesians 2, Gentiles were "alienated" from the commonwealth of Israel at the time of Jesus Christ's earthly ministry (as well as the time of Pentecost in Acts 2), so Gentiles were not brought "nigh unto God" until after "the revelation of the mystery." Before this revelation, Gentiles could only have access to God through converting to Judaism (Acts 2:10). Traditions want us to believe that Jesus Christ focused (in "the gospels") on the Body of Christ, consisting of Jews and Gentiles saved by grace, through faith in His blood and resurrection; however, if this were correct, why would Jesus declare that He was "sent to none other than to the lost sheep of the house of Israel"? This also causes us to wonder why Acts 9:15; 13:1-2; 13:46; 18:6 and 28:28 all state that God had called Paul specifically to "go to the Gentiles" with a gospel that had been "kept secret since the world began."

The so-called Great Commission had already been known before Paul's conversion, so the Great Commission couldn't have been "the revelation of the mystery" that Paul was sent "by revelation of Jesus Christ" to proclaim (Gal. 1:11-12). Peter realized God was opening the door to Gentile salvation (Acts 10), but Paul was the only "apostle to the Gentiles" named in Scripture (Rom. 11:13). God was preparing Peter for what Paul was sent to preach, and that is why James, Peter, and John gave Paul (and Barnabas) "the right hands of fellowship; that we (Paul and Barnabas) should go *unto* the heathen (Gentiles/ "uncircumcision") and they (James Peter, and John) *unto* the circumcision (Jews)" (Gal. 2:9). Did they go with the same gospel? That is the million-dollar question!

If Gentiles, apart from Judaism, were already included in God's plan of salvation from the time of Acts 2 (as well as the time of the events in the so-called "gospels"), we must wonder why Jesus Christ had to give a *special* revelation to Peter (about ten years after Pentecost), commanding him to visit a Gentile (Cornelius) in Acts 10—something Peter still considered to be a violation of the Law of Moses (Acts 10:28). Also, if Gentiles, apart from Judaism, were already included as part of Peter's gospel message at Pentecost, why would Luke declare, as late as Acts 11, that the gospel was being preached "to none but unto the Jews only" (Acts 11:19)? It is clear that "the revelation of the mystery" was still *unknown* to these scattered Jews in Acts 11. We tend to forget this fact. Simply stated: If Paul was sent to preach the Great Commission, why would Jesus give him "the revelation of the mystery, kept secret since the world began," especially if the gospel at Pentecost supposedly offered salvation by grace, through faith, *apart* from works (and even *apart* from Israel)? If there were no differences between the Jews and Gentiles at Pentecost, Acts 10 makes no sense, especially Peter's response to it being "unlawful" for him to be in the home of a Gentile.

What If the Book of Acts Didn't Exist

We should also consider how confusing it would be if the Book of Acts was omitted from the Bible. Believers would finish reading in the "gospels" about the earthly ministry of Jesus telling them to be baptized, keep the commandments, and how "the kingdom of heaven is at hand," to now reading about some previously unknown apostle (Paul) preaching, "For Christ sent me not to baptize, but to preach the gospel… lest the cross of Christ be made of none effect" (I Cor. 1:17). How confusing would it be for believers to also read from Paul: "Therefore, we conclude that a man is justified by faith, without the deeds of the Law" (Rom. 3:28)? The Book of Acts explains why this change occurred.

Where in the "gospels" did *Jesus* ever teach that salvation was "by grace, through faith (in His blood and the resurrection) without works, or the Law"? Where in Romans through Philemon did Paul ever command the "(water) baptism of repentance for the remission of sins" for salvation (Mark 1:4), specifically to Gentiles? If water baptism was necessary for the "remission of sins" in the gospel of the grace of God, shouldn't the sign gifts that accompanied the water baptism also be more evident today in all who are water baptized? When and where did Paul command justification before God by "keeping the commandments," especially for Gentiles? How confused would you be without reading Acts before Paul was declared to be "the apostle to the Gentiles" in Romans? Once again, the Book of Acts is necessary to show how the focus of salvation shifted from the gospel of the kingdom to the gospel of the grace of God. We see Israel's *decline*, while at the same time, we see the *rising* of the gospel of Christ to the Gentiles, apart from Judaism. In fact, after Acts 15, Peter is not mentioned again. The transition is apparent to all who "rightly divide the word of truth," especially in the Book of Acts.

What Epistles Were Written During Acts, and Does It Matter?

Paul's epistles can be confusing at times because he wrote some of his letters during the time of the transition from God's focus on the "Church that was at Jerusalem" (Acts 8:1) to His focus on Gentiles in the Body of Christ, which is the "new creature" (also called "the Church" (Eph. 1:22-23)). Tradition insists these churches are the same, but God's promises to Israel (Acts 1:6; 3:19-21; 7:51-60), and His calling of the Gentiles, apart from Israel (Acts 13:46; 18:6;

28:28), do not share the same means of salvation, obedience under the Law, and their eternal destinies.

In Acts 15, there is a clear distinction being made between the gospel James and Peter preached to the "circumcision," and the gospel Paul was sent to declare unto the "uncircumcision." This is evident because "the Church that was at Jerusalem" was still under the Law in Acts 15, and James, Peter, and John continued to preach to the Jews "scattered abroad" with the "gospel of the circumcision" (kingdom), which is referenced throughout their epistles (in preparation for the "last days"). Paul, on the other hand, was *not* sent to preach the so-called Great Commission (gospel of the kingdom), but rather he was sent to proclaim the gospel of the grace of God (Acts 20:24), which was not revealed until *after* Acts 9. As mentioned, after Acts 15, Peter is not mentioned once in the remaining chapters in Acts, and this is a significant change, which finally led to Paul declaring in Acts 28:28: "Be it known therefore unto you, that the salvation of God has been sent to the Gentiles, and that they will hear it." James, Peter, John, and Paul preached the same Jesus, but failing to recognize the transitional nature of the Book of Acts will only deepen the identity crisis we are already struggling to overcome within our faith.

During the Acts period, Paul wrote Galatians, I & II Thessalonians, I & II Corinthians, and Romans. In these letters, we often encounter various commands that are not doctrinally found in his later epistles (after the transition), such as healings, speaking in tongues, and water baptism. I know this disturbs believers who can't differentiate between water and spiritual baptism, but these are the same believers who do not "rightly divide the word of truth," nor do they acknowledge Paul's apostleship concerning "the preaching of Jesus Christ, according to the revelation of the mystery." They continue trying to fulfill the Great Commission, while ignoring the command "to make all men see what is the fellowship of the mystery, which from the beginning of the world hath been hid in God…" (Eph. 3:9).

Paul, during the events recorded throughout Acts, was still desperately trying to convert the Jews ("my kinsmen according to the flesh"), and he also taught how "the Jews require a sign" (Rom. 1:16; 2:9-10; 9:1-5; I Cor. 9:20). This would explain why Paul seemed to combine some concepts from the "gospels" into his teachings throughout his ministry, especially with the phrase "to the Jew first, and also to the Greek" (Rom. 1:16; 2:10). At his conversion, however, the Gentiles are mentioned first, indicating that the focus of God was about to change (Acts 9:15).

After Acts 28, we see how Paul wrote to specific Gentile churches without addressing "the Jew first," as he often did nearly ten times in the Book of Acts alone (especially when he went to synagogues first to proclaim Jesus as *the Christ*). Many of these Jews became members of the Body of Christ because they had not heard of the ministry that took place at Pentecost under the twelve apostles. In fact, Paul stated the following regarding his ministry and that of the others:

> *18 For I will not dare to speak of any of*
> *those things which Christ hath not wrought by*
> *me, to make the Gentiles obedient, by word*
> *and deed, 19 Through mighty signs and*

> *wonders, by the power of the Spirit of God; so*
> *that from Jerusalem, and round about unto*
> *Illyricum, I have fully preached the gospel of*
> *Christ. 20 Yea, so have I strived to preach the*
> *gospel, not where Christ was named, lest I*
> *should build upon another man's foundation:*
> *Romans 15:18-20*

Paul did *not* demand that the Jews and proselytes (already saved under the ministry of the Twelve) convert again under his gospel; he simply preached Christ to those who had never heard and believed the gospel that any of them had been sent to preach. All the Jews and Gentiles who believed "the gospel of Christ" that Paul had been preaching would have then become members of the Body of Christ (promised a heavenly citizenship). Paul did not tread on the ministry of James, Peter, and John (to the "circumcision") because he understood that he was sent as "the apostle to the Gentiles" (to the "uncircumcision"). James, Peter, and John continued their ministry to the Jews, especially those who had believed the gospel of the kingdom but were now "scattered abroad" throughout many regions. This agreement is explained in the following passage:

> *7 But contrariwise, when they saw that the*
> *gospel of the uncircumcision was committed*
> *unto me, as the gospel of the circumcision was*
> *unto Peter; 8 (For he that wrought effectually*
> *in Peter to the apostleship of the circumcision,*
> *the same was mighty in me toward the*

Gentiles:) ⁹ And when James, Cephas, and John, who seemed to be pillars, perceived the grace that was given unto me, they gave to me and Barnabas the right hands of fellowship; <u>*that we should go unto the heathen, and they unto the circumcision*</u>*. Galatians 2:7-9*

That stated, by the end of the events recorded in Acts, Paul had no obligation "to the Jew first" because God had fully turned to the Gentiles (and individual Jews (not the nation)) with the gospel of the grace of God (Acts 20:24; 28:28), which is now the *only* gospel by which we can be saved (from that time until now). I know this contradicts the traditions of many denominations, but many theologians still focus their teachings on the so-called "gospels," rather than the doctrines of the one apostle that Jesus sent to the Gentiles. Paul is often overshadowed by Peter in many Gentile churches, which is odd, considering Paul is "the apostle to the Gentiles." In essence, many Gentiles assume Jesus was preaching to them in "the gospels," but Jesus was clear that He came "to the lost sheep of the house of Israel."

We should also note that the "middle wall of partition" between Jews and Gentiles was not yet "broken down" until after Paul's conversion in Acts 9—not in Acts 2. Prior to Paul, there was certainly a separation between Jews and Gentiles. Jesus began to chip away at this separation when He sent Peter to the home of Cornelius, but it was Paul's gospel (regarding the "new creature") that tore it completely down, as explained in the following verses:

> *13 But now in Christ Jesus ye who sometimes were far off are made nigh by the blood of Christ. 14 For he is our peace, who hath made both one, and hath broken down the middle wall of partition between us; 15 Having abolished in his flesh the enmity, even the law of commandments contained in ordinances; for to make in himself of twain one new man, so making peace; Ephesians 2:13-15*

In Acts 2, there was a separation, even as late as Acts 11:19, but by Acts 13, the "wall of separation" had come tumbling down like the walls of Jericho.

Because of a refusal to "rightly divide" the Book of Acts, many believers continue to struggle with reconciling the teachings of the twelve apostles with the good news Paul referred to as "my gospel." To escape this confusion, various teachings (doctrines) have been invented to help justify the discrepancies between the gospel of the kingdom and the gospel of the grace of God. By making these gospels one message, and "spiritualizing" everything that doesn't fit their narrative, believers are often confused over their calling, walk, and destiny as members in the Body of Christ. This need not be! Follow 2 Timothy 2:15!

It also doesn't appear that many denominations have "graduated" beyond the Great Commission, which is often due to a failure to "rightly divide" the Book of Acts. Many believers often assume Paul's varying practices in the presence of the Jews ("the Jews require a sign" (I Cor. 1:22)) were also meant for the Gentiles. Tragically, many early

Christian leaders started to abandon much of Paul's teachings by combining both the gospel of grace with those believers still under the Law. This causes many to not differentiate between spiritual baptism and water baptism, faith and works, and they have failed miserably to separate God's promises to Israel from His promises to the Body of Christ. As previously mentioned, we can certainly understand why there is a tragic identity crisis within Christianity.

The Other Epistles of Paul at the Close of Acts and Beyond

At the time of the conclusion to the Book of Acts, which ends with the proclamation that "the salvation of God has been sent to the Gentiles, and that they will hear it," Paul also wrote (from his imprisonment in Rome) the following epistles: Ephesians, Philippians, Colossians, and Philemon, and he also wrote his pastoral letters of I & II Timothy and Titus. The letters written during the transition period in Acts (Galatians, I & II Thessalonians, I & II Corinthians, and Romans) contain information that shows the struggles the early believers were having over general doctrines regarding Law and Grace (Galatians); the Second Coming, and the so-called Rapture (Thessalonians); morality, false teachings, and divisions within the Church (Corinthians); and how Jews and Gentiles are now justified by faith, apart from the Law and works (Romans)—just to name a few of the concerns. However, in Paul's letters written at the end of, and after the close of the Acts period, we see a "pattern" emerge "to them which should hereafter believe on Him to life everlasting," and Paul finalizes much of this pattern with the following passage to the Ephesians (and to Timothy):

> *I therefore, the prisoner of the Lord, <u>beseech you that ye walk worthy of the vocation wherewith ye are called</u>, 2 With all lowliness and meekness, with longsuffering, forbearing one another in love; 3 Endeavouring to keep <u>the unity of the Spirit</u> in the bond of peace. 4 There is <u>one body</u>, and <u>one Spirit</u>, even as ye are called in <u>one hope</u> of your calling; 5 <u>One Lord, one faith, one baptism</u>, 6 <u>One God and Father of all</u>, who is above all, and through all, <u>and in you all</u>. Ephesians 4:4-6*

> *15 This is a faithful saying, and worthy of all acceptation, that Christ Jesus came into the world to save sinners; of whom I am chief. 16 <u>Howbeit for this cause I obtained mercy, that in me first Jesus Christ might shew forth all longsuffering, for a pattern to them which should hereafter believe on him to life everlasting</u>. I Timothy 1:15-16*

In Ephesians 4:4-6, which is scarcely "rightly divided" by many believers, it appears that denominations behave as if the transition in Acts never ended because we still have more than ***one body*** of believers (Catholic, Orthodox, and Protestant). Believers also tend to forget that the Body of Christ is not a denomination, but rather it is a called-out assembly of individuals who are spiritually baptized (*by* one Spirit), indwelt, and sealed with that ***one Holy Spirit*** of promise (I Cor. 6:19-20; Eph. 1:13; 4:30). The "one body" of believer is the Body of Christ, the Church of this dispensation of the grace of God (I Cor. 9:17; Eph. 3:2; Col. 1:25). We are now the "new creature" (2 Cor. 5:17; Gal. 6:15). The Body of Christ is "catholic" only in the sense that it is universal, found anywhere that believers are found to be "in Christ".

We also have confusion over other operations of the Holy Spirit today, especially with teachings regarding being "slain in the Spirit," healings, and tongues. The Holy Spirit now dwells *permanently* within believers (Eph. 2:21-22; 4:30; I Cor. 6:19-20), and He quickens us (makes us alive spiritually (Col. 2:13)); however, the Body of Christ is not a body of sign-seekers, rather we are taught that "the just shall live by faith," which is taking God at His word (Rom. 1:17). Even when Paul told the Ephesians (5:18) to "be ye filled with the Spirit," he never mentioned the sign gifts that we find throughout the Book of Acts. The Holy Spirit does not operate the same way with believers today as He once did under the Old Testament and during the gospel of the kingdom, which was dominated with many "signs and wonders" (Matt. 10:5-8). In fact, where in the nine "fruit of the Spirit" from Galatians 5:22-23 do we find the "signs and wonders" mentioned throughout "the gospels" and the Book of Acts? Yes, Paul used many signs and wonders (as described in his six letters written during Book of Acts), but by the time he wrote Ephesians 4, we see something entirely different near the end of his ministry, and the sign gifts of Pentecost are not mentioned in those last seven letters. Why?

According to Paul, "the Jews seek after a sign," and Paul gave them many until the writings of his last seven epistles where we see the "oneness" of Ephesians 4 presented to us by Paul, "the apostle to the Gentiles" (Rom. 11:13; I Cor. 1:22;13:8-11). By the end of Paul's ministry, the sign gifts were not occurring, especially the gift of healing by Paul himself (even as an apostle (Phil. 2:25-27; I Tim. 5:23; 2 Tim. 4:20)). There is also no mention (in his last seven letters) about tongues and water baptism—only the "one" spiritual baptism. In fact, in I Corinthians 13 (written during the transition in Acts), Paul wrote that such signs would cease, and they did because Paul closed Acts 28 with the declaration that he was going to the Gentiles. Remember, it was the Jews who "require a sign" (I Cor. 1:22).

As Ephesians 4 states, there is only *one body* and *one Spirit*, as well as *"**one hope** of your calling,"* but many denominations are somewhat confused over *the hope* associated with that calling (I Tim. 1:1). Instead of realizing that the Body of Christ has a completely different calling than that of "the lost sheep of the house of Israel," believers from various denominations have taken God's promises of an earthly kingdom to Israel (Gen. 15:18) and claimed those promises as their own. Many believers have replaced a *literal* kingdom to Israel with a different doctrine that abandons the intent and promises to that nation, as proclaimed under the teachings of the patriarchs, the prophets, John the Baptist, Jesus, and the twelve apostles, especially when they taught, "the kingdom of heaven is at hand" (Matt. 3:2; 4:17; 10:5-7). Now, many denominations boast how the "kingdom of God" exists only "in the hearts of believers," and they often base this thought on Luke 17:20-21 (quoted below), which had nothing to do with the Body of Christ (the Church), which was still "hid in God" during the time this event took place during Christ's earthly ministry.

> *20 And when he was demanded of <u>the Pharisees</u>, when the kingdom of God should come, <u>he answered them</u> and said, The kingdom of God cometh not with observation:*
> *21 Neither shall they say, Lo here! or, lo there! for, <u>behold, the kingdom of God is within you</u>.*
> *Luke 17:20-21*

First, according to *biblehub.com.*, the Greek word *entos* is not translated "within you," but rather it is translated as "in the midst" (of them). Secondly, considering "to whom" Jesus was speaking—the Pharisees—it would seem odd that Jesus would tell them that the kingdom of God existed *within them*, especially since they never recognized Jesus as *the Christ* (the Messiah).

For the Body of Christ, our *hope* is heavenly because we have been baptized *by* one Spirit, which places us *into Christ*, where we are "seated in heavenly places" with Him (Eph. 2:6). We look forward to the day when we will finally "meet Him in the air," which many believers deny will ever happen, even though it is unique only within the epistles of "the apostle to the Gentiles" (I Thes. 4:13-18). Again, for those who do not "rightly divide the word of truth" between the gospel of the kingdom and the gospel of the grace of God, we must wonder where they place their hope (Heaven or Earth), especially since many still believe they will have to endure the Tribulation. Again, our hope is in Christ who saves us, will resurrect us, and has "made us sit together in heavenly places in Christ" (Eph. 2:6).

Tragically, the "oneness" of Ephesians 4 has been replaced by many traditions where two different ministries of Jesus (the **one Lord**) are being proclaimed. Christ is the Head of the Church, the Savior of the Body, but in the gospel of the kingdom, He was to be King of kings and Lord of lords, sitting on the throne of David in the New Jerusalem, which will one day come down out of Heaven (Revelation 21). We know Christ as the risen, glorified Savior and Head of the Body, but many still attempt to "walk in the footsteps of Jesus" when He was ministering to the "lost sheep of the house of Israel" on Earth. In other words, many believers attempt to follow the Lord under His *earthly* ministry, not His *heavenly* ministry given to Paul. The following verse explains this:

> *16 Wherefore henceforth know we no man after the flesh: yea, though we have known Christ after the flesh, <u>yet now henceforth know we him no more</u>. 2 Corinthians 5:16*

As stated, the Twelve and Paul served the same Jesus, but two different commissions were given by Him to each (Matthew 28:16-20 and 2 Corinthians 5:14-21). Sadly, many believers still attempt to follow and combine (into one gospel) the commands to "repent and be baptized for the remission of sins" with "be ye reconciled (restored to fellowship) to God" through "the redemption that is in Christ Jesus." This is offered to the world "by grace, through faith… not of works." Currently, we have believers attempting to follow the commands of Jesus in "the gospels," and we also have others who follow Jesus as He is presented through "the revelation of the mystery." Yes, the "gospels," and Paul's epistles, have only "one Lord," but many believers are confused over whether they should follow Jesus when He was "after the flesh" (2 Cor. 5:16), or whether they should follow Jesus, who is now "seated at the right hand of God, making intercession for us" (Rom. 8:34). The Body of Christ is not commanded to follow "Christ after the flesh," but rather we are the "new creature," which was revealed by Jesus Christ to and through the "apostle to the Gentiles," who said, "Be ye followers of me, even as I also am of Christ" (I Cor. 11:1).

What about the *one faith* Paul mentioned in Ephesians 4? Is the believer's faith the primary focus in this passage from Ephesians 4:4-6, or is it the faithfulness of Jesus Christ that establishes the one true faith Paul commanded for today? For over two millennia, many believers have boasted about their faith in Christ through various sacraments and other religious rites, but is this the faith Paul meant? In Romans 3:22, Paul stated, "Even the righteousness of God, which is by faith *of* Jesus Christ unto all and upon all them that *believe*, for there is no difference (between Jews and Gentiles)." We can only be justified through faith in the finished work (death, burial, and resurrection) of Jesus Christ, who was faithful in completing the work of redemption for all sinners (2 Cor. 5:21). The faith that saves today is the faithfulness of Christ, and our faith in the finished work He did on our behalf (Rom.

1:17). There is only "one faith" today, not a combination of the gospel of the kingdom and the gospel of the grace of God.

There are certainly two baptisms (spiritual and water) being preached and practiced today, and only one of these baptisms (*by* one Spirit) identifies us with Jesus Christ's death, burial, and resurrection (Rom. 6:1-4; I Cor. 12:13). Again, for today, there is only **one baptism**, and it has nothing to do with some water rite performed by a religious leader. Our baptism today is the work and operation of God (Col. 2:12) *by* one Spirit, not *by* men, and there is absolutely no justification for practicing water baptism, especially since the time of "the revelation of the mystery," which did not (and does not) include works for salvation. Some attempt to redefine water baptism as having nothing to do with a work, but this is only because they are ignorant of "rightly dividing the word of truth." We are called to have "faith in His blood" for "the remission of sins," not "repent and be baptized for the remission of sins." There is also *no* teaching in Scripture that promotes water baptism to "show an outward sign of an inward grace." Again, this is nothing more than a tradition invented by theologians who refuse to "rightly divide the word of truth." I will devote an entire chapter to baptism, but for now, if Paul was sent to carry out the so-called Great Commission, it seems odd that he would declare the following:

> *17 <u>For Christ sent me not to baptize, but to</u>*
> *<u>preach the gospel</u>: not with wisdom of words,*
> *lest the cross of Christ should be made of none*
> *effect. 18 For <u>the preaching of the cross</u> is to*

them that perish foolishness; but unto us which
are saved it is the power of God.
I Corinthians 1:17-18

The gospel of the kingdom (the Great Commission) certainly included water baptism, so what other *gospel* could Paul be referring to in this passage? Remember, by the end of Paul's ministry, he clearly stated that there is only "one baptism," and since his last seven letters do not include water baptism, it is obvious that he was referencing the baptism *by* one Spirit.

Finally, there are various beliefs about our **one God**, which are often inconsistent with Scripture. God is not "the Man upstairs"; He is the Triune God who is restoring both Heaven and Earth through His prophecies to and through Israel (since the world began), and the "revelation of the mystery," which was revealed to the Body of Christ (kept secret since the world began). Most skeptics begin their arguments with a flawed understanding of the nature and character of God, but this is understandable because they are relying on their human reasoning to explain the Divine.

The Church has been called to show Israel and the world the means through which humanity can be "blessed with all spiritual blessings in heavenly places in Christ" (Eph. 1:3). Instead, of recognizing the "high calling of God" (Phil. 3:14), both Jews and Gentiles have gone about "to establish their own righteousness," just as Paul described of Israel in Romans 10:3. God remains elusive to billions of people, and our identity crisis bears most of the blame.

The Difference Between Knowing "In Part" and "Fully Known"

As we are near the end of this chapter, it is important for us to understand the differences between what Peter and Paul knew early in their ministries, and what they taught later after the transition of the Book of Acts had ended.

> *8 Charity never faileth: but whether there be prophecies, they shall fail; whether there be tongues, they shall cease; whether there be knowledge, it shall vanish away. 9 For we know in part, and we prophesy in part. 10 But when that which is perfect is come, then that which is in part shall be done away. 11 When I was a child, I spake as a child, I understood as a child, I thought as a child: but when I became a man, I put away childish things. 12 For now we see through a glass, darkly; but then face to face: now I know in part; but then shall I know even as also I am known.*
> *I Corinthians 13:8-12*

Paul, in Ephesians 4:1-6 (quoted previously) taught the "oneness" of the Church, but it would be helpful to examine that passage through the context of I Corinthians 13:8-11 and Colossians 1:25 also. These passages help to explain some of the various aspects of the transition within the Book of Acts. As we examine these passages, we must remember to consider what the apostles (in the New Testament) knew "in part," and what they had "fully known" at the time they experienced different events and were inspired to write about them.

Peter, at first, only knew the gospel of the kingdom (Great Commission), but he *didn't* know the gospel of the grace of God until Paul taught it to him years later (Galatians 1:15-18; 2:1-9). Peter only knew that Jesus died and rose again, but he did not know, even at Pentecost, that salvation would eventually be offered to both Jews and Gentiles by grace, through faith in the death and resurrection, apart from the works of the Law (including water baptism). Peter never preached the gospel of the grace of God at Pentecost, nor to Corneilus (Acts 10), even though theologians attempt to force such traditions into Scripture to help them justify their belief in the Bible having only "one gospel" and "one Church."

Was the Church that was at Jerusalem, and the Body of Christ the same, especially since Paul persecuted the Church at Jerusalem (Acts 8:1-2), but he was later called to lay the foundation for the Church, the Body of Christ after Acts 9? What about the Church in the wilderness that Stephen mentioned in Acts 7:38? Again, I ask how the Church in the wilderness, which was given the Law, could be the same Church (the Body of Christ) that was never "under the Law"?

To further this point, after the meeting with Paul (and Barnabas) in Galatians 2, James, Peter, and John gave Paul and Barnabas the "right hands of fellowship," as they recognized *to whom* each were being sent ("the gospel of the circumcision" (Peter), and "the gospel of the uncircumcision" (Paul)). If they were the same gospel, why would Paul have to teach his revelation (from Jesus Christ) to James, Peter, and John, which is explained when Paul stated "...they added nothing to me" (Gal. 2:6)? The following passage explains this:

> *6 But of these who seemed to be somewhat, (whatsoever they were, it maketh no matter to me: God accepteth no man's person:) for they who seemed to be somewhat in conference added nothing to me: 7 But contrariwise, when they saw that the gospel of the uncircumcision was committed unto me, as the gospel of the circumcision was unto Peter; 8 (For he that wrought effectually in Peter to the apostleship of the circumcision, the same was mighty in me toward the Gentiles:) 9 And when James, Cephas, and John, who seemed to be pillars, perceived the grace that was given unto me, they gave to me and Barnabas the right hands of fellowship; that we should go unto the heathen, and they unto the circumcision.*
> *Galatians 2:6-9*

It was through the teachings of Paul (Gal. 1:11-12) that Peter had "fully known" that salvation had come to all the world through the gospel of the grace of God, which was "the preaching of Jesus Christ, according to the revelation of the mystery, which was kept secret since the world began." Peter could not have known this mystery, especially at Pentecost, because Paul had not yet been converted until at least a year later. Peter still preached (at Pentecost), "repent (for the crucifixion) and be baptized (cleansed (Leviticus 14)) for the remission (forgiveness) of sins" (Acts 2:36-38). Peter was still a practicing Messianic Jew; and once he had learned the gospel of the grace of God from Paul (about salvation by grace, through faith in the blood and resurrection, apart from works), he finally began to share to those "twelve tribes scattered abroad" about the "sprinkling of the blood" and "a lively hope by the resurrection of Jesus Christ from the dead," as he stated in I Peter 1:1-3. In fact, Peter confirmed Paul's gospel in 2 Peter 3:15-16, even stating, "which are some things hard to be understood." After all, Paul's gospel was quite foreign to what Peter had been sent earlier to preach by Jesus (Matt. 28:16-20; Acts 2:38-41).

Paul, in his six epistles (written *during* Acts) only knew "in part" the full revelation of the gospel of grace, and this is why we see various practices involving the sign gifts, circumcision, and water baptism being mentioned in those Acts epistles Paul wrote during that time; however, he stated, "...but when that which is perfect (fully revealed/mature) is come, then that which is in part shall be done away" (I Cor. 13:10). This is why Paul later declared (*after* the Book of Acts):

> *25 Whereof I am made a minister, according to*
> *the dispensation of God which is given to me*
> *for you, <u>to fulfil the word of God</u>; 26 <u>Even the</u>*
> *<u>mystery which hath been hid from ages and</u>*
> *<u>from generations, but now is made manifest to</u>*
> *<u>his saints:</u> 27 To whom God would make known*
> *what is the riches of the glory of this mystery*

> *among the Gentiles; which is Christ in you, the*
> *hope of glory: Colossians 1:25-27*

> *6 For I am now ready to be offered, and the*
> *time of my departure is at hand. 7 I have fought*
> *a good fight, I have finished my course, I have*
> *kept the faith: 2 Timothy 4:6-7*

At the end of the transition in the Book of Acts, Paul could finally declare: one body, one Spirit, one hope, one Lord, one faith, one baptism, and one God and Father of all (Ephesians 4:1-6). Once again, Paul (during Acts), only knew "in part" what was being revealed to him by Jesus Christ (Gal. 1:11-12; I Cor. 13:8-11), but he later stated how he had been sent to "fulfill the word of God" (Col. 1:25), and as a result, those things done "in part" during the Book of Acts where now "fully known" by Paul's last seven letters, and Ephesians 4:4-6 helps to prove that.

Paul began his ministry by being water baptized (Acts 9:18), but he revealed later to the Corinthians about the spiritual baptism "by one Spirit" (I Cor. 12:13), and he concluded his ministry by declaring only "one baptism" for the Church today (Eph. 4:5). Paul circumcised Timothy (Acts 16:1-3) because of the "Jews in that region," but he later declared, "For in Christ Jesus neither circumcision availeth anything, nor uncircumcision, but a new creature" (Gal. 6:15). Remember, Paul was saved around AD 34, but the events recorded in Acts did not conclude for nearly 30 years. Acts also began with the apostles asking, "Lord, wilt thou at this time restore *again* the kingdom to Israel?" (Acts 1:6), but

Acts ends with Paul declaring, "…for the salvation of God is sent unto the Gentiles, and they will hear it" (Acts 28:28). What happened to cause this change (transition) from a focus on Israel to a focus on the Gentiles, apart from Israel?

At the time Paul wrote his epistle to the Corinthians, which occurred during the transition in the Book of Acts, he was still dealing with the Jews who "require a sign." This is why we see Paul addressing the sign gifts of tongues (I Cor. 14:1-6), healings (I Cor. 12:1-11), and even the subject of water baptism (I Cor. 1:14-17) with the Corinthians, but these doctrines are not a part of Paul's seven epistles written at the end of Acts. So, why did the Corinthian letter address tongues, healings, and water baptism? Given the proximity of the Corinthian church (in the home of Gaius (Titius Justus)), and the Jewish synagogue, which was next door (Acts 18:7), the sign gifts would have been used to persuade the Jews about Jesus. Without such signs and wonders, it would have been harder to convince the Jews that Paul's ministry was truly of God.

19 For though I be free from all men, yet have I made myself servant unto all, that I might gain the more. 20 And unto the Jews I became as a Jew, that I might gain the Jews; to them that are under the law, as under the law, that I might gain them that are under the law; 21 To them that are without law, as without law, (being not without law to God, but under the law to Christ,) that I might gain them that are without law. 22 To the weak became I as weak,

> *that I might gain the weak: I am made all*
> *things to all men, that I might by all means*
> *save some. 23 And this I do for the gospel's*
> *sake, that I might be partaker thereof with you.*
> *I Corinthians 9:19-23*

Many believers are still tempted to try this combined approach to gain souls for Christ, and as noble as this might be, we are not to place ourselves under the Law of Moses to gain the Jews, but instead, we are to tell them that Christ is the fulfillment of the Law, and that it is by grace, through faith in His finished work of redemption that they, too, can be "reconciled to God" through the death of His Son. Paul reminded the Jews of this in the following passage:

> *Brethren, my heart's desire and prayer to God*
> *<u>for Israel</u> is, that they might be saved. 2 For I*
> *bear them record that they have a zeal of God,*
> *but not according to knowledge. 3 For they*
> *being ignorant of God's righteousness, and*
> *going about to establish their own*
> *righteousness, <u>have not submitted themselves</u>*
> *<u>unto the righteousness of God. 4 For Christ is</u>*
> *<u>the end of the law for righteousness to every</u>*
> *<u>one that believeth.</u> Romans 10:1-4*

Are we to "repent and be baptized" to influence others to come to Christ? Of course not, because we are *now* "baptized *by* one Spirit into one body" (I Cor. 12:13), and we certainly do not want to "make the cross of Christ of none effect" (I

Cor. 1:17). Remember, I Corinthians 9 was written during the transition period in Acts, and Paul was still attempting to influence the Jews for the sake of Jesus. This is why Ephesians 4 is so vital because we *now* know that there is only "one body, one Spirit, one hope, one Lord, one faith, one baptism, and one God and Father, who is above all, through all, and in you all." Sadly, a vast number of believers have never made the full transition over from the gospel of the kingdom to the gospel of the grace of God, and this is why they insist on a combination of doctrines from Matthew to Revelation rather than "rightly dividing the word of truth."

Many theologians only tell "part of the truth" when they blatantly omit further revelation given to Paul for us in the Body of Christ. To say, "keep the commandments to be saved," or to command water baptism for salvation, is neglecting to share Paul's further teachings I previously quoted from Colossians 2:13-15. The Law was "nailed to the cross," which we should make known to all. And yes, I do believe water baptism was the commission of the twelve apostles, but not for Paul. Tongues were "for a sign," but for today, "…the just shall live by faith." Paul is the only apostle who could declare that he was sent "by revelation of Jesus Christ" to "fulfil the word of God" (Col. 1:25), and the Book of Acts helps us see this transition from a focus on restoring the kingdom to Israel in "the gospels" and early Acts, and God's heavenly citizenship for the Body of Christ. I will further explain this "two-fold" purpose of God in subsequent chapters.

Chapter Conclusion

In the next chapter of our study about the transition in the Book of Acts, we will examine again the gospel Peter preached in Acts 2, what did and should have happened in Acts 7, why Peter was sent to Cornelius in Acts 10, the gospel Paul preached in Acts 13, why Paul performed signs and wonders, why he circumcised Timothy (but not Titus), why he did some water baptisms, and why we conclude Acts with Paul declaring that God had "turned to the Gentiles."

Without rightly dividing the word of truth throughout the Book of Acts, we will never fully understand why God turned to the Gentiles with the gospel of the grace of God (Acts 20:24).

CHAPTER 4

A Brief Journey Through Acts

*38 Be it known unto you therefore, men and
brethren, that through this man is preached
unto you the forgiveness of sins: 39 And by him
all that believe are justified from all things,
from which ye could not be justified by the law
of Moses. Acts 13:38-39*

A Brief Journey Through Acts

Before the ascension of Jesus Christ, the apostles asked
in Acts 1:6: "Lord, wilt though at this time restore
again the kingdom to Israel?" This is in relationship
to the earthly kingdom still promised to Israel, which John the
Baptist, Jesus, and the Twelve declared to be "at hand" during
the time Jesus preached on the earth. Not one of them in Acts
1:6 would have been anticipating some *spiritual* kingdom
only existing in the "hearts of Jewish and Gentile believers,"
as it is widely circulated throughout many denominations.
Gentiles, after all, were still "aliens from the commonwealth
of Israel, strangers from the covenants of promise…and
without hope" in Acts 1:6, so the apostles would have never

considered such an allegorical fulfillment of their promised kingdom. This tradition stems from not "rightly dividing the word of truth."

In the next verse (Acts 1:7), Jesus replied, "It is not for you to know the times or the seasons, which the Father put in His own power." What no one knew, and Jesus certainly did not reveal it at that time, was that a new Church (a "new creature/ creation" (2 Cor. 5:17; Gal. 6:15)) was to be formed after Israel fell spiritually in Acts 7. This is one of the main reasons why a study of the Book of Acts is necessary, especially if we are to understand why God brought about "the gospel of the grace of God" through Paul, a previously unknown apostle (Acts 20:24). Those believers, in early Acts, *never* knew of such a body of believers made up of both Jews and Gentiles saved by grace, through faith in the blood and resurrection of Jesus Christ (apart from works). They knew nothing about how this new creature would be baptized *by* one Spirit, placing them into one body with a heavenly citizenship. This is why Paul refers to his gospel (given by Jesus Christ) as "the revelation of the mystery, kept secret since the world began." Since it was "my gospel," as he declared (Rom. 16:25), it could *not* have been preached prior to Paul's conversion in Acts 9. This gospel was *not* revealed in Acts 2, despite what theologians often try to force into the pages of the Bible, thanks to their traditions.

We *now* have the luxury of knowing that "before the foundation of the world," God had predestinated a different body of believers (the new creature), and again, it was to this "called out assembly" that He would give a *heavenly* citizenship (Eph. 1:3-4; 2:6; Phil. 3:20). In Acts 1:6, the apostles were expecting a citizenship in the kingdom on the earth, which was declared to be "at hand" just weeks before. To take what we know now and force it into the "gospels" and the early chapters of Acts, is not only wrong, but it has led to one of the worst identity crises imaginable. After all, Paul made it abundantly clear that the gospel he preached was "kept secret since the world began." This means that none of the "apostles and prophets" knew the entire redemptive plan of God for both Heaven and Earth until Paul was converted and preached the gospel of the grace of God, which came "by (direct) revelation of Jesus Christ" (Gal. 1:11-12).

The *Unsearchable* Riches of Christ

Many Gentile believers, even at the time of Paul himself, had already abandoned some of what Paul referred to as "the preaching of Jesus Christ, according to the revelation of the mystery." In fact, he even declared to Timothy: "This thou knowest, that all they which are in Asia be turned away from me…" (2 Tim. 1:15). Is this not what has occurred throughout most of Church history as well? Paul was saved to reveal "the *unsearchable* riches of Christ," which none of the apostles and prophets knew prior to the conversion of Paul in Acts 9. We cannot find Paul's gospel of the grace of God (the "revelation of the mystery") in the Scriptures prior to Paul's conversion, and this is why this particular gospel is "unsearchable," or not able to be traced. There is a vast difference between what was prophesied about Jesus Christ, and what we have learned about the Savior through the "revelation of the mystery, which was kept secret since the world began." In other words, Paul was sent to tell us about the *unprophesied* gospel of Jesus Christ, which has *now* been "...made known unto His holy apostles and prophets by the Spirit" (Eph. 3:5). Remember, the gospel Jesus revealed to Paul was "hid in God...before the foundation of the world" (Eph. 1:4; 2 Tim. 1:8-9). This is why it was *unsearchable*.

Most believers are confounded by the following passage:

> *8 <u>Unto me</u>, who am less than the least of all saints, <u>is this grace given</u>, that <u>I should preach among the Gentiles the unsearchable riches of Christ;</u> 9 <u>And to make all men see what is the fellowship of the mystery, which from the beginning of the world hath been hid in God</u>, who created all things by Jesus Christ:*
> *Ephesians 3:8-9*

Paul's gospel was *not* speaking against anything that Jesus taught on the earth to the "lost sheep of the house of Israel," as some assume; nor was he attempting to refute what Jesus delivered to the apostles at His ascension; however, we do know that Paul was speaking on behalf of Jesus when he declared that salvation was "by grace, through faith...apart from works" (Gal. 1:11-12; Eph. 2:8-9). This "revelation of the mystery, kept secret...but is now made manifest (revealed)" (Rom. 16:25-26) offers both Jews and Gentiles salvation through faith in the shed blood of Christ and His resurrection. Gentiles can now be "fellow heirs" with Jesus, *apart* from Israel instead of *through* Israel. This is why we must "rightly divide" the Book of Acts as well as all other Scripture!

For What Purpose Did God Save Paul?

When studying Peter's and Paul's actions throughout the Book of Acts, believers must determine "to whom" these apostles spoke, and "for what purpose." As for the earthly ministry of Jesus Christ (to the lost sheep of the house of Israel), we read:

> *8 Now I say that Jesus Christ <u>was a minister of the circumcision</u> for the truth of God, <u>to confirm the promises made unto the fathers:</u> 9 And that the <u>Gentiles might glorify God</u> for his mercy; as it is written, For this cause I will confess to thee among the Gentiles, and sing unto thy name. Romans 15:8-9*

Jesus came to fulfill the unconditional promises God made with Abraham (Gen. 12:1-7; 13:15-16; 15:18; 17:4-9), David, and the prophets (I Chr. 17:11-14; 2 Chr. 6:16; 2 Sam. 7:10-13; Jer. 23:5; Isa. 9:6-7). This was all regarding the earthly kingdom promised to the "seed of Abraham" (the Jews who descended from Isaac, Jacob, David, etc.). In Paul's address to the Jews in Romans 2:24-29, he reminds them how their pious works have caused the Gentiles to "blaspheme the name of God," and he reminds them that not all Jews are truly "circumcised in heart," just because of their nationality. He also warned that religious works *do not* mean you are saved. How many religious people take pride in their works, forgetting that God is more interested in the "heart of man," especially since we now walk after the Spirit (Rom. 8:1-4).

As I stated, Jesus proclaimed this kingdom (Acts 1:6) to be "at hand," and it was through the gospel of the kingdom that Jews could bring salvation to the Gentiles, as the previous passage declared (Rom. 15:8-9). Did this happen? Are we saved through the gospel (of the kingdom) Jesus preached to "the lost sheep of the house of Israel," and the "Great Commission" given at His ascension, or are we saved through the gospel that Jesus revealed to Paul concerning "the revelation of the mystery, which was kept secret since the world began"? Paul does not contradict what Jesus taught to the Jews; he *adds* to what they didn't know, which was how Gentiles would be saved because of Israel's "fall," instead of their "rising," as it is stated in Isaiah.

> *Arise, shine; for thy light is come, and the glory of the LORD is risen upon thee. 2 For, behold, the darkness shall cover the earth, and gross darkness the people: but the LORD shall arise upon thee, and his glory shall be seen upon thee. 3 <u>And the Gentiles shall come to thy light, and kings to the brightness of thy rising</u>. Isaiah 60:1-3 (to Israel)*

> *11 I say then, Have they stumbled that they should fall? God forbid: <u>but rather through their fall salvation is come unto the Gentiles</u>, for to provoke them to jealousy. Romans 11:11*

The Book of Acts explains how Israel was offered the kingdom (and the Messiah), how they rejected this, and how and why God saved Paul for the purpose of sending him to the Gentiles, "to provoke Israel to jealousy." The Body of Christ has received by grace what God will eventually give to Israel by promise (Jer. 31:31-36). God's unconditional covenants made with Israel will be fulfilled *after* "the fulness of the Gentiles be come in" (Rom. 11:25). Most of Christendom (often the combination of Scripture and tradition) has attempted to replace Israel with the Church, but we are not promised an earthly kingdom, but rather we are already "blessed with all spiritual blessings in heavenly place in Christ" (2 Cor. 5:1-2; Eph. 1:3; 2:6; Phil. 3:20). Remember, the Church Paul was called to "lay the foundation" for (I Cor. 3:10) was the same Church that was "kept secret" until after his conversion.

> *10 According to the grace of God which is given unto me, as a wise masterbuilder, I have laid the foundation, and another buildeth thereon. But let every man take heed how he buildeth thereupon. 11 For other foundation can no man lay than that is laid, which is Jesus Christ. I Corinthians 3:10-11*

How Tradition Often Still Robs Us of Truth

Traditions, rather than "right division" of the Scripture, has infiltrated most of what we call Christianity today. The embracing of traditions, over the truth of Scripture itself, occurred even during the time of Jesus, as well as into the ministry Jesus gave to Paul for the Body of Christ (Matt. 15:3,6; Mk. 7:9; Gal. 1:6-9; Col. 2:8; 2 Tim. 1:15). Many of those traditions continue to detract from the "revelation of the mystery," and believers today often uphold their traditions, even if they contradict the clear teachings of God's word (Isa. 55:11; Lk. 24:27; John 5:39; Rom. 15:4; Gal. 3:21-22; 2 Tim. 3:16-17; Heb. 4:12-13; 2 Pet. 1:19-21; 3:15-16; I John5:13). I know it is hard for some to believe, but many traditions can be practiced for millennia, but that doesn't make them scriptural in their foundation.

We now understand that when Israel rejected the Messiah, this kingdom would be delayed due to a different gospel "hid in God," which was "the preaching of Jesus Christ, according to the revelation of the mystery, which was kept secret since the world began." As I previously mentioned, many in the Church today believe they are (or will be) the fulfillment of God's promises to Israel, but Paul spoke to the Body of Christ about "the hope which is laid up for you (us) in heaven" (Col. 1:5), *not on the earth.* We need to know the differences if we are going to know our current purpose, service, and our eternal destiny. The main question is this: Was the Body of Christ, with its purpose, service, and destiny, revealed at Pentecost in Acts 2? If so, it is mysteriously absent from the text.

Why Acts 2 *Can't* Be the "Beginning of the Church"
Acts 2 is a crucial chapter, especially since there are so many theologians who insist that "the Church began at Pentecost," which is an old tradition that is widely accepted, but not thoroughly vetted in the context of Acts 2 and the eventual "revelation of the mystery" after Acts 9. If we do not "rightly divide the word of truth," such traditions form and often get

merged into our theology—never to be questioned. As I mentioned in Chapter 1 of this book, a Church was already in existence in Acts 2, and it was the 'little flock," which were true Messianic believers from the earthly ministry of Jesus (Luke 12:32). These believers accepted Jesus as the Messiah, and they anticipated the coming kingdom, which was offered to them, beginning in Acts 2. The "little flock" (the Messianic Church) was already there at Pentecost, so Jesus was offering them and their fellow Israelites the kingdom promised to them through "the fathers" (Rom. 15:8). This was promised to Israel long before there was ever a Body of Christ found in Paul's epistles.

The "little flock" consisted of those who truly believed Jesus was *the* Christ (the Messiah) during His earthly ministry, which would have included members such as the apostles, Mary (mother of Jesus), Mary Magdalene, Mary and Martha, Lazarus, Elizabeth, Mark, Stephen, and Levi (to name a few). This "little flock," which number about 120 (Acts 1:15), was already at Pentecost, and three thousand souls were *added* to the Church that was at Jerusalem on that day. This was the Church at Jerusalem (a "flock" of believers in Jesus as the Messiah), and they had been scattered after the incident with Stephen (Acts 8:1-2). Again, these believers trusted in the name of Jesus as the Messiah of Israel because they had not yet heard about the gospel of the grace of God. Note the following passages regarding them:

> *32 Fear not, little flock; for it is your Father's*
> *good pleasure to give you the kingdom.*
> *Luke 12:32*

> *27 My sheep hear my voice, and I know them, and they follow me: 28 And I give unto them eternal life; and they shall never perish, neither shall any man pluck them out of my hand. 29 My Father, which gave them me, is greater than all; and no man is able to pluck them out of my Father's hand. 30 I and my Father are one. 31 Then the Jews took up stones again to stone him. John 10:27-30*

Not only did Jesus affirm the security of the "little flock" in this passage, but after declaring Himself to be God ("I and my Father are one"), the Jews picked up stones to kill Him. Even though many in Israel did not follow Jesus, Acts Chapter 1 confirms the number of the "little flock" who'd continued with Him after His death and the resurrection.

> *15 And in those days Peter stood up in the midst of the disciples, and said, (the number of names together were about an hundred and twenty,) Acts 1:15*

As we explore the beginning of the Book of Acts, we realize that those at Pentecost were the "little flock," so Acts 2 should be examined with this in mind.

Is Pentecost "the beginning of a new Church," or was it the partial fulfillment of a prophecy found in Joel 2:28-32? The "little flock" was experiencing the "last days," prior to "the great and notable day of the Lord." The Church that was already at Jerusalem was *not* the beginning of a new dispensation, but rather it was in relationship to a prophetic promise to Israel in Joel 2. Peter reminds them of his in Acts 2.

> *14 But Peter, standing up with the eleven, lifted up his voice, and said unto them, <u>Ye men of Judaea, and all ye that dwell at Jerusalem</u>, be this known unto you, and hearken to my words: 15 For these are not drunken, as ye suppose, seeing it is but the third hour of the day. 16 <u>But this is that which was spoken by the prophet Joel; 17 And it shall come to pass in the last days</u>, saith God, I will pour out of my Spirit upon all flesh: and your sons and your daughters shall prophesy, and your young men shall see visions, and your old men shall dream dreams: 18 And on my servants and on my handmaidens <u>I will pour out in those days of my Spirit</u>; and they shall prophesy: 19 And I will shew wonders in heaven above, and signs in the earth beneath; blood, and fire, and vapour of smoke: 20 The sun shall be turned into darkness, and the moon into blood, <u>before the great and notable day of the Lord come</u>: 21 And it shall come to pass, that whosoever shall call on the name of the Lord shall be saved. Acts 2:14-21*

We know those dwelling at Jerusalem for that feast day (Pentecost) were mainly Jews, along with some proselytes (Acts 2:10), and as the Spirit was "poured out" upon them, they were witnessing the "last days...before the great and notable day of the Lord." The next prophetic event to take place would have been the Tribulation and Second Coming of Jesus Christ before His Millennial reign in Jerusalem (Isa. 2:1-4; Jer. 3:17; Eze. 20:40; Psalm 2:6-9; Zech. 14:2-5). We know this applies to Israel, because Peter continually refers to them during his Acts 2 address with such phrases as, "Ye men of Judaea...ye men of Israel...men and brethren...therefore, let the house of Israel know assuredly...." Peter recaps much of Jewish history (the Body of Christ would have had no history because it was still "unsearchable" and "kept secret" in Scripture until Paul), and Peter does so to prove that Jesus was *the Christ* (the Messiah) whom they had crucified. What was their response?

> *36 Therefore let <u>all the house of Israel</u> know assuredly, that God hath made the same Jesus, <u>whom ye have crucified</u>, both Lord and Christ. 37 Now when they heard this, <u>they were pricked in their heart</u>, and said unto Peter and to the rest of the apostles, <u>Men and brethren, what shall we do?</u> 38 Then Peter said unto them, <u>Repent, and be baptized every one of you in the name of Jesus Christ for the remission of sins</u>, and ye shall receive the gift of the Holy Ghost. Acts 2:36-38*

If Peter and Paul preached the same message of salvation, why would Paul later reveal the following to the Jews and proselytes at Rome?

> *24 <u>Being justified freely by his grace through the redemption that is in Christ Jesus</u>: 25 Whom God hath set forth to be a propitiation <u>through faith in his blood</u>, to declare his righteousness for the remission of sins that are past, through the forbearance of God; 26 <u>To declare, I say, at this time his righteousness</u>: that he might be just, and the justifier of him which believeth in Jesus…28 <u>Therefore we conclude that a man is justified by faith without the deeds of the law.</u>*
> *Romans 3:24-26 and 28*

Peter proclaimed, "repent and be baptized for the remission of sins," but Paul preached, "…being justified freely (without cost to you) by His grace, through the redemption ("through faith in His blood") that is in Christ Jesus." One of the reasons we know that Israel, specifically the "little flock," was being offered the kingdom (as Jesus promised in Luke 12:32) is because he stated in Acts 2 the following:

> *39 <u>For the promise is unto you, and to your children</u>, and <u>to all that are afar off [Acts 2:8-10]</u>, even as many as the LORD our God shall call. 40 And with many other words did he testify and exhort, saying, Save yourselves*

> *from this untoward generation. [41] <u>Then they</u>*
> *<u>that gladly received his word were baptized</u>:*
> *and the same day there were <u>added unto them</u>*
> *<u>about three thousand souls.</u>*
> *Acts 2:39-41 (brackets by author)*

Three thousand souls were "added" to the approximate 120 Messianic believers (the "little flock") who were already there to witness what Peter declared to be the "last days" and this pouring out of the Holy Ghost, which was "spoken by the prophet Joel." Pentecost was *not* the beginning of a new Church; it was the *last days* of what the prophets foretold would happen before that "great and notable day of the Lord," which would be the Tribulation and Second Coming of Jesus Christ. These saints, in preparation for the "last days," which Jesus described in Mattew 24, sold their possessions and "had all things common," which would have given them the funds to endure the Tribulation when they would not be able to "buy or sell" (Revelation 13). This is why Jesus said to pray for "our daily bread...lead us not into temptation... deliver us from evil" in Matthew 6 with the so-called Lord's Prayer. The Body of Christ has nothing to do with the Sermon of the Mount because the Body was still "kept secret" at that time. "The meek shall inherit the earth" (Matt. 5:5) is vastly different from our "citizenship, which is in Heaven" (Phil. 3:20).

Because the Tribulation did not happen, at that time, these members of the "Church at Jerusalem" later needed assistance, which led Paul to Jerusalem numerous times. Had Israel received Christ and the Kingdom, the Tribulation would have occurred, followed by the Second Coming. In other words, Paul would not have been needed simply because the Twelve were already called to "go into all the world" with the gospel of the kingdom (Matt. 24:14). There was no need for "the apostle to the Gentiles" because the "uncircumcision" would have been blessed through Israel. After Acts 7, we now know that "through their fall, salvation has come unto the Gentiles" (Rom. 11:11).

For those theologians who *still* insist Acts 2 is "the beginning of the Church (the Body of Christ)," they lack the evidence to support this belief simply because the Body of Christ, the Church, is not found in Scripture until Paul first addressed it in his letter to the Corinthians (I Cor. 12:12-27), which was about 20 years after Pentecost. Let us never forget how this "new creature" (the Body of Christ) was predestined "before the world began" (Eph. 3:9; I Tim. 1:9), but it was "kept secret" until after Israel fell spiritually in Acts 7. It was *after* the conversion of Paul in Acts 9 that we first learn about "the dispensation of the grace of God."

A Significant Message in Acts 13

If Acts 2 is our "Great Commission" for today, we must wonder why (in Acts 13) Paul and Barnabas were separated for a special purpose when the Holy Ghost spoke to believers at Antioch (not Jerusalem).

> *Now there were in the church that was at*
> *Antioch certain prophets and teachers; as*
> *Barnabas, and Simeon that was called Niger,*
> *and Lucius of Cyrene, and Manaen, which had*

> *been brought up with Herod the tetrarch, and*
> *Saul. ² As they ministered to the Lord, and*
> *fasted, <u>the Holy Ghost said, Separate me</u>*
> *<u>Barnabas and Saul for the work whereunto I</u>*
> *<u>have called them.</u> Acts 13:1-2*

Acts 13 later records Paul's first sermon (about 15 years after Pentecost), and if he was taught by Peter, and they preached the same message, then Paul should have instructed the Jews and proselytes at Antioch to "repent and be baptized for the remission of sins." He would have also taught these followers to "keep the commandments," just as Jesus did in the "gospels." However, to the surprise of the Jews, and the delight of the Gentile proselytes, Paul taught something *new* in Acts 13 than what Peter did in Acts 2:38 to the Jews and proselytes at Jerusalem.

> *³⁸ Be it known unto you therefore, men and*
> *brethren, that through this man is preached*
> *unto you the forgiveness of sins: ³⁹ And by him*
> *all that believe are justified from all things,*
> *from which ye could not be justified by the law*
> *of Moses. Acts 13:38-39*

What was the response of these Jews, and especially the Gentile proselytes?

> *⁴² And when the Jews were gone out of the*
> *synagogue, <u>the Gentiles besought that these</u>*
> *<u>words might be preached to them the next</u>*

> *sabbath. 43 Now when the congregation was broken up, <u>many of the Jews and religious proselytes followed Paul and Barnabas</u>: who, speaking to them, <u>persuaded them to continue in the grace of God</u>. 44 And the next sabbath day came almost the whole city together to hear the word of God. 45 But when the Jews saw the multitudes, they were filled with envy, and spake against those things which were spoken by Paul, contradicting and blaspheming. 46 <u>Then Paul and Barnabas waxed bold, and said, It was necessary that the word of God should first have been spoken to you: but seeing ye put it from you, and judge yourselves unworthy of everlasting life, lo, we turn to the Gentiles.</u>*
> *Acts 13:42-46*

Even with this passage from Acts 13, there are many theologians who carelessly suggest that since Peter mentioned the crucifixion and resurrection in Acts 2, they insist that "he (Peter) most certainly taught the same gospel as Paul" in Acts 13 at Antioch. Ignorance and traditions may push such a narrative, but does the Scripture itself promote this as fact? Where in Acts 2 did Peter ever command the hearers at Pentecost to place *their faith* in the blood and resurrection for the remission of sins, apart from the works of the Law? He didn't! He told them to "repent (for their rejection (Acts 2:36-37)) and be baptized (a work) for the remission of sins." On the other hand, Paul declared "Therefore, we conclude that a man is justified by faith, without the deeds of the Law" (Rom. 3:28). Which "good news" should we obey today? "Right division" teaches us one way, but tradition insists on another.

Did Israel Repent as a Nation?

We know in Acts 2, God was offering Israel the opportunity to repent for their rejection of the Messiah, leading to His crucifixion, and had they done so, Jesus would have returned and given them the kingdom, which He declared to be "at hand" during His earthly ministry. This is when Israel will be "born again" as a nation.

In Acts 3, Peter continued his preaching from Acts 2 shortly after Pentecost, and this is what he declared to the Jews:

19 Repent ye therefore, and be converted, that your sins may be blotted out, <u>when the times of refreshing shall come from the presence of the Lord</u>. 20 <u>And he shall send Jesus Christ, which before was preached unto you</u>: 21 Whom the heaven must receive <u>until the times of restitution of all things, which God hath spoken by the mouth of all his holy prophets since the world began.</u> 22 For Moses truly said unto the fathers, A prophet shall the Lord your God raise up unto you of your brethren, like unto me; him shall ye hear in all things whatsoever he shall say unto you. 23 And it shall come to pass, that every soul, <u>which will</u>

> *not hear that prophet, shall be destroyed from*
> *among the people. Acts 3:19-23*

The "restitution of all things" in in direct reference to Old Testament prophecies regarding the restoring of Israel, which was promised "by the mouth of all His holy prophets, since the world began" (Jer. 30:3 and 10-12; 31:31-36; Eze. 36:26-27; 37:12-22). On the other hand, the Body of Christ is the Church never prophesied, but rather it was "the revelation of the mystery, kept secret since the world began. Remember, in Acts 3, Peter had never heard about the Body of Christ where Jews and Gentiles would be baptized "by one Spirit into one body…by the cross" (I Cor. 12:13).

Throughout Acts 4, 5, and 6, the apostles (excluding Paul, who had not yet been converted), were being persecuted, and some imprisoned. For men who had been defeated and terrified because of the death of Jesus, the apostles were now boldly insisting that the Messiah rose from the dead, even in the face of threats from the leaders of Israel. Regardless, the apostles continued to call for repentance, even though they were directed not to by Israel's leaders (Acts 4:18; 5:12-16). Again, this does not mean the apostles were preaching *faith* in the death and resurrection for salvation, apart from works of the Law. They continued to preach the same message that was delivered at Pentecost because it was the only commission they knew at that time.

A Vision from Heaven No One Expected
Acts 7 is the key to understanding why the transition in the Book of Acts had to take place. Since blasphemy of the Holy

Ghost is "unpardonable," (Matt. 12:31-32), something new had to come about to redeem Israel, once they blasphemed the Holy Ghost in Acts 7. Even Paul referred to himself as a blasphemer (I Tim. 1:13), so he, too, would have been complicit in this "unpardonable sin," even though he did it "in ignorance" (I Tim. 1:13), just as many Jews had done as well. Both Jews and Gentiles were all declared to be "under sin" especially in Acts 7, but thankfully, through the "revelation of the mystery," God could and did have "mercy upon us all" (Rom. 11:32).

In Acts 6, Stephen was introduced. He was one of the seven men chosen to assist with supplying food to widows (of the Church (at Jerusalem)), and he was said to be a man "full of faith and the Holy Spirit." Remember, there was no Church, the Body of Christ at that time. The Jewish leaders targeted him, accusing him of falsehoods (breaking one of the commandments they'd sworn to uphold), and when Stephen preached to them about their sin of murdering the Messiah, as well as "resisting the Holy Ghost (blasphemy)" they knew the consequences of his charges against them, so they had him put to death.

Before I address Acts 7, I would like to briefly introduce a parable that Jesus taught to His disciples. It is directly related to the offer of the kingdom from Acts 1 to Acts 7.

> *6 He spake also this parable; A certain man*
> *had a fig tree planted in his vineyard; and he*
> *came and sought fruit thereon, and found*
> *none. 7 Then said he unto the dresser of his*
> *vineyard, Behold, these three years I come*

> *seeking fruit on this fig tree, and find none: <u>cut it down</u>; why cumbereth it the ground? ⁸ And he answering said unto him, Lord, <u>let it alone this year also</u>, till I shall dig about it, and dung it: ⁹ <u>And if it bear fruit, well: and if not, then after that thou shalt cut it down.</u> Luke 13:6-9*

We know from the Old Testament that the fig tree and vineyard is in relationship to Israel (Hos. 9:10; Jer. 8:13; Isa. 5:1-7). The "dresser" of the vineyard pleaded with the owner to spare the fig tree (Israel) for one year. We know Jesus pleaded from the cross, "Father, forgive them, for they know not what they do," and here in this parable, we see a plea from the "dresser" (Christ) of the vineyard to spare the fig tree. If it did not produce fruit, *after one year*, it would then perish. We know the earthly ministry of Jesus lasted over three years, and from Pentecost in Acts 2, to the stoning of Stephen in Acts 7, that was an additional year. Israel, as a nation, did not bear the fruit of repentance, so it was time for it to be "cut down." The time of Jacob's Trouble (during the Tribulation) was now upon them (Jer. 30:7-9; Matt. 24:15).

As I stated, Acts 7 was the conclusion to that addition year, and the "fig tree" was still in rebellion against God, bearing no national fruit of repentance.

In Stephen's address to the Sanhedrin (Jewish leaders), we read the following:

> *⁵¹ Ye stiffnecked and uncircumcised in heart and ears, <u>ye do always resist the Holy Ghost</u>: as your fathers did, so do ye. ⁵² Which of the*

> *prophets have not your fathers persecuted?*
> *and they have slain them which shewed before*
> *of the coming of the Just One; <u>of whom ye*
> *have been now the betrayers and murderers:</u>*
> *53 Who have received the law by the disposition*
> *of angels, and have not kept it. 54 <u>When they*
> *heard these things, they were cut to the heart</u>,*
> *and they gnashed on him with their teeth.*
> *55 <u>But he, being full of the Holy Ghost, looked*
> *up stedfastly into heaven, and saw the glory of*
> *God, and Jesus standing on the right hand of*
> *God,</u> 56 And said, Behold, I see the heavens*
> *opened, and the Son of man <u>standing</u> on the*
> *right hand of God. 57 Then they cried out with*
> *a loud voice, and stopped their ears, and ran*
> *upon him with one accord, 58 And cast him out*
> *of the city, and stoned him: <u>and the witnesses*
> *laid down their clothes at a young man's feet,*
> *whose name was Saul.</u> 59 And they stoned*
> *Stephen, calling upon God, and saying, Lord*
> *Jesus, receive my spirit. 60 And he kneeled*
> *down, and cried with a loud voice, <u>Lord, lay*
> *not this sin to their charge</u>. And when he had*
> *said this, he fell asleep.*
> *Acts 7:51-60*

In the parable of the "fig tree," it was to be "cut down" if it did not "bear fruit" after one additional year, and in this passage from Acts 7, we see Jesus "standing at the right hand of God," ready to bring judgment upon the nation of Israel.

Prior to the parable in Luke 13:6-9, Jesus stated twice that if Israel (the Jews) did not repent, they would perish (Luke 13:3,5). As a result of their rebellion, the Sanhedrin had Stephen stoned to death after they had blasphemed the Holy Ghost, so the next prophetic event that should have occurred would have been the Tribulation, where God's wrath would have been poured out upon the world. As Peter taught in Acts 2, "that great and notable day of the Lord" was coming. They were, at Pentecost, witnessing the "last days."

Because of Acts 7, there are many who believe God is done with Israel, as a nation, but this is unbiblical. Isaiah prophesied of a remnant of Israel that would exist at the time of the Tribulation, and Jeremiah stated how this remnant would be saved at the end of that time of wrath.

> *20 And it shall come to pass in that day, that the remnant of Israel, and such as are escaped of the house of Jacob, shall no more again stay upon him that smote them; but shall stay upon the LORD, the Holy One of Israel, in truth. 21 The remnant shall return, even the remnant of Jacob, unto the mighty God. 22 For though thy people Israel be as the sand of the sea, yet a remnant of them shall return: the consumption decreed shall overflow with righteousness. 23 For the Lord GOD of hosts shall make a consumption, even determined, in the midst of all the land. Isaiah 10:20-23*

*8 And it shall come to pass, that <u>in all the land,</u>
saith the LORD, two parts therein shall be cut
off and die; <u>but the third shall be left therein.</u>
9 <u>And I will bring the third part through the</u>
<u>fire</u>, and will refine them as silver is refined,
and will try them as gold is tried: they shall
call on my name, and I will hear them: I will
say, It is my people: and they shall say,
The LORD is my God. Zechariah 13:8-9*

*13 But he that shall endure unto the end, <u>the</u>
<u>same shall be saved</u>. 14 And this gospel of the
kingdom shall be preached in all the world for
a witness unto all nations; and then shall the
end come. Matthew 24:13-14*

In Matthew 24:14, Jesus taught that the "gospel of the kingdom" would be proclaimed in all the world, "and then the end shall come," and indeed, this was the gospel still being proclaimed in Acts 7; however, we know that during those dreadful seven years (Tribulation), a tremendous evangelistic event will also occur, which is carried out by a remnant of believers described in Revelation 7:4, which is going to be the 144,000 Jews (12,000 from the twelve tribes of Israel), along with the two "witnesses." This remnant of believers will help lead Israelites to Christ, along with Gentiles who believe and assist Israel at that time (Matthew 25). Unfortunately, not all Jews and Gentiles will believe during the Tribulation, and they will perish in the end (Revelation 20). We don't know who that promised remnant will be, but

Paul did state in Romans 11:5 that "at this present time, there is a remnant according to the election of grace." Again, God has always had a remnant of Israelites, such as the "little flock," and these special souls will be used in a mighty way to lead the people of Israel back to God (Rom. 11:25-29). For now, God is dealing with the Gentiles because the nation of Israel has been blinded (in part) in unbelief.

> *25 For I would not, brethren, that ye should be ignorant of this mystery, lest ye should be wise in your own conceits; that blindness in part is happened to Israel, until the fulness of the Gentiles be come in. 26 And so all Israel shall be saved: as it is written, There shall come out of Sion the Deliverer, and shall turn away ungodliness from Jacob: 27 For this is my covenant unto them, when I shall take away their sins. 28 As concerning the gospel, they are enemies for your sakes: but as touching the election, they are beloved for the father's sakes. 29 For the gifts and calling of God are without repentance. Romans 11:25-29*

Never forget that God's "gifts and calling" are irrevocable (Lev. 26:40-45; Jer. 31:10; 31:31-36; Eze. 11:19).

Stephen, in Acts 7, said a prayer, which God certainly answered: "Lord, lay not this sin to their charge." Jesus Christ prayed similarly from the cross. Thankfully, God did not pour out His wrath upon the world, but instead, He poured out His grace when He called Saul (Paul) to "the preaching of Jesus

Christ, according to the revelation of the mystery, which was kept secret since the world began." Yes, the gospel of the grace of God was about to be revealed to the world through the "revelation of Jesus Christ" given to the most unlikely person to preach it to the world: Paul—the one who is introduced and also consented to the death of Stephen in Acts 7.

The Church That Was "at Jerusalem"

In Acts 8, we see that the persecution of the Messianic Jews was about to get worse. Paul was hired by the Jewish leaders to track down and imprison those who named the name of Jesus Christ.

> *And Saul was consenting unto his death. And at that time there was a great persecution against the church which was at Jerusalem; and they were all scattered abroad throughout the regions of Judaea and Samaria, except the apostles. 2 And devout men carried Stephen to his burial, and made great lamentation over him. 3 As for Saul, he made havock of the church, entering into every house, and haling men and women committed them to prison. 4 Therefore they that were scattered abroad went every where preaching the word.*
>
> *Acts 8:1-4*

It is important to notice a few key points from this passage. Paul (Saul) was persecuting "the church which was at

Jerusalem." The Church, the Body of Christ, had *not yet* been revealed, especially since Paul was not even a convert until after Acts 9. So, there was already a Church in existence *before* the Body of Christ. That Church was the Messianic Kingdom Church at Jerusalem, consisting of the "little flock" and all who were "added" on and after the day of Pentecost. This Church was saved through repentance and baptism (and certainly belief in the name of Jesus as *the* Messiah). The gospel of the kingdom was also the gospel still taught by those who were "scattered abroad" after Stephen's death in Acts 11:19. It was the only gospel they had known. Paul persecuted this Church and anyone who was associated with the "church that was at Jerusalem."

> *13 For ye have heard of my conversation in time past in the Jews' religion, how that beyond measure <u>I persecuted the church of God, and wasted it</u>: 14 And profited in the Jews' religion above many my equals in mine own nation, being more exceedingly zealous of the traditions of my fathers. Galatians 1:13-14*

On the other hand, Paul was sent (later), by Jesus Christ, to proclaim how both Jews and Gentiles could be baptized *by* one Spirit and placed into one body (the Body of Christ). Paul even stated in Ephesians 2 how the "middle wall of partition" had been torn down, and at that point, there was no difference between the Jews and Gentiles; they could all be "one new man…in Christ" (Eph. 2:15). This is all "by grace, through faith…not of works." The "called out assembly" (the Body of

Christ) was still "kept secret since the world began" (even at Pentecost), especially since Paul was still on a mission to destroy the believers who had been scattered from the Church that was at Jerusalem. The "new creature" (the Body of Christ) that Paul proclaimed was certainly not introduced at Pentecost in Acts 2. Paul "laid the foundation" of the Church, the Body of Christ, but Peter never knew of this Church until it was taught to him by Paul.

> [10] *According to the grace of God which is given unto me, as a wise masterbuilder, I have laid the foundation, and another buildeth thereon. But let every man take heed how he buildeth thereupon.* [11] *For other foundation can no man lay than that is laid, which is Jesus Christ.*
> *I Corinthians 3:10-11*

> [15] *But when it pleased God, who separated me from my mother's womb, and called me by his grace,* [16] *To reveal his Son in me, that I might preach him among the heathen; immediately I conferred not with flesh and blood:* [17] *Neither went I up to Jerusalem to them which were apostles before me; but I went into Arabia, and returned again unto Damascus.* [18] *Then after three years I went up to Jerusalem to see Peter, and abode with him fifteen days.*
> *Galatians 1:17-18*

> *Then fourteen years after I went up again to*
> *Jerusalem with Barnabas, and took Titus with*
> *me also. ² And I went up by revelation, and*
> *communicated unto them that gospel which I*
> *preach among the Gentiles, but privately to*
> *them which were of reputation, lest by any*
> *means I should run, or had run, in vain… ⁶ But*
> *of these who seemed to be somewhat,*
> *(whatsoever they were, it maketh no matter to*
> *me: God accepteth no man's person:) for they*
> *who seemed to be somewhat in conference*
> *added nothing to me: Galatians 2:1-2 and 6*

The Body of Christ is built upon foundational truths that Jesus gave to Paul, such as I Corinthians 15:3-4 and Ephesians 2:8-9 (by grace, through faith in the death, burial, and resurrection of Christ, apart from works). It was the "pattern" revealed "first" to him, according to I Timothy 1:16. If the Church that was at Jerusalem was the same as the Church, the Body of Christ, then we have Paul "persecuting" the very Church God called him to "lay the foundation" for after his conversion in Acts 9. How could there possibly be only one Church in the New Testament, especially when the timeline doesn't match between the Bible and the traditions of men? After all, Paul persecuted one Church, but he was called to "lay the foundation" of another.

It is important to explain the following from Acts 8:

> *¹² But when they believed Philip preaching the*
> *things concerning the kingdom of God, and the*

> *name of Jesus Christ, they were baptized, both*
> *men and women. 13 Then Simon himself*
> *believed also: and when he was baptized, he*
> *continued with Philip, and wondered,*
> *beholding the miracles and signs which were*
> *done. 14 Now when the apostles which were at*
> *Jerusalem heard that Samaria had received*
> *the word of God, they sent unto them Peter*
> *and John: 15 Who, when they were come down,*
> *prayed for them, that they might receive the*
> *Holy Ghost: 16 (For as yet he was fallen upon*
> *none of them: only they were baptized in the*
> *name of the Lord Jesus.) 17 Then laid they their*
> *hands on them, and they received the Holy*
> *Ghost. Acts 8:12-17*

These believers had already been water baptized before Peter arrived (Acts 8:12), so all Peter did was "lay hands on them, and they received the Holy Ghost." Did they need to be baptized *again* to receive the Spirit, or was the "laying on" of hands sufficient to do this by Peter?

This same occurrence happened in Acts 19, which is stressed by many to be a *rebaptism* of the twelve believers at Ephesus. However, is that what occurred? If so, it is the only recording of believers needing this *rebaptism*. I will address this again, especially in the chapter dealing with baptism.

Paul's Conversion

Acts 9 set into motion a change in the "house rules" (dispensation), especially in relationship to a revelation that was "kept secret since the world began." Israel was to be the blessing to the world; however, it was through their fall that salvation had come to the Gentiles (Rom. 11:11). How could Israel bless the Gentile nations, as promised to Abraham and the prophets, especially if Israel temporarily forfeited all the blessings God promised them? Again, compare the following passages:

> *Arise, shine; for thy light is come, and the*
> *glory of the LORD is risen upon thee. ² For,*
> *behold, the darkness shall cover the earth, and*
> *gross darkness the people: but the LORD shall*
> *arise upon thee, and his glory shall be seen*
> *upon thee. ³ And the Gentiles shall come to thy*
> *light, and kings to the brightness of thy rising.*
> *Isaiah 60:1-3*

> *¹¹ I say then, Have they stumbled that they*
> *should fall? God forbid: but rather through*
> *their fall salvation is come unto the Gentiles,*
> *for to provoke them to jealousy.*
> *Romans 11:11*

From a prophetic perspective, Gentiles are to come to Israel's light (and "in the ages to come" many will), but from the perspective of the "mystery," they can *now* be blessed *apart* from Israel. Paul describes this best in the following:

> *³ For I delivered unto you first of all that which*
> *I also received, how that Christ died for our*

> *sins according to the scriptures; 4 And that he*
> *was buried, and that he rose again the third*
> *day according to the scriptures: 5 And that he*
> *was seen of Cephas, then of the twelve: 6 After*
> *that, he was seen of above five hundred*
> *brethren at once; of whom the greater part*
> *remain unto this present, but some are fallen*
> *asleep. 7 After that, he was seen of James; then*
> *of all the apostles. 8 <u>And last of all he was seen</u>*
> *<u>of me</u> also, <u>as of one born out of due time.</u>*
> *I Corinthians 15:3-8*

Thanks to the "revelation of the mystery," Gentiles can *now* receive "all spiritual blessings in heavenly places in Christ" through the gospel of grace (Eph. 1:3; Rom. 5:2). We are saved *ahead* of the prophetic time in which Gentiles are to be blessed *through* Israel. Yes, we are "as of one born out of (before) due time." We do not have to wait for the spiritual blessings of the new covenant to be given *through* Israel, which will happen for future Jews and Gentiles in the Tribulation. We are graciously receiving the spiritual blessings (since the time Paul's gospel was given to Him). Again, we are "as ones born out of (before our) due time." This is why Paul was called as "the apostle to the Gentiles," and "an able minister of the new testament (covenant)" (2 Cor. 3:6). The following passage is quite profound about our relationship to God through the blood of the New Testament:

> *5 Not that we are sufficient of ourselves to*
> *think any thing as of ourselves; but our*

sufficiency is of God; ⁶ <u>Who also hath made us able ministers of the new testament</u> [Jer. 31:31-34; Matt. 26:28]; not of the letter [the Law], but of the spirit: for the letter killeth, but the spirit giveth life. ⁷ But if the ministration of death, written and engraved in stones [the Law of Moses], was glorious, so that the <u>children of Israel</u> could not stedfastly behold the face of Moses for the glory of his countenance; which glory was to be done away [the Law]: ⁸ How shall not the ministration of the spirit be rather glorious?
2 Corinthians 3:5-8 (brackets by author)

It was *to* Paul that the "preaching of the cross" (the shed blood of the New Covenant) was *first* given, along with the truth that "God was in Christ, reconciling the world to Himself" (2 Cor. 5:19). Paul was also the first to reveal that we have the "forgiveness of sins…through faith in His blood" (Rom. 3:24-26). Thanks to "the mystery," all who believe are justified from all things "from which you could not be justified by the Law of Moses" (Acts 13:38-39). The Law only brought death, but thankfully, Jesus fulfilled the Law and died in our place (Col. 2:13-14). Now we have "the law of the Spirit of life in Christ Jesus." We are "alive in Christ" through the Spirit.

No, God is not "finished with Israel," but rather He has delayed the restoration of the earth (still promised to Israel) in order to restore Heaven with the Body of Christ, which was "kept secret since the world began." If you believe in the future Tribulation, you must accept Matthew 24 and 25, and especially Revelation as God's future prophecies for the restoration of the nation of Israel. If not, then you've not taken the time to "rightly divide the word of truth."

The Road to Damascus

Acts 9 begins with Paul receiving permission to continue his pursuit of Messianic believers who'd been "scattered abroad" after the persecution that "arose about Stephen" (Act 11:19). On this trip, Paul encountered Jesus Christ.

> *3 And as he journeyed, he came near*
> *Damascus: and suddenly there shined round*
> *about him a light from heaven: 4 And he fell to*
> *the earth, and heard a voice saying unto him,*
> *Saul, Saul, why persecutest thou me? 5 And he*
> *said, Who art thou, Lord? And the Lord said, I*
> *am Jesus whom thou persecutest: it is hard for*
> *thee to kick against the pricks. Acts 9:3-5*

When Christ called Paul to be an apostle (Eph. 1:1), He also began giving His "chief enemy" a revelation that no one knew prior to Acts 9. Unlike humanity, God is able to keep a secret! We are also introduced in this chapter to Ananias, a disciple at Damascus. Jesus spoke directly to him.

> *13 Then Ananias answered, Lord, I have heard*
> *by many of this man, how much evil he hath*
> *done to thy saints at Jerusalem: 14 And here he*
> *hath authority from the chief priests to bind all*

that call on thy name. [15] But the Lord said unto him, Go thy way: <u>for he is a chosen vessel unto me, to bear my name before the Gentiles, and kings, and the children of Israel</u>: [16] For I will shew him how great things he must suffer for my name's sake. Acts 9:13-16

After Paul's conversion, the believers were amazed when Paul preached in the synagogues that Jesus was the Christ, the Messiah (Acts 15:20-22; Gal. 1:23). The conversion of Paul has often been identified as a definitive proof to the resurrection of Jesus. Paul, at this point, had not yet preached about faith alone in the shed blood and resurrection for justification; that was yet future, but we know the "dispensation of the grace of God" (Eph. 3:2) was beginning at this time in Acts 9. Those prior to Paul's conversion, also preached that Jesus was the Messiah, but they had not yet heard of the gospel of the grace of God. Faith was preached "in His name," but faith in the finished, redemptive work of the cross and His resurrection for salvation was yet "kept secret" (Matt. 16:21-23; Luke 18:31-34). Paul, being a Pharisee, would have known the Old Testament scriptures regarding the Messiah, and after his conversion on the "road to Damascus," he was able to completely repent and see that Jesus was the fulfillment of what the prophets foretold.

As some have suggested, Paul's conversion would be equivalent to Hitler converting to Judaism. It would take such an encounter with Jesus to change Paul's heart. Preaching Jesus as *the Christ* was the faith he once destroyed; now he was preaching it (Gal. 1:23). In this aspect, Peter and Paul preached the same Jesus, but not the same means of salvation to both Jews and Gentiles.

Around the same time, Peter had brought Tabitha (a disciple) back to life (Acts 9:39-42) in Joppa, but little did he know something very profound was about to happen with a certain Gentile from Caesarea, along with a very distinct vision while Peter was in Joppa.

Cornelius, the Gentile

Acts 10 is one of the most controversial chapters simply because it is not carefully studied within the context of its timing. In essence, Jesus Christ, by special revelation, sent Peter to the home of a Gentile to show Peter what God was about to do through Paul, "the apostle to the Gentiles." Acts 10 takes place nearly a decade after Pentecost, and although many believers preach that Jesus Christ immediately did away with the Law for believers when He died on the cross, they never pause to realize that it wasn't until the "revelation of the mystery" that such *good news* was proclaimed concerning the Law and its fulfillment. Yes, Christ said He came to fulfill the Law, but it was "grace and truth" that was to be revealed to and through Paul, especially for Gentiles. In other words, Peter continued to place himself under the Law of Moses, having never known what Paul would later teach to him: "For sin shall not have dominion over you, for you are not under the law, but under grace" (Rom. 6:14). In fact, when Peter entered the home of Cornelius, a Gentile, he stated:

> *28 And he said unto them, Ye know how that it*
> *is an unlawful thing for a man that is a Jew to*
> *keep company, or come unto one of another*
> *nation; but God hath shewed me that I should*
> *not call any man common or unclean.*
> *Acts 10:28*

If Peter knew the gospel of grace proclaimed by Paul, he would have never made such a statement, because Paul's gospel message was clear that there is no difference between Jews and Gentiles. Again, it wasn't until Acts 13:38-39 that we read:

> *38 Be it known unto you therefore, men and*
> *brethren, that through this man is preached*
> *unto you the forgiveness of sins: 39 And by him*
> *all that believe are justified from all things,*
> *<u>from which ye could not be justified by the law</u>*
> *<u>of Moses</u>. Acts 13:38-39*

It was during the "sheet vision" Peter received earlier in Acts 10:10-15 that revealed to him that nothing should be called "common," and this would also include, as he was eventually shown, the Gentiles. It is often taught that Peter was the apostle to the Gentiles, since he was the one Jesus had chosen first to go to the home of Cornelius; however, what gospel did Peter proclaim to these Gentiles? At this point in Acts 10, did Peter know about salvation "by grace, through faith, apart from works"? Acts 10 never reveals such knowledge on the part of Peter.

Something different also occurred with these Gentiles that Peter did not expect. Did Corneilus, and those in his home, repent and get baptized *before* receiving the Holy Ghost?

> *36 <u>The word which God sent unto the children</u> <u>of Israel</u>, preaching peace by Jesus Christ: (he is Lord of all:) 37 That word, I say, ye know, which was published throughout all Judaea, and began from Galilee, <u>after the baptism</u> <u>which John preached</u>; 38 How God anointed Jesus of Nazareth with the Holy Ghost and with power: who went about doing good, and healing all that were oppressed of the devil; for God was with him. Acts 10:36-38*

According to Peter, to whom was "the word of God sent"? Peter recognized that it was sent to the "children of Israel" (Matthew 10:5-7; 15:24; Rom. 15:8), not to the Gentiles. Peter proceeded to explain in Acts 10 how the Jews crucified Jesus and how He rose again the third day, but Peter did *not* preach to these Gentiles anything about faith in the shed blood and resurrection for justification! So, what occurred after Peter had shared what he had already known?

> *43 To him give all the prophets witness, <u>that</u> <u>through his name</u> whosoever believeth in him shall receive remission of sins. 44 <u>While Peter</u> <u>yet spake these words, the Holy Ghost fell on</u> <u>all them which heard the word.</u> 45 And they of <u>the circumcision</u> which believed <u>were</u>*

> *astonished, as many as came with Peter,*
> *because that on the Gentiles also was poured*
> *out the gift of the Holy Ghost. 46 For they*
> *heard them speak with tongues, and magnify*
> *God. Then answered Peter, 47 Can any man*
> *forbid water, that these should not be baptized,*
> *which have received the Holy Ghost as well as*
> *we? 48 And he commanded them to be baptized*
> *in the name of the Lord. Then prayed they him*
> *to tarry certain days. Acts 10:43-48*

At Pentecost, the believers repented and were baptized *before* the Holy Ghost came upon them; however, the opposite occurred here. Peter still preached water baptism, not because it was going to remain a continuing practice for Gentiles, but rather it was due to the fact that Peter had only known the gospel of the kingdom, so that is what he preached. Also, if this is the "pattern" (I Tim. 1:16) that we are to proclaim today as Gentiles, shouldn't all Jews and Gentiles, who are baptized, have the gift of tongues just as these Gentiles did in Acts 10? Again, Peter did not tell these Gentiles anything about salvation being by grace, through faith in the shed blood and resurrection of Jesus, apart from works. That was reserved to and through the Apostle Paul, whose title would become "the apostle to the Gentiles" (Rom. 11:13), even with the events from Acts 10.

When Peter was confronted by the "circumcision" upon his return to Jerusalem (Acts 11), especially when he was accused of defiling himself when he entered the home of a Gentile, Peter explained the incident and concluded, "…what was I, that I could withstand God?" In other words, in Acts 11:17, he didn't fully understand the extent of this special calling yet, but he also acknowledged that he had no means by which to argue with God. This incident eventually led to him, James, and John giving Paul and Barnabas the "right hands of fellowship." They agreed that James, Peter and John would go to the Jews while Paul was called to go to the Gentiles (Gal. 2:7-9). Most believers ignorantly state that Peter and Paul preached the same gospel, but they preached it to two different audiences. If this were correct, why did Paul and Barnabus have to argue their case (in Acts 15) about Gentile salvation, apart from the Law?

In Acts 10, God was preparing Peter for a dramatic change in God's dealings with both Jews and Gentiles. Remember, Acts 10 followed the events of Acts 7. The only Gentiles Peter had dealt with, until that time, were those who had converted to Judaism (proselytes)—not the "heathen Gentiles" that Paul was sent to convert. Many believers insist that Peter "opened the door" to the Gentiles for salvation, and in one way he did, but this is a contradiction to what Luke wrote about Paul's return to Antioch in Acts 14.

> *[27] And when they were come, and had gathered*
> *the church together, they rehearsed all that*
> *God had done with them, <u>and how he had</u>*
> *<u>opened the door of faith unto the Gentiles</u>.*
> *Acts 14:27*

Had Acts 10 not occurred, it would have been difficult for Peter to accept the gospel that Paul was given for the

Gentiles, especially since the command to "go ye into all the world" was already given to the twelve apostles to carry out the gospel of the kingdom. Why was there a need for Paul in the first place? Couldn't the twelve apostles have handled Gentile salvation through "repent and be baptized," and "teaching them to observe all that I (Jesus) have commanded" as well?

Many believers are convinced, thanks to Church traditions, that the "heathen" Gentiles (aside from being proselytes) were always included in the gospel that was preached at Pentecost ("repent and be baptized for the remission of sins."). However, if this were the case, it seems odd that as late as Acts 11 we would read the following:

> *19 Now they which were scattered abroad upon*
> *the persecution that arose about Stephen*
> *travelled as far as Phenice, and Cyprus, and*
> *Antioch, <u>preaching the word to none but unto</u>*
> *<u>the Jews only</u>. 20 And some of them were men*
> *of Cyprus and Cyrene, which, when they were*
> *come to Antioch, spake unto the Grecians,*
> *[Greek-speaking Jews] preaching*
> *the LORD Jesus. 21 And the hand of the Lord*
> *was with them: and a great number believed,*
> *and turned unto the Lord.*
> *Acts 11:19-21 (brackets by author)*

> *25 Then departed Barnabas to Tarsus, for to*
> *seek Saul: 26 And when he had found him, he*
> *brought him unto Antioch. And it came to pass,*

> *that a whole year they assembled themselves*
> *with the church, and taught much people. <u>And</u>*
> *<u>the disciples were called Christians first in</u>*
> *<u>Antioch.</u> Acts 11:25-26*

There is a difference between preaching salvation through faith in the shed blood and the resurrection, versus preaching salvation "in the name of Jesus" as Messiah. Yes, genuine believers also recognize that Jesus is the Messiah of Israel, but they also realize that it is faith in what Jesus accomplished on Calvary's cross (and the resurrection) that made salvation possible for all. That was not preached until the "revelation of the mystery." Again, both Peter and Paul preached Jesus Christ, as these Jews did in Acts 11; however, did these disciples know anything about the "new creature" (the Body of Christ) that would consist of both Jews and Gentiles, saved by grace, through faith, apart from the Law of Moses? Did they know about the breaking down of the "middle wall of partition" between Jews and Gentiles? Apparently not, since they were still "preaching the word to none but unto the Jews only." Did they know about the baptism *by* (not with) one Spirit, placing believers into "one body," as taught in I Corinthians 12:13? Of course not, because it was still hidden from them, even in Acts 10. Paul would later begin to reveal these truths when he visited Peter sometime after *three years* of his conversion in Acts 9 (Gal. 1:18). Besides, if Peter and Paul preached the same gospel, Peter would not likely have declared Paul's gospel to be "hard to understand" in 2 Peter 3:15-16.

In Acts 12, we continue to see the plight and victories of Peter as he continued to proclaim that Jesus was "the Christ," the Messiah. Tragically, James (one of the apostles), was killed by Herod, and when he saw that it pleased the Jews, Herod's persecution of believers increased. With the death of one of the twelve apostles, this also indicated that a transition was taking place concerning the fulfillment of God's kingdom promises to and through Israel. After the death of Herod, a peculiar one at the end of Acts 12, we see Paul and Barnabus returning to Antioch where a drastic change in message was about to be recorded.

Paul's First Recorded Sermon: Well Over a Decade After Pentecost

Acts 13 begins with the Holy Spirit speaking to a group of men at Antioch.

> *Now there were in the church that was at*
> *Antioch certain <u>prophets and teachers</u>; as*
> *Barnabas, and Simeon that was called Niger,*
> *and Lucius of Cyrene, and Manaen, which had*
> *been brought up with Herod the tetrarch, and*
> *Saul. ² As they ministered to the Lord, and*
> *fasted, <u>the Holy Ghost said, Separate me</u>*
> *<u>Barnabas and Saul for the work whereunto I</u>*
> *<u>have called them.</u> ³ And when they had fasted*
> *and prayed, and laid their hands on them, they*
> *sent them away. Acts 13:1-3*

In Acts 13:9, Saul's name is referred to as Paul at that time, and at Antioch in Pisidia, Paul enters the synagogue and declares the following:

16 Then Paul stood up, and beckoning with his
hand said, Men of Israel, and ye that fear God,
give audience.
Acts 13:16 (to Jews and proselytes)

Paul took them on a journey through Israel's history, giving them specific scriptures that point to the death and resurrection of the Messiah, how Jesus was of the seed of David, and how John's baptism was for all Israel. Paul also made the declaration that Jesus was indeed "the Son," begotten of God (13:33). Paul continued to explain how Jesus did not see corruption in death, unlike David, which he explained in the following verses:

35 Wherefore he saith also in another psalm,
Thou shalt not suffer thine Holy One to see
corruption. 36 For David, after he had served
his own generation by the will of God, fell on
sleep, and was laid unto his fathers, and saw
corruption: 37 But he, whom God raised again,
saw no corruption. 38 Be it known unto you
therefore, men and brethren, that through this
man is preached unto you the forgiveness of
sins: 39 And by him all that believe are justified
from all things, from which ye could not be
justified by the law of Moses. Acts 13:35-39

This is *not* the same message that was preached in Acts 2 by Peter. At Pentecost, all who believed that they were guilty of the sin of having crucified their Messiah, were indeed "pricked in their hearts," and they repented and were baptized (and received the Holy Ghost). Peter never mentioned anything about justification apart from the Law of Moses, especially since Peter was condemned by the Jews (Acts 11) for having entered the home of a Gentile in Acts 10 (about ten years after Pentecost). Obedience to the Law of Moses was still expected for Jews and proselytes.

Paul, on the other hand, was preaching to both Jews and proselytes in Acts 13, but he offered them justification by faith (Acts 13:17-37), apart from the Law of Moses. Again, what was the reaction of the Jews and Gentiles?

42 And when the Jews were gone out of the synagogue, <u>the Gentiles besought that these words might be preached to them the next sabbath.</u> 43 Now when the congregation was broken up, <u>many of the Jews and religious proselytes followed Paul and Barnabas</u>: who, speaking to them, <u>persuaded them to continue in the grace of God</u>. 44 And the next sabbath day came almost the whole city together to hear the word of God. 45 <u>But when the Jews saw the multitudes, they were filled with envy, and spake against those things which were spoken by Paul, contradicting and blaspheming.</u> 46 <u>Then Paul and Barnabas waxed bold, and said, It was necessary that the</u>

> *word of God should first have been spoken to*
> *you: but seeing ye put it from you, and judge*
> *yourselves unworthy of everlasting life, lo, we*
> *turn to the Gentiles.*
> *Acts 13:42-46*

For the first time, Paul stated the following: "It was necessary that the word of God should first have been spoken to you (to the Jew first) …lo, we turn to the Gentiles." He stated the same to the Jews in Acts 18 and Acts 28.

> *⁴ And he reasoned in the synagogue every*
> *sabbath, and persuaded the Jews and the*
> *Greeks. ⁵ And when Silas and Timotheus were*
> *come from Macedonia, Paul was pressed in*
> *the spirit, and testified to the Jews that Jesus*
> *was Christ. ⁶ And when they opposed*
> *themselves, and blasphemed, he shook his*
> *raiment, and said unto them, Your blood be*
> *upon your own heads; I am clean; from*
> *henceforth I will go unto the Gentiles.*
> *Acts 18:4-6*

> *²⁷ For the heart of this people is waxed gross,*
> *and their ears are dull of hearing, and their*
> *eyes have they closed; lest they should see with*
> *their eyes, and hear with their ears, and*
> *understand with their heart, and should be*
> *converted, and I should heal them. ²⁸ Be it*
> *known therefore unto you, that the salvation of*

*God is sent unto the Gentiles, and that they
will hear it. ²⁹ And when he had said these
words, the Jews departed, and had great
reasoning among themselves.*
Acts 28:27-29 (quoting Isaiah)

Tradition attempts to persuade believers that Paul maintained the same gospel that Peter preached at the beginning of Acts; however, as I have stated, Peter never mentioned anything about justification apart from the Law of Moses. He did not mention salvation by grace, through faith in the death and resurrection of Jesus until after Paul revealed it to him, as explained in Galatians 1 and 2. In fact, Peter suddenly disappeared from the narrative of Acts in the fifteenth chapter when Paul went to Jerusalem with funds to help the struggling Jews who had sold their possession in preparation for the Tribulation (last days) as Peter preached in Acts 2:16-20 and 44-46. Paul did not tell Gentiles to "sell their possessions" and "have all things common," but rather, he commanded believers in I Timothy 5:8 to "provide for your own house…" or "he has denied the faith…and is worse than the infidel." These are not the same gospel messages!

The Dispute of Acts 15

As a reminder, many believers never consider the reason why the Jews in Acts 2 sold all their possessions and had all things common. If we recall in Acts 2:16-20, Peter tells them how they were in the "last days," so having all things common was their way of protecting themselves from the coming Tribulation, which Jesus warned them about in Matthew 24.

However, the Tribulation did not come, so they were running out of resources and required assistance from the Gentile churches that Paul had founded. This "relief fund" is why Paul ended up in Jerusalem in Acts 15, which led to the issue concerning the Gentiles and the Law.

> *And certain men which came down from*
> *Judaea taught the brethren, and said, Except*
> *ye be circumcised after the manner of Moses,*
> *ye cannot be saved. 2 When therefore Paul and*
> *Barnabas had no small dissension and*
> *disputation with them, they determined that*
> *Paul and Barnabas, and certain other of them,*
> *should go up to Jerusalem unto the apostles*
> *and elders about this question.*
> *Acts 15:1-2 (same concern as in Galatia)*

When Paul and his companions arrived in Jerusalem, they encountered a dispute that needed to be settled. Again, if Peter and Paul were preaching the same gospel, there would have been no issue over obedience to the Law of Moses for Gentiles ("teaching them to observe all that I have commanded" (John 14:15; Matt. 28-16-20)). It was through Paul that the Church at Jerusalem learned that Gentiles were not under the Law in the gospel he had been preaching.

> *4 And when they were come to Jerusalem, they*
> *were received of the church, and of the*
> *apostles and elders, and they declared all*
> *things that God had done with them. 5 But*

there rose up certain of the sect of <u>the Pharisees which believed</u>, saying, <u>That it was needful to circumcise them, and to command them to keep the law of Moses.</u> 6 And the apostles and elders came together for to consider of this matter. 7 And when there had been much disputing, <u>Peter rose up, and said unto them, Men and brethren, ye know how that a good while ago God made choice among us, that the Gentiles by my mouth should hear the word of the gospel, and believe.</u> 8 And God, which knoweth the hearts, bare them witness, giving them the Holy Ghost, even as he did unto us; 9 <u>And put no difference between us and them, purifying their hearts by faith.</u> 10 Now therefore why tempt ye God, to put a yoke upon the neck of the disciples, <u>which neither our fathers nor we were able to bear? 11 But we believe that through the grace of the Lord Jesus Christ we shall be saved, even as they.</u> Acts 15:4-11

Most believers read this passage through the eyes of their doctrines rather than through the eyes of those who were at this counsel at Jerusalem. Interestingly, this is the last we hear of and from Peter in the Book of Acts. This seems odd, especially if Peter and Paul were proclaiming the same means for "the remission of sins." Was this not God's way of showing the transition from the gospel of the kingdom (preached by Peter) to the gospel of the grace of God (preached by Paul)?

After hearing the arguments about Paul's gospel to the Gentiles, Peter concluded: "But we believe that *through the grace of the Lord Jesus Christ* we shall be saved, *even as they.*" This is a profound statement from Peter who had preached the "baptism for the remission of sins." Peter did not tell Gentiles, in previous passages in Acts, about anyone *not* being "under the Law"; however, he certainly concluded this to be the case after this encounter with Paul. Peter wisely realized that even the Jews were incapable of obedience to the Law of Moses, especially when he declared "…we shall be saved, *even as they,*" which was by "the grace of the Lord Jesus Christ." Since Peter did not know or preach such a gospel in Acts 2, should any theologian insert current knowledge of the gospel Paul preached into Peter's message at Pentecost, especially when "the revelation of the mystery" had not yet been revealed to Peter or the other apostles?

What James concluded, as the leader of the Church at Jerusalem (not Peter), was quite interesting. He determined that salvation was now open to the Gentiles," but that did not mean Peter was being called "the apostle to the Gentiles." James also shared how Gentiles were to be saved through what the prophets had proclaimed "from the beginning of the world" (Acts 15:13-18). Yes, Gentiles were and are to be blessed *through Israel,* as the prophets foretold, but what no one knew (both the apostles and prophets) was that God would save the Gentiles, *apart from Israel,* in what Paul would refer to as "my gospel, and the preaching of Jesus Christ, according to the revelation of the mystery," which was "not made known to the sons of men as it is now revealed unto his holy apostles and prophets" (Rom. 11:11; 16:25; Eph. 3:5). Now, in Acts 15, they knew this gospel regarding the Gentiles, and as a result, Peter concluded: "…we shall be saved, even as they" by "the grace of Jesus Christ." He also confessed that the Jews were not able to bear the burden of the Law, so why force the Gentiles to bear it?

What was James' conclusion for the Gentiles, for whom Paul was converting to faith in Jesus Christ?

19 Wherefore my sentence is, that we trouble not them, which from among the Gentiles are turned to God: 20 But that we write unto them, that they abstain from pollutions of idols, and from fornication, and from things strangled, and from blood. Acts 15:19-20

James even sent letters to Antioch with Paul and Barnabas, stating:

22 Then pleased it the apostles and elders with the whole church, to send chosen men of their own company to Antioch with Paul and Barnabas; namely, Judas surnamed Barsabas and Silas, chief men among the brethren: 23 And they wrote letters by them after this manner; The apostles and elders and brethren send greeting unto the brethren which are of the Gentiles in Antioch and Syria and Cilicia. 24 Forasmuch as we have heard, that certain

> *which went out from us have troubled you with*
> *words, subverting your souls, saying, Ye must*
> *be circumcised, and keep the law: <u>to whom we</u>*
> *<u>gave no such commandment:</u>*
> *Acts 15:22-24*

It causes us to wonder why many believers today, often guided by the traditions of other counsels throughout the centuries, have abandoned this clear teaching from the apostles themselves concerning Gentiles and the Law of Moses. Is it possible that the early Patristic Church Fathers (after the original apostles) did indeed force the *gospel of the kingdom* upon the Body of Christ instead of *the gospel of the grace of God* (I Cor. 4:16; 11:1; I Tim. 1:16)? Isn't the evidence more probable that the Patristic Church Fathers did not "rightly divide the word of truth," and as a result, this has forced many more denominations to occur because certain Church traditions did not congeal with the truth of God's word, causing many believers to "protest" and depart from the Catholic and Orthodox faiths? Any Church council (after Acts 15) that commands works for salvation, especially works of the Law, is not adhering to the very apostles who were taught directly by Jesus Christ. Many of these later councils were outside the will of God the moment they contradicted the clear teachings of Scripture itself. Acts 15 does not need any further Church councils to clarify what is obvious. It seems the motivation for such councils was for the promotion of Church traditions, not "rightly dividing the word of truth."

Why was Timothy Circumcised?

As I have been explaining, the Book of Acts is a transitional book, and there are specific actions by Peter and Paul that show the transitional nature of their gospel messages. Acts 16 is one such example.

Then came he to Derbe and Lystra: and, behold, a certain disciple was there, named Timotheus, the son of a certain woman, which was a Jewess, and believed; but his father was a Greek: 2 Which was well reported of by the brethren that were at Lystra and Iconium. 3 Him would Paul have to go forth with him; and took and circumcised him <u>because of the Jews which were in those quarters</u>: for they knew all that his father was a Greek. Acts 16:1-3

However, we read the following in Galatians 2:

Then fourteen years after I went up again to Jerusalem with Barnabas, and took <u>Titus</u> with me also. 2 And <u>I went up by revelation, and communicated unto them that gospel which I preach among the Gentiles</u>, but privately to them which were of reputation, lest by any means I should run, or had run, in vain. 3 <u>But neither Titus, who was with me, being a Greek, was compelled to be circumcised:</u> Galatians 2:1-3

Paul also water baptized several Jews (Crispus, who was the leader of the synagogue in Corinth), and Gaius, (likely a Gentile), but he happened to live next to the synagogue. However, we should understand these actions in light of the fact that "the Jews require a sign" (I Cor. 1:22), which Paul gave to them in circumcision and water baptism for the purpose of winning some of them to Christ. This was not his commission, but he did win many Jews to Christ Jesus by signs and wonders, which the Jews required in order to assess the legitimacy of Paul's apostleship.

The Gospel of the Grace of God

Jesus preached the gospel of the kingdom, but in Acts 20, Paul is very clear that the gospel he preached (from Jesus) was "the gospel of the grace of God," which he described in detail in his letters, especially those written at the end of Acts 28 and beyond. Yes, both gospels were given by Jesus Christ, but a dramatic change took place after Paul's conversion.

> *24 But none of these things move me, neither count I my life dear unto myself, so that I might finish my course with joy, and the ministry, which I have received of the Lord Jesus, to testify the gospel of the grace of God. 25 And now, behold, I know that ye all, among whom I have gone preaching the kingdom of God [not the gospel of the kingdom from heaven], shall see my face no more. 26 Wherefore I take you to record this day, that*

I am pure from the blood of all men. ²⁷ For I have not shunned to declare unto you all the counsel of God. ²⁸ Take heed therefore unto yourselves [the elder of Ephesus to whom Paul spoke], and to all the flock, over the which the Holy Ghost hath made you overseers [the elders from Ephesus], to feed the church of God, which he hath purchased with his own blood. ²⁹ For I know this, that after my departing shall grievous wolves enter in among you, not sparing the flock. ³⁰ Also of your own selves shall men arise, speaking perverse things, to draw away disciples after them. Acts 20:24-30 (brackets by author)

Again, what was the ministry God had given to Paul? He stated it was "to testify the gospel of the grace of God." Is this the same as the gospel of the kingdom that John the Baptist, Jesus, and the twelve apostles preached? If it were, we know the gospel of the kingdom taught nothing about Jews and Gentiles being baptized *by* one Spirit into one body with a "citizenship in heaven." The gospel of the kingdom is about the kingdom promised to Israel "since the world began." The "kingdom of God," which Paul mentioned in Acts 20, encompasses both the earthly and heavenly kingdom of God. This is not the same meaning as the "kingdom of heaven" proclaimed in "the gospels" and Revelation 21, which was (and is) to come down to Israel from Heaven. Many pastors and priests quote John 14 at funerals, but quite frankly, should they, especially knowing the Body of Christ was not yet known at that time Jesus promised His disciples the "kingdom of heaven" in the so-called "gospels"? Remember, the following passage about the kingdom of heaven promised by Jesus to the Jews could not have included the Body of Christ:

> *Let not your heart be troubled: ye believe in God, believe also in me. 2 In my Father's house are many mansions: if it were not so, I would have told you. I go to prepare a place for you. 3 And if I go and prepare a place for you, I will come again, and receive you unto myself; that where I am, there ye may be also.*
> *John 14:1-3*

Paul also stated that he had not "shunned to declare unto you all the counsel of God" (Col. 1:25), and this certainly included the gospel of the grace of God, which was "kept secret since the world began" until after Paul's conversion in Acts 9 (when it was "first" revealed to him as a "pattern" (I Tim. 1:16)).

Paul called for the elders of the church *at Ephesus*, and it was to them he declared, "Take heed, therefore unto yourselves, and to all the flock, over the which the Holy Ghost *hath made you overseers*, to feed the church of God, which He hath purchased with His own blood." Where do the claims of the Roman Catholic Church fit into this passage? Was Rome the official "overseer" of all the churches Paul established at that time (or at any time)? The Scripture is certainly silent about such a tradition. Besides, if the hierarchy of Roman officials were appointed to be "overseers" of all the churches, why are they not fully adhering to the commands of "the apostle to the Gentiles," especially Paul's teachings in his epistle to the Romans regarding salvation by grace, through faith, "apart from works" (Rom. 3:21-28; 4:5; 11:6)? Again, where did Paul command "repent and be baptized for the remission of sins" in his epistles?

Throughout the Book of Acts, it was Paul who was sent—by God—to be "the apostle to the Gentiles," and as he concluded his teachings in the Book of Acts (Acts 28), it was to the Gentiles that salvation has been sent, apart from Israel (Acts 28:28). Peter never received the gospel of the grace of God—only Paul did, and Luke shows how the Book of Acts began with the Twelve asking about the restoration of the kingdom to Israel (Acts 1:6), and how the declaration was given to Paul, not the Twelve, to bring salvation to the Gentiles, apart from Israel. If you can study the entire Book of Acts and somehow conclude that Rome (through Peter) was in charge of all the churches at that time, then we must wonder why Peter disappears from the narrative in Acts 15, especially if he was such an important apostle to the Body of Christ, which he never knew anything about until Paul taught it to him years later.

As traditions continue to rob us of important truths, it now makes sense why Paul explained to the Ephesian elders about the "grievous wolves," which he said would come in and devour the flock, obviously leading many away from the gospel of the grace of God. We certainly have proof of that today, thanks to Church traditions!

Final Events in Acts

The "vow" that Luke references in Acts 18 and Acts 21 should be viewed in the context of the following passage to the Corinthians:

> *19 For though I be free from all men, yet have I made myself servant unto all, that I might gain the more. 20 And unto the Jews I became as a Jew, that I might gain the Jews; to them that are under the law, as under the law, that I might gain them that are under the law; 21 To them that are without law, as without law, (being not without law to God, but under the law to Christ,) that I might gain them that are without law. I Corinthians 9:19-21*

Many believers are confused over the vow that Luke discussed in Acts 21, which seems to certainly imply a Nazarite vow taken by Paul, which is ascribed to the Law in Numbers 6. James was concerned about the reports that Paul was attempting to persuade the Jews "which were among the Gentiles to *forsake* (depart from) Moses... (the Law)" (Greek: *apostasia* (root: *aphistemi*)). This same word for "forsake" means *departure* in both Acts 21:21 and 2 Thessalonians 2:3 when Paul discussed the "departure" of believers prior to the revelation of the antichrist. Paul never persuaded the Jews to rebel ("defect from the truth") of Moses; he (along with James and Peter) simply agreed that the Gentiles were never given the Law, nor were they under the Law of Moses (Acts 15).

Paul also never persuaded the Jews (who were saved under the twelve apostles' ministry concerning the gospel of the kingdom) to ever get "resaved" under the gospel of the grace of God. In fact, Romans 15, as I have previously mentioned, stated the following to both Jews and Gentiles:

18 For I will not dare to speak of any of those things which Christ hath not wrought by me, to make the Gentiles obedient, by word and deed, 19 Through mighty signs and wonders, by the power of the Spirit of God; so that from Jerusalem, and round about unto Illyricum, I have fully preached the gospel of Christ. 20 Yea, so have I strived to preach the gospel, not where Christ was named, lest I should build upon another man's foundation:
Romans 15:18-20

The passage from Acts 21 gives us a great indication that Paul was not preaching the same gospel as the Twelve, for had he been doing so, such debates and concerns over the Law would not have been an issue, and Paul would not have worried about "building upon another man's foundation."

Paul likely engaged in this "vow" to win the Jews over to the acknowledgment that Jesus was indeed the Messiah of Israel. Was he correct in taking part in this "vow," even after being warned by the Spirit not to go to Jerusalem in the first place (Acts 21:4)? Perhaps not (like the error Peter made in Galatians 2:11-14), but such controversial passages are important because they show us how the inspired writers of the books of the Bible recorded what had occurred—not just filtering the events through a personal, biased narrative. The *words* recorded by the writers of the Bible are inspired, but this does not mean the apostles and prophets lost their humanity, especially when they recorded their own sinful choices throughout their lives. In other words, if the Bible were simply nothing more than the ramblings of human beings, they certainly didn't write narratives that made themselves out to be "larger than life" characters.

As for Paul, even with his dark past, he still persuaded many Jews to acknowledge that Jesus was the Messiah, and many unbelieving Jews became members of the Body of Christ as well, but Paul was not attempting to convince Jews who had already been saved under the gospel of the kingdom to be saved *again* under the gospel of the grace of God, especially in light of Galatians 2:7-9 where James, Peter, and John gave Paul and Barnabas the "right hands of fellowship" that they (James, Peter, and John) should confine their ministry to the *Circumcision*, and Paul to the *Uncircumcision*. James, Peter, and John continued to preach and write to the "twelve tribes scattered abroad" concerning the precepts they had already proclaimed before Paul was ever saved.

Paul was also able to use his dual identity as both a Roman citizen and a Jew to eventually land himself in Rome before Felix and Festus (governors), and ultimately before Caesar. In the final chapters in the Book of Acts, Paul was able to share the faith he preached to a mighty audience of Jews and Gentiles during his imprisonments, even though his journey to the region brought about the shipwreck and a bite from a poisonous snake (from which he suffered no ill effects).

These events simply show us the truth that when God has a plan for your life, nothing will stand in its way. Until his last breath, Paul proclaimed the very gospel that still saves the world today: Jesus died for us, was buried, and rose again on the third day (I Cor. 15:3-4). The Bible does not record how Paul died, but we know it was likely accomplished through a beheading, which was common punishment in those days.

May we all conclude our journey of faith, according to the words of Paul:

> *I charge thee therefore before God, and the Lord Jesus Christ, who shall judge the quick and the dead at his appearing and his kingdom; 2 Preach the word; be instant in season, out of season; reprove, rebuke, exhort with all long suffering and doctrine. 3 For the time will come when they will not endure sound doctrine; but after their own lusts shall they heap to themselves teachers, having itching ears; 4 And they shall turn away their ears from the truth, and shall be turned unto fables. 5 But watch thou in all things, endure afflictions, do the work of an evangelist, make full proof of thy ministry. 6 For I am now ready to be offered, and the time of my departure is at hand. 7 I have fought a good fight, I have finished my course, I have kept the faith: 8 Henceforth there is laid up for me a crown of righteousness, which the Lord, the righteous judge, shall give me at that day: and not to me*

only, but unto all them also that love his
appearing. 2 Timothy 4:1-8

Conclusion to This *Abridged Version* of the Book of Acts
In the beginning of the Book of Acts, we see the offering of the kingdom to Israel, which was the same kingdom Jesus declared to be "at hand" during His earthly ministry. The apostles began in Acts 1 by asking the following:

6 When they therefore were come together, they
asked of him, saying, <u>Lord, wilt thou at this</u>
<u>time restore again the kingdom to Israel?</u> 7 And
he said unto them, It is not for you to know the
times or the seasons, which the Father hath
put in his own power. Acts 1:6-7

However, the Book of Acts concludes with the following words from a previously unknown apostle:

28 Be it known therefore unto you, that <u>the</u>
<u>salvation of God is sent unto the Gentiles</u>, and
that they will hear it. 29 And when he had said
these words, the Jews departed, and had great
reasoning among themselves.
Acts 28:28-29

What happened that would cause such a dramatic change between God's promises to Israel (and the offering of the kingdom to them), and the conclusion that the "salvation of God is sent to the Gentiles, and that they will hear it"? At

Pentecost, in Jerusalem, the Jews were told to "repent and be baptized…for the remission of sins," but Paul later preached at Antioch that "all who believe are justified from all things from which you could not be justified by the Law of Moses"? James declared faith and works for salvation (James 2:17, 24), and yet Paul stated in Romans 4:5 that God justifies sinners by faith without works. We must "rightly divide the word of truth" to make sense of it all.

Israel had blasphemed the Holy Ghost in Acts 7, but in Acts 9, we see the conversion of another apostle, and his commission was to go to the Gentiles, kings, and also the Jews. Notice how the Gentiles are mentioned first? We also see Peter preaching the gospel of the kingdom to Cornelius in Acts 10, but Paul stated in Acts 20 how he was called to preach the gospel of the grace of God. There are many who insist these are the same gospel; however, one gospel only promised a kingdom on earth, while the other gospel promised a citizenship in heaven.

The transitional nature of the Book of Acts has caused many of the disputes between believers who do not "rightly divide the word of truth," especially in the Book of Acts. It seems this is why believers are often bitter toward one another, as well as why we have such an identity crisis within our faith. The Book of Acts presents many teachings that contradict the "traditions of men," but when we see the reason for God's dispensational change in the middle of the Book of Acts (with the saving of Paul), we can begin to reconcile what only appears to be contradictions.

I understand how and why there are so many other teachings in Acts that should be explored; however, my purpose in highlighting the specific chapters and passages was to show the reason why Acts is truly a transitional book, and it should be studied with the command of "rightly dividing" in mind. As much as the traditions of men are successful in robbing us of vital truths, we must guard against the same warnings that Paul gave to the elders at Ephesus about wolves devouring the flock. We know Satan's purpose is to "steal, kill, and destroy," but when we "rightly divide the word of truth," it weaponizes the Body of Christ with the "sword of the Spirit, which is the word of God" (Eph. 6:17). Christ defeated Satan, and the gospel of the grace of God specifically proves that!

As we study more about the practical application of what it is we should know and do as believers, may we never forget how and why the transition described throughout the Book of Acts was necessary. Israel's rejection of Jesus left Gentiles "without hope," but thanks be to God for the gospel of grace He revealed to the "chief of sinners," beginning in Acts 9. Now, we have been "brought nigh unto God by the blood of Jesus Christ" (Eph. 2:13).

CHAPTER 5

Unscriptural Assumptions

44 Ye are of your father the devil, and the lusts
of your father ye will do. He was a murderer
from the beginning, and abode not in the truth,
because there is no truth in him. When he
speaketh a lie, he speaketh of his own: for he
is a liar, and the father of it.
John 8:44

Some Hard Questions That Need Answered

The opening Scripture to this chapter is still the tremendous truth Jesus revealed to the unbelieving Pharisees concerning the very nature of Satan, and given what Paul stated about these same religious practitioners, it applies to all who go about "to establish their own righteousness" (Rom. 10:3). We have become accustomed to accepting whatever has "a form of godliness," while at the same time, we ignore the power of the gospel to free us from the lies of Satan. There is no doubt that many believers fail to "rightly divide" when it comes to the various teachings in the Bible, and they do not realize how "the gospel of Jesus Christ, according to the revelation of the mystery" has been "hid from them…in whom the god of this world has blinded their minds" (2 Cor. 4:3-4). The greatest tool Satan often uses for such confusion is religion itself.

Thankfully, through the gospel Paul proclaimed, we have learned how salvation (for individual Jews and Gentiles) is now by grace, through faith, not of works so no one can boast. This particular gospel was *not* preached prior to the "revelation of the mystery" given to Paul. We must "search the scriptures daily," as the Bereans did (Acts 17:11) if we are to grow in this grace. The glorious truth of the "revelation of the mystery" is "unsearchable" (Eph. 3:8) prior to Paul's conversion and his subsequent letters, and it was "not made known unto the sons of men" (Eph. 3:5) until Jesus Christ revealed it to Paul over a period of about three decades, as we had learned throughout Acts (Gal. 1:11-12). Salvation was once by faith and obedience to various commands of God, but now it is by grace, through faith, apart from works. Christ completed the work of redemption, and it is now our "reasonable service" to live for Him (Rom. 12:1-3). The following passage shows that this gospel message was given to Paul for the Body of Christ:

> *3 For this is good and acceptable in the sight*
> *of God our Saviour; 4 Who will have all men to*
> *be saved, and to come unto the knowledge of*
> *the truth. 5 For there is one God, and one*
> *mediator between God and men, the man*
> *Christ Jesus; 6 Who gave himself a ransom for*
> *all, to be testified in due time. 7 Whereunto I*
> *am ordained a preacher, and an apostle, (I*

speak the truth in Christ, and lie not;) a
teacher of the Gentiles in faith and verity. I
Timothy 2:3-7

Paul was made a preacher, and an apostle, to testify that Jesus gave Himself as a "ransom for all," and it is through the gospel Jesus Christ gave to Paul that we now have the hope of salvation, based on the shed blood of Calvary's cross. This "preaching of the cross" is foolishness to many.

18 For the preaching of the cross is to them that
perish foolishness; but unto us which are
saved it is the power of God.
I Corinthians 1:18

Have you ever seriously considered what works of righteousness *you* could possibly perform that could *add* to the righteousness of God, which is given to you freely (at no cost to you) by faith in the completed work of Christ? Are we not *already* "complete in Him" (Col. 2:10), and "sealed with that Holy Spirit of promise" (Eph. 1:13)? Is the blood of Christ sufficient to save you, or is there some work or ritual (sacrament) you could or should perform to obtain and maintain your salvation? Sure, there are works we *should* add to our walk as believers (Rom. 12:1-2; Eph. 2:10; 4:1; 2 Tim. 1:8-9), but we should never forget how God made Christ "to be sin for us…that we might be made the righteousness of God in Him" (2 Cor. 5:21). Believers are to "*work out* your own salvation" rather than "*work to earn* your own salvation." You can't work out what you do not already possess, and you can't boast about something you did not earn.

Quite often, Catholicism, Orthodox, and Protestant teachings attempt to return to the "gospels" of Matthew, Mark, Luke, and even John for their salvation and obedience, which were still under the "gospel of the kingdom" and the Law of Moses (Matt. 4:17; John 14:21). Did Jesus send Paul with the command for Gentiles to "repent and be baptized for the remission of sins"? Did Paul ever command the Church to be "born of water and of the Spirit," as many insist upon for salvation? No, because Paul was sent by Jesus Christ (Gal. 1:11-12) to proclaim salvation *by faith* in the blood of Jesus for the remission of sins (Rom. 3:24-26), including His resurrection for our justification (Rom. 4:25), which is all apart *from* works we might perform for salvation (Eph. 2:8-9). If you recall, I showed many passages in previous chapters that indicated clearly that faith, plus obedience to specific commands, were a part of the salvation experience to many, prior to the "revelation of the mystery." The "revelation of the mystery" changed how salvation was dispensed to humanity since the conversion of Paul.

For those who insist upon water baptism for salvation, we must remember that John the Baptist was sent to baptize *with* water, Jesus baptized *with* the Holy Spirit, but Paul proclaimed our baptism *by* the Holy Spirit, which places (immerses) us into one body called the Body of Christ, which was "kept secret since the world began." Water baptism is a work done by humanity, but baptism *by* one Spirit is the work of God upon all those who, by faith, believe the gospel of the grace of God outlined in I Corinthians 15:1-4.

Paul also taught, "But to him who works *not*, but believes on Him that justifies the ungodly, *his faith is counted as righteousness*" (Rom. 4:5), so we must all be careful not to add personal works to earn God's righteousness, "lest the cross of Christ should be made of none effect" (I Cor. 1:17; Eph. 4:5). Many believers confuse their positional sanctification (God separates us from the world) with their practical sanctification (where believers separate themselves from the world). There is a difference! Justification (declaring us righteous) occurs when we believe the gospel, allowing us to obtain the righteousness of Christ, but sanctification is an ongoing process where the character of Christ is manifested in and through us.

Many believers say they are saved by grace, but they also believe their salvation must include works for their justification to be complete, especially on the judgment day. Faith alone in Christ's redemption completes our righteousness, but the process of sanctification is daily as we strive to "mortify (put to death) the deeds of the body" (Rom. 8:13). According to Romans 8:29-30, we will already have been justified and glorified when we appear before Jesus Christ at the Judgment Seat of Christ (2 Cor. 5:10), which is only for members of the Body of Christ.

> *29 For whom he did foreknow, he also did predestinate to be conformed to the image of his Son, that he might be the firstborn among many brethren. 30 Moreover whom he did predestinate, them he also called: and whom*

he called, them he also justified: and whom he
justified, them he also glorified.
Romans 8:29-30

Therefore being <u>justified by faith</u>, we have
peace with God through our Lord Jesus
Christ: ² By whom also we have access by faith
into this grace <u>wherein we stand</u>, and rejoice
in hope of the glory of God. Romans 5:1-2

Born Again, or Believe the Gospel?

According to the "gospels," and the General Epistles of James, Peter, and John (and Jude), one of the vital requirements of being "born again" is to acknowledge that Jesus is the Messiah (the Christ). To the Jews "scattered abroad," John stated:

<u>Whosoever believeth that Jesus is the Christ is</u>
<u>born of God</u>: and every one that loveth him
that begat loveth him also that is begotten of
him. ² By this we know that we love the
children of God, when we love God, <u>and keep</u>
<u>his commandments</u>. ³ For this is the love of
God, <u>that we keep his commandments</u>: and his
commandments are not grievous.
⁴ For whatsoever is born of God
overcometh the world: and this is the victory
that overcometh the world, even our faith.
⁵ <u>Who is he that overcometh the world, but he</u>
<u>that believeth that Jesus is the Son of God?</u>

> *⁶ This is he that came <u>by water and blood</u>, even Jesus Christ; not by water only, <u>but by water and blood</u>. <u>And it is the Spirit that beareth witness, because the Spirit is truth</u>. I John 5:1-6*

The Holy Spirit testifies (bears witness) to the world that Jesus is both human and divine. This occurred when Jesus identified with humanity in water baptism, even though He had no sins from which He needed to be cleansed. Jesus told John that He was being baptized "to fulfill all righteousness" (under the Law (John 5:17; Gal. 4:4)). The Holy Spirit also gave witness of Jesus to the world when our Savior shed His blood. Remember, Jesus also declared "…I have a baptism to be baptized with" in reference to His death (Luke 12:50).

However, because this passage from I John 5 also commands believers to "keep the commandments," we must question whether this passage was written directly to the Body of Christ, especially considering the following passages from "the apostle to the Gentiles":

> *²⁴ Being justified freely by his grace through the redemption that is in Christ Jesus: ²⁵ Whom God hath set forth to be a propitiation through faith in his blood, to declare his righteousness for the remission of sins that are past, through the forbearance of God; ²⁶ To declare, I say, at this time his righteousness: that he might be just, and the justifier of him which believeth in Jesus. ²⁷ Where is boasting then? It is*

excluded. By what law? of works? Nay: but by the law of faith. 28 Therefore we conclude that a man is justified by faith without the deeds of the law.
Romans 3:24-28

4 Now to him that worketh is the reward not reckoned of grace, but of debt. 5 But to him that worketh not, but believeth on him that justifieth the ungodly, his faith is counted for righteousness. Romans 4:4-5

13 But now in Christ Jesus ye who sometimes were far off are made nigh by the blood of Christ. 14 For he is our peace, who hath made both one, and hath broken down the middle wall of partition between us; 15 Having abolished in his flesh the enmity, even the law of commandments contained in ordinances; for to make in himself of twain one new man, so making peace; Ephesians 2:13-15

13 And you, being dead in your sins and the uncircumcision of your flesh, hath he quickened together with him, having forgiven you all trespasses; 14 Blotting out the handwriting of ordinances that was against us, which was contrary to us, and took it out of the way, nailing it to his cross; Colossians 2:13-15

> *8 If we say that we have no sin, we deceive*
> *ourselves, and the truth is not in us. 9 If we*
> *confess our sins, he is faithful and just to*
> *forgive us our sins, and to cleanse us from all*
> *unrighteousness.*
> *I John 1:8-9*

What must the Body of Christ do to find approval with God today?

> *15 <u>Study to shew thyself approved unto God</u>, a*
> *workman that needeth not to be ashamed,*
> *<u>rightly dividing the word of truth</u>.*
> *2 Timothy 2:15*

Where in the previous passages did Paul state to "keep the commandments"? Where did he also command, "repent and be baptized for the remission of sins"? Did he tell believers to be "born of water and of the Spirit" or they wouldn't "see the kingdom of God"? Must the Body of Christ confess their sins to be forgiven, or are they called to place their faith in Jesus Christ and His redemptive work on the cross and His resurrection for their forgiveness? Remember, the whole world's sins were already imputed (put to Christ's charge) long before any of us ever committed a single one of them. Paul does not contradict what Jesus taught to the other apostles; he simply added a further revelation they weren't aware of "in times past." Paul was not sent to preach two gospels; he was sent to preach "one body, one Spirit, one hope, one Lord, one faith, one baptism, and one God" (Eph.

4:4-6). Most of Christendom ignores this "oneness," which should be found within the Church, the Body of Christ. Is it? Was "the mystery" revealed to others before Paul?

> *For this cause I Paul, the prisoner of Jesus Christ for you Gentiles, 2 If ye have heard of the dispensation of the grace of God which is given me to you-ward: 3 How that by revelation he made known unto me the mystery; (as I wrote afore in few words, 4 Whereby, when ye read, ye may understand my knowledge in the mystery of Christ) 5 Which in other ages was not made known unto the sons of men, as it is now revealed unto his holy apostles and prophets by the Spirit; 6 That the Gentiles should be fellowheirs, and of the same body, and partakers of his promise in Christ by the gospel: 7 Whereof I was made a minister, according to the gift of the grace of God given unto me by the effectual working of his power. 8 Unto me, who am less than the least of all saints, is this grace given, that I should preach among the Gentiles the unsearchable riches of Christ; 9 And to make all men see what is the fellowship of the mystery, which from the beginning of the world hath been hid in God, who created all things by Jesus Christ: 10 To the intent that now unto the principalities and powers in heavenly places might be known by the church the manifold wisdom of God,*

*¹¹ According to the eternal purpose which he
purposed in Christ Jesus our Lord:
Ephesians 3:1-11*

Israel was to be a "light to the Gentiles," bringing blessings "to all nations," which is what prophecy clearly teaches; however, Gentiles are now "blessed with all spiritual blessings in heavenly places in Christ," *apart* from the nation of Israel—due to the nation's "fall" (Rom. 11:11). This is why the "revelation of the mystery, which was kept secret since the world began" had to be revealed "*in due time*." Israel was offered the kingdom in early Acts, but by Acts 7, they had "resisted the Holy Ghost," along with the Messiah, and therefore, they were placed into "blindness" (Rom. 11:25) "until the fulness of the Gentiles be come in," which will occur when the Body is "caught up" and judged at the Judgment Seat of Christ (Rom. 14:10; 2 Cor. 5:10). We should also note that the Judgment Seat of Christ is not mentioned before Paul's conversion, and it is not mentioned outside of his epistles, which means it is unique to "the revelation of the mystery" for the Body of Christ, just as the so-called Rapture is unique to us as well (I Thes. 4:13-18; I Cor. 15:51-52). Most believers do not understand that the so-called Rapture is unique only to Paul's epistles, and that is why it is highly debated in many denominations. When you "rightly divide the word of truth," the closing of the "dispensation of the grace of God" becomes quite apparent, especially against the backdrop of prophecies yet to be fulfilled regarding Israel and the nations "in the ages to come."

The Body of Christ is already indwelt and sealed with the Holy Spirit, and we are already "in Christ," whereas the saints "in times past" had to "keep the commandments," sacrifice, and "confess their sins" to be "forgiven" when they did not obey and follow what was commanded of them (I John 1:8-9). "But now," we are already fully forgiven (Col. 2:13-15), and the Holy Spirit dwells within us when we believe the gospel. This is grace! Paul was an "able minister of the new testament (covenant)," which he preached concerning the shedding of the blood of Christ for atonement (I Cor. 5:7). Yes, Jesus died and paid the full price for our salvation before Paul was saved, but this does not mean the gospel of the kingdom revealed salvation "by grace, through faith, not of works" at that time. Acts 2, at Pentecost, says nothing about this means of salvation, only "repent and be baptized for the remission of sins," which is what Jesus commanded them to preach, beginning at Jerusalem. Again, the Body of Christ is already sealed *with* the Holy Spirit.

> *19 What? know ye not that your body is the*
> *temple of the Holy Ghost which is in you,*
> *which ye have of God, and ye are not your*
> *own? 20 For ye are bought with a price:*
> *therefore glorify God in your body, and in your*
> *spirit, which are God's. I Corinthians 6:19-20*

> *13 In whom ye also trusted, after that ye heard*
> *the word of truth, the gospel of your salvation:*
> *in whom also after that ye believed, ye were*
> *sealed with that holy Spirit of promise,*

*14 Which is the earnest of our inheritance until
the redemption of the purchased possession,
unto the praise of his glory.
Ephesians 1:13-14*

*30 And grieve not the holy Spirit of God,
whereby ye are sealed unto the day of
redemption. Ephesians 4:30*

When believers in the Body of Christ, the Church, return to the "gospels" and early Acts for their salvation and obedience, they place themselves back under the Law of Moses, and they seek now an earthly kingdom promised to Israel, which they *spiritualize* to mean "the kingdom that exists within our hearts." We are to "seek those things which are above."

*If ye then be risen with Christ, seek those
things which are above, where Christ sitteth on
the right hand of God. 2 Set your affection on
things above, not on things on the earth. 3 For
ye are dead, and your life is hid with Christ in
God. 4 When Christ, who is our life, shall
appear, then shall ye also appear with him in
glory.
Colossians 3:1-4*

The Body of Christ is the "new creature," and yet, many believers desire to overwhelmingly return to the gospel Jesus taught "after the flesh" (2 Cor. 5:16), and not the "revelation of the mystery" Jesus revealed to Paul from Heaven. Many believers combine the salvation message of Jesus to "the lost sheep of the house of Israel" with the salvation message He revealed to Paul about salvation being by grace, through faith in His shed blood and resurrection. The result has been nothing but confusion for millions. Many believers also insist on "repentance and baptism" and "keeping the commandments" simply because that is what Jesus preached in "the gospels." Jesus also taught Paul ("by revelation"), but this is often ignored for the sake of the traditions that many were raised to believe are for their obedience today.

Paul wrote the following to the Jews about the Law, which many believers today insist that we are still under for obedience (Rom. 6:14):

> *Brethren, my heart's desire and prayer to God for Israel is, that they might be saved. 2 For I bear them record that they have a zeal of God, but not according to knowledge. 3 For they being ignorant of God's righteousness, and going about to establish their own righteousness, have not submitted themselves unto the righteousness of God. 4 <u>For Christ is the end of the law for righteousness to every one that believeth.</u> Romans 10:1-4*

Believers will also argue that the Ten Commandments are God's moral laws, and therefore, we should keep them for our justification, but what they do not realize is that the Jewish sabbath is part of those commandments, and yet Paul tells us not to be subject unto such observances (Col. 2:16-23). Yes, Paul emphasizes nine of the ten commandments, but he condensed them even more with the command (from Jesus) to "love thy neighbor as thyself" (Gal. 5:14). Remember, we also "establish the law" by being "in Christ" (Rom. 3:31), and because we walk in the Spirit (Rom. 8:9), we are to maintain the "fruit of the Spirit" (Gal. 5.22-23). We must always remember that we are "justified by faith, without the deeds of the law" (Rom. 3:28).

Since many Gentile believers feel it is necessary to place themselves under the "gospels" and early Acts for their commission (the so-called Great Commission), then what are they to do with the "ministry of reconciliation" given to Gentiles in the Body of Christ, which says nothing about "repent and be baptized for the remission of sins"? The sacrifice of Jesus brought a fulfillment to the Law of Moses, but that doesn't mean such a message was revealed at the time Jesus preached on Earth, or at Pentecost. Given the importance of what Paul revealed to the Jews at Rome about Jesus being "the end to the Law for righteousness to everyone that believes" (Rom. 10:4), we should be emphasizing these same truths. It was later in that same chapter (Romans 10) that Paul declared to the Jews and proselytes (see Rom. 9:1-5 also):

9 That if thou shalt confess with thy mouth the
Lord Jesus, and shalt believe in thine heart
that God hath raised him from the dead, thou
shalt be saved. 10 For with the heart man
believeth unto righteousness; and with the

> *mouth confession is made unto salvation.*
> *[11] For the scripture saith, Whosoever believeth*
> *on him shall not be ashamed. [12] For there is no*
> *difference between the Jew and the Greek: for*
> *the same Lord over all is rich unto all that call*
> *upon him. [13] For whosoever shall call upon the*
> *name of the Lord shall be saved.*
> *Romans 10:9-13*

As I stated, many believers tend to read themselves into everything written in the New Testament; however, we must realize that Jesus came first "to the lost sheep of the house of Israel…to fulfill the promises made unto the fathers," and this would include the command Jesus said to Nicodemus in John 3 about being "born of water and of the Spirit." Nicodemus should have also recognized that Israel was "baptized unto Moses" in the Red Sea (I Cor. 10:1-4), and that Jesus, who was standing in front of him, was indeed that Rock from which the nation of Israel drank at that time. Due to Israel's "blindness," they will not, as a nation, be "born again" until Jesus appears in His glory at the Second Coming.

> *[24] For I will take you from among the heathen,*
> *and gather you out of all countries, and will*
> *bring you into your own land. [25] Then will I*
> *sprinkle clean water upon you, and ye shall be*
> *clean: from all your filthiness, and from all*
> *your idols, will I cleanse you. [26] A new heart*
> *also will I give you, and a new spirit will I put*
> *within you: and I will take away the stony*

heart out of your flesh, and I will give you an heart of flesh. 27 And I will put my spirit within you, and cause you to walk in my statutes, and ye shall keep my judgments, and do them. 28 And ye shall dwell in the land that I gave to your fathers; and ye shall be my people, and I will be your God. Ezekiel 36:24-28

8 In that day shall the LORD defend the inhabitants of Jerusalem; and he that is feeble among them at that day shall be as David; and the house of David shall be as God, as the angel of the LORD before them. 9 And it shall come to pass in that day, that I will seek to destroy all the nations that come against Jerusalem. 10 And I will pour upon the house of David, and upon the inhabitants of Jerusalem, the spirit of grace and of supplications: and they shall look upon me whom they have pierced, and they shall mourn for him, as one mourneth for his only son, and shall be in bitterness for him, as one that is in bitterness for his firstborn.
Zechariah 12:8-10 (at the Second Coming)

13 Wherefore gird up the loins of your mind, be sober, and hope to the end for the grace that is to be brought unto you at the revelation of Jesus Christ; 14 As obedient children, not fashioning yourselves according to the former

> *lusts in your ignorance: 15 But as he which*
> *hath called you is holy, so be ye holy in all*
> *manner of conversation; 16 Because it is*
> *written, Be ye holy; for I am holy. 17 And if ye*
> *call on the Father, who without respect of*
> *persons judgeth according to every man's*
> *work, pass the time of your sojourning here in*
> *fear…23 Being born again, not of corruptible*
> *seed, but of incorruptible, by the word of God,*
> *which liveth and abideth for ever.*
> *I Peter 1:13-17 and 23 (preparing Israel for*
> *the return of Jesus)*

Israel will also be "born of the Spirit" at the Second Coming of Jesus Christ. They will inherit all the "spiritual blessings" of the New Covenant (testament) at that time (Jer. 31:31-36). However, the Body of Christ has "all spiritual blessings in heavenly places in Christ" (Eph. 1:3) *at this time*, thanks to the grace of God. Please note, again, the following:

> *5 And that he was seen of Cephas, then of the*
> *twelve: 6 After that, he was seen of above five*
> *hundred brethren at once; of whom the greater*
> *part remain unto this present, but some are*
> *fallen asleep. 7 After that, he was seen of*
> *James; then of all the apostles. 8 And last of all*
> *he was seen of me also, <u>as of one born out of</u>*
> *<u>due time</u>. I Corinthians 15:5-8:*

The Body of Christ (kept secret since the world began) is currently receiving *by grace* what Israel will inherit through *the promises* known "*since* the world began." The Body of Christ was also known by God "*before* the foundation of the world," which no one knew this truth until Paul was given "the revelation of the mystery." This is why we should not assume the "gospels" and early Acts were written directly to the Church that Paul "laid the foundation" for through his ministry (I Cor. 3:10). It was Paul who was *first* called to proclaim salvation through faith in the shed blood of Jesus Christ, which He proclaimed to be "the blood of the new testament" (Matt. 26:26-28).

Did the disciples understand what Jesus meant by this? Remember, had Satan known the "revelation of the mystery," he would not have had Christ crucified (I Cor. 2:7-8). Even in Acts 2 at Pentecost, Peter and the other apostles did not preach salvation by grace, through faith in the blood of Jesus Christ, apart from works of the Law. Again, "in due time," this was revealed later to and through Paul by Jesus Christ (Gal. 1:11-12).

I challenge you to find where anyone—before Paul—preached salvation by faith in the blood and resurrection of Jesus, along with having a heavenly citizenship as a member of the Body of Christ. We also find nothing preached about believers being "baptized *by* one Spirit into one body" until Paul was sent to reveal it by Jesus Christ (after Israel's fall in Acts 7). For most, they assume this gospel message began in Matthew, but please note the following passage regarding the "blood of the new covenant (testament)" and to whom God made "an able minister" of it.

> *2 Ye are our epistle written in our hearts,*
> *known and read of all men: 3 Forasmuch as ye*
> *are manifestly declared to be the epistle of*
> *Christ ministered by us, written not with ink,*
> *but with the Spirit of the living God; not in*
> *tables of stone, but in fleshy tables of the*
> *heart. 4 And such trust have we through Christ*
> *to God-ward: 5 Not that we are sufficient of*
> *ourselves to think any thing as of ourselves;*
> *but our sufficiency is of God; 6 Who also hath*
> *made us able ministers of the new testament;*
> *not of the letter, but of the spirit: for the letter*
> *killeth, but the spirit giveth life.*
> *2 Corinthians 3:2-6*

> *6 To the praise of the glory of his grace,*
> *wherein he hath made us accepted in the*
> *beloved. 7 In whom we have redemption*
> *through his blood, the forgiveness of sins,*
> *according to the riches of his grace; 8 Wherein*
> *he hath abounded toward us in all wisdom and*
> *prudence; 9 Having made known unto us the*
> *mystery of his will, according to his good*
> *pleasure which he hath purposed in himself:*
> *Ephesians 1:6-9*

During the earthly ministry of Jesus, He was a "minister of the circumcision," and the nations were to be blessed *through* Israel; however, thanks to the "revelation of the mystery," individual Gentiles from all nations can *now* possess "all spiritual blessings" apart from Israel. This is why Paul stated in I Corinthians 15:8 that he was "as of one born out of (before) due time." We are saved *apart* from Israel, not *through* Israel. There were Gentiles saved *before* the gospel of the grace of God (through Israel), and there will still be Gentiles saved *after* the Church is called to "meet Him in the air." Sadly, Jew and Gentile salvation will be very difficult during the Tribulation, but thankfully, both Jews and Gentiles can be saved by grace, through faith in the shed blood of Jesus Christ and His resurrection *at this time*. All who believe become members of the Body of Christ, and they have a heavenly citizenship. It was Paul and his companions *first*, not Peter, who was called to become "able ministers of the new testament (covenant)." Peter preached "repentance and water baptism for the remission of sins," while Paul preached "faith in the blood of Jesus Christ for the remission of sins." Why was this?

> *11 I say then, Have they stumbled that they*
> *should fall? God forbid: but rather through*
> *their fall salvation is come unto the Gentiles,*
> *for to provoke them to jealousy.*
> *Romans 11:11*

Thanks to religious traditions, very few Israelites are ever jealous of what we have, mostly because millions of believers themselves aren't' fully aware of what they do possess by grace, through faith, thanks to the "preaching of Jesus Christ, according to the revelation of the mystery." We must be doing something wrong because the Jews always sought to kill Paul for what he proclaimed about Gentiles possessing "all spiritual blessings in heavenly places in Christ." Instead, we have provoked Israel to anger through the denominational teachings of "Replacement Theology," which seek to replace Israel altogether. The majority of believers do not recognize "the mystery," so they simply combine Jesus Christ's earthly ministry to Israel with the ministry He gave to Paul for the Body of Christ—claiming it as one gospel (while denying the promises God still has for the nation of Israel when they will be "born again"). Gentiles do not need to wait to receive "all spiritual blessings," as described in Jeremiah 31 because we have now become "able ministers of the new testament" through the gospel of the grace of God. It wasn't until after Paul taught Peter the "gospel which I preach among the Gentiles" (Gal. 2:2; Eph. 3:8) that Peter mentioned the blood and resurrection in the context of salvation to all, as taught in his two epistles to the "strangers scattered throughout..." (which was the Circumcision).

The Apostle John insisted that if the Jews continued to "walk in light," they, too, could be "cleansed by the blood of Jesus Christ." If they didn't, they were told to "confess their sins."

> *7 But if we walk in the light, as he is in the*
> *light, we have fellowship one with another, and*
> *the blood of Jesus Christ his Son cleanseth us*
> *from all sin. 8 If we say that we have no sin, we*
> *deceive ourselves, and the truth is not in us.*
> *9 If we confess our sins, he is faithful and just*
> *to forgive us our sins, and to cleanse us from*

all unrighteousness. 10 If we say that we have not sinned, we make him a liar, and his word is not in us. I John 1:7-10 (to the Circumcision)

*Whosoever believeth <u>that Jesus is the Christ is born of God</u>: and every one that loveth him that begat loveth him also that is begotten of him. 2 <u>By this we know that we love the children of God, when we love God, and keep his commandments.</u> 3 For this is the love of God, that we keep his commandments: and his commandments are not grievous.
I John 5:1-3 (to the Circumcision)*

*28 Therefore we conclude that a man is justified by faith without the deeds of the law.
Romans 3:28*

Paul was "made an able minister of the new testament (covenant)" through "the preaching of Jesus Christ, according to the revelation of the mystery, which was kept secret since the world began." Again, many believers insist that because *Peter* mentioned the death and resurrection in Acts 2, that somehow indicates that he also preached that salvation could be obtained by faith in the finished work of Jesus Christ, apart from the deeds of the law. He did not. Acts 2 does not contain the gospel of I Corinthians 15:1-4; only "repent and be baptized for the remission of sins."

Today, however, there is only one means of salvation for both Jews and Gentiles:

> *8 For by grace are ye saved through faith [in*
> *the death, burial, and resurrection]; and that*
> *not of yourselves: it is the gift of God: 9 Not of*
> *works, lest any man should boast.*
> *Ephesians 2:8-9 (brackets by author)*

"But now" clearly indicates a change from what was commanded prior to Paul's writing to the believers in Rome. Both Jews and Gentiles can be saved today "through faith in His blood." "In times past," Gentiles were not a part of God's plan of salvation without first converting to Judaism. That all changed when Paul was "made an able minister of the new testament (covenant)."

> *11 Wherefore remember, that ye being in time*
> *past Gentiles in the flesh, who are called*
> *Uncircumcision by that which is called the*
> *Circumcision in the flesh made by hands;*
> *12 That at that time ye were without Christ,*
> *being aliens from the commonwealth of Israel,*
> *and strangers from the covenants of promise,*
> *having no hope, and without God in the world:*
> *13 But now in Christ Jesus ye who sometimes*
> *were far off are made nigh by the blood of*
> *Christ. 14 For he is our peace, who hath made*
> *both one, and hath broken down the middle*
> *wall of partition between us;*
> *Ephesians 2:11-14*

This is "the revelation of the mystery," and the specific formation of the "new creature," which is the Body of Christ, the Church. This was "kept secret since the world began," so you will search in vain to find this "called out assembly" of believers in any writings prior to Paul. We are now saved by grace, through faith (in the finished work of Jesus Christ), apart from works (especially the Law of Moses). Believers are now declared to be "complete in Him" (Col. 2:10) when they place their faith in the shed blood and resurrection of Jesus Christ. We have now become "the righteousness of God in Him" by faith, not of works. The Law is fulfilled in us because we are now "in Christ" (Rom. 3:31). Now, that's grace!

> *There is therefore now no condemnation to them which are in Christ Jesus, who walk not after the flesh, but after the Spirit. 2 <u>For the law of the Spirit of life in Christ Jesus hath made me free from the law of sin and death.</u> 3 For <u>what the law could not do</u>, in that it was weak through the flesh, God sending his own Son <u>in the likeness of sinful flesh, and for sin, condemned sin in the flesh:</u> 4 <u>That the righteousness of the law might be fulfilled in us</u>, who walk not after the flesh, but after the Spirit. Romans 8:1-4*

How is it possible for us to do this? Thankfully, God declared us "dead to sin" so we can "walk in newness of life."

> *What shall we say then? Shall we continue in sin, that grace may abound? 2 God forbid.*

> *How shall we, that are dead to sin, live any longer therein? ³ Know ye not, that so many of us as were baptized into Jesus Christ were baptized into his death? ⁴ Therefore we are buried with him by baptism into death: that like as Christ was raised up from the dead by the glory of the Father, even so we also should walk in newness of life. ⁵ For if we have been planted together in the likeness of his death, we shall be also in the likeness of his resurrection: ⁶ Knowing this, that our old man is crucified with him, that the body of sin might be destroyed, that henceforth we should not serve sin.* Romans 6:1-6

Even though we still sin, God has declared us to be "dead" to it! Sin was put to death when God "baptized (us) *by* one Spirit into Jesus Christ." He stated that we were also "baptized into His death."

I've always been intrigued by the words "know ye not" in this passage. In other words, we should know better, but thanks to unscriptural traditions, some believers "bathe" this passage from Romans 6 in water baptism, which Paul already taught to the Corinthians (prior to writing to the Romans) the baptism "*by* one Spirit into one body" (I Cor. 12:13). Why would Paul retreat to water baptism after declaring previously to the Corinthians the "spiritual baptism" done by God (*by* one Spirit")? I often refer to such individuals as "waterlogged Christians" because they seem to insert water baptism into every passage that mentions the word *baptism*. They forget about the other seven or so baptisms in the Bible that have nothing to do with water.

If Romans 6 infers water baptism, as many insist, then it clearly teaches that water baptism is necessary for salvation. Are we truly baptized "into Christ" by water? If so, then Paul was wrong when he taught the following to the Galatians:

> *24 Wherefore the law was our schoolmaster to bring us unto Christ, <u>that we might be justified by faith</u>. 25 But after that faith is come, we are no longer under a schoolmaster. 26 For ye are all the children of God <u>by faith in Christ Jesus</u>. 27 For as many of you as have been <u>baptized into Christ have put on Christ</u>.*
> *Galatians 3:24-27*

Galatians was written even before Corinthians and Romans, so Paul made it clear in his first writings that faith justifies us, as well as baptizes us "into Christ," and water had nothing to do with this. If it did, then salvation isn't by faith; it is by water baptism, which is what many believers place their faith in to save them. Tragically, how many believers are convinced they are saved simply because they were "water baptized"? For those who do not believe salvation is by water baptism, they often still insist it should be performed because "Jesus was baptized." After four decades of biblical studies, I have yet to find a command to be water baptized as a "symbol" of "an inward change" and an "outward sign" to others of that change. Water baptism, from the time of John the Baptist, was for the "remission of sins," so for those who insist on this traditional "symbolic" and unbiblical practice of water baptism ("outward sign of an inward change"), we must wonder why we would need the "blood of Christ" for the forgiveness of sins, especially if water takes care of this concern. It did prior to the cross! John the Baptist, Jesus, and the twelve apostles did not teach that water baptism was only a "sign of dying to self and raising to newness of life"; they taught it, during the earthly ministry of Jesus, as the basis of "the remission of sins."

The cross, not the Jordan River, is where "the remission of sins" took place for "all who believe" (Rom. 10:4), and after Paul began preaching, we know water baptism "for the remission of sins" was replaced (I Cor. 1:17) with "faith in His blood for the remission of sins" (Rom. 3:24-26). Many churches are still practicing two baptisms, even though Paul stated there is only one baptism (Eph. 4:5), which he clearly defines as being done "*by* one Spirit." Paul, in due time, revealed that faith in the blood of the cross is what forgives us, not water (I Cor. 1:17-18). After all, the Bible is silent on the notion of any believers being *buried in water*, or that we are buried *like* Christ. By faith in the blood, we are buried "with Christ...*by* one Spirit." Our "newness of life" (Rom. 6:4) is not associated with water baptism, but rather it is associated with His resurrection. Yes, water baptism was once a requirement for the "lost sheep of the house of Israel," *but now*, as an "able minister of the new testament (in His blood)," Paul declared only "one baptism," which we learn in his letters to be "*by* one Spirit." This is how we are baptized into His death, burial, and resurrection. (I will address water baptism in a separate chapter, but the traditions surrounding Romans 6 forced a brief commentary at this time.)

Chapter Conclusion

I know I continue to introduce various subjects that are not often "rightly divided" within denominationalism, but without 2 Timothy 2:15, we will continue to add to the list of new denominations over time, especially when various sects break away from one church to form another. This is not unity, nor is it the will of God to have such divisions.

Believers are commanded to "make all men see what is the fellowship of the mystery," but this, too, is often overlooked and outright condemned by those who cling to "Christian" covenants that are, at best, inferred into the Scriptures. The Old and New Testaments (covenants) were made by God with the "house of Israel," but many Gentiles who don't "rightly divide" somehow feel compelled to take those covenants promised to Israel and claim them as their own—relacing Israel altogether. The "revelation of the mystery" takes such a need away.

By commanding people to be "born again," most believers aren't even aware of the direct context that phrase has to the nation of Israel. The Body of Christ is told to "believe" (the gospel of the grace of God) to be "justified from all things from which you could not be justified by the Law of Moses." If we do not "rightly divide the word of truth," which is associated with the "gospel of our salvation" (Eph. 1:13), then we will continue to deepen the identity crisis we are currently suffering within our faith.

CHAPTER 6

"Know Ye Not..."

*³ As I besought thee to abide still at Ephesus,
when I went into Macedonia, that thou
mightest charge some that they teach no other
doctrine, ⁴ Neither give heed to fables and
endless genealogies, which minister questions,
rather than godly edifying which is in faith: so
do. I Timothy 1:3-4*

Traditions or Truth:

As I have taught, all the major denominations tend to combine the "gospel of the kingdom" (Mark 1:14-15) with the "gospel of the grace of God" (Acts 20:24; Gal. 2:2; 2:7; Eph. 6:19) which means they believe salvation is ultimately by grace, but they often continue to insist on repentance and water baptism, being "born again," and "keeping the commandments" to *fully* save them. To them, their works are necessary so they may strive in cooperation with God's grace (not realizing the differences between justification and sanctification). In other words, most believers from almost all denominations are apt to "follow in the footsteps of Jesus," according to His teachings found in the so-called "gospels," but too often, they never recognize the "greater commission" given to Paul for the Body of Christ, which is "the ministry of reconciliation" where God made Christ "to be sin for us…that we might become the righteousness of God in Him" (2 Cor. 5:18-21).

Remember, grace is the *unmerited* favor of God, and in "the dispensation of the grace of God," works are not sufficient to save us (or keep us saved), rather it is the sufficiency of faith in the shed blood of Jesus Christ that makes us "the righteousness of God in Him." If you feel you must earn your salvation, then you trust more in the sufficiency of your own works rather than the sufficiency of the blood of Christ to save you from the eternal penalty of your sins. Faith in His blood brings about the remission of sins (Rom. 3:24-26), not works (Eph. 2:8-9).

The "gospels" do not contain the gospel of the grace of God, which was first revealed to us through the gospel Jesus gave to Paul (I Tim. 1:16). Most believers do not recognize this fact.

> *[37] If any man think himself to be a prophet,*
> *or spiritual, let him acknowledge that the*
> *things that I write unto you are the*
> *commandments of the Lord. [38] But if any man*
> *be ignorant, let him be ignorant.*
> *I Corinthians 14:37-38*

If you "follow in the footsteps of Jesus," found throughout the "gospels," would you not be considered a practicing Jew or proselyte under Judaism and the Law (Gal. 4:4-5)? Any Gentile who followed the religion of Jesus (Judaism) during

His earthly ministry was called a proselyte. Would this not mean that Gentiles should still convert to Judaism to be saved, just as Gentiles did under the earthly ministry of Jesus Christ? Could a Gentile, during the earthly ministry of Jesus, ever claim to be saved by grace, through faith in the shed blood and resurrection of Jesus Christ, especially apart from works of the law? Remember, even the Twelve did not know or understand the words of Jesus (about His death and resurrection) in Matthew 16:21-23 or Luke 18:31-34, so how could any Gentile comprehend it? Paul reminded us in 2 Corinthians 5:16 "…yea, though we have known Christ after the flesh, yet now henceforth know we Him no more." Since the time of Paul, we know Jesus Christ as the risen, glorified Savior, and He is the Head of the Body, a title not found outside of Paul's epistles.

The "revelation of the mystery" teaches how we are saved *apart* from Israel and the Law, and this revelation, given to Paul, was not taught at the time Jesus was on the earth; it was taught to Paul beginning at least a year after Jesus was risen and ascended into Heaven. He later appeared to Paul, as Acts 9 teaches, which was after Israel's *fall* in Acts 7. Israel stumbled at the cross (I Cor. 1:23), but they hadn't *fallen* into spiritual blindness until the stoning of Stephen in Acts 7.

If *uncircumcised* Gentiles were in *one body* with the Jews prior to Paul's conversion, why would Paul state in his first sermon (Acts 13:46), "Seeing you (Jews)…judge yourselves unworthy of everlasting life, lo we turn to the Gentiles"? This hardly makes sense, especially since no such gospel message was yet "made known unto the sons of men" prior to the conversion of Paul and "the revelation of the mystery." No believer was ever told they were "baptized *by* one Spirit" and placed "into one body" until after Acts 9. Pentecost was a partial fulfillment of prophecy (Joel 2; Acts 2:14-21), not the "revelation of the mystery."

Again, I ask, if Peter and Paul were preaching the same gospel (the Great Commission), why would Paul refer to his gospel as the "revelation of the mystery…which in other ages was not made known unto the sons of men as it is now revealed" (Eph. 3:3-5)? As mentioned already, Paul specifically stated that he learned the gospel of the grace of God "by revelation of Jesus Christ," not the twelve apostles:

> *[11] But I certify you, brethren, that the gospel which was preached of me is <u>not after man</u>.*
> *[12] <u>For I neither received it of man, neither was I taught it, but by the revelation of Jesus Christ.</u> Galatians 1:11-12*

As I have been explaining, before the conversion of Paul in Acts 9, Christ came to Israel (the circumcision) to prepare the nation for their King and His Kingdom, as well as to provide the message whereby they could receive both (Acts 2:38; 3:19-21). How can anyone read the Old Testament, especially after Genesis 12, and not see what God promised to accomplish through Israel, not only for that nation, but also for the Gentile nations that were to be blessed through Abraham and his seed? This *kingdom of heaven*, which Jesus and the apostles preached during Christ's earthly ministry, was promised to Abraham and his seed, and it offered blessings to the nations who blessed Israel (Gen. 12:1-3).

Now, through Abraham's Seed (Jesus Christ), salvation is available to all through the gospel of the grace of God (Gal. 3:16), apart from the Law of Moses (Gal. 3:13, 24).

Let us remember, in Acts there was the gospel of the kingdom and the gospel of the grace of God running simultaneously for a while. While James, Peter, and John continued their ministry with the Circumcision, Paul continued establishing churches mainly with Gentiles (the Uncircumcision), which we read about in Galatians 2:7-9. There was water baptism and spiritual baptism. There were works performed under the Law, and the directive from Peter and James (Acts 15) that declared that Gentiles were not under the Law (Acts 15:10, 19, 24; Rom. 9:1-5). I find it baffling that the same people who insist believers today must adhere to James 2:21-24 are also the same believers who forget what James also stated in Acts 15 about Gentiles *not* being "under (the works of) the Law." Paul wrote Galatians 3 to help illustrate how Gentile salvation could be obtained strictly by faith without the Law, just as Abraham was declared "righteous by faith" hundreds of years before the Law. Abraham had never known the gospel of the grace of God; he simply believed God and it was "counted unto him for righteousness."

From Genesis 12 to Acts 7, Israel was the primary focus of God's attention, especially if the Gentile nations were to be blessed through Abraham's seed (Israel) as God promised to do (Rom. 15:8). However, when Israel rejected the Messiah and the Kingdom, we know how this left the Gentiles: "without hope" (Eph. 2:11-12).

Are We Still Without Hope?

Thankfully, individual Jews and Gentiles now have hope through the "revelation of the mystery," which God revealed to and through Paul. What is known *now* by the Body of Christ was "not made known" until the conversion of Paul, so we shouldn't force our current knowledge of the truth upon certain believers in the past who were not yet made aware of the "revelation of the mystery." For those theologians and believers who insist there is only one Church and one gospel *throughout* the entire Bible, they may want to consider again what Paul stated about "the mystery" being "kept secret since the world began." If there had only been one gospel throughout the Bible, then we are left to wonder what Paul meant about his gospel message being "kept secret since the world began," especially when there had been a gospel being preached long before Paul was converted in Acts 9.

Believers may also want to consider why the gospel of the kingdom and the gospel of the grace of God do not teach the same means of salvation, the same destiny for Israel (Earth) and the Body of Christ (Heaven), and why there are several different judgments (the Judgment Seat of Christ, the judgment and resurrection of the "just and the unjust," and the Great White Throne Judgment)? Are these the same judgments? Revelation 20 deals with the two judgments of prophecy, so where does the Judgment Seat of Christ fit into prophecy (Rom. 14:10; 2 Cor. 5:10)? It doesn't, because it was only a part of the "revelation of the mystery" given to Paul, "the apostle to the Gentiles." Does "repent and be baptized for the remission of sins," and "by grace, through faith, without works" seem to offer salvation the same way?

How can we still say there is only one Church and one gospel from Genesis to Revelation? Invented covenants are often used to help provide answers to these important questions; however, "rightly dividing the word of truth" ultimately provides solutions for those not wanting "to be ashamed."

Sure, theologians could invent teachings to address these questions, and they certainly have, but why invent anything when the word of God simply needs to be "rightly divided"? We have wasted precious time wrongly dividing the word of truth to satisfy theologies that are completely unnecessary. Paul commanded the right division of Scripture two thousand years ago, but Catholicism did not apply this command, and 1500 years later, the Protestant Reformation gave us several new covenants not taught within Scripture. We can find "the dispensation of the grace of God" in Paul's epistles, and we can find numerous covenants God made with various biblical characters, but I have yet to find the Covenants of Redemption, Works, and Grace. I suppose we could infer them, but not without *spiritualizing* passages that require us to abandon the contextual and literal understanding of the passages themselves. Is this not how we eventually ended up with the belief that the Body of Christ somehow became "spiritual Israel"?

But Now!

It wasn't until the "revelation of the mystery" to Paul that he could declare "but now," meaning something new was being introduced. The Great Commission was already being proclaimed, *but now*, it is the gospel of the grace of God that is able to save us.

25 Now to him that is of power to stablish you according to <u>my gospel</u>, and <u>the preaching of Jesus Christ, according to the revelation of the mystery, which was kept secret since the world began,</u> 26 <u>But now is made manifest</u>, and by the scriptures of the prophets [adj. prophetic writings of Paul;], according to <u>the commandment of the everlasting God, made known to all nations for the obedience of faith:</u> 27 To God only wise, be glory through Jesus Christ for ever. Amen.
Romans 16:25-27 (brackets by author)

25 Whereof I am made a minister, according to <u>the dispensation of God which is given to me for you, to fulfil the word of God;</u> 26 <u>Even the mystery which hath been hid from ages and from generations, but now</u> is made manifest to his saints: 27 To whom God would make known what is the riches of the glory of <u>this mystery among the Gentiles; which is Christ in you, the hope of glory:</u> Colossians 1:25-27

8 Be not thou therefore ashamed of the testimony of our Lord, nor of me his prisoner: but be thou partaker of the afflictions of the gospel according to the power of God; 9 <u>Who hath saved us, and called us with an holy calling, not according to our works, but according to his own purpose and grace,</u>

> *which was given us in Christ Jesus before the
> world began,* [10] *But is now made manifest by
> the appearing of our Saviour Jesus Christ,
> who hath abolished death, and hath brought
> life and immortality to light through the
> gospel:* [11] *Whereunto I am appointed a
> preacher, and an apostle, and a teacher of the
> Gentiles.* 2 Timothy 1:8-11

"But now" are two powerful words in the context of Scripture. The gospel of the kingdom was already being preached during the earthly ministry of Jesus (Matt. 4:23; Mk. 1:14), *but now*, we are to "make all men see what is the fellowship of the mystery, which from the beginning of the world hath been hid in God…" (Eph. 3:9).

Failing to "rightly divide the word of God" has caused the utter chaos and disunity in the Church. Gentiles were already "given over to a reprobate mind" (Rom. 1:28), *but now*, Gentiles have been made "joint heirs with Christ" (Rom. 8:16-17). "Repent and be baptized for the remission of sins" was proclaimed at Pentecost, *but now*, we are to proclaim, "Be ye reconciled (restored to fellowship) with God… through faith in His blood" (Rom. 3:25; 2 Cor. 5:18-21). The means by which we can be restored to fellowship is "…by grace, through faith…apart from works." Again, failure to recognize these differences has caused a debilitating identity crisis within believers throughout most of Christian history. When the Bible became widely available to the "common man," divisions within the Church accelerated because the truth of Scripture called into question many of the traditions that had been forced upon millions of believers.

Again, if there has only been one body of believers, or "call-out assembly" throughout the entire Bible, along with only one gospel through which salvation can be obtained, we can honestly conclude that the Bible *does* contradict itself (it certain does not). It is one thing to say that salvation has always been by grace, through faith; however, it is important to understand the timing in which this was first made known "unto the sons of men," apart from works. Abraham, Moses, the twelve apostles, and even Jesus did not proclaim this specific "good news" about salvation being by grace, through faith in what Christ accomplished for us (death and resurrection). It wasn't until after "the revelation of the mystery" by Paul that such a gospel was "made known unto the sons of men" (Eph. 3:5).

But now, both Jews and Gentiles are baptized *by* one Spirit into one body, and we are now "joint heirs" with Christ, having been given a heavenly citizenship. No one knew of such a body of believers (Body of Christ) until Paul was commissioned to establish and preach it (I Cor. 3:10). Remember, "in times past" the Gentiles were left with "having no hope, and without God in the world"; however, thanks to the revelation given to Paul by Jesus Christ, we would have never known about salvation being made available to Gentiles, despite Israel's "fall" (Romans 11:11), which should have brought about "the great and notable Day of the Lord" (Tribulation and Second Coming). Instead of God's wrath, He gave us grace, and a "citizenship in heaven," but most believers are trained to return to the "gospels" and

Pentecost for their hope and salvation. However, as I have questioning, where in the "gospels" and at Pentecost were believers told that salvation was "by grace, through faith in the death and resurrection of Christ…apart from works" for salvation? Where were believers, prior to "the revelation of the mystery," told they were "seated in heavenly places in Christ" (Eph. 2:6)? This is why we must "rightly divide the word of truth."

As a final reminder, the "revelation of the mystery," along with Israel's unfaithfulness, does not mean God will, or has abandoned His *unconditional* covenants of an everlasting kingdom to Israel, which He made with Abraham and his descendants through Isaac and Jacob (and David)—long before Israel's spiritual fall in Acts 7.

> *18 In the same day the LORD made a*
> *covenant with Abram, saying, Unto thy seed*
> *have I given this land, from the river of Egypt*
> *unto the great river, the river Euphrates:*
> *Genesis 15:18*

Yes, God knew Israel would reject Jesus and the offers of the kingdom, but He also knew He had a "hidden wisdom" for individual Jews and Gentiles (not involving whole nations), which was to be "testified in due time." It was Paul who was made a "preacher and an apostle" for this purpose (I Tim. 2:5-7). Again, why did God delay the gospel Paul preached, regarding "the revelation of the mystery"?

> *⁶ Howbeit we speak wisdom among them*
> *that are perfect: yet not the wisdom of this*
> *world, nor of the princes of this world, that*
> *come to nought: ⁷ But we speak the wisdom of*
> *God in a mystery, even the hidden wisdom,*
> *<u>which God ordained before the world unto our</u>*
> *<u>glory</u>: ⁸ Which none of the princes of this*
> *world knew: <u>for had they known it, they would</u>*
> *<u>not have crucified the Lord of glory</u>.*
> *I Corinthians 2:6-8*

Remember, God promised Abraham how the nations that blessed Israel would also be blessed through the covenant God made with him and his seed in Genesis 12:1-3, as well as the following passages:

> *⁶ And he said, It is a light thing that thou*
> *shouldest be my servant to raise up the tribes*
> *of Jacob, and to restore the preserved of*
> *Israel: <u>I will also give thee for a light to the</u>*
> *<u>Gentiles, that thou mayest be my salvation</u>*
> *<u>unto the end of the earth</u>.*
> *Isaiah 49:6 (to Israel)*

> *Arise, shine; for thy light is come, and the*
> *glory of the LORD is risen upon thee. ² For,*
> *behold, the darkness shall cover the earth, and*
> *gross darkness the people: but the LORD shall*
> *arise upon thee, and his glory shall be seen*

*upon thee. ³ <u>And the Gentiles shall come to thy
light, and kings to the brightness of thy rising</u>.
Isaiah 60:1-3 (to Israel)*

*⁸ <u>Now therefore so shalt thou say unto my
servant David, Thus saith the LORD of hosts</u>, I
took thee from the sheepcote, from following
the sheep, <u>to be ruler over my people, over
Israel:</u> ⁹ And I was with thee whithersoever
thou wentest, and have cut off all thine
enemies out of thy sight, and have made thee a
great name, like unto the name of the great
men that are in the earth. ¹⁰ <u>Moreover I will
appoint a place for my people Israel, and will
plant them, that they may dwell in a place of
their own, and move no more; neither shall the
children of wickedness afflict them any more,
as beforetime.</u> ¹¹ And as since the time that I
commanded judges to be over my people
Israel, and have caused thee to rest from all
thine enemies. <u>Also the LORD telleth thee that
he will make thee an house</u>. ¹² And when thy
days be fulfilled, <u>and thou shalt sleep with thy
fathers, I will set up thy seed after thee, which
shall proceed out of thy bowels, and I will
establish his kingdom</u>. ¹³ <u>He shall build an
house for my name, and I will stablish the
throne of his kingdom for ever.</u> ¹⁴ I will be his
father, and he shall be my son. If he commit
iniquity, I will chasten him with the rod of men,*

and with the stripes of the children of men:
¹⁵ But my mercy shall not depart away from
him, as I took it from Saul, whom I put away
before thee. ¹⁶ <u>And thine house and thy
kingdom shall be established for ever before
thee: thy throne shall be established for ever.</u>
2 Samuel 7:8-16 (to Israel)

⁴ He that sitteth in the heavens shall laugh:
the LORD shall have them in derision. ⁵ Then
shall he speak unto them in his wrath, and vex
them in his sore displeasure. ⁶ Yet have I set my
king upon my holy hill of Zion. ⁷ I will declare
the decree: the LORD hath said unto me, Thou
art my Son; this day have I begotten thee. ⁸ Ask
of me, and <u>I shall give thee the heathen for
thine inheritance, and the uttermost parts of
the earth for thy possession.</u>
Psalm 2:4-8

There is coming a future Tribulation, the Second Coming of Christ, and the giving of a Messianic Kingdom to the promised seed of Abraham (and Gentile proselytes (not the Body of Christ)), and when Jesus began His ministry to the "lost sheep of the house of Israel," He began with this message:

¹⁷ From that time Jesus began to preach,
and to say, Repent: <u>for the kingdom of heaven
is at hand.</u> Matthew 4:17

Jesus came to His own to fulfill all that God had promised to Israel, which would have brought blessings to the nations as well, and this is why Jesus came to the "lost sheep of the house of Israel" (Rom. 9:1-5). It is also the reason He came, preaching "repent, for the "kingdom of heaven is at hand" (Matt. 3:2; 4:17; Mark 1:15). If we recall, right before the ascension of Jesus, His apostles asked if Jesus would restore the kingdom unto Israel (Acts 1:6-7).

It was during Christ's ministry, to the "circumcision" that we learn of the "baptism of repentance for the remission of sins" by John, the "Sermon on the Mount," the so-called "Lord's Prayer," the Tribulation and Second Coming of Christ, the Great Commission, the pouring out of the Holy Ghost (prophesied by Joel and others (Num. 11:29; Prov. 1:23; Isa. 32:15)), and also the coming Messianic Kingdom to Israel. Believers today still insist Jesus was referring to Jewish and Gentile "Christians" in "one body" during those events recorded in "the gospels" and early Acts, even though Gentile salvation, apart from Israel, had not yet been made known until after Paul's conversion in Acts 9. Also, no one was called a "Christian" prior to Acts 11.

> *19 Now they which were scattered abroad upon*
> *the persecution that arose about Stephen*
> *travelled as far as Phenice, and Cyprus, and*
> *Antioch, preaching the word to none but unto*
> *the Jews only...25 Then departed Barnabas to*
> *Tarsus, for to seek Saul: 26 And when he had*
> *found him, he brought him unto Antioch. And it*
> *came to pass, that a whole year they*

> *assembled themselves with the church, and*
> *taught much people. And the disciples were*
> *called Christians first in Antioch.*
> *Acts 11:19 and 25-26*

These events took place before Paul's first sermon to Jews and proselytes at Antioch, where Paul declared (for the first recorded time) the following:

> *38 Be it known unto you therefore, men and*
> *brethren, that through this man is preached*
> *unto you the forgiveness of sins: 39 And by him*
> *all that believe are justified from all things,*
> *from which ye could not be justified by the law*
> *of Moses. Acts 13:38-39*

Had Peter and Paul been preaching the same gospel of "repent and be baptized for the remission of sins," Paul apparently forgot this. Also, the Gentiles were very happy to hear this message, which Paul delivered the next sabbath. This is also when Paul first stated:

> *45 But when the Jews saw the multitudes, they*
> *were filled with envy, and spake against those*
> *things which were spoken by Paul,*
> *contradicting and blaspheming. 46 Then Paul*
> *and Barnabas waxed bold, and said, It was*
> *necessary that the word of God should first*
> *have been spoken to you: but seeing ye put it*

from you, and judge yourselves unworthy of
everlasting life, lo, we turn to the Gentiles.
Acts 13:45-46

Did Paul turn to the Gentiles with the exact same gospel as Acts 2? There is no evidence of this, especially in Acts 13.

As promised, if Israel had repented, the Lord would have returned and established this promised Messianic Kingdom to Israel (after the Tribulation). Jesus also told His disciples how He would "go and prepare a place for them" (John 14:1-3), so if the kingdom was only intended to exist "in their hearts," this does not fit the context of the passage in John 14, especially considering also the promise of Revelation 21 when the New Jerusalem comes down out of Heaven. I've heard this passage (from John 14) preached at many funerals; however, Jesus was not discussing the "citizenship in Heaven" for the Body of Christ (still hidden in God), but rather He was preparing Israel for the Messianic Kingdom that was to be established on Earth. Peter (and John) continued to look for this promise given by Christ during His earthly ministry to Israel, as demonstrated in the following passages:

10 But the day of the Lord will come as a
thief in the night; in the which the heavens
shall pass away with a great noise, and the
elements shall melt with fervent heat, the earth
also and the works that are therein shall be
burned up. 11 Seeing then that all these things
shall be dissolved, what manner of persons

> *ought ye to be in all holy conversation and godliness, [12] Looking for and hasting unto the coming of the day of God, wherein the heavens being on fire shall be dissolved, and the elements shall melt with fervent heat?*
> *[13] <u>Nevertheless we, according to his promise, look for new heavens and a new earth, wherein dwelleth righteousness.</u> [14] Wherefore, beloved, seeing that ye look for such things, be diligent that ye may be found of him in peace, without spot, and blameless.* 2 Peter 3:10-14

> *And I saw a new heaven and a new earth: for the first heaven and the first earth were passed away; and there was no more sea.*
> *[2] And I John saw the holy city, new Jerusalem, coming down from God out of heaven, prepared as a bride adorned for her husband.* Revelation 21:1-2

Without recognizing the "revelation of the mystery," countless theologians have had to invent a place for the Body of Christ in passages intended for Israel and Israel alone. There is no "time machine" capable of transporting the Body of Christ into the time of the saints of the Old Testament, or when Jesus was "sent to none other than to the lost sheep of the house of Israel." Sure, we can learn about the events that led Christ to the cross (throughout the entire Bible), but the gospel that states that salvation is by grace, through faith in the shed blood of Christ and His resurrection is not found until Paul was commissioned, by Jesus Christ, to preach it to the world. Again, this is why Paul's gospel is called "the revelation of the mystery…kept secret since the world began." It is also called "the dispensation (stewardship) of the grace of God." Believers have an identity crisis because they can't seem to refrain from embedding themselves into God's dealings and promises to and with Israel, especially in the "gospels" and the early chapters in Acts. They ignorantly use the statement, "When you see the word *Israel*, it means *all the people of God*."

The Whole Counsel of God

Right now, Israel is in temporary blindness (Rom. 11:25) "until the fulness of the Gentiles be come in" (Rom. 11:25), but when the Tribulation occurs, it will become the greatest evangelistic effort ever known to humanity. Again, the Jews were told to repent, and the "times of refreshing" would come "from the presence of the Lord" (Acts 3). Did that happen? The current condition of the world, and the ongoing blindness of Israel toward her Messiah should confirm how they are not experiencing the "times of refreshing from the presence of the Lord." Thanks, however, to the *unconditional* promises of God, this will happen for the "promised seed" of Abraham, just as prophecy stated millennia before Jesus "came to His own and His own received Him not" (John 1:11).

For now, we are to share the gospel of the grace of God with the world, which is how we are reconciled (restored to fellowship) with God. Gentiles do not have to be saved *through* Israel, but rather they are saved *apart* from Israel

(Rom. 11:11). This is why Paul was called into the ministry, "to declare unto you all the counsel of God."

> *24 But none of these things move me, neither count I my life dear unto myself, <u>so that I might finish my course with joy, and the ministry, which I have received of the Lord Jesus, to testify the gospel of the grace of God.</u> 25 And now, behold, I know that ye all, among whom I have gone preaching the kingdom of God, shall see my face no more. 26 Wherefore I take you to record this day, that I am pure from the blood of all men. 27 <u>For I have not shunned to declare unto you all the counsel of God.</u>*
> *Acts 20:24-27*

According to the so-called Great Commission, weren't the Twelve commissioned to "go ye into all the world"? Paul, on the other hand, was commissioned to reveal to both Jews and Gentiles the entire plan of God for both Heaven and Earth. Until Paul, Israel knew God's eternal plans for the Messianic Kingdom that was to be established on Earth; however, no one knew God would also reveal the gospel of the grace of God, which would reveal a "new creature" called the Body of Christ (2 Cor. 5:17). We have our citizenship in Heaven (Phil. 3:20), which is completely foreign in Scripture until Paul revealed it. Before God completes His prophecies regarding the "new heavens and the new earth," He must remove the Church, the Body of Christ, because we are *not* a part of His prophetic program for Israel and the future Gentile *nations*, in which many are to be saved, *in the ages to come*, under the "gospel of the kingdom" (Matt. 24:14). Remember, we are "as of ones born out of due time" (I Cor. 15:8), so the Body of Christ is receiving by grace what Israel will be given by promise when they are "born again of the Spirit" (John 3:5) at the Second Coming of Christ.

God's eternal plan is to unify both Heaven and Earth under Christ's authority (as both King and Head of the Body), but this does not mean God revealed His eternal purpose for Heaven at the time Jesus Christ was on the earth. That would seem odd, considering that Jesus proclaimed, "the kingdom of heaven is at hand," which His disciples asked whether it would be restored to them on Earth (Acts 1:6). God's plan for Heaven, however, was to be testified in due time." Never forget that Jesus came to "the circumcision…to confirm the promises made unto the fathers" (Rom. 15:8). As I have already stated, we should never force what we know currently from Paul into what was not yet "made known unto the sons of men," especially during the earthly ministry of Christ. Paul stated the following regarding our position in Christ "in the ages to come":

> *16 For by him were all things created, that*
> *are in heaven, and that are in earth, visible*
> *and invisible, whether they be thrones, or*
> *dominions, or principalities, or powers: all*
> *things were created by him, and for him:*
> *17 And he is before all things, and by him all*
> *things consist. 18 And he is the head of the*
> *body, the church: who is the beginning, the*

> *firstborn from the dead; <u>that in all things he</u>*
> *<u>might have the preeminence</u>. [19] For it pleased*
> *the Father that in him should all fulness dwell;*
> *[20] And, <u>having made peace through the blood</u>*
> *<u>of his cross, by him to reconcile all things unto</u>*
> *<u>himself; by him, I say, whether they be things</u>*
> *<u>in earth, or things in heaven.</u>*
> *Colossians 1:16-20*

This blessed truth about God's restoration of all things was not made known until the "revelation of the mystery," especially in regard to the Body of Christ in relationship to the restoration of Heaven. This is one reason why Paul declared in Colossians 1:25 that he was sent "to fulfill the word of God." And now, all believers are "complete in Him" (Col. 2:10), and in Christ, believers find "all the fulness of God." This is all "according to the eternal purpose which He purposed in Christ Jesus our Lord" (Eph. 3:11). Israel is awaiting the Messianic Kingdom to be establish on this earth, while the Body of Christ has already been "seated in heavenly places in Christ" (Eph. 2:6), thanks to our "citizenship in heaven," which we already possess "in Christ" (Phil. 3:20). We are ambassadors for Christ in this foreign land (Earth), and it is our duty to represent our Savior as we daily make ourselves a "living sacrifice" (Rom. 12:1-2).

This unity could not have occurred until God removed the enmity (hostility) between Himself and humanity (by the cross), and between the enmity that existed between both Jews and Gentiles. God, through the "revelation of the mystery," has revealed how He has "broken down the middle wall of partition" that separated both Jews and Gentiles (Eph. 2:12-17). We are now members of the *One True Church*, the Body of Christ, which is not the Church referenced in Matthew 16. If it were, then the "revelation of the mystery," which revealed the "new creature" (The Body of Christ), was not a mystery at all, especially if it was somehow introduced in "the gospels." We don't need to investigate too far into various theologies to figure out who is behind such scriptural manipulation and *"spiritual lies."*

Covenant Theology is very subtle in its redefining and *spiritualization* of Scripture in relationship to Israel and the Body of Christ. Where Covenant Theology sees "the revelation of the mystery" as the fulfillment of God's covenant promises through the Church, which is now "spiritual Israel," Paul showed a clear distinction between God's purpose for the Church and His covenant promises to the nation of Israel.

> *I say then, Hath God cast away his people?*
> *God forbid. For I also am an Israelite, of the*
> *seed of Abraham, of the tribe of Benjamin.*
> *2 God hath not cast away his people which he*
> *foreknew…25 For I would not, brethren, that ye*
> *should be ignorant of this mystery, lest ye*
> *should be wise in your own conceits; <u>that</u>*
> *<u>blindness in part is happened to Israel, until</u>*
> *<u>the fulness of the Gentiles be come in</u>.*
> *Romans 11:1-2 and 25*

By redefining "Israel" to mean "all the people of God" throughout the entire Bible, any interpretation can be applied to support whatever inferred covenants that Covenant theologians desire, along with the denominations that support its theology. We know God will still call 144,000 Jews from "the twelve tribes of Israel" at the time of the Tribulation (Rev. 7:1-8), so it is evident that God is not yet finished with the nation of Israel, even though Covenant theologians believe God's covenant promises will only be fulfilled through the Church—not a revived nation of Israel. Will the Church and the 144,000 remnant believers from Israel work cooperatively at the time of the Tribulation? Interestingly, I have never known there to be twelve tribes in the Body of Christ.

If Covenant Theology were based on solid biblical exegesis, why must its theologians *infer* at least three *new* covenants *not* found in Scripture; admit to the fact that God's covenant promises will *not* be fulfilled through Israel, but rather through the Church (which clearly shows they did recognize this distinction between Israel and the Church at one time); and if there has only been "one Church" throughout all of the Bible, why was it necessary for Paul to write in Ephesians 2 that his gospel had "broken down the middle of wall of partition" between the Israelites and Gentiles long after Pentecost in Acts 2? Is this not when Covenant Theology insists the Church began, even though they teach that Israel, in the Old Testament, was truly "all the people of God" already? They may believe this, but does Scripture truly show such a Church in existence millennia ago?

Also, if Covenant Theology were a "sound doctrine," where did Paul ever teach that the Body of Christ (the Church) would inherit the earthly kingdom promised to Israel, especially in the Old Testament, the "gospels," and early Acts? Isn't the Body of Christ promised a citizenship in Heaven (Phil 3:20)? Besides, if there were only one Church and one gospel, why does the Bible identify several churches, such as the Church in the Wilderness (Acts 7:38), the Church that was at Jerusalem (Acts 8:1-2), and the Body of Christ (the Church), which was "kept secret since the world began"? If there were only one gospel, and Paul's gospel was "kept secret," we must wonder what gospel was preached to the Church in the Wilderness and the Church that was at Jerusalem, which existed before the Body of Christ? (I will address this further in a chapter that addressed the notion of a "spiritual Israel.")

What Paul Specifically Taught Us in the Body of Christ
As I stated previously, Paul was called and sent to "lay the foundation" for the Body of Christ (I Cor. 3:10) so God could reveal His eternal purpose for both Heaven and Earth.

> *9 Having made known unto us <u>the mystery of his will</u>, according to his good pleasure which he hath purposed in himself: 10 <u>That in the dispensation of the fulness of times he might gather together in one all things in Christ, both which are in heaven, and which are on earth; even in him:</u> 11 In whom also we have obtained an inheritance, <u>being</u>*

> *predestinated according to the purpose of him*
> *who worketh all things after the counsel of his*
> *own will: 12 That we should be to the praise of*
> *his glory, who first trusted in Christ.*
> *Ephesians 1:9-12*

Paul's gospel was never known in the Old Testament, the "gospels," and in early Acts (1-12). However, as I previously asked, did Israel repent and receive the "times of refreshing," which Peter described in Acts 3:19-21? After all, Israel's leaders beheaded John the Baptist, crucified Jesus, stoned Stephen to death, and even hired Saul (Paul) to hunt down and persecute anyone who followed Christ as the Messiah. They obviously did not repent, and this left the nations "without hope, and without God in this world."

The "dispensation of the grace of God" (Eph. 3:2) was known only by God "before the world began," and this is why believers shouldn't be leaping at the opportunity to "follow in the footsteps of Jesus" during His earthly ministry to the "lost sheep of the house of Israel." Yes, we should always support and agree with what Jesus taught, of course, but *only* through the "right division" of the Scriptures written to the Body of Christ, which was still "kept secret" during the time Jesus Christ walked on this earth. There are, in fact, many things that Jesus taught during His earthly ministry which can still apply to the Body of Christ, but we must be careful that our application does not "frustrate grace" (Gal. 2:21), which we often do through our traditions.

For example, when Jesus declared in John 14:6 that He was "the way, the truth, and the life: no man comes to the

Father, but by me," is this not also truth for the time when Paul proclaimed the gospel of the grace of God? Can believers today find a way to God apart from Christ? Of course not, even though some have suggested otherwise. When Jesus commanded Peter to preach at Pentecost how they should "repent and be baptized for the remission of sins," should this be followed today as well? If so, why didn't "the apostle to the Gentiles" ever command this for believers in the Body of Christ? Paul mostly referred to the baptism "*by one Spirit*," and yet many believers feel the need to always add water to Paul's references to baptism. They do so by sheer ignorance of the word "rightly divided." After all, was the Body of Christ "born of water" in the Red Sea with Moses, and must we wait until the Second Coming of Jesus to be "born again"? Of course not!

There are also many theologians who attempt to make the Body of Christ "spiritual Israel" to justify their belief that there is only one Church and one gospel. Again, what about the Church in the wilderness, the Church that was at Jerusalem, and the Church, which is the Body of Christ? Did these all consist of one "called out assembly"? Did God start the Body of Christ in the Sinai wilderness? Did He give the Body of Christ the Law of Moses for our obedience? Did He begin the Body of Christ at Pentecost, which is always in reference to "the Church that was at Jerusalem"? Are we to command the world to "repent and be baptized for the remission of sins" as they did at Pentecost? Thankfully, God had something hidden in Himself, and "the revelation of the mystery" eventually brought salvation to individual Gentiles (and even Jews) apart from the nation of Israel and that nation's promises of an earthly kingdom. This "hidden wisdom" for the Body of Christ was all revealed in "the gospel of the grace of God." It is "unsearchable" elsewhere! The gospel of the kingdom that John the Baptist, Jesus, and His disciples preached, never revealed "the mystery." The Body of Christ is the "new creature" that Jesus revealed to and through Paul.

Tragically, many theologians have failed to recognize what God was doing through Paul, and to avoid "rightly dividing the word of truth," they find it much easier to invent "covenants" that might, at best, be implied in the Scriptures for believers. They see only one gospel from Genesis to Revelation, which they assume applies to all believers, regardless of the time in which a particular "good news" was revealed. They have even assumed God has turned all His promises to Abraham and Israel's Kingdom over to the Gentiles in the Body of Christ. This is a deliberate failure to recognize God's prophetic promises to Israel, and His "revelation of the mystery" to and through Paul—by direct revelation of Jesus Christ.

We know God is not "slack concerning His promises" to Israel as "some men count slackness" (2 Pet. 3:9), and even though many pastors and priests insist God has abandoned His unconditional promises to Israel—by giving them to the Church—this does not mean they are correct. They simply refuse to "rightly divide the word." God has *not* replaced Israel with the Church; otherwise, why should the Body of Christ be called a "new creature" if it is to be associated with the previously revealed promises to Israel as a nation?

To Conclude…

It was necessary to review this material after we examined these concepts throughout the Bible. We can never underestimate the importance of "rightly dividing the word of truth." I believe it is one of the best cures for the identity crisis we have within our faith as believers. Gentile salvation is still available today through the gospel of the grace of God, not the gospel of the kingdom Jesus gave to the twelve apostles.

For those who only see one Church and one gospel throughout the Bible, they are left to figure out what gospel would have been preached to the Church in the Wilderness and the Church that was at Jerusalem, especially since Paul, who was saved in Acts 9, declared that his gospel was "the revelation of the mystery, which was kept secret since the world began." How could Paul's gospel be proclaimed to any other Church prior to his conversion? We must "rightly divide."

CHAPTER 7

God's Eternal Purpose

⁹ Having made known unto us the mystery of his will, according to his good pleasure which he hath purposed in himself: ¹⁰ That in the dispensation of the fulness of times he might gather together in one all things in Christ, both which are in heaven, and which are on earth; even in him: ¹¹ In whom also we have obtained an inheritance, being predestinated according to the purpose of him who worketh all things after the counsel of his own will:
Ephesians 1:9-11

"Well, Jesus Said…"

There are millions of believers who insist all "Christians" were the focus of the earthly ministry of Jesus, even though Jesus proclaimed He was sent to "none other than to the lost sheep of the house of Israel," which we have recorded in Matthew and Romans (Matt. 10:5-7; 15:24; Rom. 15:8)? Millions of Gentile believers simply can't resist reading themselves into every command

Jesus gave in Matthew, Mark, Luke, John, and early Acts, even though Jesus was clear "to whom" He was sent (Rom. 9:1-5). They do this because religious traditions insist that whatever Jesus commanded, they must "follow in His footsteps." The common belief that the Old Testament was "for the Jews," and the New Testament is "for all Christians" is not entirely accurate; in fact, it has devastated the walk of many believers who, for good reason, can't reconcile all that Jesus said to both the twelve apostles and to Paul. Even biblical scholars struggle to reconcile Paul's ministry with that of the Twelve, and this is also because they have failed to recognize the importance of 2 Timothy 2:15.

One such example comes from John 3:1-6. Jesus spoke directly to Nicodemus, a Pharisee, about the need to be "born of water and of the Spirit." Millions of believers, especially pastors, go about commanding that people must be "born again," and they often enthusiastically add water baptism into this command ("born of water"), even though Nicodemus clearly understood Jesus to mean physical birth. However, was John 3 written to members of the Body of Christ? If so, why the need for "the revelation of the mystery" given to Paul (several years after John 3)?

The command to Nicodemus is simple to understand when you "rightly divide the word of truth." During the Exodus, Israel was born as a nation in the Red Sea (Exodus 14-15, Psalm 136, I Cor. 10), but this did not mean that every Israelite was automatically promised eternal life by their physical birth; they had to be "born of the Spirit." Even John the Baptist declared that God could make children of Israel "out of stones" (Matt. 3:9; Luke 3:8) if He chose to do so.

Paul also stated, "For they are not all Israel, which are of Israel" (Rom. 9:6). Again, this is another passage many believers attempt to apply directly to themselves, even though Paul was writing directly to Israelites who assumed their physical birth met the criteria for being given all the promises of God (Romans 9:1-5). They had to believe "on His name" as their Messiah (John 3:16) to receive the blessings of the promises "made unto the fathers" (Rom. 15:8). Gentiles were never born the "children of God," so how can Gentiles be "born again" (Eph. 2:11-12)? Besides, if believers in the Body of Christ are to be "born again," why didn't Paul *ever* give such a command to us?

At the time Jesus spoke to Nicodemus in John 3, salvation (apart from Israel), was *not* yet made available to Gentiles unless they converted to Judaism, so during the earthly ministry of Jesus, it was necessary for a person to have first been "born of water" from the womb of a Jewish woman, because "salvation is of the Jews" (John 4:22). This is why Jesus told Nicodemus that he had to be "born again." Do you see the need to "rightly divide the word of truth" between the earthly ministry of Jesus "to the lost sheep of the house of Israel" and His heavenly ministry to the "new creature" (consisting of both Jews and Gentiles) in Paul's epistles?

As I have maintained, our identity crisis exists because pastors, priests, and millions of believers are not "rightly dividing the word of truth." In fact, most disagreements among believers often begin with the statement, "Well, Jesus said…"; however, these same believers never seem to consider "to whom" Jesus was speaking, "at what time," and for "what purpose." It would solve so many disagreements within Christianity if we would understand that Jesus came to fulfill the "promises made unto the fathers" regarding the *earthly kingdom* to Israel. However, when Israel rejected Jesus and the kingdom that was "at hand," especially in Acts 7, this led to the conversion of Paul for the Gentiles (Acts 9:15). He was given a special purpose concerning a *heavenly citizenship* for a "new creature" that was "kept secret since the world began." As for the earthly kingdom promised to Israel, God is always faithful, even though Israel is in temporary blindness toward Him at this time (Rom.11:25). God, however, is not "slack concerning His promises."

If the Body of Christ (the Church) was the focus of the "gospels" and early Acts, we must certainly "repent and be baptized for the remission of sins," and we must also strictly obey the Law of Moses as Jesus commanded (Matt. 6:14-15; 19:16-17; 28:16-20; Luke 18:18-22; John 14:150). How many believers would balk at such an idea that water baptism was necessary, as well as "keeping the commandments," to be saved? After all, Jesus did command these under the gospel of the kingdom He preached while on the earth. In other words, if you insist that the Body of Christ is in the "gospels," then the Church would be under the Law, even though Jesus taught Paul that we are "not under the Law, but under grace" (Rom. 6:14).

As concerning the "lost sheep," we read:

> *23 And Jesus went about all Galilee, teaching in their synagogues, and preaching <u>the gospel of the kingdom</u>, and healing all manner of*

sickness and all manner of disease among the people. Matthew 4:23

5 These twelve Jesus sent forth, and commanded them, saying, <u>Go not into the way of the Gentiles</u>, and into any city of the Samaritans enter ye not: 6 <u>But go rather to the lost sheep of the house of Israel.</u> 7 And as ye go, preach, saying, <u>The kingdom of heaven is at hand.</u> 8 <u>Heal the sick, cleanse the lepers, raise the dead, cast out devils</u>: freely ye have received, freely give. Matthew 10:5-8

16 Then <u>the eleven disciples</u> went away into Galilee, into a mountain where Jesus had appointed them. 17 And when they saw him, they worshipped him: but some doubted. 18 And Jesus came and spake unto them, saying, All power is given unto me in heaven and in earth. 19 <u>Go ye therefore, and teach all nations, baptizing them in the name of the Father, and of the Son, and of the Holy Ghost:</u> 20 <u>Teaching them to observe all things whatsoever I have commanded you</u>: and, lo, I am with you always, even unto the end of the world. Amen. Matthew 28:16-20

Does your church preach these same commands? Again, shouldn't all believers be water baptized, do all that Jesus commanded under the Law, heal the sick, cleanse lepers, raise the dead, cast out devils, and freely give whatsoever it is that we have in abundance (see I Tim. 5:8)? After all, "Jesus said…" these things, didn't He? Do you also celebrate all the holy days and sabbaths of the Hebrew calendar as Jesus did under the Law? If so, why would Jesus later teach the Body of Christ (through Paul's epistle to the Colossians) that we should "not be judged in respect to holy days…and sabbaths…which are a shadow of things to come, but the body is of Christ" (Col. 2:16-23)? Something new had occurred with the conversion of Paul in Acts 9, and religious denominations are failing to fully recognize it.

As I have stated, if we do what "Jesus said" in the "gospels," this would mean water baptism, keeping the commandments, having the "sign gifts," keeping the Sabbath, observing feasts and other holy days, religious acts of purity, celebrating the necessity of the sacrifice of Passover, and whatever else Jesus said to do (Matt. 28:16-20). Usually, believers immediately insist that Jesus fulfilled the Law, and indeed He did, but when did He reveal this to Gentiles, and when did He remove the Jews from obedience to the Law? Remember, even as late as Acts 10 (nearly a decade after Pentecost), Peter was still under the Law, and years later, he was rebuked by Paul for attempting to cause the Gentiles "to live as do the Jews."

> *14 But when I saw that they walked not*
> *uprightly <u>according to the truth of the gospel</u>, I*
> *said unto Peter before them all, If thou, being*
> *a Jew, livest after the manner of Gentiles, and*
> *not as do the Jews, why compellest thou the*

*Gentiles to live as do the Jews? [15] We who are
Jews by nature, and not sinners of the
Gentiles, [16] <u>Knowing that a man is not justified
by the works of the law, but by the faith of
Jesus Christ, even we have believed in Jesus
Christ, that we might be justified by the faith of
Christ, and not by the works of the law: for by
the works of the law shall no flesh be justified</u>.
Galatians 2:14-16 (Paul speaking to Peter)*

This same argument could apply in many ways between believers who still insist we are to be in obedience to the commands of Jesus in "the gospels," and those believers who are obedient to the gospel of Jesus Christ presented by Paul as "the apostle to the Gentiles." Very few believers ever pause to also consider what Paul meant by "according to the truth of the gospel" in Galatians 2:14. What gospel did Paul give to the Galatians that caused such a statement by him? If it were the Great Commission, why would there be an issue with Peter "compelling the Gentiles to live as do the Jews"? After all, the Great Commission, given by Jesus, commanded all believers to "observe all that I have commanded you," which instructed them to "keep the commandments."

What about the "gospel" Paul mentioned to the Corinthians in the following passage? Was it the same as what Peter preached about water baptism? Not at all!

*[17] <u>For Christ sent me not to baptize, but to
preach the gospel</u>: not with wisdom of words,*

> *lest the cross of Christ should be made of none effect*. *I Corinthians 1:17*

Could John the Baptist and the twelve apostles ever make the statement, "For Christ sent me not to baptize"? Of course not, because the gospel they were given (gospel of the kingdom) included water baptism for the "remission of sins."

As we have read, the gospel Paul was sent to preach, especially to the Gentiles, did not include water baptism; otherwise, Paul would have commanded it for all believers today. Water baptism, in Paul's epistles, was replaced with the "one baptism" of Ephesians 4:5, which taught the Corinthians the following: "For *by* one Spirit are we all baptized into one body" (I Cor. 12:13). Paul, a short time after his epistle to the Corinthians, stated to the Romans (Jews and Gentiles) that it is "...through faith *in His blood*, to declare His righteousness for the remission of sins..." (Rom. 3:24-26). Water baptism cannot "remit sins" today, even though many still insist it can. It's only by faith in His blood!

Many Protestant denominations, which do not require water baptism for salvation, will attempt to get around Matthew 28:16-20 by strongly *encouraging* water baptism as a symbol of "dying to self and raising to newness of life." They generally base this theology on what Paul taught in Romans 6:1-4 and Romans 8:1-4. However, in Romans 3:24-26, we understand that it is "faith in His blood" (initiating the baptism *by* the Spirit) that allows us to become members of one body (the "new creature"), and water has nothing to do with it. Our baptism (*by* one Spirit) is the work of God, not the work of men.

Paul introduced the baptism *by* one Spirit (I Cor. 12:13) before he wrote his epistle to the Romans, so why would Paul infer (or even revert to) water baptism to the Romans after explaining to the Corinthians that the baptism he taught was spiritual—not with water? Again, Paul stated to the Corinthians: "...for Christ sent me not to baptize, but to preach the gospel." Theologians who do not "rightly divide" the doctrines associated with baptism are the same theologians who ignore the last part of I Corinthians 1:17 where Paul boldly taught, "...lest the cross of Christ should be made on none effect." The blood of Christ is sufficient to save us, not water baptism.

Many of the Patristic Church Fathers, in the first few centuries after the apostles, did not "rightly divide the word of truth" very well on the subject of water baptism (and other doctrines), and as a result, they devoted much of their teachings and obedience on the "gospels," not upon the teachings of "the apostle to the Gentiles," who declared that he was "not sent to (water) baptize, but to preach the gospel." The "Great Commission" included water baptism, so what "gospel" was Paul referencing in his letter to the Corinthians? Since there is little evidence that the majority of the Patristic Church Fathers understood "the preaching of Jesus Christ, according to the revelation of the mystery, which was kept secret since the world began," it is easy to see why their writings were often "saturated" with water baptism simply because they assumed the words Jesus taught in "the gospels" were far superior to the words He revealed to Paul regarding the Gentiles (Gal. 1:11-12). I believe this fatal error is why their teachings are often inconsistent with both the Bible and with one another. May we never forget, however, that their writings did help preserve the word of God in the so-called New Testament, and for that, we must be grateful for their courage to share it, even though they didn't "rightly divide."

Justification by Faith

Paul was also sent to proclaim "righteousness, apart *from* the Law" (Rom. 3:21), which was accomplished through the blood of Jesus Christ. This was all testified "in due time." Here are a few of those passages Jesus sent him to proclaim to the Body of Christ (concerning the Law of Moses):

> *16 Knowing that a man is not justified by the works of the law, but by the faith of Jesus Christ, even we have believed in Jesus Christ, that we might be justified by the faith of Christ, and not by the works of the law: for by the works of the law shall no flesh be justified...21 I do not frustrate the grace of God: for if righteousness come by the law, then Christ is dead in vain. Galatians 2:16 and 21*

> *10 For as many as are of the works of the law are under the curse: for it is written, Cursed is every one that continueth not in all things which are written in the book of the law to do them. 11 But that no man is justified by the law in the sight of God, it is evident: for, The just shall live by faith. Galatians 3:10-11*

22 But the scripture hath concluded all under sin, <u>that the promise by faith of Jesus Christ might be given to them that believe</u>. 23 But <u>before faith came</u>, we were kept under the law, shut up unto the faith which should afterwards be revealed. 24 Wherefore the law was our schoolmaster to bring us unto Christ, <u>that we might be justified by faith</u>. Galatians 3:22-24

16 This I say then, Walk in the Spirit, and ye shall not fulfil the lust of the flesh. 17 For the flesh lusteth against the Spirit, and the Spirit against the flesh: and these are contrary the one to the other: so that ye cannot do the things that ye would. 18 <u>But if ye be led of the Spirit, ye are not under the law.</u> Galatians 5:16-18

28 Therefore we conclude that a man is justified by faith without the deeds of the law. Romans 3:28

4 Now to him that worketh is the reward not reckoned of grace, but of debt. 5 But to him that worketh not, but believeth on him that justifieth the ungodly, his faith is counted for righteousness. Romans 4:4-5

> *[14] For sin shall not have dominion over you:*
> *<u>for ye are not under the law, but under grace</u>.*
> *Romans 6:14*

No such passages were taught to believers under the earthly ministry of Jesus Christ, especially since Jesus continued to insist they "keep the commandments." It wasn't until Paul's gospel (given to him by Jesus Christ) that we learn how the Law was given so that "the whole world would become guilty before God" (Rom. 3:9 and 19). In one of the previous passages on this topic, Paul stated that "the Law *was* our (the world's) schoolmaster to bring us unto Christ, that we might be justified by faith" (Gal. 3:24). "In times past," faith and works defined obedience, "but now," faith without works justifies the sinner.

There are more passages on this same subject about faith and the Law, and most pastors and priests are already aware of these passages existing in the Bible, but if they have to "spin" the literal meaning of these words to justify their denomination's practices, then they are attempting to indemnify their religion, not the Word! They need to "rightly divide," not privately interpret what is very clear from Scripture (2 Pet. 1:20-21). "All Scripture is given by inspiration of God..." (not the traditions of men). It is easy to lead congregations into an identity crisis, especially with a priest or pastor who doesn't "rightly divide the word of truth."

Jesus came specifically to Israel, which is something most believers don't seem to understand, even though He stated this clearly in the "gospels," along with other writings from Paul, as noted in the following passages:

> *22 And, behold, a woman of Canaan came out of the same coasts, and cried unto him, saying, Have mercy on me, O Lord, thou son of David; my daughter is grievously vexed with a devil. 23 But he answered her not a word. And his disciples came and besought him, saying, Send her away; for she crieth after us. 24 <u>But he answered and said, I am not sent but unto the lost sheep of the house of Israel.</u> Matthew 15:22-24 (to a Gentile woman)*

> *I say the truth in Christ, I lie not, my conscience also bearing me witness in the Holy Ghost, 2 That I have great heaviness and continual sorrow in my heart. 3 For I could wish that myself were accursed from Christ for my brethren, <u>my kinsmen according to the flesh</u>: 4 <u>Who are Israelites</u>; to whom pertaineth the adoption, and the glory, and the covenants, and the giving of the law, and the service of God, and the promises; 5 Whose are the fathers, <u>and of whom as concerning the flesh Christ came</u>, who is over all, God blessed for ever. Romans 9:1-5*

Were Gentiles given the covenants...the Law...the promises (Rom. 9:4-5)? Paul declared that these were given to Israel, *not* Gentile nations. All the promises in those two verses from Romans 9 were given and written in the Old Testament (and continued into the "gospels" and early Acts), and under what status (condition) were Gentiles *at that time*?

12 That at that time ye were without Christ,
being aliens from the commonwealth of Israel,
and strangers from the covenants of promise,
having no hope, and without God in the world:
Ephesians 2:12

Again, we should understand that Jesus was sent to fulfill Israel's promises "made unto the fathers," which were spoken throughout the Old Testament, and this is why He was a "minister of the circumcision" (Rom. 15:8). It was to "the lost sheep of the house of Israel" that John the Baptist, Jesus, and the twelve apostles preached "the kingdom of heaven is at hand." God's covenants to Israel promised that the Gentile nations would be blessed at the time of *Israel's rising* (Isa. 60:1-3); however, when Israel "resisted the Holy Ghost," as Stephen announced, God finally gave the world "the revelation of the mystery" through *another* apostle. Through God's marvelous grace, Paul declared how Gentiles have obtained salvation because of Israel's *fall* (Acts 7:51-60; Rom.11:11). Israel was supposed to take "the salvation of God to the end of the earth" (Isa. 49:6), but their rejection brought about salvation to the Gentiles, apart from Israel. Remember, the gospel Paul preached was "hid in God… before the world began," so it wasn't the gospel of the kingdom that he was sent to proclaim, especially since that

258

gospel had already been taught prior to Paul's conversion. Again, the gospel of the kingdom (Great Commission) wasn't the revelation of "the mystery", but rather it was the confirmation of what God promised to Israel through the fathers (Rom. 15:8). The Body of Christ consists of both Jews and mostly Gentiles, and this makes Paul an interesting choice to be the "apostle to the Gentiles," especially since he was both a Roman citizen, as well as an Israelite. This "dual citizenship" also saved Paul from imprisonment and death on different occasions.

God's Eternal Purpose: What is It?

What many believers do not seem to consider is God's eternal purpose for both "heaven and earth," which He intends to "restore" through both Israel (Earth) and the Body of Christ (Heaven). I mentioned the previous points in this chapter to show how important it is to recognize the differences between the purposes for which Jesus came to the "lost sheep of the house of Israel," and His purpose for saving and sending Paul to the Gentiles, with "the revelation of the mystery, which was kept secret since the world began." God intends to bring Heaven and Earth back into the original "good" state in which it was first created.

Eternity will not proceed with a corrupted Heaven and Earth. God will restore both, and He has chosen Israel and the Body of Christ for this purpose. Interestingly, the phrase "… there was evening, and there was morning" does not appear on the seventh day in the Genesis account. God created for six days and rested from creation on the seventh, having determined that the creation was "very good." Now, however,

God is in the process of "restoration" after the corruption Satan caused in both "heaven and earth." Without recognizing (and "rightly dividing") God's purpose for Israel, and His purpose for the Body of Christ, we will *not* fully understand God's purpose for our individual lives. We must know God's eternal plan for both Heaven and Earth, which is something many believers have combined into one religious tradition, leading most believers into an identity crisis where they don't know if they are the Body of Christ, the Bride of Christ, or "spiritual Israel." They assume these titles are synonymous, but only one of these titles (the body of Christ) is found within Scripture.

God's Eternal Plan for Earth
The following passages address how God has revealed His eternal plan for Earth over time:

*In the beginning God created
the heaven and the earth.
Genesis 1:1 (two realms revealed by God)*

*14 And the LORD God said unto the serpent, Because thou hast done this, thou art cursed above all cattle, and above every beast of the field; upon thy belly shalt thou go, and dust shalt thou eat all the days of thy life: 15 And I will put enmity between thee and the woman, and between thy seed and her seed; it shall bruise thy head, and thou shalt bruise his heel.
Genesis 3:14-15 (set into motion for Earth)*

Now the LORD had said unto <u>Abram</u>, Get thee out of thy country, and from thy kindred, and from thy father's house, unto a land that I will shew thee: [2] *<u>And I will make of thee a great nation</u>, and I will bless thee, and make thy name great; <u>and thou shalt be a blessing</u>: [3] And I will bless them that bless thee, and curse him that curseth thee: <u>and in thee shall all families of the earth be blessed.</u> Genesis 12:1-3 (chosen people for Earth)*

[18] *In the same day the LORD made a covenant with Abram, saying, Unto thy seed have I given this land, <u>from the river of Egypt unto the great river, the river Euphrates</u>: Genesis 15:18 (the land God promised to His people Israel)*

[6] *And I will make thee exceeding fruitful, and I will make nations of thee, and kings shall come out of thee.* [7] *And <u>I will establish my covenant</u> between me and thee <u>and thy seed after thee in their generations for an everlasting covenant</u>, to be a God unto thee, and to thy seed after thee.* [8] *And I will give unto thee, and to thy seed after thee, <u>the land wherein thou art a stranger, all the land of Canaan, for an everlasting possession</u>; and I will be their God. Genesis 17:6-8 (God establishes His covenant with Abraham)*

> *19 And God said, Sarah thy wife shall bear thee*
> *a son indeed; and thou shalt call his name*
> *Isaac: and I will establish my covenant with*
> *him for an everlasting covenant, and with his*
> *seed after him. 20 And as for Ishmael, I have*
> *heard thee: Behold, I have blessed him, and*
> *will make him fruitful, and will multiply him*
> *exceedingly; twelve princes shall he beget, and*
> *I will make him a great nation. 21 <u>But my</u>*
> *<u>covenant will I establish with Isaac, which</u>*
> *<u>Sarah shall bear unto thee at this set time in</u>*
> *<u>the next year.</u> Genesis 17:19-21*
> *(covenant promised to Isaac)*

Please notice in the Book of Acts 3:19-21, Peter offered Israel the kingdom, which was ultimately promised to the seed of Isaac and Jacob (Israel):

> *19 Repent ye therefore, and be converted, that*
> *your sins may be blotted out, when the times of*
> *refreshing shall come from the presence of the*
> *Lord. 20 And he shall send Jesus Christ, which*
> *before was preached unto you: 21 Whom the*
> *heaven must receive until the times of*
> *restitution of all things, which God hath*
> *spoken <u>by the mouth of all his holy prophets</u>*
> *<u>since the world began.</u> Acts 3:19-21*

God's promise, "since the world began," is to give Israel the kingdom promised to Abraham and his seed (Isaac, Jacob,

David, etc.), and it is a kingdom that will be located in a physical piece of real estate (Nile River to the Euphrates River).

Israel, in the following passages, is also called to be a "kingdom of priests," which is the same title Peter mentioned in his epistle he wrote to the Jews scattered abroad (I Pet. 1:1). Paul never referred to the Body of Christ as a "kingdom of priests," nor does Jesus, through Paul, offer the Body of Christ a kingdom on Earth.

> *3 And Moses went up unto God, and*
> *the LORD called unto him out of the mountain,*
> *saying, <u>Thus shalt thou say to the house of*
> *Jacob, and tell the children of Israel</u>; 4 Ye have*
> *seen what I did unto the Egyptians, and how I*
> *bare you on eagles' wings, and brought you*
> *unto myself. 5 Now therefore, <u>if ye will obey my*
> *voice indeed, and keep my covenant</u>, then ye*
> *shall be a <u>peculiar treasure unto me</u> above all*
> *people: for all the earth is mine: 6 And ye shall*
> *be unto me <u>a kingdom of priests, and an holy*
> *nation</u>. These are the words which thou shalt*
> *speak <u>unto the children of Israel</u>.*
> *Exodus 19:3-6 (Moses to Israel)*

> *9 But ye are <u>a chosen generation, a royal*
> *priesthood, an holy nation, a peculiar people</u>;*
> *that ye should shew forth the praises of him*
> *who hath called you out of darkness into his*
> *marvellous light; 10 Which in time past <u>were*

not a people, but are now the people of God: which had not obtained mercy, but now have obtained mercy. I Peter 2:9-10 (speaking to the "circumcision," not the Body)

[10] Moreover <u>I will appoint a place for my people Israel</u>, and will plant them, that they may dwell in a place of their own, <u>and move no more; neither shall the children of wickedness afflict them any more, as beforetime,</u> [11] And as since the time that I commanded judges to be over my people Israel, and have caused thee to rest from all thine enemies. <u>Also the LORD telleth thee that he will make thee an house</u>…[16] And thine house and thy kingdom <u>shall be established for ever before thee: thy throne shall be established for ever.</u> [17] According to all these words, and according to all this vision, <u>so did Nathan speak unto David.</u> 2 Samuel 7:10-11 and 16-17 (regarding David's throne)

The word that Isaiah the son of Amoz saw concerning Judah and Jerusalem. [2] And it shall come to pass <u>in the last days,</u> that the mountain of the LORD's house shall be established in the top of the mountains, and shall be exalted above the hills; <u>and all nations shall flow unto it.</u> [3] And many people shall go and say, Come ye, and let us go up to

the mountain of the LORD, <u>to the house of the</u>
<u>God of Jacob</u>; and he will teach us of his
ways, and we will walk in his paths: for out of
Zion <u>shall go forth the law, and the word of</u>
<u>the LORD from Jerusalem</u>.
Isaiah 2:1-3 (in the "end times")

14 Behold, <u>the days come</u>, saith the LORD, that I
will perform that good thing <u>which I have</u>
<u>promised unto the house of Israel and to the</u>
<u>house of Judah</u>. 15 In those days, and at that
time, will I cause <u>the Branch of righteousness</u>
<u>to grow up unto David</u>; and <u>he shall execute</u>
<u>judgment and righteousness in the land</u>. 16 <u>In</u>
<u>those days shall Judah be saved</u>, and
Jerusalem shall dwell safely: and this is the
name wherewith she shall be called,
The LORD our righteousness. Jeremiah
33:14-16 (all Israel will be saved)

26 <u>And so all Israel shall be saved: as it is</u>
<u>written</u>, There shall come out of Sion the
Deliverer, and shall turn away ungodliness
from Jacob: 27 For this is my covenant unto
them, when I shall take away their sins. 28 As
concerning the gospel, they are enemies for
your sakes: but as touching the election, they
are beloved for the father's sakes. 29 For the
gifts and calling of God are without
repentance. Romans 11:26-29 (still future)

31 And, behold, thou shalt conceive in thy womb, and bring forth a son, and shalt call his name JESUS. 32 He shall be great, and shall be called the Son of the Highest: and the Lord God shall give unto him the throne of his father David: 33 <u>And he shall reign over the house of Jacob for ever; and of his kingdom there shall be no end</u>.
Luke 1:31-33

6 For <u>unto us</u> a child is born, <u>unto us</u> a son is given: and the government shall be upon his shoulder: and his name shall be called Wonderful, Counsellor, The mighty God, The everlasting Father, The Prince of Peace. 7 Of the increase of his government and peace <u>there shall be no end, upon the throne of David, and upon his kingdom, to order it, and to establish it with judgment and with justice from henceforth even for ever</u>. The zeal of the LORD of hosts <u>will perform this</u>. Isaiah 9:6-7 (God's sovereignty concerning Israel)

Arise, shine; for thy light is come, and the glory of the LORD is risen upon thee. 2 For, behold, the darkness shall cover the earth, and gross darkness the people: but the LORD shall arise upon thee, and his glory shall be seen upon thee. 3 <u>And the Gentiles shall come to thy</u>

> *light, and kings to the brightness of thy*
> *rising…* [19] *The sun shall be no more thy light by*
> *day; neither for brightness shall the moon give*
> *light unto thee: but the LORD shall be unto thee*
> *an everlasting light, and thy God thy glory.*
> [20] *Thy sun shall no more go down; neither*
> *shall thy moon withdraw itself: for*
> *the LORD shall be thine everlasting light, and*
> *the days of thy mourning shall be ended.* [21] *Thy*
> *people also shall be all righteous: they shall*
> *inherit the land for ever, the branch of my*
> *planting, the work of my hands, that I may be*
> *glorified. Isaiah 60:1-3 and 19-21*
> *(the coming kingdom)*

The Apostle Paul declared "to whom" Jesus came to fulfill these promises, so the "nations" could also be blessed through Israel:

> [6] *And he said, It is a light thing that thou*
> *shouldest be my servant to raise up the tribes*
> *of Jacob, and to restore the preserved of*
> *Israel: I will also give thee for a light to the*
> *Gentiles, that thou mayest be my salvation*
> *unto the end of the earth. Isaiah 49:6*

> [8] *Now I say that Jesus Christ was a minister of*
> *the circumcision for the truth of God, to*
> *confirm the promises made unto the fathers:*
> [9] *And that the Gentiles might glorify God for*

> *his mercy; as it is written, For this cause <u>I will</u>*
> *<u>confess to thee among the Gentiles</u>, and sing*
> *unto thy name. Romans 15:8-9*

It was not a mystery that Gentiles would also be saved, because this is revealed throughout prophecy; however, "the mystery" revealed a way in which they *would* be saved during what Paul referred to as "the dispensation of the grace of God" (Eph. 3:2). When Paul stated "but now" in numerous passages from his writings, he was clearly showing a change is the way God would be dealing with Gentiles (through both prophecy and "the revelation of the mystery"). Gentiles are *now* "blessed with all spiritual blessings in heavenly places in Christ," *apart* from Israel. Israel was the chosen vessel to bring God's "salvation to the end of the earth," but after the nation's spiritual fall in Acts 7, God saved Paul and gave to him "the revelation of the mystery" whereby Gentiles are now saved apart from the Law of Moses, water baptism, and works. This was "kept secret since the world began." Tragically, instead of embracing this glorious gospel of the grace of God, many believers have been convinced they are under the Great Commission, which places them back under the Law, even if they aren't aware of this fact (Gal. 5:1).

To fulfill the promises from God to Israel, Jesus had to come into this world to save "the lost sheep of the house of Israel." Without this, the uncircumcised Gentiles would have been left with "no hope," because the only gospel they had for salvation was through conversion to Judaism (John 4:22). Paul revealed that Jesus "came into the world to save sinners," and He offers salvation (since the time of Paul's gospel) by grace, through faith, not of works. Because of the virgin birth, Jesus did not inherit the Adamic nature, and this is why it was revealed *first* to Paul that "He (God the Father) made Him (God the Son (Jesus)) to be sin for us, who knew no sin, that we might be made the righteousness of God in Him" (2 Cor. 5:21).

The Earthly Ministry of Jesus Christ

Jesus came into this world "to save sinners," but how this *applied* to both Jews and Gentiles had remained a "hidden wisdom" until God converted Paul (Rom. 16:25; Eph. 3:1-10; Col. 1:23-28; I Tim. 1:16). We know Jesus came to proclaim the kingdom to Israel, which was spoken "by the mouth of all His holy prophets since the world began," and we also know the gospel He preached "to the lost sheep of the house of Israel" was first revealed in the "gospels." Note the following:

> *16 The people which sat in darkness saw great light; and to them which sat in the region and shadow of death light is sprung up. 17 From that time Jesus began to preach, and to say, Repent: for the kingdom of heaven is at hand.*
> *Matthew 4:16-17*

Over 30 times in Matthew alone, the "kingdom of heaven" is named. This title does not appear again until the Book of Revelation. This is also the same gospel He sent His disciples (apostles) to preach. Once again, please notice "to whom" this gospel was sent!

5 These twelve Jesus sent forth, and commanded them, saying, <u>Go not into the way of the Gentiles, and into any city of the Samaritans enter ye not</u>: 6 But go rather <u>to the lost sheep of the house of Israel</u>. 7 And as ye go, preach, saying, <u>The kingdom of heaven is at hand</u>. 8 Heal the sick, cleanse the lepers, raise the dead, cast out devils: freely ye have received, freely give.
Matthew 10:5-8

24 But he answered and said, <u>I am not sent but unto the lost sheep of the house of Israel</u>.
Matthew 15:24 (in the encounter with the Gentile woman)

17 Think not that I am come to destroy the law, or the prophets: <u>I am not come to destroy, but to fulfil.</u> 18 For verily I say unto you, Till heaven and earth pass, one jot or one tittle shall in no wise pass from the law, <u>till all be fulfilled</u>. 19 <u>Whosoever therefore shall break one of these least commandments</u>, and shall teach men so, he shall be called the least in the kingdom of heaven: <u>but whosoever shall do and teach them</u>, the same shall be called great in the kingdom of heaven. 20 For I say unto you, <u>That except your righteousness shall exceed the righteousness of the scribes and</u>

Pharisees, ye shall in no case enter into the
kingdom of heaven. Matthew 5:17-20
(what Jesus came to do for Israel)

⁴ But when the fulness of the time was come,
God sent forth his Son, made of a woman,
made under the law, ⁵ To redeem them that
were under the law, that we might receive the
adoption of sons. Galatians 4:4-5
(the time it was revealed)

We know that the Law was still in effect during the time Jesus preached to "the lost sheep of the house of Israel." In fact, it wasn't until *after* the conversion of Paul in Acts 9 that we understand that the Law of Moses was fully paid for by the atoning sacrifice of Jesus. Jesus said He came to fulfill all things, but it had not yet been revealed *when* this would be fully known to all, including Gentiles. The gospel of the kingdom (the Great Commission) was to be proclaimed "beginning at Jerusalem," which shows Israel prominence in God's prophetic plans for the earth.

⁴⁴ And he said unto them, These are the words
which I spake unto you, while I was yet with
you, that all things must be fulfilled, which
were written in the law of Moses, and in the
prophets, and in the psalms, concerning me.
⁴⁵ Then opened he their understanding, that
they might understand the scriptures, ⁴⁶ And
said unto them, Thus it is written, and thus it

> *behooved Christ to suffer, and to rise from the*
> *dead the third day:* ⁴⁷ *And that repentance and*
> *remission of sins should be preached in his*
> *name among all nations, beginning at*
> *Jerusalem. Luke 24:44-47*

Does this passage mean the "remission of sins" was preached "by faith in His blood," or was the "remission of sins" preached "in His name" as Messiah (John 3:16)? Paul revealed the following to the Romans many years *after* Luke 24 was spoken by Jesus:

> ²⁴ *Being justified freely by his grace through*
> *the redemption that is in Christ Jesus:* ²⁵ *Whom*
> *God hath set forth to be a propitiation through*
> *faith in his blood, to declare his righteousness*
> *for the remission of sins that are past, through*
> *the forbearance of God;* ²⁶ *To declare, I say, at*
> *this time his righteousness: that he might be*
> *just, and the justifier of him which believeth in*
> *Jesus. Romans 3:24-26*

Does the phrase "being witnessed by the law and the prophets" (see also Matt. 26:56) mean they had already known Paul's gospel? Of course not, especially considering the fact Paul stated, "but now" several times in his epistles, which meant his gospel message was being revealed *for the first time* (I Tim. 1:16). What the "law and the prophets" could certainly provide a "witness" to was the coming Messiah and how no one could fulfill the Law of Moses. The "law and the prophets" knew nothing about Paul's gospel, even though they testified of the coming Messiah who would "take away the sin of the world," as promised through Israel (John 1:29).

> *4 For whatsoever things were written aforetime were written for our learning, that we through patience and comfort of the scriptures might have hope. 5 Now the God of patience and consolation grant you to be likeminded one toward another according to Christ Jesus: 6 That ye may with one mind and one mouth glorify God, even the Father of our Lord Jesus Christ. Romans 15:4-6*

Again, the prophets knew of God's plan to restore Earth, but they couldn't have known God's plan for restoring Heaven because it was "kept secret since the world began." "Faith in His blood" for the "remission of sins," was also not known until the "revelation of the mystery." We know His death, burial, and resurrection was preached in the Old Testament, as well as the "gospels" and early Acts, but "faith in His blood and resurrection" for salvation was not preached until Paul (Rom. 4:25; I Cor. 15:3-4), nor can we find the "new creature" where both Jews and Gentiles are baptized *by* one Spirit into one body with a heavenly citizenship. This was all a part of what Paul called "my gospel, and the preaching of Jesus Christ, according to the revelation of the mystery, which was kept secret since the world began." The "revelation of the mystery" does not replace what God promised Israel in prophecy. Israel and the Body of Christ have two different destinies.

Jesus also revealed the following (during His earthly ministry):

38 For I came down from heaven, not to do mine own will, but the will of him that sent me. 39 And this is the Father's will which hath sent me, that of all which he hath given me I should lose nothing, but should raise it up again at the last day. 40 And this is the will of him that sent me, that every one which seeth the Son, and believeth on him, may have everlasting life: and I will raise him up at the last day.
John 6:38-40

Jesus came into the world at the time of "the last days," and this is why Jesus (and His apostles) preached "the kingdom of heaven is *at hand*." This same gospel continued into Peter's sermon in Acts 2 when he affirmed the following truth at Pentecost:

16 But this is that which was spoken by the prophet Joel; 17 And it shall come to pass in the last days, saith God, I will pour out of my Spirit upon all flesh: and your sons and your daughters shall prophesy, and your young men shall see visions, and your old men shall dream dreams: 18 And on my servants and on my handmaidens I will pour out in those days

> *of my Spirit; and they shall prophesy:* [19] *<u>And I will shew wonders in heaven above, and signs in the earth beneath</u>; blood, and fire, and vapour of smoke:* [20] *<u>The sun</u> shall be turned into darkness, and <u>the moon</u> into blood, <u>before the great and notable day of the Lord come:</u>*
> *Acts 2:16-20*

Pentecost is not the beginning of a long, two-thousand year "grace period" with the "new creature" known as the Body of Christ (the Church), but rather it is the time prior to that "great and notable day of the Lord," which includes the Tribulation, ending with the Second Coming of Jesus Christ. No one knew anything about what Paul would be called to preach ("the revelation of the mystery" regarding Gentile salvation *apart* from Israel). The Body of Christ involves the eternal purpose of God for Heaven, not Earth, and failure to recognize this has caused an identity crisis (especially regarding our purpose in Christ, involving a citizenship in Heaven). We are now "ambassadors for Christ," not proselytes to Judaism, even though some resemble such a status.

We know that Jesus did fulfill all that God sent Him to do for redemption, but this does not mean it was revealed during His earthly ministry to "the Circumcision." Even Peter and the other apostles weren't aware, at first, of the redemption available through faith in the shed blood and the resurrection of Jesus, which I explained in the chapter with the commentary on the Book of Acts.

God's Eternal Purpose for Heaven

Surprisingly, to most believers, the Old Testament does not contain one mention of believers from Israel ever going to Heaven. However, to the Apostle Paul, Jesus revealed the following about our *heavenly* calling:

For we know that if our earthly house of this tabernacle were dissolved, we have a building of God, an house not made with hands, <u>eternal in the heavens</u>. 2 For in this we groan, earnestly <u>desiring to be clothed upon with our house which is from heaven</u>:
2 Corinthians 5:1-2 (to the Body of Christ)

3 Blessed be the God and Father of our Lord Jesus Christ, who hath blessed us with all spiritual blessings <u>in heavenly places in Christ</u>:
Ephesians 1:3 (to the Body of Christ)

4 But God, who is rich in mercy, for his great love wherewith he loved us, 5 Even when we were dead in sins, hath quickened us together with Christ, (by grace ye are saved;) 6 <u>And hath raised us up together, and made us sit together in heavenly places in Christ Jesus:</u> 7 <u>That in the ages to come</u> he might shew the exceeding riches of his grace in his kindness toward us through Christ Jesus.
Ephesians 2:4-7 (to the Body of Christ)

8 Unto me, who am less than the least of all saints, is this grace given, that I should preach among the Gentiles the unsearchable riches of Christ; 9 And to make all men see what is the fellowship of the mystery, which from the beginning of the world hath been hid in God, who created all things by Jesus Christ:
Ephesians 3:8-11 (to the Body of Christ)

20 For our conversation is in heaven; from whence also we look for the Saviour, the Lord Jesus Christ: 21 Who shall change our vile body, that it may be fashioned like unto his glorious body, according to the working whereby he is able even to subdue all things unto himself. Philippians 3:20-21
(to the Body of Christ)

3 We give thanks to God and the Father of our Lord Jesus Christ, praying always for you, 4 Since we heard of your faith in Christ Jesus, and of the love which ye have to all the saints, 5 For the hope which is laid up for you in heaven, whereof ye heard before in the word of the truth of the gospel; 6 Which is come unto you, as it is in all the world; and bringeth forth fruit, as it doth also in you, since the day ye heard of it, and knew the grace of God in truth:
Colossians 1:3-6 (to the Body of Christ)

*18 And the Lord shall deliver me from every
evil work, and <u>will preserve me unto his
heavenly kingdom:</u> to whom be glory for ever
and ever. Amen. 2 Timothy 4:18 (Paul to
Timothy)*

Why was it necessary to reveal this new eternal purpose regarding Heaven to a new apostle, who was also sent to establish a "new creature" called the Body of Christ? As you recall, when Israel blasphemed the Holy Ghost by rejecting the kingdom and the Messiah (in Acts 7), this left Gentiles with "no hope," even though prophecy still declared "all Israel shall be saved," including those Gentiles who *will be saved* through Israel "in the ages to come." Gentiles today are saved by grace, through faith, but "in the ages to come," we know how difficult it will be for those "left behind" to face the Tribulation. Many will be saved during the Tribulation, but a reading of Revelation 6-18 tells us what they must endure. I prefer this "early bird" special that God has given to us "freely" (at no cost to you and me). As Paul declared, he (we) are "as of ones born out of (before) due time." Indeed, today is "the day of salvation" (2 Cor. 6:2). "The revelation of the mystery" to Paul revealed salvation *now* to all who believe the gospel of the grace of God. We are not told to "repent and be baptized for the remission of sins," but rather we are told to "be ye reconciled to God," as the following passages explains to the "new creature":

*16 Wherefore henceforth know we no man after
the flesh: yea, though we have known Christ*

after the flesh, yet now henceforth know we him no more. [17] Therefore if any man be in Christ, <u>he is a new creature</u>: old things are passed away; behold, all things are become new. [18] And all things are of God, who hath reconciled us to himself by Jesus Christ, <u>and hath given to us the ministry of reconciliation;</u> [19] To wit, that God was in Christ, reconciling the world unto himself, not imputing their trespasses unto them; <u>and hath committed unto us the word of reconciliation</u>.
2 Corinthians 5:16-19

[14] But God forbid that I should glory, save in the cross of our Lord Jesus Christ, by whom the world is crucified unto me, and I unto the world. [15] For in Christ Jesus neither circumcision availeth any thing, nor uncircumcision, <u>but a new creature</u>. [16] And as many as walk according to this rule, peace be on them, and mercy, and upon the Israel of God. Galatians 6:14-16

I will address the "Israel of God" in a subsequent chapter, but it *doesn't* mean what many theologians attempt to enforce through Replacement Theology. The "new creature" is the Body of Christ where both Jews and Gentiles have been baptized *by* one Spirit into one Body, based solely on faith in the following gospel (apart from works):

> *Moreover, brethren, <u>I declare unto you the</u>*
> *<u>gospel which I preached unto you, which also</u>*
> *<u>ye have received, and wherein ye stand</u>; ² By*
> *which also ye are saved, if ye keep in memory*
> *what I preached unto you, unless ye have*
> *believed in vain. ³ <u>For I delivered unto you</u>*
> *<u>first of all that which I also received</u>, how that*
> *<u>Christ died for our sins</u> according to the*
> *scriptures; ⁴ And that <u>he was buried</u>, and*
> *that <u>he rose again the third day</u>*
> *according to the scriptures:*
> *I Corinthians 15:1-4*

This is one of the earliest creeds known to have circulated after the resurrection, likely within the decade after Jesus rose again. After all, Paul began his ministry about a year after the resurrection (Acts 9). In fact, hundreds of those who had seen the risen, glorified Jesus could have easily testified to the truth of this gospel message from I Corinthians 15:3-4. It was in this same chapter (I Cor. 15:6) that Paul placed a challenge to any skeptic concerning the testimony of the hundreds of eyewitnesses still alive when Paul taught the Corinthians (Acts 18). I can almost hear Paul asking the following: *How can you say there is no resurrection of the dead when there are still hundreds of eyewitnesses to this fact?* (I Cor. 15:12-14).

As I have written, it was *not* "the mystery" that Jesus would die, be buried, and raise again on the third day; however, it was "the revelation of the mystery" where we discover *how* this redemption through Jesus Christ could and would impact the world. This gospel was given by Jesus Christ to Paul for individual Jews and Gentiles (not nations) who believe this gospel (Gal. 1:11-12). This gospel was *not* announced until after Israel, as a nation, fell into spiritual blindness (Acts 7:51-60; Rom. 11:25), and "the apostle to the Gentiles" was saved and sent to the world.

The gospel of the kingdom had been rejected, but this does not mean God is done with Israel as a nation. It was God who made His convents with Israel, and even though the covenant of the Law was conditional, God's promises (beginning with Abraham) were given at least four centuries before there was a Law of Moses. Remember, God's "gifts and calling are without repentance (irrevocable)" (Rom. 11:29), so God's covenants to Abraham, Isaac, Jacob, and David were and are still eternal and unconditional. This is stated in the following passage to the Jews:

> *I say then, <u>Hath God cast away his people?</u>*
> *<u>God forbid</u>. For I also am an Israelite, of the*
> *seed of Abraham, of the tribe of Benjamin.*
> *2 <u>God hath not cast away his people which he</u>*
> *<u>foreknew</u>. Wot ye not what the scripture saith*
> *of Elias? how he maketh intercession to God*
> *against Israel saying, 3 Lord, they have killed*
> *thy prophets, and digged down thine altars;*
> *and I am left alone, and they seek my life…*
> *5 <u>Even so then at this present time also there is</u>*
> *<u>a remnant according to the election of grace.</u>*
> *6 <u>And if by grace, then is it no more of works</u>:*
> *otherwise grace is no more grace. But if it be*

> *of works, then it is no more grace: otherwise*
> *work is no more work. Romans 11:1-3 and 5-6*

This remnant is also described as the "twelve tribes" of Israel in Revelation 7:1-8.

God's eternal purpose for Heaven, however, was revealed when Israel failed to be "a light to the Gentiles," and "God's salvation to the end of the earth." Romans 11 reveals the result.

> *[11] I say then, <u>Have they stumbled that they*
> *should fall? God forbid: but rather through*
> *their fall salvation is come unto the Gentiles,*
> *for to provoke them to jealousy.</u> [12] <u>Now if the*
> *fall of them be the riches of the world, and the*
> *diminishing of them the riches of the Gentiles;*
> *how much more their fulness?</u> [13] For I speak to*
> *you Gentiles, inasmuch as <u>I am the apostle of*
> *the Gentiles,</u> I magnify mine office: [14] If by any*
> *means <u>I may provoke to emulation them which*
> *are my flesh, and might save some of them.</u>*
> *[15] For if the casting away of them be the*
> *reconciling of the world, <u>what shall the*
> *receiving of them be, but life from the dead?</u>*
> *Romans 11:11-15 (Israel's "fall")*

When Paul stated in Galatians 6:16 about "peace be on them, and mercy, *and* the Israel of God," he was speaking about peace and mercy on two different groups: the believing remnant of Israel, as well as the Body of Christ. This is why the word "and" is used in Galatians 6:16, indicating two separate groups. Paul stated in Romans 9:3-4, "For I could wish myself accursed from Christ for my brethren, my kinsmen according to the flesh, who are Israelites…," and he also declared in Romans 11:14, "If by any means I may provoke to emulation them which are my flesh, and might save some of them," so it must be obvious that Paul always prayed for the "Israel of God," even though he was "the apostle to the Gentiles." Would it be wrong for Paul to pray for Israel? Of course not, just as believers should be praying for Israel, to whom Jesus Christ will return "in the ages to come."

God revealed to Paul that those who are in the Body of Christ already have a "citizenship" (conversation) in Heaven, which is where he also taught in Ephesians 2:6-7 that we are "seated in heavenly places in Christ, that in the ages to come He might show the exceeding riches of His grace in His kindness toward us through Christ Jesus."

The following verses also describes God's eternal purpose for Heaven, which He will restore using the Body of Christ.

> *9 Having made known unto us the mystery of*
> *his will, according to his good pleasure which*
> *he hath purposed in himself: 10 That in the*
> *dispensation of the fulness of times he might*
> *gather together in one all things in Christ,*
> *both which are in heaven, and which are on*
> *earth; even in him: 11 In whom also we have*
> *obtained an inheritance, being predestinated*

> *according to the purpose of him who worketh*
> *all things after the counsel of his own will:*
> *Ephesians 1:9-11*

There are those who insist God has only one destiny for believers, but this is not supported by Scripture. The Old Testament, and other passages from the "gospels" and early Acts, clearly indicate that God has a purpose for Earth through His promises "made unto the fathers," and this is why Jesus was "a minister of the circumcision." He preached "the kingdom of heaven is at hand," whereas Paul proclaimed we have "a citizenship in heaven." These are not the same!

After Satan and his angels are cast completely out of Heaven, and the "high places" that they occupy at this time (Eph. 6:12; Rev. 12:7-9), this is when the Body of Christ will be used to fulfill God's *heavenly* purpose for eternity, which has been vacated by those angels. I do not know exactly what we will be doing after the Judgment Seat of Christ (Rom. 14:10; 2 Cor. 5:10), but faithful service on Earth will bring about greater rewards and responsibilities, especially when we finally realize the reality of Heaven "in person."

We did a study in the Book of Revelation many years ago, and I remember the victory over Satan described in the following verses:

> *[7] And there was war in heaven: Michael and*
> *his angels fought against the dragon; and the*
> *dragon fought and his angels, [8] And prevailed*
> *not; neither was their place found any more in*
> *heaven. [9] And the great dragon was cast out,*

that old serpent, called the Devil, and Satan,
which deceiveth the whole world: he was cast
out into the earth, and his angels were cast out
with him. Revelation 12:7-9

As many believers look forward to our "heavenly home," we should have even more resolve with the importance of sharing the gospel with our loved ones. "This world in not my home, I'm just a passin' through" (written by Albert E. Brumley). No good soldier of God willingly leaves someone behind. Tell as many people as possible that they can be "reconciled (restored to fellowship) to God through our Lord Jesus Christ."

To Conclude about God's Eternal Purpose
May we never forget the eternal purposes of God, which He promised to both Israel and the Body of Christ, and how He will one day bring all things together in Christ, "both which are in heaven, and which are on earth, even in Him." Sadly, many believers have not been taught about "rightly dividing the word of truth," and therefore, they are often robbed of such blessed truths regarding their position in Christ, how they are to live and walk in the Spirit today, and where they will finally grasp their eternal citizenship.

Replacement Theology emerged under the Patristic Church Fathers in the first few centuries because many of them were not "rightly dividing" the "promises made unto the fathers" in the Old Testament. It appears they assumed that since Israel rejected Jesus Christ, God was finished with that nation and eventually gave the promise of a kingdom to the Gentiles. If we obey 2 Timothy 2:15, we need not tamper with God's unconditional promises to Israel, especially since Jesus taught Paul that "God has not cast away His people, which He foreknew." There is a remnant that will go into the Tribulation (Rev. 7:1-8), and yes, there will be Gentiles saved as well (as prophecy states), but we are "as of ones born out of due time," having been saved by grace, through faith in His blood…for the remission of sins" at this time.

The Body of Christ is not found in prophecy, and therefore, the Church is told "For God has not appointed us to wrath, but to obtain salvation by our Lord Jesus Christ" (I Thes. 5:9). We are living under what Paul called "the dispensation of the grace of God" (Eph. 3:2), and he also reassures us that we are "now justified by His blood," and as a result, "we shall be saved from wrath through Him" (Rom. 5:9). Let us remember and share the glorious hope we have in Jesus Christ.

In Paul's letter to Titus, he again reminds us of our blessed hope, which should strengthen our resolve to "make all men see what is the fellowship of the mystery, which from the beginning of the world has been hid in God, who created all things through Christ Jesus." To Titus, Paul wrote:

> *11 For the grace of God that bringeth salvation*
> *hath appeared to all men, 12 Teaching us that,*
> *denying ungodliness and worldly lusts, we*
> *should live soberly, righteously, and godly, in*
> *this present world; 13 Looking for that blessed*
> *hope, and the glorious appearing of the great*
> *God and our Saviour Jesus Christ; 14 Who*
> *gave himself for us, that he might redeem us*

*from all iniquity, and purify unto himself a
peculiar people, zealous of good works.
15 These things speak, and exhort, and rebuke
with all authority. Let no man despise thee.
Titus 2:11-15*

Don't let anyone or anything, especially any religious theology based upon the traditions of men, hold you back from what God has in store for you in Heaven.

*If ye then be risen with Christ, seek those
things which are above, where Christ sitteth on
the right hand of God. 2 Set your affection on
things above, not on things on the earth. 3 For
ye are dead, and your life is hid with Christ in
God. 4 When Christ, who is our life, shall
appear, then shall ye also appear with him in
glory. Colossians 3:1-4*

One final closing thought:
   *24 Know ye not that they which run in a race
   run all, but one receiveth the prize? So run,
   that ye may obtain. I Corinthians 9:24*

CHAPTER 8

The "One New Man"

19 And what is the exceeding greatness of his power to us-ward who believe, according to the working of his mighty power, 20 Which he wrought in Christ, when he raised him from the dead, and set him at his own right hand in the heavenly places, 21 Far above all principality, and power, and might, and dominion, and every name that is named, not only in this world, but also in that which is to come: 22 And hath put all things under his feet, and gave him to be the head over all things to the church, 23 Which is his body, the fulness of him that filleth all in all. Ephesians 1:19-23

Is There Only One Church in the Bible?

Tragically, the Church at-large has not "rightly divided" Scripture, and as a result, many in the Body of Christ, as I have stated, believe the Church has replaced Israel by combining the entire New Testament (and even the Old Testament) into one gospel and one Church (Acts 7:38; 8:1;

Rom. 12:5). If this were correct, we must wonder if the "Church that was a Jerusalem" (Acts 8:1) is the same Church as the Body of Christ (Eph. 1:22-23), which was *first* mentioned by Paul *after* Acts 9. What about the "Church in the wilderness" Stephen mentioned in Acts 7:38 to the Sanhedrin? Is it the same Church as the Church that was at Jerusalem or the Church, which is the Body of Christ? Were Gentiles in the Body of Christ *first* formed as a Church in the dry baptism of the Red Sea? If so, why did Paul refer to the Body of Christ as a "new creature," which was "kept secret since the world began"? After all, the Exodus account was written long before Paul is ever referenced in the Bible, so how could the Body of Christ be the "new creature" if there has only been one Church throughout the entire word of God?

As a warning to the Corinthians about their immoral conduct, Paul reminded them of the overthrow of "the Church in the wilderness" by God (due to their immoral behaviors) after He led them "by the hand" out of Egypt.

> *Moreover, brethren, I would not that ye should*
> *be ignorant, how that all our fathers were*
> *under the cloud, and all passed through the*
> *sea; 2 And were all baptized unto Moses in the*
> *cloud and in the sea; 3 And did all eat the same*
> *spiritual meat; 4 And did all drink the same*
> *spiritual drink: for they drank of that spiritual*
> *Rock that followed them: and that Rock was*
> *Christ. 5 But with many of them God was not*
> *well pleased: for they were overthrown in the*
> *wilderness. I Corinthians 10:1-5*

Regardless of which Church God established with Israel, in both the Old and New Testaments, He has always maintained a remnant of Jewish believers who did not bow to the false gods that Israel had come to serve at various times throughout the Old Testament. They were often judged harshly by God for their disobedience because they promised to follow the Law, but they violated it throughout their history, especially as they went about "to establish their own righteousness" (Rom. 10:3). Many believers aren't aware that God was (and will be again) "an Husband unto you (Israel)," and He had even "divorced Israel" for her spiritual adultery at one time (Isa. 54:5; Jer. 3:6-14; 31:32; Hos. 3:1).

We should also remember that God did not condone the sinful practices of ancient cultures, and just because there are regulations (in the Law) associated with those sinful practices, that does not mean God created or excused them. Do we not have to enact various laws in our own culture due to civil disobedience? Just as God provides a way of escape for sin today (I Cor. 10:13), He set forth regulations in the Law that led people from bondage to their sin as well. Many still mock the moral and civil principles of the Law that God gave to Israel, and they often refer to God as a tyrant for His judgments upon those who violated it (specifically Israel); however, this only proves their ignorance for the reason why God gave the Law in the first place. Paul was the first apostle to reveal these glorious truths:

> *19 Now we know that what things soever the law saith, it saith to them who are under the law: that every mouth may be stopped, and all*

the world may become guilty before God.
20 Therefore by the deeds of the law there shall
no flesh be justified in his sight: for by the law
is the knowledge of sin.
Romans 3:19-20

20 Moreover the law entered, that the offence
might abound. But where sin abounded, grace
did much more abound:
Romans 5:20

3 For what the law could not do, in that it was
weak through the flesh, God sending his own
Son in the likeness of sinful flesh, and for sin,
condemned sin in the flesh:
Romans 8:3

24 Wherefore the law was our schoolmaster to
bring us unto Christ, that we might be justified
by faith. Galatians 3:24

Human morality can never compare to the holy and righteous standards of God, and even though we may try, we always fall short of God's glory (Rom. 3:23). Because of their sin, God had provided various ways for Israel to address their trespasses through temporary sacrifices (Heb. 10:4), and may we never forget that it was the Law of Moses that sent Jesus Christ to the cross to pay for all the world's sins.

*13 Christ hath redeemed us from the curse of
the law, being made a curse for us: for it is
written, Cursed is every one that
hangeth on a tree:
Galatians 3:13*

*21 For he [God] hath made him [Jesus Christ]
to be sin for us, who knew no sin; that we
might be made the righteousness of God in
him. 2 Corinthians 5:21 (brackets by author)*

As for the Gentiles, we "did not want to retain God in our knowledge," so we were "given over to a reprobate mind" (Rom. 1:28), and that is still evident, especially today. Gentiles became a "law unto themselves," and this has evolved into the secular forms of morality dominating our culture in these modern times. There seems to be "a form of godliness," but Christ is not likely found anywhere within its structure (John 8:44). As I have stated numerous times, we do not get to invent our own morality and then demonize those who fail to live up to those standards.

*14 For when the Gentiles, which have not the
law, do by nature the things contained in the
law, these, having not the law, are a law unto
themselves: 15 Which shew the work of the law
written in their hearts, their conscience also
bearing witness, and their thoughts the mean
while accusing or else excusing one another;)
Romans 2:14-15*

> *14 But the natural man receiveth not the things*
> *of the Spirit of God: for they are foolishness*
> *unto him: neither can he know them, because*
> *they are spiritually discerned.*
> *I Corinthians 2:14*

What Happened to the Church in the Wilderness?

The remnant from the Church in the wilderness was maintained throughout the times of "the Law and the prophets" in Israel's history, and by the time Jesus was ministering to "the lost sheep of the house of Israel," we know the New Testament remnant as "the little flock" (in reference to Luke 12:32). It was to this "little flock" that the kingdom was promised. The "Church that was at Jerusalem" was based upon the Jewish *remnant* of believers who trusted in Jesus as their Messiah, and on the day of Pentecost, about three thousand souls were *added* to this "little flock," which numbered about 120 in the Upper Room, prior to the pouring out of the Holy Ghost in Acts 2 (Lk. 12:32; Acts 1:15; 2:41). This is why John the Baptist (the last of the Old Testament prophets), Jesus Himself, and the Twelve went about, proclaiming "the kingdom of heaven is at hand." Had Israel received this promised kingdom, the prophecy of Isaiah 11 would have been fulfilled at that time.

> *11 And it shall come to pass in that day, that the*
> *Lord shall set his hand again the second time*
> *to recover the remnant of his people, which*
> *shall be left, from Assyria, and from Egypt,*
> *and from Pathros, and from Cush, and from*

> *Elam, and from Shinar, and from Hamath, and*
> *from the islands of the sea. 12 And he shall set*
> *up an ensign for the nations, and shall*
> *assemble the outcasts of Israel, and gather*
> *together the dispersed of Judah from the four*
> *corners of the earth. Isaiah 11:11-12*

Although there are similarities and differences between the Church in the wilderness and the Church that was at Jerusalem, there was still a continuity of a believing remnant from the birth of that nation in the Red Sea to the Church Jesus taught to the "little flock" in Matthew 16:16-18. The Church in the wilderness worshipped God in the Tabernacle, but the Church that was at Jerusalem worshipped in the Temple. Today, the "temple of the Holy Spirit" is within members of the Body of Christ (I Cor. 6:19-20). Sacrifices were made in the Tabernacle and the Temple, but today, the members of the Body of Christ are to be "living sacrifices" (Rom. 12:1-2). As I have stated, God maintained a remnant of believers in the Old Testament, and there was also a remnant of believers in the New Testament (Rom. 11:5-6). They were all associated directly with the nation of Israel, not the Body of Christ. The Body of Christ had no remnant because it began as a "new creature" after Acts 9, and anyone who believes the gospel of the grace of God today still becomes a part of the "one new man." The Body of Christ has no prior history because this Church was "unsearchable" (Eph. 3:8) and "kept secret since the world began."

This is a fact that is often overlooked because of Church traditions, which places the Body of Christ at Pentecost, rather than the time of "the revelation of the mystery," which occurred after the conversion of Paul in Acts 9. In order to support the teaching that the Church "began at Pentecost," it is often done through *implied* covenants that God supposedly made with Himself and all believers throughout the entire Bible, even though Gentiles were "aliens from the commonwealth of Israel, and strangers from the covenants of promise (to Israel") in times past (Eph. 2:11-12). To support such a theology of certain *implied* covenants, these theologians rename the Israel of God to mean "all God's people." Yes, according to these theologians, if I read about Israel in Isaiah, that no longer means the descendants of Issac and Jacob; it now includes both Jews and Gentiles as "all God's people." In other words, the Body of Christ, which was "kept secret since the word began" (until Acts 9) was supposedly revealed to the prophets long before Paul, which completely undermines his entire ministry, and it violates Ephesians 2:11-12 in every possible way. This kind of nonsense is why we must "rightly divide the word of truth."

If the Church "began at Pentecost," we shouldn't be surprised that many believers are also unaware that Peter stated in Acts 2:16 that what they were witnessing (the pouring out of the Holy Spirit) in the Church at Jerusalem (at Pentecost) was the prophesied "last days" (from Joel) concerning Israel's covenant promises from God—not the beginning of a new dispensation where God's grace would be poured out upon the world, instead of His wrath (Acts 7:55-56).

The apostles also expected Matthew 24:34 to occur in their lifetime, which stated how their generation would see the

Tribulation and Second Coming of Jesus Christ. This is why much of the material in the writings of James, Peter, John, and Jude focused so much on the "last days (times)," and *how* the "scattered strangers" (twelve tribes of Israel) were to live in the world prior to the return of Jesus Christ, especially in the presence of Gentiles during that future time (Jas. 1:1; I Pet. 1:1; 2:12; 4:3; 3 John 1:7). However, under the gospel of the grace of God, there is no Jew or Gentile because we are in one body, through faith in the shed blood of the cross. We are "baptized *by* one Spirit into one body." Besides, Paul "persecuted and wasted" the Church of God that was at Jerusalem before he was converted (Acts 8:1-2; I Cor. 15:9; Gal. 1:13), so we must be cautious not to make the Body of Christ synonymous with the Church that was at Jerusalem. It was Paul who "laid the foundation" for the Body of Christ I Cor. 3:10), and he wasn't converted in Acts 2 at Pentecost, which is when most believers claim the Body of Christ began.

The Church in the Wilderness

The "Church in the wilderness," was revealed by God to and through Moses, just as the Messianic Kingdom Church was revealed to and through Peter, and the Body of Christ was revealed to and through Paul. No matter which Church, Jesus Christ is the solid "rock" of them all! To assume the Body of Christ was always known is a blatant violation of solid biblical exegesis, and theologians should be careful to "rightly divide" on these "called-out assemblies" taught throughout Scripture. (Keep in mind as we study: The Hebrew Old Testament used the word "congregation," but the Greek New Testament used the word "church.")

Moses was instructed by God to write the following to the "congregation" of Israel:

> *And <u>the LORD spake unto Moses and Aaron in the land of Egypt</u> saying, ² This month shall be unto you the beginning of months: it shall be the first month of the year to you. ³ <u>Speak ye unto all the congregation of Israel</u>, saying, In the tenth day of this month they shall take to them every man a lamb, according to the house of their fathers, a lamb for an house: Exodus 12:1-3 (the command of the Passover)*

> *And they took their journey from Elim, <u>and all the congregation of the children of Israel</u> came unto the wilderness of Sin, which is between Elim and Sinai, on the fifteenth day of the second month after their departing out of the land of Egypt. ² And the whole congregation of the children of Israel murmured against Moses and Aaron <u>in the wilderness:</u> Exodus 16:1-2 ("congregation" is also "church")*

> *²⁰ And thou shalt <u>command the children of Israel</u>, that they bring thee pure oil olive beaten for the light, to cause the lamp to burn always. ²¹ <u>In the tabernacle of the congregation</u> without the vail, which is before the testimony, Aaron and his sons shall order it*

> *from evening to morning before the L*ORD*: <u>it
> shall be a statute for ever unto their
> generations on the behalf of the children of
> Israel.</u> Exodus 27:20-21*

Did these instructions to this "congregation" in Exodus change during the earthly ministry of Jesus Christ who was "made of a woman, made under the Law to redeem them that were under the Law" (Gal. 4:4-5)? They did *not* because Jesus continued to command Israel to "keep the commandments," along with all the "feast days." (Matt. 19:17; John 14:15 and 21; Acts 10:28; I John 2:3; 3:22,24; 2 Jn. 1:6), just as Moses commanded in the books he wrote by inspiration of God.

> *[39] Know therefore this day, and consider it in
> thine heart, that the L*ORD *he is God in heaven
> above, and upon the earth beneath: there is
> none else. [40] <u>Thou shalt keep therefore his
> statutes, and his commandments, which I
> command thee this day</u>, that it may go well
> with thee, and with thy children after thee, and
> that thou mayest prolong thy days upon the
> earth, <u>which the L*ORD *thy God giveth thee, for
> ever</u>. Deuteronomy 4:39-40*

Stephen, in Acts 7, explained the following about this Church God revealed to Moses in the wilderness:

> *35 This Moses whom they refused, saying, Who*
> *made thee a ruler and a judge? the same did*
> *God send to be a ruler and a deliverer by the*
> *hand of the angel which appeared to him in the*
> *bush. 36 <u>He brought them out, after that he had</u>*
> *<u>shewed wonders and signs in the land of</u>*
> *<u>Egypt, and in the Red sea, and in the</u>*
> *<u>wilderness forty years.</u> 37 <u>This is that Moses,</u>*
> *<u>which said unto the children of Israel,</u> A*
> *prophet shall the Lord your God raise up unto*
> *you of your brethren, like unto me; him shall*
> *ye hear. 38 <u>This is he, that was in the church in</u>*
> *<u>the wilderness with the angel which spake to</u>*
> *<u>him in the mount Sina, and with our fathers:</u>*
> *<u>who received the lively oracles to give unto us:</u>*
> *Acts 7:35-38*

Millennia before Jesus declared to Peter, "Upon this rock, I will build my church" (Matt. 16:18), there was *already* a "Church in the wilderness" under Moses, consisting of the Israelites who were brought out of the land of Egypt. The congregation of Jews continued throughout the Old Testament, leading to the building of the Temple (twice) in Jerusalem, as well as the synagogues throughout Israel and the surrounding regions.

Which Church is for Today?

Knowing that God has always maintained a remnant of believing Israelites, we must consider the implications of these truths as we investigate which Church believers are a part of today. There will be a Jewish remnant during the Tribulation as well (Isa. 10:20-22; Eze. 12:16; Rom. 9:27; 11:1-6; Rev. 7:1-8), so we need to keep this in mind as we consider the Churches found throughout Scripture. Jesus even declared which gospel this Jewish remnant will proclaim during the Tribulation in Matthew 24:14, which is "the gospel of the kingdom." This makes sense, especially since Israel will be on the heels of the Messianic Kingdom, which Jesus said was "at hand" during His earthly ministry. Remember, no one knew about the "revelation of the mystery" and the "new creature" that would be given to Paul after Acts 9.

It is also important for me to quote once again what Paul taught the Corinthians about the Church in the wilderness.

Moreover, brethren, I would not that ye should be ignorant, how that all our fathers [Israelites] were under the cloud, and all passed through the sea [Red Sea]; 2 And were all baptized unto Moses in the cloud and in the sea [a dry baptism because they walked on dry ground]; 3 And did all eat the same spiritual meat; 4 And did all drink the same spiritual drink: for they drank of that spiritual Rock [Greek: petras] that followed them: and that Rock was Christ.
I Corinthians 10:1-4 (brackets by author)

Jesus is the "Rock" (*petras*) that was present during the Exodus (in the Church of the wilderness), and the word Paul used in this passage from I Corinthians is the same Greek word (*petras*) Jesus used in Matthew 16:18 ("upon this rock (*petras*) I will build my church"). There is no God-ordained Church in the Bile that Jesus is not the foundation of it! The name Peter, in Matthew 16:18, is *Petros*, not *petras*, which I will explain shortly. The Church Jesus mentioned in Matthew 16:18 was to be fully realized when Israel repented, which would have led to the return of Jesus Christ and the giving of the promised kingdom to Israel, which Jesus declared to be "at hand" during His earthly ministry (under the gospel of the kingdom). Peter referred to this in Acts 3 as "the restitution of all things" concerning Israel. Part of this promise was fulfilled at Pentecost with the offering of the kingdom to the "little flock," but the ultimate rejection of Jesus and that kingdom by Israel in Acts 7 is what brought about "the revelation of the mystery." Regardless, it was to the "little flock" that the kingdom was promised, but again, it will not be realized until Christ's return, and the conditions of the Tribulation will provide the right atmosphere for Israel to repent.

> *19 Repent ye therefore, and be converted, that your sins may be blotted out, when the times of refreshing shall come <u>from the presence of the Lord</u>. 20 <u>And he shall send Jesus Christ, which before was preached unto you:</u> 21 Whom the heaven must receive until the times of restitution of all things, <u>which God hath spoken by the mouth of all his holy prophets since the world began</u>. Acts 3:19-21*

Catholic, Orthodox, and Protestant churches have failed to realize these words from Peter in Acts 3. The Church of Matthew 16:18, and the Church that was at Jerusalem in Acts 2, and the Church in the wilderness will only find their prophetic fulfillment at the return of Jesus Christ, not in some "spiritual Israel" that exists only in "the hearts of believers," as many theologians erroneously teach today. The Body of Christ is a previously *unprophesied* Church known as "the new man," but thanks to the traditions of men, many believers assume the Body of Christ was always known. If it were, why did Paul declare the following to the Ephesians?

> *If ye have heard of the dispensation of the*
> *grace of God which is given me to you-ward:*
> *3 How that by revelation he made known unto*
> *me the mystery; (as I wrote afore in few words,*
> *4 Whereby, when ye read, ye may understand*
> *my knowledge in the mystery of Christ)*
> *5 Which in other ages was not made known*
> *unto the sons of men, as it is now*
> *revealed unto his holy apostles and*
> *prophets by the Spirit; Ephesians 3:2-5*

As I have stated, since the time of the "Church in the wilderness," God has always maintained a remnant of believers (Rom. 11:1-6). By the time of the earthly ministry of Jesus, there was a remnant known as "the little flock," and it was to this flock of believers that the kingdom of heaven was promised. It was also to this small assembly of Messianic Jews that Jesus instructed the following:

*17 And if he shall neglect to hear them, <u>tell it
unto the church</u>: but if he neglect to hear the
church, let him be unto thee as an heathen
man and a publican. 18 Verily I say unto you,
Whatsoever ye shall bind on earth shall be
bound in heaven: and whatsoever ye shall
loose on earth shall be loosed in heaven.
19 Again I say unto you, <u>That if two of you shall
agree on earth as touching any thing that they
shall ask, it shall be done for them of my
Father which is in heaven</u>. 20 <u>For where two or
three are gathered together in my name</u>, there
am I in the midst of them. Matthew 18:17-20*

Even though many believers claim this passage as their
own, do they fully realize that the Body of Christ was still
"hid in God" at the time Jesus was instructing this Church
known as "the little flock"? Again, what group of people in
the "gospels" were promised the kingdom, especially because
they "gathered in His name" as Messiah?

*32 <u>Fear not, little flock; for it is your Father's
good pleasure to give you the kingdom.</u> 33 <u>Sell
that ye have, and give alms</u>; provide
yourselves bags which wax not old, a treasure
in the heavens that faileth not, where no thief
approacheth, neither moth corrupteth.
Luke 12:31-32*

The "little flock" members (who believed Jesus was *the Christ*), were in the Upper Room just prior to Pentecost, and it was to this "little flock" that the "kingdom of heaven" was offered. Remember, approximately 3000 souls were *added* to this "Messianic Church (at Jerusalem)" on that day (Acts 2:41). Also, according to Acts 2:44, what were these members required to do at Pentecost? They were told to "sell all you have…and have all things common," just as Jesus stated in Luke 12:33 to this "little flock." This same "little flock" (Messianic Kingdom Church) became the Church that was at Jerusalem—the one Paul "persecuted and wasted" (Gal. 1:13), and this Church was "scattered abroad" after the stoning of Stephen. It was to these believers that James, Peter, and John later wrote in their epistles (often referred to as "The General Epistles").

The concept of a "flock of sheep" is always synonymous with Israel (Psalm 23, 77, 78; Eze. 34; Jer. 23; Mic. 2; I Pet. 5), not the Gentiles who were the enemies of the flock. This is why Jesus stated, "I am not sent but unto the lost sheep of the house of Israel." Regardless, there are still many who believe that *any* Church mentioned in the New Testament *is* the Body of Christ, but we know from Scripture (not tradition) that the "one new man" was *not* revealed in the Old Testament, nor was it taught during the earthly ministry of Jesus Christ and the early chapters in Acts.

The Body of Christ (the Church (Eph. 1:21-22)) was taught as part of the "revelation of the mystery, kept secret since the world began," so how could it have been the Church in the wilderness, the "little flock" of Luke 12, the Church Jesus mentioned in Matthew 16 to Peter, or the Church at Pentecost, especially since Paul, who "laid the foundation" for the Body, was not even an apostle during those times? We are a "Church of God," but so was the Church in the wilderness and the Church that was at Jerusalem, but those Churches were not the Body of Christ as many suppose.

As I have mentioned, there are some who continue to insist the believers mentioned in "the gospels" were the Body of Christ (Jews and Gentiles in one body), but if this were so, why would Jesus state to the Gentile woman in Matthew 15 that it was "not meet (right) to take the children's bread (Israel) and to cast it to dogs (Gentiles)," especially if Jews and Gentiles *were already* in "one body," which is not mentioned *once* in the Old Testament, the "gospels," and in early Acts? Also, keep in mind, there was only one other Gentile in the "gospels," prior to Christ's inquisition before Pilate, that Jesus had any direct contact with, and that was the Roman centurion whose servant He healed (Matthew 8 and Luke 7). When Jesus spoke to the Samaritan woman at the well, He mentioned nothing about Jews and Gentiles being in "one body," but instead, He told her in John 4:22 that "salvation is of the Jews." This would be consistent with His instructions to the Twelve in Matthew 10:5-7, especially when He told the Twelve: "Go *not* into the way of the Gentiles...but go rather to the lost sheep of the house of Israel."

So, if the Body of Christ already existed as the "one and only true Church" throughout Scripture, we must wonder why Jesus had extremely limited contact with Gentiles during His earthly ministry, especially since the Body of Christ consists mainly of Gentiles. Was the Church in the wilderness, the "little flock" of Luke 12, the Church mentioned to Peter in Matthew 16, or the Church that was at Jerusalem at Pentecost already familiar with the preaching of Paul, which taught how both Jews and Gentiles could be reconciled to God through faith in the blood of Christ, along with being baptized into "one body...by the cross"? Did they already know "the mystery"? If they were already familiar with what Paul called "my gospel," then we are left to "spiritualize" the following passage in I Corinthians 2:

> *7 But we speak the wisdom of God in a mystery,* <u>*even the hidden wisdom,*</u> <u>*which God ordained*</u> <u>*before the world unto our glory*</u>*: 8 Which none of the princes of this world knew:* <u>*for had they*</u> <u>*known it, they would not have crucified the*</u> <u>*Lord of glory*</u>*. I Corinthians 2:7-8*

"The revelation of the mystery," which proclaimed salvation to both Jews and Gentiles (who have placed their faith in the finished work of Jesus Christ) was *first* given to Paul as a *pattern* (I Tim. 1:16), and it was "not made known unto the sons of men" until after Paul was saved in Acts 9; therefore, it is impossible for the Body of Christ to have existed prior to his conversion. This is also why it is so dangerous to "spiritualize" Scripture that should be "rightly divided," especially in the context of which Church was prophesied and unprophesied in Scripture. By not "rightly dividing," we now have millions of Gentile believers attempting to "walk in the footsteps of Jesus" from a time when He was only sent to "the lost sheep of the house of Israel."

Paul was clear that the Church that he was sent to establish was indeed the "new creature," not the Church in the wilderness or the Church that was at Jerusalem (at Pentecost). Besides, both Churches were already known prior to Paul's conversion in Acts 9. Paul also clearly taught that the foundation of the Body of Christ is not Peter (*Petros*), but rather it is Jesus Christ (*petras*).

> *10 According to the grace of God which is given unto me, as a wise masterbuilder, I have laid the foundation, and another buildeth thereon. But let every man take heed how he buildeth thereupon. 11 For other foundation can no man lay than that is laid, which is Jesus Christ. I Corinthians 3:10-11*

> *16 Wherefore henceforth know we no man after the flesh: yea, though we have known Christ after the flesh, yet now henceforth know we him no more. 17 Therefore if any man be in Christ, he is a new creature: old things are passed away; behold, all things are become new. 2 Corinthians 5:16-17*

> *15 For in Christ Jesus neither circumcision availeth any thing, nor uncircumcision, but a new creature. Galatians 6:15*

The Church today (the Body of Christ) is the "new creature" of Paul's epistles to both Jews and Gentiles. To become a member of the Church, you must believe that salvation is by grace, through faith in the death, burial, and resurrection of Jesus Christ, apart from works (I Cor. 15:3-4; Eph. 2:8-9). Thankfully, God is able to save people, despite the demands of their religious denominations. If you have placed your faith in the completed work of redemption Jesus provided personally for you, you are saved, even though your denomination might demand some sacrament or other work for salvation. You have become a member of the Body of Christ, *not* the Church in the wilderness or the Messianic Kingdom Church that was at Pentecost in Acts 2, which most denominations still teach was the "beginning of the Church." Remember, the "one new man" was revealed after the conversion of Paul in Acts 9!

Many assume the teachings in the following passage have *always been known*, but have they?

> *14 For he is our peace, who hath made both one, and <u>hath broken down the middle wall of partition between us</u>; 15 Having abolished in his flesh the enmity, even the law of commandments contained in ordinances; for to make in himself of twain <u>one new man</u>, so making peace; 16 And that he might <u>reconcile both unto God in one body by the cross</u>, having slain the enmity thereby:*
> *Ephesians 2:14-16*

This separation between Jews and Gentiles was *not* preached to the Church in the wilderness, nor was it taught to the "little flock" or the Twelve. It certainly was not taught at Pentecost because there is no mention of Jews and Gentiles being reconciled into "one body by the cross." In fact, the Twelve were only addressing Israel in Acts 2 with such phrases as "Ye men of Judaea, and all that dwell at Jerusalem…ye men of Israel…let all the house of Israel know assuredly…" right before Peter commanded them to "repent and be baptized for the remission of sins." Also, it was nearly ten years after Pentecost that Peter was directed (for the first time) to the home of a Gentile in Acts 10, and he continued to insist on water baptism with Cornelius and his household. Again, the Body of Christ began with Paul, not in Genesis or Exodus as some preach. It was not revealed during the preaching of John the Baptist, or the teaching of Jesus in Matthew 16, or at Pentecost. We must "rightly divide the word of truth."

"The Church at Jerusalem"

The Church that was at Jerusalem was the Church Christ referenced to Peter in Matthew 16:16-18, which I will quote shortly. In Acts 2, however, we also learn about the context of this promised Church, which was also in relationship to King David, not the "revelation of the mystery, which David would have *never* known. Note the following:

> *29 Men and brethren, let me freely speak unto*
> *you of the patriarch <u>David</u>, that he is both*
> *dead and buried, and his sepulchre is with us*

> *unto this day. 30 Therefore being a prophet, and*
> *knowing that God had sworn with an oath to*
> *him, that of the fruit of his loins, according to*
> *the flesh, <u>he would raise up Christ to sit on his</u>*
> *<u>throne</u>; 31 He seeing this before spake of the*
> *resurrection of Christ, that his soul was not left*
> *in hell, neither his flesh did see corruption.*
> *Acts 2:29-31*

The entire context of Acts 2 is associated with the coming kingdom being offered to the Church (the "little flock" to whom the kingdom was promised), and this Church was *already* at Jerusalem on the "Day of Pentecost" (Acts 1:15). Remember, once more, that 3000 souls were "added" to the "little flock" of about 120 who were in the Upper Room in Acts 1:15. In fact, was the Body of Christ instructed to continue their daily worship in the Temple, just as the followers of Jesus did in Acts 2:46? What about the signs and wonders by those who repented and were water baptized at Pentecost? Are these true characteristics of the Church, the Body of Christ, today? I should also mention again that Israel, as a nation, will *not* be "born again" until the Second Coming of Jesus Christ (Isa. 11; Eze. 37; Rom. 11). Had the nation repented in those early chapters in Acts, Jesus would have returned (Act 3:19-21) after the Tribulation. The Church that was at Jerusalem grew in number under the gospel of the kingdom (the Great Commission), but we must understand that something happened to that Church, which was due to Israel's rejection of both the Messiah and the offer of the kingdom to that nation, which was soon "scattered abroad" after Acts 7. We discussed this in the chapters on the Book of Acts.

Before I discuss further the Church that was at Jerusalem, I think it is prudent to explain that the prophetic Israel of the Bible is not the Israel reestablished in 1948, even though a remnant is likely within that nation at this time (Rom. 11:5-6). The assumption that 1948 was a "fulfillment of prophecy" completely disregards the fact that during the Tribulation, which is before the return of Jesus to establish His kingdom in Israel (in Jerusalem), God will regather Israel in those days. The current nation of Israel was established for the Jews through a secular government, and it also consists of a majority of secular citizens. There is yet a future regathering of God's people, as described in Deuteronomy 30, Isaiah 11 and 43, Jeremiah 32, Ezekial 36 and 37, Zechariah 12, Amos 9; Matthew 24 and 25, and Romans 11. Today, we are under "the mystery," not prophecy.

What Happened to the Church at Jerusalem?
As I have already taught, by Acts 7, the nation of Israel, through its leaders, had blasphemed the Holy Ghost (7:51), and they refused to accept Jesus as their Messiah, so it was then that we were introduced to Paul (Saul), and it was *to him* that the Body of Christ, the Church, was revealed for "our glory" (I Cor. 2:7). If the Church that was at Jerusalem is the same Church as the Body of Christ, which Paul *first* introduced, we must again wonder why Luke stated the following in these passages:

And Saul [Paul] was consenting unto his death. And at that time there was a great persecution against <u>the church which was at Jerusalem</u>; and they were all <u>scattered abroad</u> throughout the regions of Judaea and Samaria, <u>except the apostles</u>. ² And devout men carried Stephen to his burial, and made great lamentation over him. ³ As for Saul, he made havock of the church [that was at Jerusalem], entering into every house, and haling men and women committed them to prison. ⁴ Therefore they that were scattered abroad went every where preaching the word.
Acts 8:1-4 (brackets by author)

Since Paul (Saul) had not yet been converted until Acts 9, what "word" were these disciples of Jesus preaching? It couldn't have been the "revelation of the mystery" because that had not yet been revealed to Paul because he was still a "chief enemy" of Jesus Christ. The only "word" these believers would have known was what the Twelve preached to them at Pentecost.

Paul, on the other hand, later wrote the following concerning the Church of God that was at Jerusalem:

¹¹ But I certify you, brethren, that <u>the gospel which was preached of me is not after man</u>. ¹² <u>For I neither received it of man, neither was I taught it, but by the revelation of Jesus Christ.</u> ¹³ For ye have heard of my

> *conversation <u>in time past in the Jews' religion</u>,*
> *how that beyond measure <u>I persecuted the</u>*
> *<u>church of God, and wasted it</u>: 14 And profited*
> *in the Jews' religion above many my equals in*
> *mine own nation, being more exceedingly*
> *zealous of the traditions of my fathers. 15 But*
> *when it pleased God, <u>who separated me from</u>*
> *<u>my mother's womb, and called me by his</u>*
> *<u>grace</u>, 16 <u>To reveal his Son in me, that I might</u>*
> *<u>preach him among the heathen; immediately I</u>*
> *<u>conferred not with flesh and blood</u>: 17 Neither*
> *went I up to Jerusalem <u>to them which were</u>*
> *<u>apostles before me</u>; but I went into Arabia, and*
> *returned again unto Damascus.*
> *Galatians 1:11-17*

There is no way the disciples, who were "scattered abroad" after the persecution of Stephen, could have been preaching the gospel that Paul was later called to preach as "my gospel," which declared faith alone in the shed blood and resurrection of Jesus Christ for justification (to declare one righteous). It was still "hid in God" to them until after Paul revealed it over time, as I explained in the chapters about the transition in the Book of Acts.

However, did James, Peter, and John continue their ministry later with the Body of Christ, or did they continue to write and instruct the "circumcision" from the Church of God that was now "scattered about" from Jerusalem? Tradition insists that James, Peter, and John wrote to the same audience as Paul, but this violates their agreement in Galatians 2.

*7 But contrariwise, when they saw that <u>the
gospel of the uncircumcision was committed
unto me, as the gospel of the circumcision was
unto Peter;</u> 8 (For he that wrought effectually
in Peter to the apostleship of the circumcision,
the same was mighty in me toward the
Gentiles:) 9 And when James, Cephas, and
John, who seemed to be pillars, perceived the
grace that was given unto me, they gave to me
and Barnabas the right hands of fellowship;
<u>that we should go unto the heathen, and they
unto the</u> circumcision. Galatians 2:7-9*

There was also no evidence that Paul forced those already saved under the gospel of the kingdom to be "resaved" under his ministry, especially considering the following passage:

*20 Yea, so have I strived to preach the gospel,
not where Christ was named, lest I should
build upon another man's foundation:
Romans 15:20*

Paul was referencing the gospel of the grace of God, according to "the revelation of the mystery," not the gospel of the kingdom, which the Twelve had already made known to "the lost sheep of the house of Israel." There was already a gospel that had been preached prior to the conversion of Paul, and Paul declared that he was not called to "build upon another man's foundation." This also indicates that another foundation was already in existence before Paul established the one given to him by Jesus Christ. He did, however, warn others about how they built upon the foundation he laid in I Corinthians 3:10!

To Whom Did James, Peter, and John Preach?
Let us examine "to whom" these three saints preached in their "General Epistles."

> *James, a servant of God and of the Lord Jesus Christ, <u>to the twelve tribes which are scattered abroad</u>, greeting. James 1:1*

> *Peter, an apostle of Jesus Christ, <u>to the strangers scattered</u> throughout Pontus, Galatia, Cappadocia, Asia, and Bithynia...*
> *I Peter 1:1-2*

> *⁹ That was the true Light, which lighteth every man that cometh into the world. ¹⁰ He was in the world, and the world was made by him, and the world knew him not. ¹¹ <u>He came unto his own, and his own received him not.</u> ¹² But as many as received him, to them gave he power to become the sons of God, even to them <u>that believe on his name</u>: ¹³ Which were born, not of blood, nor of the will of the flesh, nor of the will of man, but of God. ¹⁴ <u>And the Word was made flesh, and dwelt among us</u>, (and we*

*beheld his glory, the glory as of the only
begotten of the Father,) <u>full of grace and truth</u>.*
John 1:9-14

*My little children, these things write I unto
you, that ye sin not. And if any man sin, we
have an advocate with the Father, Jesus Christ
the righteous: 2 And he is the propitiation for
our sins: and not for ours only, but also for the
sins of the whole world. 3 And hereby we do
know that we know him, <u>if we keep his
commandments</u>. 4 He that saith, I know him,
and keepeth not his commandments, is a liar,
and the truth is not in him. 5 <u>But whoso keepeth
his word, in him verily is the love of God
perfected: hereby know we that we are in him.</u>*
I John 2:1-5

This passage appears after John wrote the following about breaking the commandments:

*6 If we say that we have fellowship with him,
and walk in darkness, we lie, and do not the
truth: 7 But if we walk in the light, as he is in
the light, we have fellowship one with another,
and the blood of Jesus Christ his Son cleanseth
us from all sin. 8 If we say that we have no sin,
we deceive ourselves, and the truth is not in
us. 9 <u>If we confess our sins, he is faithful and
just to forgive us our sins, and to cleanse us</u>*

> *from all unrighteousness.* *10 If we say that we*
> *have not sinned, we make him a liar, and his*
> *word is not in us. I John 1:6-10*

How could I John 1:6-10 be written directly to the Body of Christ, especially since Paul clearly taught that we have already been "forgiven *all* trespasses" (Col. 2:13), we are already "the righteousness of God in Him" (2 Cor. 5:21), and we are "not under the law, but under grace" (Rom. 6:14)?

Many religious traditionalists boast about some of the Patristic Church Fathers being disciples of Paul and John; however, it is more important to realize that John learned from Paul (Galatians 2) the gospel which he (Paul) preached among the Gentiles (by direct revelation of Jesus Christ (Gal. 1:11-12)). In that gospel, Paul proclaimed salvation by faith in the blood of Jesus for the remission of sins, without works; however, were James, Peter, and John instructed by Jesus to preach the gospel of the grace of God to the *uncircumcision* as Paul did? Not at all. Yes, they learned about the gospel Paul preached about "the one new man," but this does not mean they stopped preaching the gospel of the kingdom (the Great Commission), which insisted on "repent and be baptized for the remission of sins." This is why John continued to emphasize keeping the commandments in order to abide in Christ. We, on the other hand, are justified by faith without the deeds of the Law (Acts 13:38-39; Rom. 3:21-31; 4:4-5; Gal. 2:16-21). Remember, James was still writing to the "twelve tribes scattered abroad."

If we "rightly divide" as "to whom" Paul and the other apostles were writing, as I have previous quoted from James

1:1, I Peter 1, and John's letters, we should see that the instructions through the Great Commission were different from what Jesus taught to and through Paul to the Body of Christ (through "the revelation of the mystery"). Until this is recognized, our identity crisis in Christ will continue to bring confusion, and we know God is "not the Author of confusion" (I Cor. 14:33). Salvation is by grace, through faith today (or since the time of Paul), but this hasn't been the consistent message within the churches since the time of the apostles' deaths. How many souls have been lost or misguided because of ignorance on the part of believers not "rightly dividing"?

> *37 If any man think himself to be a prophet, or spiritual, let him acknowledge that the things that I write unto you are the commandments of the Lord. 38 But if any man be ignorant, let him be ignorant. I Corinthians 14:37-38*

Currently, about two billion people in the world claim to be "Christian," and of those two billion, a very small percentage of them are Jewish converts. Tragically, instead of adhering to the gospel of the grace of God (Acts 20:24; I Tim. 1:16) given to Paul (the only "apostle to the Gentiles"), the majority of Gentiles have either combined, or have even abandoned much of Paul's gospel to the Church, in favor of adhering to the traditions associated with the "gospels," which were for "the lost sheep of the house of Israel." Many believers still insist they are to follow all that was written to and for "the Church that was at Jerusalem." If anyone boasts about how they are "following in Jesus' footsteps" from His earthly ministry in "the gospels," they may want to consider "to whom" He was sent, and then they may wish to determine if they are somehow from "the lost sheep of the house of Israel." If we recall, Paul also told us "to whom" Jesus came in the following passage:

> *3 For I could wish that myself were accursed*
> *from Christ for my brethren, my kinsmen*
> *according to the flesh: 4 <u>Who are Israelites</u>; to*
> *whom pertaineth the adoption, and the glory,*
> *and the covenants, and the giving of the law,*
> *and the service of God, and the promises;*
> *5 Whose are the fathers, <u>and of whom as</u>*
> *<u>concerning the flesh Christ came</u>, who is over*
> *all, God blessed for ever. Amen.*
> *Romans 9:3-5*

Galatians 2 is also extremely important for us to "rightly divide" between the "gospel of the *uncircumcision*," and the "gospel of the *circumcision*." These gospels were not the same, nor were they given to the same audience. Scripture clearly shows us this, but the *traditions of men* must "spiritualize" these two gospels by combining them into one.

> *Then fourteen years after I went up again*
> *[now 17 years since first meeting Peter (Gal.*
> *1:18)] to Jerusalem with Barnabas, and took*
> *Titus with me also. 2 And I went up by*
> *revelation [of Jesus Christ], and*
> *communicated unto them [the apostles and*

*other disciples] that gospel which I preach
among the Gentiles [the revelation of the
mystery], but privately to them which were of
reputation [the apostles], lest by any means I
should run, or had run, in vain. ³ But neither
Titus, who was with me, being a Greek, was
compelled to be circumcised: ⁴ And that
because of false brethren unawares brought in,
who came in privily to spy out our liberty
which we have in Christ Jesus, that they might
bring us into bondage: ⁵ To whom we gave
place by subjection, no, not for an hour; that
the truth of the gospel might continue with
you. ⁶ But of these [the apostles] who seemed
to be somewhat, (whatsoever they were, it
maketh no matter to me: God accepteth no
man's person:) for they who seemed to be
somewhat in conference added nothing to me
[see Gal. 1:11-12]
Galatians 2:1-6 (brackets by author)*

Lest we forget: James, Peter, and John learned about Paul's ministry to the Gentiles from Paul, and they "added nothing to me," as Paul declared. This does not mean they added nothing because they were all preaching the same gospel, because Paul said he told them "...*that* gospel which I preach among the Gentiles." Titus, who was *not* compelled to be circumcised," was an example to them for how Gentiles were not under the Law of Moses. Again, in Acts 15, James, and Peter agreed to this conclusion regarding Gentiles and the

Law, but only *after* Paul raised the concern about the Judaizers insisting that Gentiles were under the Law.

It is, however, the next three verses that reveal something extremely important as well, which is worth repeating once more:

> *⁷ But contrariwise [the opposite], when they saw that the gospel of the uncircumcision [Gentiles] was committed unto me [Paul], as the gospel of the circumcision [Israelites] was unto Peter; ⁸ (For he that wrought effectually in Peter to the apostleship of the circumcision, the same was mighty in me toward the Gentiles:) ⁹ And when James, Cephas, and John, who seemed to be pillars [co-equal leaders], perceived the grace that was given unto me, they gave to me and Barnabas the right hands of fellowship; that we should go unto the heathen [Gentiles], and they unto the circumcision [Israelites]. ¹⁰ Only they would that we should remember the poor [at least one similarity in purpose]; the same which I also was forward to do.*
> *Galatians 2:7-10 (brackets by author)*

Some modern translations insert the words "to the" instead of using "of the" when identifying the "gospel of the *uncircumcision*" and the "gospel of the *circumcision*." Note the following:

*7 On the contrary, they recognized that I had
been entrusted with the task of preaching the
gospel <u>to the uncircumcised</u>, [a] just as
Peter had been <u>to the circumcised</u>.
Galatians 2:7 (New International Version)*

*7 On the contrary, they realized that I had been
entrusted with preaching the gospel <u>to the
uncircumcised</u>, just as Peter had been
entrusted with preaching the gospel
<u>to the circumcised</u>
Galatians 2:7 (New Catholic Bible)*

In all the original Greek uses of the article (genitive (possessive), feminine) being written before the words "uncircumcision" and "circumcision," it is always rendered "of the," not the English "to the." To use the words "to the" only implies that Peter and Paul were preaching the same gospel, but only to two different groups. If this were correct, why did Paul say the gospel he preached was not taught to him by "any man but by revelation of Jesus Christ"? Secondly, the context of Galatians 2 clearly indicated that Paul "communicated unto them the gospel which I preach among the Gentiles" and how they "added nothing to me." Finally, if what Peter and Paul preached were the same gospels, why did Peter in Acts 15 state, "We believe that through the grace of our Lord Jesus Christ, *we shall be saved, even as they*"? This certainly doesn't indicate the same gospel being preached by Peter and Paul. The context of the passage from Galatians 2:7 clearly indicates "of the" to be the appropriate Greek rendering of the words, not "to the" as the English would translate it. Follow the original Greek, and "rightly divide."

According to Galatians 1, after Paul went into Arabia and returned to Damascus, it was another three years before Paul visited Peter in Jerusalem (Gal. 1:11-12, 17-18, 21). It was another fourteen years later that we have the encounter in Galatians 2 where the "gospel of the *uncircumcision*" and the "gospel of the *circumcision*" were discussed. Most likely, Galatians was Paul's first letter, and this epistle was a letter of correction to those churches that he had already established in Galatia. There were also "scattered Jews" in those regions, for they attempted mightily to persuade many believers in the churches of Galatia to abandon Paul's gospel by returning to the "yoke of bondage" of the Law (Gal. 5:1). It is also important to note that the Galatians were indeed "mixing Law with Grace," so it is even further proof that Paul had founded several churches at Galatia before he had written his first letter of correction to them. It was his gospel that those churches were to follow—not that of the Twelve (or the Judaizers who'd insisted on observing the Law). Paul warned against teaching another gospel.

> *8 But though we, or an angel from heaven,*
> *preach any other gospel unto you than that*
> *which we have preached unto you, let him be*
> *accursed. 9 As we said before, so say I now*
> *again, if any man preach any other gospel*
> *unto you than that ye have received, let him be*
> *accursed. Galatians 1:8-9*

We know that the Body of Christ consists of believers who are "baptized *by* one Spirit into one body" (I Cor. 12:13). On the other hand, the "little flock" at Pentecost, which was the Church of God at Jerusalem, was baptized by Christ *with* the Holy Spirit, and the message in Acts 2 never mentioned how Jews and Gentiles were in one body "by the cross" with a "citizenship in Heaven." Also, no believers, prior to Paul's epistles, were ever told that their "bodies are the temple of the Holy Ghost." Even though believers at Pentecost were indwelt with the Holy Ghost, they still went to the Temple, but the "temple of the Holy Ghost" is within us today. The Body of Christ has been "forgiven all trespasses" (Col. 2:13), but the believers from the Church at Jerusalem were still instructed by John to "confess their sins" to be forgiven (I John 1:9). Remember, after the destruction of the Temple in AD 70, there was no Temple for the Jews, but through the "revelation of the mystery," we have been taught that we are now the "temple of the Holy Ghost."

> *19 Now therefore ye are no more strangers and foreigners, but fellowcitizens with the saints, and of the household of God; 20 And are built upon the foundation of the apostles and prophets, Jesus Christ himself being the chief corner stone; 21 In whom all the building fitly framed together groweth unto <u>an holy temple in the Lord</u>: 22 <u>In whom ye also are builded together for an habitation of God through the Spirit.</u> Ephesians 2:19-22*

> *19 What? know ye not that <u>your body is the</u>*
> *<u>temple of the Holy Ghost which is in you</u>,*
> *which ye have of God, and ye are not your*
> *own? 20 For ye are bought with a price:*
> *therefore glorify God in your body, and in your*
> *spirit, which are God's. I Corinthians 6:19-20*

Was this ever preached to the Church in the wilderness? What about the Church that was at Jerusalem? Again, they were water baptized and indwelt with the Holy Ghost at Pentecost, but did Peter tell them that "the temple of God is within you?" Also, Luke 17:21 does not teach that the "kingdom of heaven" was within them (the unbelieving Pharisees). That would seem impossible, especially in their unbelief. The Greek words in Luke 17:21 mean "among you," not "within you." After AD 70, there was no temple for them to worship within, but Paul had already taught the Body of Christ that they were the "temple of the Holy Ghost," and there is now no other gospel that is able to save besides the gospel of the grace of God for both Jews and Gentiles. Most churches still combine the gospel of the kingdom and the gospel of the grace of God, and they do so by ignoring the "oneness" of Paul's gospel in Ephesians 4:1-6. This fact is often overlooked because believers retreat to "the gospels" for their obedience, which places them back under the Law of Moses (Gal. 4:4-5), and currently, there is no Temple available for the sacrifices imposed by the Law.

The Church: Rightly Dividing Matthew 16 and I Corinthians 3

In the following passage from Matthew 16, we read about a Church Jesus promised to build:

> *13 When Jesus came into the coasts of Caesarea Philippi, he asked his disciples, saying, <u>Whom do men say that I the Son of man am?</u> 14 And they said, Some say that thou art John the Baptist: some, Elias; and others, Jeremias, or one of the prophets. 15 He saith unto them, But whom say ye that I am? 16 And <u>Simon Peter answered and said, Thou art the Christ, the Son of the living God.</u> 17 And Jesus answered and said unto him, Blessed art thou, Simon Barjona: for flesh and blood hath not revealed it unto thee, <u>but my Father</u> which is in heaven. 18 And I say also unto thee, <u>That thou art Peter, and upon this rock I will build my church; and the gates of hell shall not prevail against it.</u>*
>
> *Matthew 16:13-18*

Is the Body of Christ built upon the testimony of Peter in Matthew 16:16, which is when he declared, "Thou art *the Christ* (Messiah), the Son of the living God," or is the Body of Christ built upon Jesus as "Lord and Savior," who gave His life a "ransom for all" (as Paul testified to Jews and Gentiles "in due time")? Christ is now the Head of the Church, the Body of Christ (Col. 1:18; 2:19), but if Peter was the head of the Body of Christ, which Paul claimed to have "laid the foundation" for under his own ministry, then we must contemplate how Peter could be the head of a Church that was not yet revealed until after Paul laid the foundational truths for it after his conversion in Acts 9. Besides, Peter wasn't even the head of the Church that was at Jerusalem, which became the Church Jesus mentioned in Matthew 16:18. After all, it was James who was the head of the Church that was at Jerusalem, which was the one Paul "persecuted and wasted" (Gal. 1:13).

Do you see how traditions often rob us of vital truths? The entire narrative about the Catholic Church becoming (at Pentecost) the Church mentioned in Matthew 16 is completely based upon the traditions of men who failed to "rightly divide the word of truth." Protestants often fall victim to various traditions as well, which are either adapted from Catholic traditions, or they simply invent their own theological conundrums that also ignore 2 Timothy 2:15.

Again, if Peter laid the foundational truths for the Church, the Body of Christ, then Paul must have been lying to Timothy in his first pastoral letter to him.

> *15 This is a faithful saying, and worthy of all acceptation, <u>that Christ Jesus came into the world to save sinners</u>; of whom I am chief. 16 Howbeit for this cause I obtained mercy, <u>that in me first</u> Jesus Christ might shew forth all longsuffering, <u>for a pattern</u> to them <u>which should hereafter believe on him to life everlasting.</u> I Timothy 1:15-16*

At His ascension, Jesus gave the so-called "Great Commission" to the twelve apostles (eleven at the time) for their "pattern," and the intended purpose was to bring "salvation to the end of the earth" through Israel (Isa. 49:6; Matt. 28:16-20). This Messianic Kingdom Church was the Church Jesus mentioned in Matthew 16:16-18, and it was to this Church that Jesus first called to take salvation to the world (Matt. 28:16-20). Jesus included water baptism and the expectation of "teaching them to observe all that I have commanded" (from His earthly ministry under the gospel of the kingdom), and this was a directive for all to follow. This would include "keep the commandments" for their obedience, which is still found within James', Peter's, and John's writings to "the twelve tribes scattered abroad." It was to the "little flock" that Jesus promised to give the Messianic Kingdom Church, which He spoke about in Matthew 16. However, through the "fall" of Israel in Acts 7, God soon gave to Paul the "revelation of the mystery, which was kept secret since the world began," and this formed a "new creature" (the "one new man") known as the Body of Christ, the Church, which has a heavenly citizenship in eternity. The Messianic Kingdom Church, with an earthly promise (Matt. 5:5), is not the Body of Christ!

A closer examination of Matthew 16 also revealed how Jesus first referred to Peter as Simon Barjona (the name given to him by Peter's father); however, Jesus then called him "Peter" (*Petros (masculine)*). As a result of Peter's testimony that Jesus is *the Christ*, the Messiah, Jesus further stated, "upon *this rock (petras (feminine))* I will build my Church." Paul, in I Corinthians 3:11, and especially in I Corinthians

10:4, stated clearly that "the Rock" (*petras*) is Jesus Christ. *Petros* (pebble) and *petras* (cliff, boulder) do not have the same meanings exactly in the Greek, which is the language the New Testament was written in for our benefit. As I stated earlier, the same *petras* that Jesus used in Matthew 16:18 when He stated, "upon this rock," is the same *petras* Paul used in I Corinthians 10:4 when he stated, "That Rock was Christ" (according to biblehub.com). If Jesus had meant for the Messianic Kingdom Church to be built upon one man (Peter), He would have said, "Upon this *Petros*, I will build my Church." That is not the Greek word used in the New Testament.

The Messianic Kingdom Church will be fully built upon Christ as Messiah (taught throughout prophecy), just as the Church is *now* built upon Jesus Christ as the Head of the Church, which is His body (according to the "revelation of the mystery" (Rom. 16:25; Eph. 1:22-23)). The Church in Matthew 16:18 was prophetic, but the Church of Ephesians 1:22-23 was "kept secret" until Jesus saved Paul on the road to Damascus in Acts 9. Paul's epistles, quite often, annihilate many traditions within denominationalism, and this is likely why "the revelation of the mystery" is still a mystery to millions simply because traditions have been robbing believers of these vital truths for millennia.

On another matter, Israel is to be a "kingdom of priests," but the Body of Christ is called to be "ambassadors for Christ," which means our residency is elsewhere (Ex. 19:6; 2 Cor. 5:20; Phil. 3:20). I've heard many brothers and sisters in Christ refer to the Church as a "kingdom of priests," but again, this title was given millennia before the "revelation of the mystery" and the Body of Christ was ever made known. Also, Paul *never* refers to the Body of Christ as a "priesthood" in any way. To justify these traditions that the Body of Christ is "a royal priesthood" (1 Pet. 2:9), many theologians have insisted that the Church is "spiritual Israel." If theologians must alter the clear references to Israel by claiming them as our own, we must wonder what the motive is in doing so, and what other doctrines have fallen victim to such "spiritual lies."

The same thing occurs when Catholic, Orthodox, and Protestant brothers and sisters teach that the Church "began at Pentecost." If this, too, were correct, how do we explain the further need for Paul, the "new creature" (Body of Christ), and the "revelation of the mystery"? Christ is to be King of the Messianic Church, but He is only referred to as the Head of the Body in Paul's writings, which are not a part of prophecy (Eph. 3:6; Eph. 5:23; Col. 1:18). The dispensation of the grace of God began with Paul, not Peter, and there was no Church preached, prior to "the revelation of the mystery," where both Jews and Gentiles were saved by grace, through faith in the death, burial, and resurrection of Jesus Christ, apart from works. That was not preached at Pentecost to the "little flock." Also, the "middle wall of partition" had not yet been "broken down" at Pentecost, as it was through Paul's gospel of grace. If it were, then the purposes of Acts 10 were unnecessary. The Body of Christ is not built upon Jesus as the Christ (Israel's Messiah); it is built upon Jesus as the Lord and Savior of the world, who is "the Head of the body."

Paul, A Wise "Masterbuilder" for the Body of Christ Reexamined

To the Body of Christ, Paul declared:

> *8 Now he that planteth and he that watereth are one: and every man shall receive his own reward according to his own labour. 9 <u>For we are labourers together with God</u>: ye are God's husbandry, ye are God's building. 10 <u>According to the grace of God which is given unto me, as a wise masterbuilder, I have laid the foundation, and another buildeth thereon.</u> But let every man take heed how he buildeth thereupon. 11 <u>For other foundation can no man lay than that is laid, which is Jesus Christ.</u>*
> *I Corinthians 3:8-11*

What did Paul mean when he stated, "I have laid the foundation, and another buildeth thereon"? Paul was called *first*, as a *pattern* (I Tim. 1:16), to lay the foundational truths for the Body of Christ, the "new creature," and we must all be very careful how we build upon these foundational truths (the gospel of the grace of God), especially as members of the Body of Christ, the Church. Unfortunately, we are using the "traditions of men" for mortar as we build the Body of Christ.

What foundational truth did Paul *first* teach these Corinthians, who became members of the Body of Christ?

> *Moreover, brethren, <u>I declare unto you the gospel which I preached unto you</u>, which also*

*ye have received, and wherein ye stand; ² By
which also ye are saved, if ye keep in memory
what I preached unto you, unless ye have
believed in vain. ³ <u>For I delivered unto you
first of all that which I also received</u>, how that
<u>Christ died for our sins</u> according to the
scriptures; ⁴ And that <u>he was buried</u>, and that
<u>he rose again the third day</u> according to the
scriptures:
I Corinthians 15:1-4*

The twelve apostles did not know the entire purpose for the
shed blood of Jesus because it had not yet been revealed to
them, even though they were witnesses to Christ's death,
burial, and resurrection (Eph. 3:5). The Catholic, Orthodox,
and many Protestant churches still do not find much favor in
believing Paul "laid the foundation" for the Church, the Body
of Christ, especially when many believers are still convinced
that the Twelve started the Body of Christ in Acts 2 at
Pentecost. Paul clearly stated, "For other foundation can no
man lay than that is laid, *which is Jesus Christ*." Paul *first*
taught the Body of Christ that Jesus was the Head of the
Church, not Peter, who is nowhere mentioned in Scripture to
hold such a role of *any* Church.

*²² And hath put all things under his feet, and
gave him to be <u>the head over all things to the
church, ²³ Which is his body</u>, the fulness of him
that filleth all in all.
Ephesians 1:22-23*

> *18 And <u>he is the head of the body, the church</u>:*
> *who is the beginning, the firstborn from the*
> *dead; that in all things he might have the*
> *preeminence. Colossians 1:18*

> *9 For in him dwelleth all the fulness of the*
> *Godhead bodily.10 <u>And ye are complete in him,</u>*
> *<u>which is the head of all principality</u>*
> *<u>and power:</u>*
> *Colossians 2:9-10*

We are made "complete in Christ" by grace, through faith, not the traditions of any church or denomination. Please examine the following verse concerning the Church as a supporter of truth:

> *15 But if I tarry long, that thou mayest know*
> *how thou oughtest to behave thyself <u>in the</u>*
> *<u>house of God, which is the church of the living</u>*
> *<u>God, the pillar and ground of the truth.</u> 16 And*
> *without controversy great is the mystery of*
> *godliness: God was manifest in the flesh,*
> *justified in the Spirit, seen of angels, preached*
> *unto the Gentiles, believed on in the world,*
> *received up into glory. I Timothy 3:15-16*

Here is the passage often cited (I Tim. 3) as proof that the Church is the *source of truth* rather than the supporter of truth (pillar and ground). Christ is the foundation and "Chief

Cornerstone," and all members of the Church are to build upon the foundation already laid for us by "the apostle to the Gentiles" who clearly stated "Be ye followers of me, even as I also am of Christ" (I Cor. 4:16; 11:1). After all, who gave the Church the truth of the gospel? Was it the Roman Catholic Church? Who is "the Word of God"? Is it any Church found within the Bible? Of course not, because Jesus is The Word (John 1:1-2), and "All *scripture* is given by inspiration of God..." (not the inspiration of any denomination)! All believers are responsible for supporting the truth given to us "by inspiration of God." Sadly, if we don't "rightly divide the word of truth," we end up with the Catholic, Orthodox, and Protestant denominations. How well have these denominations "rightly divided the word of truth"?

An Example of How Tradition Robs Us of Truth
When theologians don't "rightly divide the word of truth," they easily find escape through "spiritualizing" the scriptures to satisfy their theologies. In other words, they can make up whatever they want Scripture to mean (2 Pet. 1:20-21). Here is an example of how many take a passage and wrongly apply it to the Body of Christ.

> *42 Jesus saith unto them, Did ye never read in the scriptures, The stone which the builders rejected, the same is become the head of the corner: this is the Lord's doing, and it is marvellous in our eyes? 43 Therefore say I unto you, The kingdom of God shall be taken from you, and given to a nation bringing forth the*

> *fruits thereof. 44 And whosoever shall fall on*
> *this stone shall be broken: but on whomsoever*
> *it shall fall, it will grind him to powder. 45 And*
> *when the chief priests and Pharisees had*
> *heard his parables, they perceived that he*
> *spake of them. 46 But when they sought to lay*
> *hands on him, they feared the multitude,*
> *because they took him for a prophet.*
> *Matthew 21:42-46*

Was the "kingdom of God" taken away from *that generation* of Israelites and "given to a nation bringing forth fruits thereof"? Yes, in one sense, but ultimately, traditions have been successful in ripping Matthew 16 and 21 from Israel and handing those promises over to a predominantly Gentile Church, which is the Body of Christ (not known until Paul). Matthew 16 is only in reference to the Messianic Kingdom Church, which Jesus promised to the "little flock," which again was the Jewish remnant at Pentecost in Acts 2. It was to this "little flock" that Matthew 21:43 is referring—not the Body of Christ! After all, the Body of Christ is not a "nation," rather it consists of individual Gentiles from many different nations.

Jesus gave the parable of the "Husbandmen and the Vineyard" to the leaders seeking to seize Him at that time (Matt. 21:33-42). His statement that "the kingdom shall be taken from you, and given to a *nation* bringing forth fruits thereof" was in direct reference to these leaders who ultimately wanted to kill Him. Jesus knew of their plot; therefore, the kingdom that was promised to Israel would not go to those in *that generation* who rejected Him, but rather it would be given to those who truly worshipped Him as *the* Christ (the Messiah), and this would be the "little flock" that was in the Upper Room prior to the pouring out of the Holy Ghost at Pentecost (Luke 12:32; Acts 1:15). This "little flock" of believers were *not* those of Israel who had cried out, "Crucify Him! Crucify Him!" About 120 members of the "little flock" were soon joined with the hundreds who had seen Jesus after His resurrection (I Cor. 15:6), and on the day of Pentecost, God began to offer them the kingdom referenced in Matthew 16. Matthew 21 had nothing to do with the predominantly Gentile Church called the Body of Christ. This Church came after the Messianic Kingdom Church at Pentecost, which is the Church of Matthew 16.

Why This Matters

Christ came and preached about the promised "kingdom of heaven" to Israel, which He, John the Baptist, and the twelve apostles said was "at hand." In Luke, we also read this:

> *Then he called his twelve disciples together,*
> *and gave them power and authority <u>over all</u>*
> *<u>devils, and to cure diseases</u>. ² And he sent them*
> *to <u>preach the kingdom of God, and to heal the</u>*
> *<u>sick</u>. ³ And he said unto them, Take nothing for*
> *your journey, neither staves, nor scrip, neither*
> *bread, neither money; neither have two coats*
> *apiece. ⁴ And whatsoever house ye enter into,*
> *there abide, and thence depart. ⁵ And*
> *whosoever will not receive you, when ye go out*

> *of that city, shake off the very dust from your*
> *feet for a testimony against them. ⁶ And they*
> *departed, and went through the towns,*
> *preaching the gospel, and healing every*
> *where. Luke 9:1-6*

Is this the same gospel we are to proclaim today? Do pastors and priests have the authority to "cure diseases and heal the sick" today? If so, why are there hospitals and nursing homes? Surely there are plenty of priests and pastors in local areas to take care of such illnesses. The Twelve were clearly preaching "the gospel" in Luke 9, but were they sharing the "preaching of the cross" gospel as Paul was commissioned to do after his conversion in Acts 9? Did the gospel in Luke 9 include anything about faith in the blood (death) and resurrection of Jesus Christ for the remission of sins? If so, Luke 18, which occurred quite some time after Luke 9, still doesn't make sense.

> *³¹ Then he took unto him the twelve, and said*
> *unto them, Behold, we go up to Jerusalem, and*
> *all things that are written by the prophets*
> *concerning the Son of man shall be*
> *accomplished. ³² For he shall be delivered unto*
> *the Gentiles, and shall be mocked, and*
> *spitefully entreated, and spitted on: ³³ And they*
> *shall scourge him, and put him to death: and*
> *the third day he shall rise again. ³⁴ And they*
> *understood none of these things: and this*

*saying was hid from them, neither knew they
the things which were spoken. Luke 18:31-34*

How could the Twelve proclaim the same gospel as Paul's when they were preaching in Luke 9, especially when they didn't understand anything about the "preaching of cross" in Luke 18? It wasn't until sometime after Paul's conversion in Acts 9 that the Twelve finally understood salvation to be "by grace, through faith (in the death and resurrection), apart from works," which is all based on "faith in His blood…for the remission of sins." In other words, there is not just *one gospel* presented throughout the New Testament, as many still insist. The gospel of the kingdom and the gospel of the grace of God are *not* the same, and these passages in Luke 9 and 18 prove that. Our remission of sins comes through faith in the blood of Christ, not repentance and water baptism.

*24 Being justified freely by his grace through
the redemption that is in Christ Jesus: 25 Whom
God hath set forth to be a propitiation through
faith in his blood, to declare his righteousness
for the remission of sins that are past, through
the forbearance of God; 26 To declare, I say, at
this time his righteousness: that he might be
just, and the justifier of him which believeth in
Jesus. Romans 3:24-26*

It wasn't until *after* Pentecost (the supposed "beginning of the Church") that Christ finally appeared to Paul on the road to Damascus, calling him into a specific ministry for the

Gentiles (Acts 9:15). There was a Church already in existence before Jesus spoke to Peter in Matthew 16, and there was a Church at Jerusalem before Paul was ever converted to and by Jesus Christ. Again, Christ was a "minister of the circumcision, to confirm the promises made unto the fathers" (Rom. 15:8), which was the promise of a Messianic Kingdom that would one day come down from Heaven (Revelation 21), and Peter was told he would be given the "keys to the Kingdom." On the other hand, members of the Body of Christ (the Church) are promised a citizenship in Heaven.

If Matthew 16 and 21 are referencing the Body of Christ, where does this leave the apostles who were promised to "sit on twelve thrones, judging the twelve tribes of Israel" in the kingdom promised to Israel (Matt. 19:28)? Was Peter ever called to be the "apostle to the Gentiles" (Rom. 11:13)? Did Peter know about the Body of Christ, which was still "hid in God" before Paul's conversion? Certainly not, because Paul presented his gospel message as "the revelation of the mystery, which was kept secret since the world began." We must "rightly divide" Matthew 16 and 21, and I Corinthians 3:10-11; otherwise, we will continue this endless identity crisis.

Honestly, it is not my intention to offend my Catholic brothers and sisters, but the Catholic interpretation of Matthew 16 completely disregards the intended purpose of Christ's earthly ministry to the "lost sheep of the house of Israel," as well as the promises God made to "the fathers" in the Old Testament. The Body of Christ was never preached prior to Paul, so Matthew 16 couldn't be referencing *this*

Church. Traditions of men insist upon this interpretation, but the word of God obliterates such nonsense.

Many Protestant brethren do this as well with Matthew 21:43, when they claim the promises of God are now given over to the Church, the Body of Christ, which they insist is "spiritual Israel." When we "rightly divide the word of truth" in Matthew 16 and 21, we will not need to alter these passages from the unconditional and prophetic nature of them, which is for the promised nation of Israel, where Jesus is *the* Christ (Messiah), which Peter eloquently declared in Matthew 16:16. Again, the "Body of Christ" was still a mystery to the world during the earthly ministry of Jesus Christ, as well as the promises to and from the Old Testament prophets (Rom. 16:25; Eph. 3:1-10; Col. 1:23-27).

A Final Note about the Churches Explained in This Chapter

The Church in the wilderness, the "little flock," the Church mentioned in Matthew 16, the Church at Pentecost at Jerusalem, and the Body of Christ can be confusing when they are not "rightly divided." The Church in the wilderness was clearly Israel only. The remnant in the New Testament was called "the little flock," to whom the kingdom was promised and offered at Pentecost. This, too, was for Israel. Paul persecuted this "Church that was at Jerusalem" before he was saved and sent to "lay the foundation" for the "one new man," the Body of Christ.

Even though most believers don't seem to be aware of these Churches, they are all taught within Scripture, but unless we realize "to whom" and for "what purpose" these

Churches (assemblies) were called out, we will forever argue over which Church we are members of today, and how we can become members of it.

CHAPTER 9

The Body or the Bride?

*35 Thus saith the LORD, which giveth the sun
for a light by day, and the ordinances of the
moon and of the stars for a light by night,
which divideth the sea when the waves thereof
roar; The LORD of hosts is his name: 36 If those
ordinances depart from before me, saith
the LORD, then the seed of Israel also shall
cease from being a nation before me for ever.
37 Thus saith the LORD; If heaven above can be
measured, and the foundations of the earth
searched out beneath, I will also cast off all
the seed of Israel for all that they have done,
saith the LORD. Jeremiah 31:35-37*

*28 There is neither Jew nor Greek, there is
neither bond nor free, there is neither male nor
female: for ye are all one in Christ Jesus.
29 And if ye be Christ's, then are ye Abraham's
seed, and heirs according to the promise.
Galatians 3:28-29*

Is God Done with Israel?

Before we assume Galatians 3:29 supports the theology that the Body of Christ is somehow "spiritual Israel," we should remember that we are not a "replacement" for Israel in God's eyes, but rather we are a completely "new creature," consisting of both Jews and Gentiles (spiritually baptized into one body). All who *believe* the gospel of Jesus Christ, according to the "revelation of the mystery," have been saved by grace, through faith, and baptized into the Body of Christ—"not of works, lest any man should boast." We have a heavenly citizenship (Phil. 3:20), and the Church (the Body of Christ) is *never* found within the prophecies God addressed concerning Israel, so this is why the Body was revealed as "the mystery" after Acts 9 (following the conversion of Paul). The only way for some theologians to avoid this simple truth is for them to "replace" Israel with the Church, and this greatly impacts our salvation, walk (obedience), and destiny as believers. God's promises to Israel ("since the world began") were given to that promised seed of Abraham (through Isaac) long before the "revelation of the mystery" was ever taught to Paul by Jesus Christ. May we never forget that the Body of Christ was "chosen in Him *before* the foundation of the world" (Eph. 1:4), not like the nation of Israel, which was called out "*since* the world began" (Gen. 12:1-3; Acts 3:19-21). The Body of Christ was not taught until after Acts 9.

"The Mystery" revealed that Gentiles could now become "fellow heirs" with Jesus *apart* from Israel. It is through Israel's "fall," *not* that nation's "rising" that we have received the atonement through faith in the shed blood and resurrection of Jesus Christ, apart from works. The Body is not an extension of what God has already revealed; otherwise, we would not be called "the one new man," which was "kept secret since the world began." God was not building upon what has always been, but rather He revealed something completely new with the Body of Christ.

Gentiles, in *prophecy*, were to come to God through Israel's *rising* (Isa. 60:1-3), but under "the revelation of the *mystery*," Gentiles are "as of one(s) born out of (before) due time" (I Cor. 15:8), having received by grace *now* what Israel and future Gentiles will receive by promise after the Body of Christ is "caught up to meet the Lord in the air" (I Thes. 4:13-18). Again, this all came about because of Israel's *fall* (Rom. 11:11). Many proclaim "the mystery" as God's revelation that the Church will inherit the promises of the kingdom that God ordained for Israel; however, "the mystery" says nothing about the Church being a replacement for God's promises to Israel:

> *I say then, Hath God cast away his people?*
> *God forbid. For I also am an Israelite, of the*
> *seed of Abraham, of the tribe of Benjamin.*
> *2 God hath not cast away his people which he*
> *foreknew...25 For I would not, brethren, that ye*
> *should be ignorant of this mystery, lest ye*
> *should be wise in your own conceits; that*
> *blindness in part is happened to Israel, until*
> *the fulness of the Gentiles be come in.*
> *Romans 11:1-2 and 25*

If God were done with the nation of Israel, why would Paul focus deeply on the Israelites in Romans 9 through 11—promising that they will be saved because God's "gifts and calling are without repentance (irrevocable)"? Why would Paul remind the Roman Jews that "God hath not cast away His people, which He foreknew," if, in fact, the Church has replaced Israel? Romans 11:25 does not make sense as well, especially if God were officially done with the nation of Israel. He reminded the Israelites that "blindness in part (temporarily) is happened to Israel, *until* the fulness of the Gentiles be come in." After the Church is "caught up to meet the Lord in the air," we see God dealing with the nation of Israel once again, and the nations will yet be blessed through the seed of Abraham (Gen. 22:18). Since the "revelation of the mystery," individual Jews and Gentiles are able to be saved into one Body; however, in the "ages to come," God will once again complete His promises to the *nation* of Israel, along with the *nations* that will be blessed through Israel (Gen. 12:1-3; 22:18; Isa. 49:6; 60:1-3; Zech. 8:12-13; Rom. 15:8-12; Gal. 3:8-9). The "revelation of the mystery" teaches us that it is through Israel's *fall* that we have been "blessed with all spiritual blessings" in Christ.

Paul specifically reminded the Israelites in Romans 11:26-29 that "all Israel shall be saved...for this in *My* covenant unto them, when I shall take away their sins," and yes, this would include the sin of their rebellion against their own Messiah (Rom. 11:26-27). In "the ages to come," why would God bother to "take away their sins" if He were finished with that nation forever? Why call a remnant from the twelve tribes of Israel in Revelation 7 if God replaced that nation with the Church?

Since the "preaching of the cross," all who *believe* are now justified (declared righteous) in the sight of God. Thankfully, God did not impute the world's sins unto us when He placed them *all* on Christ (2 Cor. 5:19), and this is how God is able to forgive "all trespasses," which He has done, especially for those who believe the gospel (Col. 2:13-15). However, has Israel reconciled itself to God so they may receive the spiritual blessings of the New Covenant (Testament)? Has the Gentile world all been saved through belief in the finished work of Jesus Christ? Of course not; it only applies to those who believe the gospel, which is explained in the following passages:

> *19 To wit, that God was in Christ, reconciling*
> *the world unto himself, not imputing their*
> *trespasses unto them; and hath committed unto*
> *us the word of reconciliation.*
> *2 Corinthians 5:19*

> *10 For therefore we both labour and suffer*
> *reproach, because we trust in the living God,*
> *who is the Saviour of all men, specially of*
> *those that believe. I Tmothy 4:10*

After the Body of Christ is "caught up to meet the Lord in the air" (perhaps soon), God will then fulfill His promises to Israel through the "remnant" elected by grace (Rom. 11:5-6;

Rev. 7:1-8). Again, this is because God's promises to Israel are irrevocable (Rom. 11:29).

> *⁵ Even so then at this present time also there is a remnant according to the election of grace. ⁶ And if by grace, then is it no more of works: otherwise grace is no more grace. But if it be of works, then it is no more grace: otherwise work is no more work. Romans 11:5-6*

> *²⁵ For I would not, brethren, that ye should be ignorant of this mystery, lest ye should be wise in your own conceits; that blindness in part is happened to Israel, until the fulness of the Gentiles be come in. ²⁶ And so all Israel shall be saved: as it is written, There shall come out of Sion the Deliverer, and shall turn away ungodliness from Jacob: ²⁷ For this is my covenant unto them, when I shall take away their sins. ²⁸ As concerning the gospel, they are enemies for your sakes: but as touching the election, they are beloved for the father's sakes. ²⁹ For the gifts and calling of God are without repentance. Romans 11:25-29*

> *And after these things I saw four angels standing on the four corners of the earth, holding the four winds of the earth, that the wind should not blow on the earth, nor on the sea, nor on any tree. ² And I saw another angel*

ascending from the east, having the seal of the living God: and he cried with a loud voice to the four angels, to whom it was given to hurt the earth and the sea, ³ Saying, Hurt not the earth, neither the sea, nor the trees, till we have sealed the servants of our God in their foreheads. ⁴ <u>And I heard the number of them which were sealed: and there were sealed an hundred and forty and four thousand of all the tribes of the children of Israel.</u>
Revelation 7:1-4

As I have stated at different times, if God were officially done with Israel forever, it seems strange that He would seal 144,000 Jews from the twelve tribes of Isreal for the purpose of evangelizing the world during the Tribulation, which is yet future. We also know that the "gospel of the kingdom" will be proclaimed at that time as well, and then the "end shall come" (Matt. 24:14).

On the other hand, the so-called Rapture is exclusively for the Body of Christ (who are currently under God's grace), but soon this grace will give way to God's wrath and judgment, which will be poured out upon this Christ-rejecting world. The Church, however, has been "saved from wrath through Him" (Rom. 5:9). God offers salvation "freely (at no cost to you) by His grace," but sadly, there are still millions who will reject God's gift of salvation. No one will ever go to Hell without having first been loved by God, who sent Jesus Christ to die in their place.

> *3 For this is good and acceptable in the sight*
> *of God our Saviour; 4 Who will have all men to*
> *be saved, and to come unto the knowledge of*
> *the truth. 1 Timothy 2:3-4*

A Few Questions to Consider

There are a couple questions we should consider before we insist the Church has replaced God's promises to Israel: (1) If the Church is supposed to go through the Tribulation, and there is currently no distinction between Jews and Gentiles within the Church, why would God specifically call out a remnant from the twelve tribes of Israel at that future time, especially if He no longer has an eternal purpose for Israel as a nation (Rev. 7:5-8)? (2) If the Church must "endure to the end" of the Tribulation to be saved, why *wouldn't* Jesus instruct Paul (in his epistles) to prepare the Church for this time of God's wrath? (3) Was Paul somehow giving false hope when he reassured believers that they would be "saved from wrath through Him" (Rom. 5:8-11)? We should also consider the fact that our sins were paid for *completely* on the cross, and it is our Savior who endured the penalty of death for our sins—not us (Rom. 6:23). Faith in His shed blood is sufficient to save us, and this is why "God has not appointed us to wrath" (I Thes. 5:9).

As for the passage from Jeremiah 31, which was quoted in the opening words of this chapter, the prophet stated that if the sun, moon, and the stars cease to give their light, Israel will cease to be a nation before God forever. This is a promise from God to Israel, and yet many denominations teach that God has indeed broken His prophetic, unconditional promises to that nation by replacing Israel with the Church, the Body of Christ. There is nothing "spiritual" about this type of teaching, which comes from theologians who have failed to "rightly divide the word of truth." Have the sun, moon, and stars ceased to give their light? Of course not, so Israel has not ceased to be a nation before God, even though they are temporarily blinded by their unbelief.

Covenant theologians insist they do not adhere to Replacement Theology, and yet these same pastors claim that God's promises to Israel have been given over to the Church for their fulfillment, especially when they claim that "Israel" now means "all God's people." This is also why some of these same theologians have removed the literal meanings of God's promises by over-spiritualizing them into something God never intended—claiming the "kingdom is only in the hearts of believers." If God did, in fact, give His promises to Israel over to the Church, should we not expect a piece of real estate for our eternal home between the Nile and Euphrates rivers (Gen. 15:18)? This is why the theology of many denominations forces them to change the nation of Israel (in both the Old and New Testaments) to mean "all God's people," calling us what we now know as "spiritual Israel." If the Church is the "true Israel" (or "spiritual Israel"), then we have no choice but to irradicate the teachings of a *literal* fulfillment of the Abrahamic and Davidic covenants given to and through Abraham's seed (Israel).

Is It *Really* Spiritual Maturity to Believe the Church is "Spiritual Israel"?

In previous chapters, I have presented many passages from Scripture to show how Israel, as a "chosen nation," is both the genealogical descendants of Abraham through Isaac, as well as the Bride to whom God was "married" and will be again (Jer. 3:8,14; 31:32; Isa. 54:5; Hosea 2; Eze. 16; Rev. 21). If Replacement Theology were biblical, we must somehow "spiritualize" the people John referenced as the "twelve tribes" in Revelation 7. Are there *really* "twelve tribes" in the Body of Christ? Even after Israel's rejections of the Messiah and Kingdom (Acts 7), Peter still called them "a chosen race, a royal priesthood" in I Peter 2:9-10. Paul never refers to the Body as such.

Many believers in the Body of Christ insist Peter was writing to them; however, I Peter 1:1-5 is clear *to whom* Peter was addressing. Besides, Peter also agreed to continue his ministry with the "circumcision," not the "uncircumcision" (Gal. 2:7-9). Acts 28:28 shows that Paul later confined his ministry to the "uncircumcision." Yes, there are many blessed truths within the "General Epistles" of James, Peter, and John that are for our understanding, but we must be careful not to "frustrate grace" (Gal. 2:21) when applying them (James 2:21-24; 2 Pet. 3:15-17; I John 3:24; 5:2-3).

Our Walk as Believers Today

Our walk as believers today is greatly impacted when we do *not* recognize the differences between the Body of Christ and God's Bride (Israel). We battle over how to be saved, how to be obedient to God's word in our daily lives, and our eventual destiny as believers. If 2 Timothy 2:15 is applied during our reading of Scripture, Paul is clear to the Body of Christ (mainly Gentiles) that salvation is "not of works," even though James—as the representative of the Jews in the Church at Jerusalem—was keeping the Law (James 2:10; 21-24). James insisted his audience was "the strangers (from the twelve tribes) scattered abroad," and he was never called to be "the apostle to the Gentiles." Under Paul's ministry, Gentiles did (do) not need to convert to Judaism (especially circumcision) to be saved, and James and Peter confirmed this in Acts 15.

Many theologians tend to forget that there were still many "kingdom saints" (the Israel of God) in existence at the same time Paul wrote his epistles, so the "General Epistles" of James, Peter, and John (and Jude) continued to address these saints. They did, after all, give Paul and Barnabas the "right hands of fellowship." Remember, James, Peter, and John all agreed to preach to the "circumcision, while Paul and Barnabas agreed to go to the "uncircumcision" (in Galatians 2:7-9). We must "rightly divide the word of truth" before applying various passages that may or may not be written to the Body of Christ, especially for our obedience.

What We Must "Rightly Divide" as the Body of Christ (Not the Bride)

To the Jews in Acts 2, Peter stated the following about salvation:

> *36 Therefore let all the house of Israel know*
> *assuredly, that God hath made the same Jesus,*

whom ye have crucified, both Lord and Christ.
37 Now when they heard this, they were pricked
in their heart, and said unto Peter and to the
rest of the apostles, Men and brethren, what
shall we do? 38 Then Peter said unto them,
<u>Repent, and be baptized every one of you in</u>
<u>the name of Jesus Christ for the remission of</u>
<u>sins</u>, and ye shall receive the gift of the Holy
Ghost. Acts 2:36-38

To the Body of Christ, Paul stated (concerning salvation):

3 <u>For I delivered unto you first of all that which</u>
<u>I also received</u>, how that <u>Christ died for our</u>
<u>sins</u> according to the scriptures; 4 And that <u>he</u>
<u>was buried</u>, and that <u>he rose again</u> the third
day according to the scriptures:
I Corinthians 15:3-4

24 <u>Being justified freely by his grace through</u>
<u>the redemption that is in Christ Jesus</u>: 25 Whom
God hath set forth to be a propitiation <u>through</u>
<u>faith in his blood, to declare his righteousness</u>
<u>for the remission of sins</u> that are past, through
the forbearance of God; 26 To declare, I say, at
this time his righteousness: that he might be
just, and <u>the justifier of him which believeth in</u>
<u>Jesus</u>. Romans 3:24-26

Concerning obedience, the Jews were still commanded by James the following:

21 Was not Abraham our father justified by works, when he had offered Isaac his son upon the altar? 22 Seest thou how faith wrought with his works, and by works was faith made perfect? 23 And the scripture was fulfilled which saith, Abraham believed God, and it was imputed unto him for righteousness: and he was called the Friend of God. 24 <u>Ye see then how that by works a man is justified, and not by faith only.</u> James 2:21-24

To the Jews and proselytes at Antioch (and also Rome), Paul declared:

38 Be it known unto you therefore, men and brethren, that through this man is preached unto you the forgiveness of sins: 39 <u>And by him all that believe are justified from all things, from which ye could not be justified by the law of Moses.</u> Acts 13:38-39

What shall we say then that Abraham our father, as pertaining to the flesh, hath found? 2 For if Abraham were justified by works, he hath whereof to glory; but not before God. 3 For what saith the scripture? Abraham believed God, and it was counted unto him for righteousness. 4 Now to him that worketh is the

*reward not reckoned of grace, but of debt.
⁵ But to him that worketh not, but believeth on
him that justifieth the ungodly, his faith is
counted for righteousness. Romans 4:1-5*

What about our destinies between the Bride (Israel) and the Body of Christ? Are they the same in eternity?

*¹⁸ In the same day the LORD made a covenant
with Abram, saying, Unto thy seed have I
given this land, from the river of Egypt unto
the great river, the river Euphrates:
Genesis 15:18*

*⁶ And I will make thee exceeding fruitful, and I
will make nations of thee, and kings shall
come out of thee. ⁷ And I will establish my
covenant between me and thee and thy seed
after thee in their generations for an
everlasting covenant, to be a God unto thee,
and to thy seed after thee. ⁸ And I will give
unto thee, and to thy seed after thee, the land
wherein thou art a stranger, all the land of
Canaan, for an everlasting possession; and I
will be their God. Genesis 17:6-8*

*¹⁴ He is the LORD our God; his judgments are
in all the earth. ¹⁵ Be ye mindful always of his
covenant; the word which he commanded to a
thousand generations; ¹⁶ Even of the covenant*

> *which he made with Abraham, and of his oath*
> *unto Isaac;* [17] *And hath confirmed the same to*
> *Jacob for a law, and to Israel for an*
> *everlasting covenant,* [18] *Saying, Unto thee will*
> *I give the land of Canaan, the lot of your*
> *inheritance; I Chronicles 16:14-18*

These are just a few of the promises that Jesus Christ came into the world to fulfill for "the lost sheep of the house of Israel" (Rom. 15:8).

Israel is the Bride, according to the following passages:

> [19] *And I will betroth thee unto me for ever; yea,*
> *I will betroth thee unto me in righteousness,*
> *and in judgment, and in lovingkindness, and in*
> *mercies.* [20] *I will even betroth thee unto me in*
> *faithfulness: and thou shalt know the LORD.*
> *Hosea 2:19-20*

> [14] *Turn, O backsliding children, saith*
> *the LORD; for I am married unto you: and I*
> *will take you one of a city, and two of a family,*
> *and I will bring you to Zion:*
> *Jeremiah 3:14*

> *And I saw a new heaven and a new earth: for*
> *the first heaven and the first earth were passed*
> *away; and there was no more sea.* [2] *And I John*
> *saw the holy city, new Jerusalem, coming*

down from God out of heaven, prepared as a
bride adorned for her husband.
Revelation 21:1-2

To the Body of Christ, however, Jesus gave these promises:

3 Blessed be the God and Father of our Lord
Jesus Christ, who hath blessed us with all
spiritual blessings in heavenly places in
Christ: Ephesians 1:3

6 And hath raised us up together, and made us
sit together in heavenly places in Christ Jesus:
7 That in the ages to come he might shew the
exceeding riches of his grace in his kindness
toward us through Christ Jesus.
Ephesians 2:6-7

20 For our conversation is in heaven; from
whence also we look for the Saviour, the Lord
Jesus Christ: 21 Who shall change our vile
body, that it may be fashioned like unto his
glorious body, according to the working
whereby he is able even to subdue all things
unto himself.
Philippians 3:20-21

Every verse Jesus commanded *is truth*, but is every truth in the Bible written to the same audience? If I change the word

"Israel" to mean "all the people of God," this *really* confuses these previous passages in this section of the chapter. Will the Body of Christ inherit the Earth, or does it currently possess a citizenship in Heaven? Yes, some *individual* Jews will inherit their heavenly citizenship as members of the Body of Christ, but the *nation* of Israel will "inherit the Earth" (Matt.5:5).

In all the previous verses about salvation, our obedience, and our destiny, we must "rightly divide" or we will continue to confuse the salvation message, not know whether our faith requires works of obedience for justification, whether we are to "keep the commandments," or whether will we inherit the Earth or have a citizenship in Heaven. This is what happens when we don't distinguish between the messages to both the Body of Christ and the Bride of Christ.

The Purpose of Galatians 3

The reason why the letter to the Galatians was written was due to the Judaizers who had insisted that the Gentile converts (under Paul's ministry) were to be circumcised under the ordinance of the Law. Paul gave no such command to Gentiles, especially in the churches of Galatia, nor did James and Peter (in Acts 15) command Gentiles to be obedient to the Law of Moses, especially after Paul had shared with them even more about the "revelation of the mystery," which he had been preaching among the Gentiles for approximately 15 years at the time Acts 15 occurred (Gal. 2:1-6).

Paul and Barnabas went to Jerusalem to help resolve the matter over the Law of Moses and Gentiles. Since Paul had also revealed the "preaching of the cross" to these "pillars" of the Church at Jerusalem (Galatians 2), Peter eventually realized that the Jews could be saved by faith, "even as they" (the Gentiles). This means that Peter was not fully aware of this prior to the revelation given to him by Paul, who received it by revelation of Jesus Christ (Gal. 1:11-12). Peter finally recognized that neither Jew nor Gentile could live by the Law, especially when Paul revealed that "Christ is an end of the Law… to everyone that believes" (Rom. 10:4). This does not mean the apostles were told about justification apart from the Law in Matthew 28 or Acts 2. In fact, Peter (in Acts 10:28) was still under the Law at that time (some 8-10 years *after* Pentecost). Galatians 3 should have put an end to any "works-based" religious practices to maintain salvation, but has it?

The New Creature

The Church consists of an *invisible* membership of believers who trust that Jesus died for them and rose again, and by attaching "Israel" to the term "spiritual Israel," this ultimately aligns the Church with a particular nation and people, which is not what Paul taught concerning the Church being "neither Jew nor Gentile." The Body of Christ is more "catholic" than any so-called denomination in Christendom today (calling itself Catholic) because of its inclusivity to anyone who believes the gospel Paul was sent—by Christ—to preach. Sure, the Body of Christ consists of individual Jews and Gentiles, bond and free, males and females, but God has made us all one "in Christ," with no distinctions, especially in the context of the following verses:

> *4 There is one body, and one Spirit, even as ye*
> *are called in one hope of your calling; 5 One*

Lord, one faith, one baptism, ⁶ One God and
Father of all, who is above all, and through
all, and in you all.
Ephesians 4:4-6

On the other hand, in many denominations (which combine faith, sacraments, and traditions), there are often several requirements for a person to become a member of their churches. For some denominations, water baptism is their "entrance" into that church's membership, as well as the Body of Christ; however, in the Body of Christ, our baptism is a work of God, not humans, which is accomplished *by* one Spirit, baptizing us into one body—not baptizing us into "one denomination" (I Cor. 12:13; Col. 2:11-12). We know there is "only one Mediator (Jesus Christ) between God and man" (I Tim. 2:5), but there are still some denominations that force themselves also into the role as a mediator. Such arrogance!

As mentioned, anyone who believes Jesus died for them (to pay for their personal sins), and rose again (for their justification), they are saved and become a member of the *invisible* Body of Christ—the "universal (catholic) Church." Under the "dispensation of the grace of God," no church should demand a work to be performed by any believer *for salvation* (or Church membership into the one Body). We are saved by grace, through faith in Christ's *completed* work, apart from works we might perform in an attempt to earn God's favor. Grace is the unmerited favor of God, and it is given freely (at no cost to us). It is through faith (taking God at His word) that salvation is realized by the sinner. After being baptized *by* one Spirit, placing believers into one body, it is, however, our "reasonable service" to present our bodies as "a living sacrifice" (Rom. 12:1-2). The following passages reflect these points:

12 For there is no difference between the Jew and the Greek: for the same Lord over all is rich unto all that call upon him. 13 For whosoever shall call upon the name of the Lord shall be saved. 14 How then shall they call on him in whom they have not believed? and how shall they believe in him of whom they have not heard? and how shall they hear without a preacher? 15 And how shall they preach, except they be sent? as it is written, How beautiful are the feet of them that preach the gospel of peace, and bring glad tidings of good things! 16 But they have not all obeyed the gospel. For Esaias saith, Lord, who hath believed our report? 17 So then faith cometh by hearing, and hearing by the word of God.
Romans 10:12-17

13 In whom ye also trusted, after that ye heard the word of truth, the gospel of your salvation: in whom also after that ye believed, ye were sealed with that holy Spirit of promise, 14 Which is the earnest of our inheritance until the redemption of the purchased possession, unto the praise of his glory.
Ephesians 1:13-14

8 For by grace are ye saved through faith; and
that not of yourselves: it is the gift of God:
9 Not of works, lest any man should boast.
10 For we are his workmanship, created in
Christ Jesus unto good works, which God hath
before ordained that <u>we should walk in them</u>.
Ephesians 2:8-10

4 Now to him that worketh is the reward not
reckoned of grace, but of debt. 5 <u>But to him</u>
<u>that worketh not</u>, but believeth on him that
justifieth the ungodly, <u>his faith is counted for</u>
<u>righteousness.</u> Romans 4:4-5

26 For ye are all the children of God <u>by faith in</u>
<u>Christ Jesus</u>. 27 For as many of you as have
been baptized into Christ have put on Christ.
28 There is neither Jew nor Greek, there is
neither bond nor free, there is neither male nor
female: for ye are all one in Christ Jesus.
29 <u>And if ye be Christ's, then are ye Abraham's</u>
<u>seed, and heirs according to the promise.</u>
Galatians 3:26-29

Again, Galatians 3 was written specifically to show how justification (declaring someone righteous in the sight of God) is strictly by grace, through faith, and not of works (especially of the Law, which Christ fulfilled). Paul uses Abraham to show how he was "justified by faith" over 400 years *before* the Law of Moses ever existed. Abraham, being a Gentile, "believed God, and it was counted unto him for righteousness," and in like manner, Gentiles (under the gospel of the grace of God) are declared "righteous" *through* faith without the Law as well. So, since a believer becomes a "son of Abraham" (who was the *father of faith*), would this not make the believer a "spiritual Gentile," especially since Abraham was justified by faith as a Gentile? Remember, Galatians 3 was Paul's rebuttal to the Judaizers who insisted that Gentiles could not be justified without the Law, but before we assume Abraham was justified by faith in the shed blood of Jesus Christ, like we are today, we must consider that Abraham knew nothing about "the revelation of the mystery, which was kept secret since the world began." Abraham simply "believed God (what He said), and it was counted unto his for righteousness." We must do the same.

Many believers attempt to argue against the writings of Paul (especially in Galatians 3) by insisting that since Jesus said to "keep the commandments" (Matt. 28:16-20; John 14:15), we should do the same. However, these same believers also forget that Jesus taught Paul "by direct revelation" (Gal. 1:11-12), and He never instructed Paul to teach the Gentiles that they "were under the law" (Acts 15; Rom. 6:14). This is why we must "rightly divide the word of truth" so we can determine *what* Jesus said, *to whom* He said it, and *at what time* Jesus taught His words. Yes, Jesus did teach "the circumcision" to "keep the commandments," especially since He was "made of a woman, made under the Law" (Gal. 4:4), but Paul was clear when he stated, "Therefore, we conclude that a man is justified by faith, without the deeds of the Law" (Rom. 3:28). Such a revelation was "not made known unto the sons of men" until after Paul was saved in Acts 9. The Bible does not contradict itself; it compliments itself when it is "rightly divided."

Is the Body of Christ the Only Path for Fulfillment of God's Promises?

It is deceptive on the part of theologians who still insist the Church (the Body of Christ) is the *only* path to the fulfillment of God's promises in the Old Testament, the "gospels," and the early part of Acts (when the kingdom was being offered to Israel). This concept of "spiritual Israel" is closely tied to Replacement Theology, which seems to have been conveniently invented to explain away God's *unfulfilled* promises to the nation of Israel after the destruction of Jerusalem in AD 70. The early Church Fathers did not faithfully consider the "dispensation of the grace of God," which was "kept secret since the world began." After all, "the mystery" is still a mystery today for millions of believers, and that is the fault of many theologians within the Body of Christ. Sure, many believe dispensationalism was recently invented, but why did Paul teach the "dispensation of the grace of God, 2,000 years ago? Just as Martin Luther revived "justification by faith," other theologians rediscovered the content I have presented throughout this book, which is supported from Paul's epistles long before Catholic, Orthodox, and Protestant denominations came into existence.

This also proves the Church is *not* the source of truth, but rather we are to be the protectors of it (from "right division" of the word of God). If the Catholic Church is the "source of truth," as it claims, then it should be proclaiming "the dispensation of the grace of God" and "rightly dividing the word of truth." Most believers in various denominations have never heard of either truth from God's word, and that would include believers in the thousands of Catholic, Orthodox, and Protestant churches scattered throughout the world. The only consistent thing about Church history is that it hasn't always been consistent! Since God has not fulfilled (yet) His promises to Israel concerning the Millennial Kingdom, the early Church Fathers appear to have assumed He "replaced" Israel with the Church, and therefore, the Body of Christ was eventually declared as "spiritual Israel." One simple error in not applying 2 Timothy 2:15 has changed the entire theology of the Body of Christ, which has led to our identity crisis today. This is not God's will; He desires unity, and the Church is failing miserably to bring that about. I ask: Is it possible that what Jesus said to the Pharisees in John 8:44 could also apply to some religious teachers today?

> *[44] Ye are of your father the devil, and the lusts of your father ye will do. He was a murderer from the beginning, and abode not in the truth, because there is no truth in him. When he speaketh a lie, he speaketh of his own: for he is a liar, and the father of it. John 8:44*

So, Is the Body of Christ the *True Israel* in the Bible?

By teaching that the Church is the only "true Israel," this allows theologians to spiritualize many passages to justify this claim (Rom. 2:28-29; Rom. 9:6-7; Gal. 3:28-29; Gal. 6:16). Sadly, it only proves their ignorance regarding "rightly dividing the word of truth." The doctrine of the Church being "spiritual Israel" is *not* biblical; however, it has become the only well-known alternative explanation for many theologians who insist God is using the Church to fulfill His future and unconditional promises to Israel. If God intended to give all of Israel's blessings over to the Church forever, He would not have declared (through Jeremiah) that if the sun, moon, and stars ceased to give their light, Israel would cease to be a nation before Him "forever." Satan's aim has been the destruction of Israel, and yes, he can "transform himself into an angel of light" (2 Cor. 11:14), which means he is fully capable of using certain theologies to accomplish this. Ephesians 6:17 teaches that "the sword of the Spirit" is the word of God, but when the word of God is not "rightly divided," it can be used to kill the unity God intended for the Body of Christ. Remember, in the "last days," there will be "a form of godliness," but many will "deny the power" (the might, the truth, and the ability) to support it. Replacement Theology eliminates God's promises to the nation of Israel, which implies that He could also eliminate His promises to the Church, especially with salvation. If you are a believer who fears the loss of salvation, then you are trusting more in the sufficiency of yourself than the sufficiency of the blood of Christ to save all who believe, including yourself.

The Body of Christ has been given the *spiritual blessings* of God *by grace*, and we are blessed *apart* from Israel, not *through* Israel.

> *[11] I say then, Have they stumbled that they*
> *should fall? God forbid: but rather through*

their fall salvation is come unto the Gentiles, for to provoke them to jealousy. [12] Now if the fall of them be the riches of the world, and the diminishing of them the riches of the Gentiles; how much more their fulness? [13] For I speak to you Gentiles, inasmuch as I am the apostle of the Gentiles, I magnify mine office: [14] If by any means I may provoke to emulation them which are my flesh, and might save some of them. [15] For if the casting away of them be the reconciling of the world, <u>what shall the receiving of them be, but life from the dead?</u>
Romans 11:11-15

[25] For I would not, brethren, that ye should be ignorant of this mystery, lest ye should be wise in your own conceits; that blindness in part is happened to Israel, until the fulness of the Gentiles be come in. [26] And so all Israel shall be saved: as it is written, There shall come out of Sion the Deliverer, and shall turn away ungodliness from Jacob: [27] For this is my covenant unto them, when I shall take away their sins. [28] As concerning the gospel, they are enemies for your sakes: but as touching the election, they are beloved for the father's sakes. [29] For the gifts and calling of God are without repentance.
Romans 11:25-29

God is using the Body of Christ, the Church, to show Israel the richness of His spiritual blessings (to provoke them to jealousy), and He promised these spiritual blessings to Israel in Jeremiah 31:31-37. He obviously didn't need the Church when He made the New Covenant with Israel in Jeremiah 31, nor does He need the Church to fulfill any of the unconditional promises He made with Israel in the Old Testament. Remember, the Church (the Body of Christ) was "kept secret since the world began." In other words, God made His unconditional covenants with Israel long before the Body of Christ was known, and He can accomplish His promises to Israel without the Church even after it was revealed to Paul. We are a "heavenly people"; Israel is "earthly."

Since the time of Paul's direct teachings, we are to obey the following:

8 Unto me, who am less than the least of all saints, is this grace given, that I should preach among the Gentiles the unsearchable riches of Christ; 9 And to make all men see what is the fellowship of the mystery, which from the beginning of the world hath been hid in God, who created all things by Jesus Christ: 10 To the intent that now unto the principalities and powers in heavenly places might be known by the church the manifold wisdom of God, 11 According to the eternal purpose which he purposed in Christ Jesus our Lord: 12 In whom

> *we have boldness and access with confidence*
> *by the faith of him.*
> *Ephesians 3:8-12*

The Body of Christ is not the "true Israel" that it manifested in many traditions today, but rather we are the "fulness of Him that filleth all in all" as the "new creature" (Eph. 1:22-23).

Abraham's Seed and the Body of Christ

In Galatians 3:29, Paul stated that we are "Abraham's seed," and "heirs according to the promise," not because we have become the "Israel of God," or "spiritual Israel," but rather we have become members of Christ's Body, the Church, to whom Paul declared:

> *22 But the scripture hath concluded all under*
> *sin, that the promise by faith of Jesus Christ*
> *might be given to them that believe.*
> *Galatians 3:22*

All things are complete in and through Christ (including the Old and New covenants), and even though the Law condemned the world, all who trust in the faithfulness of Christ are made "complete in Him" (Col. 2:10). It was the "letter of the Law" that condemned the world, but it was also through the shed "blood of the new testament (covenant)" that salvation for all can be freely given to those who believe in the completed work of Christ for them (death, burial, and resurrection). Paul (not Peter) stated the following:

¹⁰ For therefore we both labour and suffer reproach, because we trust in the living God, who is the Saviour of all men, <u>specially of those that believe</u>. I Timothy 4:10

²¹ For after that in the wisdom of God the world by wisdom knew not God, it pleased God by the foolishness of preaching <u>to save them that believe</u>. I Corinthians 1:21

³ Forasmuch as ye are manifestly declared to be the epistle of Christ ministered by us, <u>written not with ink, but with the Spirit of the living God; not in tables of stone, but in fleshy tables of the heart</u>. ⁴ And such trust have we through Christ to God-ward: ⁵ Not that we are sufficient of ourselves to think any thing as of ourselves; but our sufficiency is of God; ⁶ <u>Who also hath made us able ministers of the new testament; not of the letter, but of the spirit: for the letter killeth, but the spirit giveth life.</u>
2 Corinthians 3:3-6

We are only the "seed of Abraham" because we are in Christ, and Christ is the ultimate Seed of Abraham (Gal. 3:16). This blessing comes to us now by grace, but the nations are promised to be blessed through the regenerated Israel in the future, and this is given by promise to Abraham. Remember, we, the Body of Christ, are "as of ones born out of due time" (I Cor. 15:8). God intends to fulfill His promises to Israel because He is always faithful to His word. Would He still be God if He wasn't faithful to His promises? The concept of the Church being "spiritual Israel" completely undermines God's promises—all for the sake of a theology that is, at best, only implied in the Scripture.

No one in the Old Testament ever heard of the Church, the Body of Christ, nor did they know about the "revelation of the mystery" because it was "kept secret since the world began." Through the "preaching of the cross," which is based upon the shedding of the blood of the new covenant, Paul was made an "able minister of the new testament (covenant)," and Christ's blood is the major focus of the gospel of the grace of God, not the Great Commission, which teaches nothing about salvation being "by grace, through faith in His shed blood and resurrection, apart from works (or Israel)". Jesus *did not* teach the apostles (in Matthew 28:16-20) to "Go ye into all the world and preach salvation by grace, through faith in My blood and the resurrection," nor did He teach them that "all who believe are justified from all things from which you could not be justified by the Law of Moses" (Acts 13:38-39; Eph. 2:8-9). In fact, Jesus told them to go into all the world and preach water baptism and the observance of all that He had commanded, which would have included "keep the commandments." The Great Commission and the gospel of the grace of God have the same Jesus, but they do not contain the same commands for salvation, our walk, and our eternal destiny.

As I have mentioned, the Church consists of a "new" and invisible "creature" made up of anyone who has placed their faith in the shed blood and resurrection of Jesus Christ. There are no Catholic, Orthodox, or Protestant denominations in the Bible (nor will there be any denominations in Heaven), even though religionists insist their denomination is the "one true Church." Remember, in the Body of Christ, there is neither Jew nor Gentile, only the "new creature." The "new creature" is the Church, the Body of Christ—not some nonbiblical teaching ("spiritual Israel') that insists the Church is the fulfillment of God's Old and New Testament promises that He once gave to the nation of Israel (Rom. 15:8). Most theologians are trying to fill a kingdom for which it was never promised to them in the first place. The Body of Christ was yet a mystery when God gave those promises to Israel, so it is impossible for us to be "spiritual Israel," especially since the Messianic Kingdom was never promised to us.

Again, the Body of Christ was hidden until Paul, so there is no way God intended the word "Israel" to mean "all the people of God" at a time when Gentiles had been "given over to a reprobate mind" (Rom. 1:28), and they were "aliens from the commonwealth of Israel, strangers from the covenants of promise, and having no hope" (Eph. 2:11-12). Honestly, how could "Israel" mean "all the people of God" when the only people of God were the descendants of Abraham's physical seed? The only Israel in the Bible was the Israel God established through the lineage of Isaac and Jacob. We are the Body of Christ—not Israel; otherwise, Christ would have to be called "spiritual Israel" as well, because we are "in Him." So, who then will The Lamb marry in Revelation 21? Will He be marrying Himself? This may seem irrational, but no more irrational than calling the Body of Christ "spiritual Israel."

Are Members of the Church the *Real* Jews?

I need to explore a few of the passages often used by some believers to justify the theology that the Church, the Body of Christ, is the "*true Israel* (Jews)" or "spiritual Israel." One such passage is found in Romans 2. After Romans 1 declared that God "gave them (Gentile world) over to a reprobate mind" because they refused to "retain God in their knowledge," Paul set his sights on the "religious" man (the Jew) who insisted his works of the Law would justify him before God. Remember, Galatians 3 clearly taught that Gentiles are "sons of Abraham" by faith, not the Law, which did not exist at the time Abraham was justified and later circumcised (about 15 years later) after "he believed God, and it was counted unto him as righteousness" (Gen. 15:6). How can we be "spiritual Israel" and "sons of Abraham" at the same time, especially since there was no Israel at the time Abraham was called to be "the father of many nations"? Are we *really* the "true Jews" as many claim?

Note the following passage:

> *24 For the name of God is blasphemed <u>among the Gentiles through you [Jews]</u>, as it is written. 25 For circumcision verily profiteth, if thou keep the law: but if thou be <u>a breaker of the law, thy circumcision is made uncircumcision</u>. 26 Therefore if the uncircumcision keep the righteousness of the law, <u>shall not his uncircumcision be counted for circumcision?</u> 27 And shall not uncircumcision which is by nature, if it fulfil*

the law, judge thee, who by the letter and
circumcision dost transgress the law? ²⁸ <u>*For he*</u>
<u>*is not a Jew, which is one outwardly; neither is*</u>
<u>*that circumcision, which is outward in the*</u>
<u>*flesh:*</u> ²⁹ <u>*But he is a Jew [right with God],*</u>
<u>*which is one inwardly; and circumcision is*</u>
<u>*that of the heart, in the spirit, and not in the*</u>
<u>*letter;*</u> *whose praise is not of men, but of God.*
Romans 2:24-29 (brackets by author)

I have often marveled at how anyone could somehow use this passage to justify the theology that the Church is "spiritual Israel," especially when it was referencing *real* Israelites. Paul was addressing the "religious Jew" who believed his "circumcision" and birth made him "right with God," even though he sought to continually break the Law of Moses. Paul restated this in Romans 10:

³ *For they being ignorant of God's*
righteousness, and <u>*going about to establish*</u>
<u>*their own righteousness,*</u> *have not submitted*
themselves unto the righteousness of God.
⁴ *For Christ is the end of the law for*
righteousness to every one that believeth.
Romans 10:3-4

This is why Paul stated in Romans 2:24, "For the name of God is blasphemed among the Gentiles through *you* (Jews), as it is written." This clearly indicated "to whom" Paul was addressing: the Israelites. Many religious Jews felt they were "right with God" through their "circumcision," but Paul reminded them that when they broke the Law, they became just as the "uncircumcision" (Gentiles). Paul was not stating that believing Gentiles were "true Jews" because they attempted to follow the laws of God in their conscience (by nature), rather Paul was setting up the Jews and Gentiles at Rome for the following truths:

> *9 What then? are we better than they? No, in*
> *no wise: for we have before proved both Jews*
> *and Gentiles, that they are all under sin...*
> *19 Now we know that what things soever the*
> *law saith, it saith to them who are under the*
> *law: that every mouth may be stopped, and all*
> *the world may become guilty before God.*
> *20 Therefore by the deeds of the law there shall*
> *no flesh be justified in his sight: for by the law*
> *is the knowledge of sin. Romans 3:9 and 19-20*

Paul finally revealed the purpose of the Law, which was to point to the need for our Savior, Jesus Christ. For over 1500 years, the Israelites attempted to be justified through the Law, but instead, "...they went about to establish their own righteousness." As for the Gentiles (nations), they were given over to a "reprobate mind" because they refused to "retain God in their knowledge." God did this so He could "have mercy upon all" (Rom. 11:32).

Romans 2 does not declare believers in the Church to be "spiritual Israel"; Paul simply taught that the religious Jews were no better than the "uncircumcised" Gentiles. It would be a gross ignorance for Gentiles to compare themselves to the Jews being described in the Romans 2 passage, especially in the context of their (the Israelites) behavior under the Law. Remember, in the Body of Christ, there is "neither Jew nor Gentile," so it is wrong for theologians to push the narrative that believers are somehow "the true Jews" today. Remember, Paul was writing to Jews and proselytes in Rome, not exclusively to Gentiles in the Body of Christ. By Romans 3:9, Paul showed in the first two chapters of Romans that "both Jews and Gentiles are under sin."

Does Romans 9 Prove We Are "Spiritual Israel" As Many Claim?

Romans 9 is another passage often used by various theologians to promote the teaching that the Body of Christ is "spiritual Israel."

> *6 Not as though the word of God hath taken*
> *none effect. <u>For they are not all Israel,</u>*
> *<u>which are of Israel:</u>*
> *Romans 9:6*

Before I provide the entire context of this passage from Romans 9, I must wonder if it would be accurate for me to assume that anyone who refers to themselves as a "Christian" is truly a believer in Jesus Christ as their Savior? Of course not, because having an *intellectual knowledge* about Jesus Christ does not make someone saved from their sins. After all, many atheists believe in the historical accounts that Jesus died by crucifixion, He was buried in a wealthy man's tomb, and that tomb was empty three days and three nights later. Does this acknowledgment make them "Christians," even though they do not believe Jesus Christ is God incarnate? Should we assume all Jews are the "children of God," even if they do not acknowledge Jesus as *the Christ*, the Messiah? Let us keep this in mind as we read the following passage (in its context):

> *I say the truth in Christ, I lie not, my conscience also bearing me witness in the Holy Ghost, 2 That I have great heaviness and continual sorrow in my heart. 3 For I could wish that myself were accursed from Christ for my brethren, <u>my kinsmen according to the flesh: 4 Who are Israelites; to whom pertaineth the adoption, and the glory, and the covenants, and the giving of the law, and the service of God, and the promises; 5 Whose are the fathers, and of whom as concerning the flesh Christ came, who is over all, God blessed for ever.</u> Amen. 6 Not as though the word of God hath taken none effect. <u>For they are not all Israel, which are of Israel: 7 Neither, because they are the seed of Abraham, are they all children: but, In Isaac shall thy seed be called.</u> 8 That is, <u>They which are the children of the flesh</u>, these are <u>not the children of God: but the children of the promise are counted for the seed. 9 For this is the word of promise</u>, At this time will I come, and <u>Sarah shall have a son</u>.*

> *10 And not only this; but when <u>Rebecca also</u>*
> *<u>had conceived by one, even by our father</u>*
> *<u>Isaac</u>; 11 (For the children being not yet born,*
> *neither having done any good or evil, that the*
> *purpose of God according to election might*
> *stand, not of works, but of him that calleth;)*
> *Romans 9:1-11*

Paul was obviously concerned and prayed for those who are Israelites, "according to the flesh," so Romans 9 was *not* written directly to or about the Gentiles in the Body of Christ (the Church). Paul was speaking to Israelites because he desired strongly that they, too, would come to know Jesus Christ as their Savior. In like manner, we are also called to pray for Israel because God's promises for blessings to the whole world are prophetically through that nation, and if we recall, there will be a sealed remnant from the twelve tribes of Israel during the Tribulation (Psalm 122:6; John 4:22; Rom. 11:5-6; Rev. 7:1-8). Also notice that Paul stated that "the adoption, the glory, the covenants, the Law, and the service and promises" were all given to Israel. Had Israel accepted the kingdom that Christ said was "at hand," and offered in Acts, the world would have been blessed and could have been saved through the gospel of the kingdom (Isa. 60:1-3; Matt. 24:14; Rom. 15:8-12). God knew this rejection by Israel would occur, but in Genesis, He promised a Messiah and a Kingdom, and He had to offer both to Israel before "the revelation of the mystery."

Nothing takes God by surprise. Just because God foreknows something, that does not mean He forces humanity to abandon the free agency He has given to us. God foreknew Adam would sin, but did He prevent it from happening? God already had a redemptive plan for humanity before the foundation of the world, and "when the fulness of time was come, God sent forth His Son..." to fulfill it (Gal. 4:4-5). Israel was free to reject Jesus Christ and the Messianic Kingdom, but God's faithfulness will indeed bring about Israel's future redemption, and He has already sealed the 144,000 Israelites for this task (during the Tribulation). This will open the possibility for salvation to Israel and the nations at that time. God works "all things after the counsel of His own will," even while humanity is in rebellion against Him. Does this mean every Jew will be saved because of the evangelism that will take place "in the ages to come"? Doesn't Romans 9:7 explain that the "chosen seed" will come through the lineage of Isaac?

The Twelve could have evangelized the world through the Great Commission, but since Israel rejected the Messiah, and the offering of the Kingdom of Heaven promised to them "since the world began," this left the Gentiles without hope, "and without God in the world" (Eph. 2:11-12). Again, no one knew, but God, that Paul would be *the* chosen vessel to go to the Gentiles with a message of salvation that did not involve Gentiles converting to Judaism first (becoming proselytes). Christ's gospel message through Paul was a direct result of Israel's "fall" from their standing with God (Romans 11:11). This *new* gospel, proclaimed by Paul, was a mystery "hid in God" until Paul received it by direct revelation from Jesus Christ (Galatians 1:10-12).

The specific verse regarding "For they are not all Israel, which are of Israel" (Rom. 9:6) needs no "spiritual" interpretation or identity at all. Not all Jews are the true believers of the promises made to and through Abraham, Issac, and Jacob, even though they were born of Israelite heritage. To imply that Romans 9:6 has to do with the Body of Christ (or Gentiles specifically) is both ignorant and deceptive on the part of those who proclaim such a teaching, especially given the context of Romans 9:1-5, which focuses on Israelites only (according to the flesh). Again, not all Jews will be believers, even at the end of the Tribulation. Yes, Paul stated in Romans 11:26 that "all Israel shall be saved," but Romans 9:7 explains specifically who Paul was referencing as "all Israel."

7 Neither, because they are the seed of Abraham, <u>are they all children</u>: <u>but, In Isaac shall thy seed be called.</u> Romans 9:7

In other words, not all Israelites are (or will be) believers just because they came through the lineage of Abraham. This is all the apostle Paul is stating in Romans 9:6. He is not implying that the Body of Christ is somehow "spiritual Israel," especially since the Gentiles are not once mentioned until Romans 9:24. Even in that verse, Paul distinguished between the Jews and Gentiles, so this would cause us to question how some theologians could claim the Body of Christ are the "true Jews," especially when two separate groups of people are being named by Paul in Romans 9:24. So, "…they are not all Israel, which are of Israel" is like saying, "…not all people who call themselves "Christian" are true believers in Christ as their Savior.

What about the "Israel of God" in Galatians 6?

In all the dozens of instances in the Old and New Testaments where we encounter the word "Israel," it is in reference only to the ethnic Jews to whom Jesus came (Matt. 15:24; Rom. 9:3-5). If "Israel" has always meant "all the people of God," as some suppose, then why would Jesus overwhelmingly ignore Gentiles in "the gospels"; instruct His disciples to "go *not* into the way of the Gentiles"; and why would He directly state (in the presence of a Gentile) that He was "*not* sent but unto the lost sheep of the house of Israel," right before referring to Gentiles as "dogs" (Matt. 10:5-7; 15:24-26)? There doesn't seem to be anything "spiritual" about denying "to whom" Jesus came, according to "the flesh" (Rom. 9:3-5).

That stated, the other passage often used to justify the teaching that we are somehow "spiritual Israel" is found in Galatians 6:15-16. It is important to realize that it is impossible to refer to the Body of Christ as "the Israel of God" or "spiritual Israel," especially since the Body of Christ was "chosen in Him *before* the foundation of the world" (Eph. 1:4; 2 Tim. 1:8-9), which was long before Israel was ever called out in Genesis through Abraham and his seed. Again, before God called out Israel in Genesis, He had already predestined the Body of Christ "before the world began," so calling the Body of Christ "the Israel of God" or "spiritual Israel" simply replaces one body of believers known "since the world began" with another "kept secret since the world began." Again, no one knew about the Body of Christ until God revealed it to Paul. Assuming the Church is now "spiritual Israel" ignores all the Scriptures Paul stated about the Body being a "new creature," not some carryover from the past promises of God to Israel (Rom. 16:25; 2 Cor. 5:17; Gal. 6:15; Eph. 1:10; 3:1-10; Col. 1:23-28).

> *14 But God forbid that I should glory, save in the cross of our Lord Jesus Christ, by whom the world is crucified unto me, and I unto the world. 15 For in Christ Jesus neither circumcision availeth any thing, nor uncircumcision, but a new creature. 16 And as many as walk according to this rule, peace be on them, and mercy, <u>and upon the Israel of God</u>. Galatians 6:14-16*

Prior to these verses, Paul was addressing (as he did throughout his epistle to the Galatians) that mixing law with grace is detestable in the sight of God (Gal. 1:8-9). The Judaizers were attempting to force the Gentile believers to be circumcised under the Law (making them proselytes to Judaism). As a result of the persistence of the Jews, these Galatian believers were told (by Paul) not to abandon the "liberty wherewith Christ has made us (them) free" (Gal. 5:1). Do we not have this same coercion still taking place throughout various denominations that insist on "works to justify their faith," simply because they haven't "rightly divided" James' words to "the twelve tribes of Israel" from the instructions given to us by Jesus to and through Paul? Regardless, many theologians use Galatians 16:16 to justify that believers are the "Israel of God," which they claim is the Church today. Given the context of the letter to the Galatians, Paul did everything he could to keep the Gentiles separate from the Judaizers who were forcing the Law of Moses upon them. It would seem odd that Paul would insist in Galatians 6:16 that the Church was now the "true Israel," especially when he wrote in Galatians 3:28 how "There is neither Jew nor Greek…" in the Body of Christ.

In I Corinthians 10:32, which was written about five years after Galatians 6, Paul stated the following:

32 Give none offence, neither to the Jews, nor
to the Gentiles, nor to the church of God:
I Corinthians 10:32

If Paul's intent was to teach that the Church was "the Israel of God" in Galatians 6, why would he later still show a distinction between Jews, Gentiles, and the Church of God in his letter to the Corinthians? Besides, if you read the beginning of I Corinthians 10, Paul revisits the history of Israel at the parting of the Red Sea. The Church established under "the revelation of the mystery" by Paul was certainly *not* involved in that ancient event, which only involved the "Church in the wildness" (ethnic Israel) mentioned by Stephen in Acts 7:38. This previous Church in the wilderness did not evolve into the Body of Christ because the Body of Christ is "a new creature: old things are passed away; behold, all things are become new" (2 Cor. 5:17).

The word "Israel of God" is never used by Paul in reference to the Body of Christ, and yet, for some reason, theologians insist on such an interpretation because their theology demands this forced meaning. Why is it necessary for some theologians to imply the reference to the "Israel of God" as Paul's attempt to somehow replace Israel with the Church today? Paul, in Romans 9, prays for his fellow countrymen (Israelites), so why is he not permitted to do the same here in Galatians 6 with the term "Israel of God"? Again, we are members of the Body of Christ, so we *do not* need to become a "spiritual" entity called the "Israel of God"? When your theology demands only "one gospel" and "one church" in the New Testament, you have no choice but to "spiritualize" many Scriptures to fit a preconceived doctrine (or theology) that is, at best, implied!

By recognizing the gospel of the grace of God (the revelation of the Mystery), you do not need to become anything but a member of the Body of Christ, and you don't have to change God's promises to Israel by arrogantly claiming God has replaced Israel with the Church today, especially through a form of theology that focuses its entire existence on covenants not defined anywhere in Scripture. You simply do not need to change anything with prophecy regarding Israel's future Messianic Kingdom, which is to be established on this earth. In fact, when Paul was addressing the Jewish leaders in Acts 28:17-23, he still referenced the "hope of Israel" to come. Why would he be dishonest about this to the Jews if, in fact, their hope would be replaced with the Church? Paul is allowed to pray that God would not only save Israel (Rom. 9), but he was also allowed to pray for Israel's protection and future salvation (Gal. 6). We should be praying for Israel, especially the remnant, because these sealed saints will one day evangelize the world with the gospel of the kingdom (Matt. 24:14).

Also, the word "and" in Galatians 6:16 should indicate that two separate entities are being discussed in this passage from Galatians 6. However, let us examine again the two verses specifically taught from the passage.

> *15 For in Christ Jesus neither circumcision availeth any thing, nor uncircumcision, but a new creature. 16 And as many as walk according to this rule, <u>peace be on them</u>, and mercy, <u>and</u> upon the <u>Israel of God</u>.*
> *Galatians 6:15-16*

Who are "them" that Paul is referencing in 6:16? Verse 15 explains that Paul is discussing the Body of Christ, the Church (the new creature), which does not differentiate between the "circumcision" (Jew) or the "uncircumcision" (Gentiles), taught under "the revelation of the mystery." Paul calls for "peace on them" who walk according to this rule that he taught to the Body of Christ. It is the true Church for today, which Paul established when he declared, "I have laid the foundation, and another builds thereon…" (I Cor. 3:10). Paul is asking for "peace be on them" who "walk according to this rule…," which refers to those who obey the gospel Paul was called to preach (the gospel of the grace of God). Remember, Galatians 1:8-9 warns against teaching any other gospel today.

He is also calling for peace on the "Israel of God," who are those Jewish saints who had been saved under the gospel of the kingdom before Paul was called to proclaim the gospel of the grace of God. Many of these Jewish saints were still alive at the time Paul wrote to the Galatians. Again, this "Israel of God" was saved under the earthly ministry of Christ and the Twelve, and they knew their hope was the promised kingdom, even though they were suffering much persecution at the time (Acts 8:1). These Jewish saints were "scattered abroad," and the letters of James, Peter, and John (and Jude) were written to these saints who were told how to live in the presence of Gentiles (I Pet. 2:12), and to look for the *"new heavens and the new earth"* (2 Peter 3:13), not a "citizenship in heaven." They were also destined to see the Tribulation (Matt. 24:34), so prayers would be warranted for them. This is what they were expecting in their lifetime, just as Paul was anticipating "the meeting in the air" for the Body of Christ. They were believers just as much as the members of the Body of Christ, so shouldn't these saints be considered "spiritual Israel" as much as the Body of Christ—if there were such a thing as "spiritual Israel" from Scripture, which there is not.

Quoting Romans 9:6 and Galatians 6:16 out of context has erroneously promulgated the belief and preaching of an entirely different gospel that is *not found* in the Bible. Remember, Paul sternly warns of this in Galatians 1:6-9. Paul was commanding peace and mercy on both the "new creature" (The Body of Christ) *and* on the "Israel of God," which consisted of kingdom believers from the earthly ministry of Jesus, as well as the early chapters in Acts (especially Pentecost). The Book of Acts details much about the fall of Israel, which brought salvation to the Gentiles (Rom. 11:11), but by Acts 28:28, Paul stated, "Be it known therefore unto you (Jews), that the salvation of God is sent unto the Gentiles, and that they will hear it." Acts 28 still identifies both the Jews and Gentiles, and this passage was written well over a decade after Galatians 6:16 mentioned "the Israel of God," which is mistakenly interpreted to mean the Church, the Body of Christ as "spiritual Israel."

If the Church of this age of grace would "rightly divide," there would be a legitimate reason for Israel to be jealous of believers today. However, by "replacing" Israel with the Church, we have horribly undermined the intent of the salvation God has offered to Gentiles through "the revelation of the mystery." Israel (and her apostles and prophets) had no idea that God would save Gentiles *apart* from Israel, nor did they know that both Jews and Gentiles would be saved into "one body by the cross" (Ephesians 2:13-16), which makes the Church the "new creature." Simply "rightly dividing the word of truth" would clear up so much heresy and confusion in the Body of Christ today, especially concerning Romans 9:6 and Galatians 6:16.

The Circumcision of Philippians 3:3
There is also another passage that has caused some in the Body to declare that we are "spiritual Israel." It is in Philippians 3.

> *Finally, my brethren, rejoice in the Lord. To write the same things to you, to me indeed is not grievous, but for you it is safe. 2 Beware of dogs, beware of evil workers, beware of the concision. 3 <u>For we are the circumcision,</u>*

*which worship God in the spirit, and rejoice in
Christ Jesus, and have no confidence in the
flesh. Philippians 3:1-3*

The "concision" in this passage is preceded by Paul's warning about "dogs" and "evil workers." Paul uses the word "concision" for these false brethren (Judaizers) who seemed to boast about their physical circumcision, but they weren't willing to completely cut off the "works of the flesh" and recognize the sufficiency of Christ's atoning sacrifice for their sins. Regardless, they influenced others (mainly Gentiles) with false practices, even demanding circumcision for salvation. At *no time* did God *ever* place Gentiles under the covenant of circumcision, let alone any covenant involving Israel. So, what "circumcision" is Paul referencing in Philippians 3:3?

The "concision" today does not come in the form of those commanding circumcision, but rather it is coming in the form of those who attempt to make us "spiritual Israel." Some have even *invented* covenants that God supposedly made with "all the people of God," hoping to solidify this ideology of the Church being "spiritual Israel" or the "true Jews." Regrettably, "evil workers" are still in operation today, and we should "beware of the concision" as well, especially those who have replaced physical circumcision with the work of water baptism, along with other ordinances for salvation.

*7 For the mystery of iniquity doth already
work: only he who now letteth will let, until he
be taken out of the way. 2 Thessalonians 2:7*

Paul also explained how we are to have "no confidence in the flesh." Those of "the concision" had a great deal of confidence in their circumcision, and this would be the circumcision made *with hands*. Our circumcision is made *without hands*, so it is a spiritual circumcision, which has cut us off from the world through faith in the death and resurrection of Christ.

> *10 And <u>ye are complete in him</u>, which is the head of all principality and power: 11 In whom also <u>ye are circumcised with the circumcision made without hands</u>, in putting off the body of the sins of the flesh <u>by the circumcision of Christ</u>: 12 <u>Buried with him in baptism</u>, wherein also <u>ye are risen with him through the faith of the operation of God</u>, who hath raised him from the dead. Colossians 2:10-12*

It has always amazed me how so many religionists are willing to accept the spiritual circumcision of believers (cut off from our "old sin nature"), and yet they immediately assume the baptism in Colossians 2:12 to be water baptism, which is a physical ordinance performed by man. Jesus Christ was "cut off" from the world at His death ("the circumcision of Christ"), and when we are baptized "*by* one Spirit," we are also placed into Christ's death, burial, and resurrection, and therefore, we, too, are "cut off" from the world as well. This is positional sanctification (to set apart as holy). Paul explained this also to the Romans.

What shall we say then? Shall we continue in sin, that grace may abound? 2 God forbid. How shall we, that are dead to sin, live any longer therein? 3 Know ye not, that so many of us as were baptized into Jesus Christ were baptized into his death? 4 Therefore we are buried with him by baptism into death: that like as Christ was raised up from the dead by the glory of the Father, even so we also should walk in newness of life. 5 For if we have been planted together in the likeness of his death, we shall be also in the likeness of his resurrection: 6 Knowing this, that our old man is crucified with him, that the body of sin might be destroyed, that henceforth we should not serve sin. Romans 6:1-6

Our circumcision and baptism are done by "the operation of God," not humans (Col. 2:12). So, in this sense, Paul referred to the Philippians as "the circumcision," and this, too, applies to the whole Body of Christ. However, does this make us "spiritual Israel?" If it did, then we must wonder why Paul considers all the works he did under Judaism (the faith of Israel) to be "dung," especially when compared to the "excellency of knowing Christ." Paul clearly taught the Body of Christ that we are saved "apart from Israel," and yet many theologians want to associate the Body with Israel by calling it "spiritual Israel."

In the following verses, Paul does not deny his Hebrew heritage, but rather he shows the folly in having "confidence in the flesh" to save him, and this included circumcision.

> *4 Though I might also have confidence in the flesh. <u>If any other man thinketh that he hath whereof he might trust in the flesh, I more:</u>*
> *5 Circumcised the eighth day, of the stock of Israel, of the tribe of Benjamin, an Hebrew of the Hebrews; as touching the law, a Pharisee;*
> *6 Concerning zeal, persecuting the church; touching the righteousness which is in the law, blameless. 7 <u>But what things were gain to me, those I counted loss for Christ.</u> 8 Yea doubtless, and I count all things but loss <u>for the excellency of the knowledge of Christ Jesus my Lord</u>: for whom I have suffered the loss of all things, and do count them but dung, that I may win Christ, 9 <u>And be found in him, not having mine own righteousness, which is of the law, but that which is through the faith of Christ, the righteousness which is of God by faith:</u>*
> *10 That I may know him, and the power of his resurrection, and the fellowship of his sufferings, being made conformable unto his death; Philippians 3:4-10*

Paul was demonstrating to those at Philippi that he had more confidence in the completeness of the "circumcision of Christ" (His death) than he did in his own "works of the flesh" in Judaism, which is the religion of the nation of Israel. Referring to the Body of Christ as "spiritual Israel," based on the passage from Philippians 3:3, only shows a gross misrepresentation of what Paul was truly teaching about the spiritual circumcision of believers, as well as our association with the "circumcision of Christ," which again, is in reference to His death (being *cut off* from the world).

The context of Philippians 3:3 does not make us *true Jews*; it only shows how believers have been "cut off" from the world through the "circumcision made *without hands*." If we were "true Jews," would this not associate us with the nation of Israel? Paul separated his works (as an Israelite) from the work of Christ on our behalf, so why should members of the Body of Christ reassociate ourselves with Israel by inventing the doctrine of us becoming "spiritual Israel"? No matter how theologians spin it, insisting that the Church is "spiritual Israel" is inherently the foundational teachings of Replacement Theology.

Today, believers do not need to be physically circumcised, or water baptized, to be saved. This is all done spiritually when we place our faith in the work of Christ ("the preaching of the cross") We have "the faith of Abraham" in "taking God at His word." This is also one reason why Paul declared that we have been "blessed with all spiritual blessings in heavenly places in Christ" (Eph. 1:3). Remember, Colossians 2:14 declared that all the "handwriting of ordinances" were "nailed to the cross," so the only circumcision and baptism today are those done completely apart from human hands. They are "the operation of God." We have been crucified with Christ, and Paul reminded believers: "Wherefore if you be dead with

Christ from the rudiments (principles) of the world, why, as though living in the world are you subject to ordinances?" (Col. 2:20). That is still a great question for most believers today!

19 For I through the law am dead to the law, that I might live unto God. Galatians 2:19

4 For Christ is the end of the law for righteousness to every one that believeth. Romans 10:4

Using Philippians 3:3 to justify the belief that the Body of Christ has become "spiritual Israel" is nothing more than Replacement Theology at its best. Israel has always meant, and will continue as such, to be the physical descendants of Isaac and Jacob. If the word "Israel" was intended to mean "all God's people," then we would clearly see this presented by the apostles themselves, which it is not. Paul even stated in Ephesians 2:11-13 that Gentiles were "aliens from the commonwealth of Israel, and strangers from the covenants of promise," but now, we have been brought nigh unto God "by the blood of Christ." So, if "Israel" has always meant "all the people of God," then explain the separation between Jews and Gentiles throughout Scripture, and the need for Paul's gospel to "break down the middle wall of partition between us."

We also cannot separate Philippians 3:3 from Romans 4. Please note the following:

⁹ Cometh this blessedness then upon <u>the circumcision only, or upon the uncircumcision also</u>? for we say that faith was reckoned to Abraham for righteousness. ¹⁰ How was it then reckoned? when he was in circumcision, or in uncircumcision? Not in circumcision, <u>but in uncircumcision</u>. ¹¹ And he received the sign of circumcision, a seal of the righteousness of the faith which he had yet being uncircumcised: <u>that he might be the father of all them that believe, though they be not circumcised; that righteousness might be imputed unto them also</u>: ¹² <u>And the father of circumcision to them who are not of the circumcision only, but who also walk in the steps of that faith of our father Abraham, which he had being yet uncircumcised.</u> Romans 4:9-12

Abraham is the "father of faith" to anyone who believes in what God said in His word. Faith is, after all, taking God at His word and relying completely on His faithfulness to fulfill it. If we are "spiritual Israel," then Abraham can't be the father of the circumcision and the uncircumcision (as the passage declared), so this would make him the father of only one group, which is conveniently referred to as "spiritual Israel." It is assumed that things *spiritual* have somehow replaced the *physical* promises of God to Israel, and this reckless theology ("spiritual Israel") completely violates Romans 4, especially in the following verses:

> *16 Therefore it is of faith, that it might be by grace; to the end the promise might be sure to all the seed; <u>not to that only which is of the law, but to that also which is of the faith of Abraham; who is the father of us all</u>, 17 (As it is written, I have made thee a father of many nations,) before him whom he believed, even God, who quickeneth the dead, and calleth those things which be not as though they were.*
> *Romans 4:16-17*

Abraham and Sarah attempted to "help God out" through inserting their own solution to God's promises He made with Abraham. They used Hagar to assist in accomplishing God's promises, and this seems similar to the way some theologians ("the concision") are attempting to do when they insist that the Body of Christ is "spiritual Israel." The belief of the Church replacing Israel did not occur until the second century A.D. by men who did not bother to "rightly divide the word of truth." They had also failed to recognize "the revelation of the mystery, which was kept secret since the world began," and the result has been disastrous to our faith. This is why we have such an identity crisis within our faith.

Philippians 3:3 is not in reference to members of the Body of Christ having become "true Jews" or "spiritual Israel"; it is only referencing believers who have been spiritually circumcised through the faithfulness and "operation of God." Abraham is the father of all who have faith in what God said in His word, both the circumcised and the uncircumcised—not one group called "spiritual Israel." Paul would mock such an idea that the members of the Body of Christ are the "true Jews" of God. There were "true Jews" who already walked "in the faith of Abraham" (Rom. 4:12) long before the Body of Christ was formed after Acts 9. Were they "spiritual Israel" also? Again, the concept of "spiritual Israel" only came into existence because the Patristic Church Fathers, and the Reformed theologians of modern-day, have both failed to "rightly divide the word of truth." Let us not reward this latest version of "the concision" by promulgating their fallacious teachings.

Concluding Thoughts

Just as Abraham was made righteous by faith, so is the Body of Christ. Remember, Abraham was already declared righteous (Gen. 15:6) before he was circumcised many years later (Gen. 17:24). It amazes me how any of the world's mainline religions (some four billion between Christianity, Islam, and Judaism) could call Abraham their "father," and yet, strive to be justified by works. Our works should be nothing more than an expression of our faith. I do not do good works to get saved; I do good works because I am saved. We are already forgiven (Col. 2:13) and "complete in Him" (Col. 2:10) as members of the Body of Christ. We do not need to resort to the replacement of Israel through an erroneous title mandated by theologians who do not "rightly divide the word of truth."

8 Beware lest any man spoil you through philosophy and vain deceit, after the tradition

of men, after the rudiments of the world, and
not after Christ. Colossians 2:8

Even though tradition, which often robs us of truth, dictates that we *must* refer to the members of the Body of Christ as "spiritual Israel," we must first recognize that the Apostle Paul, the apostle to the Gentiles (Rom. 11:13), was called out to bring the message of salvation to the world (apart from the nation of Israel). Associating us with the title "spiritual Israel" is a gross misrepresentation of the gospel of the grace of God (given through the "revelation of the mystery" (Rom. 16:25)), which no one ever knew prior to the conversion of Paul. The identity crisis in our faith has caused confusion, division, and even hatred toward one another. This, to me, is an abomination in the eyes of God who wants all of us to have "unity in the bond of peace."

16 All scripture is given by inspiration of God,
and is profitable for doctrine, for reproof, for
correction, for instruction in righteousness:
17 That the man of God may be perfect,
thoroughly furnished unto all good works.
2 Timothy 3:16-17

My goal was to present (in context) the controversial passages some use to declare us "spiritual Israel." This belief stems directly from a failure to "rightly divide the word of truth," and by not obeying 2 Timothy 2:15, we should be "ashamed." The Body is a spiritual, invisible assembly of believers, but there is nothing spiritual about replacing God's promises to Israel with the heavenly purpose He has for the Body of Christ. We are a "new creature," not a gathering of Israel into a new name commonly called "spiritual Israel."

CHAPTER 10

Water Baptism: Should We or Should We Not?

For Christ sent me not to baptize, but to
preach the gospel: not with wisdom of words,
lest the cross of Christ should be made of none
effect. [18] For the preaching of the cross is to
them that perish foolishness; but unto us which
are saved it is the power of God.
I Corinthians 1:17-18

Tradition or Truth?

Baptism is one of the most divisive and confusing doctrines of the Church, and even though I see it as a rather simple concept when determining its placement in God's program for the Church today, it has caused so much controversy that it will likely never be one of the doctrines we will ever unify over until we understand its purpose under the Great Commission, and its suspension under the gospel of the grace of God. Until then, it remains one of the most embarrassing disputes in Christianity. In this chapter, I will address several different views, and then we will "rightly divide the word of truth" to see the *one baptism* that is consistent with God's plan for the Church since the time "the revelation of the mystery" was first given to Paul by Jesus Christ.

To no one's surprise, believers might go to any given church and be told that they must be water baptized, or they can't be saved. They might go to another and be told they don't need to be water baptized, but they *should* because Jesus was baptized. Another church might immerse believers completely, while another is satisfied with sprinkling some water over them. Then, believers might be told that they *should* be water baptized to show others the "inward change" where they are "burying their old self and raised anew." Finally, believers could miraculously be told by someone who sees the distinct dispensational change given by Christ to Paul (through the "revelation of the mystery") that there is only *one* baptism today, and this is the one done "*by* one Spirit," immersing us into *one* Body, the Body of Christ. Since the time of the early Church Fathers, *two* baptisms have been taught and maintained, even though Paul never commissioned Gentiles to "repent and be baptized for the remission of sins," especially since he was sent by Jesus to teach only *one* baptism, which is the work of God done *by* the Holy Spirit upon all who believe the gospel of the grace of God.

Perhaps you can see the level of confusion resulting from this water rite. Even though there are at least a dozen baptisms in the Bible, with only five having anything to do with water, we might do well to examine the significance of both water and spiritual baptism, which are two distinct doctrines associated with believers throughout the Bible,

402

especially in the New Testament. So, I ask: Should we, or should we not, water baptize today?

Let Us Begin with John

Many believers do not understand the baptism John performed upon Jesus in the Jordan River. They also fail to "rightly divide" this baptism, believing it is still in operation today.

> *[11] I indeed baptize you with water unto repentance. but he that cometh after me is mightier than I, whose shoes I am not worthy to bear: he shall baptize you with the Holy Ghost, and with fire: Matthew 3:11 (John the Baptist)*

> *[18] And Jesus came and spake unto them, saying, All power is given unto me in heaven and in earth. [19] Go ye therefore, and teach all nations, baptizing them in the name of the Father, and of the Son, and of the Holy Ghost: [20] Teaching them to observe all things whatsoever I have commanded you: and, lo, I am with you always, even unto the end of the world. Amen. Matthew 28:18-20*

> *[17] For Christ sent me not to baptize, but to preach the gospel: not with wisdom of words, lest the cross of Christ should be made of none effect. [18] For the preaching of the cross is to*

them that perish foolishness; but unto us which
are saved it is the power of God.
I Corinthians 1:17-18

If you ask most believers what the gospel is for today, they will likely reply that it is the so-called Great Commission Jesus gave in Matthew 28. In fact, Peter obeyed this gospel (the gospel of the kingdom) when he and the other apostles preached at Pentecost to "the house of Israel," especially in the context of Acts 2:38. So, if the Great Commission is the only gospel for today, it seems strange that Paul, "the apostle to the Gentiles," would state that he *wasn't* "sent to baptize, but to preach *the gospel*" (I Cor. 1:17). What gospel was he referring to in his letter to the Corinthians, because the Great Commission (the gospel of the kingdom) certainly included the command for the apostles to water baptize, along with observing all that Jesus commanded during His earthly ministry to "the lost sheep of the house of Israel"? As we have examined, this would have included the order to "keep the commandments"?

Before I tackle this doctrine in depth, please understand that I fully believe in water baptism for the remission of sins (as it was proclaimed by John the Baptist, Jesus, and the apostles in the "gospels" and early Acts); however, should water baptism be practiced today under the gospel of the grace of God, especially since believers are "not under the Law, but under grace"? Again, if it were a doctrine for the Body of Christ, why didn't Paul ever command—in his epistles—all believers to "repent and be baptized for the remission of sins," which would have been consistent with the so-called Great Commission? Paul did baptize *very few* during the transitional period in the Book of Acts, but we are already aware that he did this mainly in the context of the presence of Jews, especially when preaching in the local synagogues throughout the places described in the Book of Acts. In fact, he even circumcised Timothy "because of the Jews, which were in those quarters" (Acts 16:3). However, Paul never told the Gentiles to be circumcised under the Law.

We have no definitive proof that Paul continued to carry the practice of water baptism over into his gospel message, especially to Gentiles, nor did he command his fellow laborers to continue water baptism for their converts. Paul mentioned a few people he baptized in I Corinthians 1:14-16, but (as quoted already) in I Corinthians 1:17, Paul stated clearly, "For Christ sent me *not* to baptize, but to preach the gospel," which I also quoted in the introduction to this chapter. That verse alone has been spun in more ways than a thousand loads of laundry in a washing machine.

As I explained in a previous chapter related to our spiritual circumcision, as well as our spiritual baptism (I Cor. 12:13; Col. 2:11-12), we should make sure to "rightly divide the word of truth" on this matter. As the Judaizers hounded the Gentiles in Paul's day over circumcision for salvation, many theologians and their congregants today have simply replaced one legalistic rite under the Law for yet another (water baptism). Believers will spend hours debating baptism, but do they ever get to the real issue over this important doctrine?

As mentioned previously, baptism is a divisive doctrine for many, but I maintain that it is only divisive because of religious traditions, not the Bible. Tradition insists on various reasons for and against water baptism and its practices, but again, are these reasons based on the support of religious traditions, or are they based on sound biblical exegesis?

My experience over many decades has led me to understand water baptism through the dispensational change God introduced with the conversion of Paul, and his calling as the "apostle to the Gentiles." Those who do not recognize this dispensational change, beginning in Acts 9, will often find themselves unable to explain even the basic differences between water and spiritual baptism, which makes it even more difficult to have a rational conversation with them on the subject. For those who insist that Romans 6, Ephesians 4, and Colossians 2 are addressing water baptism—not spiritual baptism—there is very little we can do to assist in their understanding of Paul's ministry under "the dispensation of the grace of God" (Eph. 3:2).

The general arguments regarding water baptism involve the thief on the cross, infant baptism, why Jesus was baptized by John, and whether water baptism is an "outward sign of an inward change of heart (or inward grace)." Again, water baptism had its time and place, and it will again under the gospel of the kingdom during the Tribulation (Matt. 24:14), but since the time Paul penned his epistles, he concluded in Ephesians 4:5 that there is only *one baptism*, which he clearly stated in I Corinthians 12:13 to be *"by* one Spirit." Remember, Paul received this teaching "by revelation of Jesus Christ" (Gal. 1:10-12), and if the focus of salvation is not completely on the sufficiency of the blood of Jesus Christ, then we must wonder what other works believers must perform to be "complete in Him" (Col. 2:10).

At the giving of the so-called Great Commission, Jesus was very clear with His instructions to the apostles concerning the means of salvation. Let us examine that commission once again for context.

> *16 Then the eleven disciples went away into Galilee, into a mountain where Jesus had appointed them. 17 And when they saw him, they worshipped him: but some doubted.*
> *18 And Jesus came and spake unto them, saying, All power is given unto me in heaven and in earth. 19 Go ye therefore, and teach all nations, <u>baptizing them in the name of the Father, and of the Son, and of the Holy Ghost:</u>*
> *20 Teaching them to observe all things whatsoever I have commanded you: and, lo, I am with you always, even unto the end of the world. Amen. Matthew 28:16-20*

As I have explained, this is the so-called "Great Commission," which is "the gospel of the kingdom" that Jesus proclaimed on Earth. Water baptism, keeping the commandments, and the promised Millennial Kingdom to Israel were all a part of the *gospel of the kingdom* that John the Baptist, the Twelve, and Jesus declared to be "at hand." However, was this the gospel Paul was sent, by Jesus, to proclaim to the Body of Christ? On the contrary, Paul declared that Christ sent him "not to baptize"; that believers were "not under Law, but under grace"; and "our citizenship is in Heaven," which all seem to clearly indicate a dramatic change from the so-called Great Commission, which mentioned none of the doctrines Jesus gave to Paul. This is why we need to "rightly divide the word of truth."

Were Believers Ever Rebaptized with Water?
Had the so-called Great Commission been the only revelation given by Jesus Christ to the world, I would wholeheartedly champion the preaching of Peter in Acts 2:38: "…repent and be baptized for the remission of sins." We know that John the Baptist was sent to preach "the water baptism of repentance," and this was for "the remission of sins," just as Peter preached at Pentecost in Acts 2:38, but there is no record of anyone having been rebaptized simply because they knew only the "baptism of John."

There is strong debate, however, over the following verses from Acts 19, which some use to insist that being rebaptized with water was a practice done by the apostles, even Paul.

> *And it came to pass, that, while Apollos was at Corinth, Paul having passed through the upper coasts came to Ephesus: and finding certain disciples, 2 He said unto them, Have ye received the Holy Ghost since ye believed? And they said unto him, We have not so much as heard whether there be any Holy Ghost. 3 And he said unto them, Unto what then were ye baptized? And they said, Unto John's baptism. 4 Then said Paul, John verily baptized with the baptism of repentance, saying unto the people, that they should believe on him*

which should come after him, that is, on Christ Jesus. ⁵ When they heard this, they were baptized in the name of the Lord Jesus. ⁶ <u>And when Paul had laid his hands upon them</u>, the Holy Ghost came on them; and <u>they spake with tongues, and prophesied</u>. ⁷ And all the men were about twelve. Acts 19:1-7

Acts 19:1-7 is very challenging for some, but when the Greek rendition of this verse is explored, we discover that Paul was simply asking whether they received the Holy Spirit upon believing? In 19:3, the King James Version renders it in such a way that it implies whether these disciples even believed in the Holy Ghost, but according to Matthew 3, John the Baptist declared, this:

¹¹ <u>I indeed baptize you with water unto repentance. but he that cometh after me is mightier than I, whose shoes I am not worthy to bear: he shall baptize you with the Holy Ghost, and with fire:</u> ¹² Whose fan is in his hand, and he will throughly purge his floor, and gather his wheat into the garner; but he will burn up the chaff with unquenchable fire. ¹³ Then cometh Jesus from Galilee to Jordan unto John, to be baptized of him. ¹⁴ But John forbad him, saying, I have need to be baptized of thee, and comest thou to me? ¹⁵ And Jesus answering said unto him, Suffer it to be so now: <u>for thus it becometh us to fulfil all</u>

*<u>righteousness.</u> Then he suffered him. ¹⁶ And
Jesus, when he was baptized, went up
straightway out of the water: and, lo, the
heavens were opened unto him, <u>and he saw the
Spirit of God descending like a dove, and
lighting upon him: ¹⁷ And lo a voice from
heaven, saying, This is my beloved Son, in
whom I am well pleased.</u>*
Matthew 3:11-17

There is no doubt that if these believers knew the "baptism of John," they would have also known that John preached that Jesus would also baptize believers *with* the Holy Spirit. This is not a question whether these men in Acts 19 believed in the Holy Spirit; they simply weren't aware of the Acts 2:38 baptism in which Jesus baptized believers *with* the Holy Ghost after several thousand had been water baptized at Pentecost.

On the issue of being "rebaptized," there is one question many theologians overlook: Were the 120 "little flock" members rebaptized with water at Pentecost as well? Were they not believers already?

*³² Fear not, little flock; for it is your Father's
good pleasure to give you the kingdom.*
Luke 12:32

*¹³ And when they were come in, they went up
into an upper room, where abode both Peter,
and James, and John, and Andrew, Philip, and*

*Thomas, Bartholomew, and Matthew, James
the son of Alphaeus, and Simon Zelotes, and
Judas the brother of James. 14 These all
continued with one accord in prayer and
supplication, with the women, and Mary the
mother of Jesus, and with his brethren. 15 And
in those days Peter stood up in the midst of the
disciples, and said, (the number of names
together were about <u>an hundred and twenty</u>,) ...*
Acts 1:13-15

The "little flock" of Jewish believers (not members of the Body of Christ) were in "one accord" in the "upper room." It was to this "little flock" that Jesus promised to give the kingdom of heaven (Luke 12). However, would Jesus have offered the kingdom to them if they hadn't already repented and were water baptized for the remission of sins? Since the "little flock" consisted of believers who had been the disciples of Jesus Christ's earthly ministry, they would have already known the "baptism of John" (John 1:33), so it would seem odd for them to follow Jesus but deny their participation in water baptism. They did, after all, water baptize others during Christ's earthly ministry.

Please note the following about the day of Pentecost:

*And when the day of Pentecost was fully come,
they were all with one accord in one place.
2 And suddenly there came a sound from
heaven as of a rushing mighty wind, and it
filled all the house where they were sitting.*

> *³ And there appeared unto them cloven tongues
> like as of fire, and it sat upon each of them.
> ⁴ And they were all filled with the Holy Ghost,
> and began to speak with other tongues, as the
> Spirit gave them utterance. Acts 2:1-4*

This occurred *before* Peter commanded the nonbelievers from "the house of Israel" to "repent and be baptized for the remission of sins" in Act 2:37-28. There is no indication that those in the "upper room" were water baptized *again* before the Holy Spirit filled them. Why should they?

Once again, let us briefly explore who was water baptized on the day of Pentecost?

> *³⁶ Therefore let <u>all the house of Israel</u> know
> assuredly, that God hath made the same Jesus,
> whom ye have crucified, both Lord and Christ.
> ³⁷ Now when they heard this, <u>they were pricked
> in their heart</u>, and said unto Peter and to the
> rest of the apostles, Men and brethren, what
> shall we do? ³⁸ Then Peter said unto them,
> <u>Repent, and be baptized every one of you in
> the name of Jesus Christ for the remission of
> sins, and ye shall receive the gift of the Holy
> Ghost</u>... ⁴¹ <u>Then they that gladly received his
> word were baptized: and the same day there
> were added unto them about three thousand
> souls.</u> Acts 2:36-38 and 41*

The only people water baptized in Acts 2 were those who had not yet believed that Jesus was *the Christ*. After believing, 3000 souls were *added* to the "little flock" already there. The "little flock," in addition to the Twelve, were not rebaptized with water at Pentecost; they were only baptized with the Holy Ghost before Peter began to preach to the Jews and proselytes in Jerusalem during Pentecost (Acts 2:10). After all, who would have done the water baptizing if it weren't the apostles themselves?

The water baptism at Pentecost occurred after Peter and the apostles had preached about the guilt of the Jews for having crucified Jesus. Again, Peter did not preach salvation by grace, through faith in the death and resurrection of Jesus at Pentecost; he only preached "repent and be baptized…for the remission of sins," and for the believers to prepare for the "last days" by commanding them to "have all things common," which was in preparation for the time when believers were not going to be able to buy or sell without the "mark of the beast." Later, after Acts 7, this financial arrangement led to Paul coming to Jerusalem with offerings from several churches he had evangelized with the gospel of the grace of God.

That stated, was it required of these men in Acts 19 (likely associates of Apollos) to be rebaptized? Remember in Acts 18:26, Priscilla and Aquila took Apollos aside and added to his understanding from what they learned from Paul (see Col. 1:25). Paul did not rebaptize these twelve Ephesians with water; he simply "laid hands on them," and they received the Holy Ghost.

"Christian Baptism"

Before further inquiry into this question about rebaptism, there are some who erroneously teach that John's baptism was not "Christian baptism," and to a degree, they are correct because no Israelite was called a Christian until Acts 11:26, which was at Antioch (not Jerusalem). The typical theological view assumes these twelve men in Acts 19 needed to be rebaptized for the remission of sins because the baptism of John wasn't done the "correct way." It needed to be in accordance with the so-called Great Commission of Matthew 28, which is the full "Christian baptism" (according to those who ignore 2 Timothy 2:15). In truth, the baptism of John (addressed in Acts 19) was "just as good" as the water baptisms performed by the Twelve apostles in Acts 2.

Read the following passages again and ask whether these baptisms were the same in purpose (for repentance and remission of sins):

11 I indeed baptize you <u>with water unto repentance</u>. but he that cometh after me is mightier than I, whose shoes I am not worthy to bear: <u>he shall baptize you with the Holy Ghost, and with fire</u>: Matthew 3:11
(John the Baptist)

4 John did baptize in the wilderness, and <u>preach the baptism of repentance for the remission of sins</u>. Mark 1:4

38 Then Peter said unto them, <u>Repent, and be baptized every one of you in the name of Jesus Christ for the remission of sins</u>, and ye shall receive the gift of the Holy Ghost. Acts 2:38

John the Baptist and Peter both preached the water baptism of "repentance for the remission of sins." What the men in Acts 19 did not know was the baptism of the Holy Spirit done *by Jesus* at Pentecost. Did this make their initial water baptism under John null and void? If so, what about all the saints who were baptized prior to Pentecost in Acts 2? If this theological nonsense about "Christian baptism" was the case, then any baptized believer, prior to Acts 2:38, should have been rebaptized at Pentecost, or thereafter. This type of thinking is similar to some denominations which require water baptism again if it is not performed according to their church doctrines (sprinkling vs. dunking, or in the name of Jesus or the Trinity).

As far as calling Acts 2:38 a "Christian baptism," I find this interesting, especially since believers were not called "Christians" until Antioch in Acts 11:25-26, and even then (also in Acts 11) it also stated the following:

19 Now they which were scattered abroad upon the persecution that arose about Stephen travelled as far as Phenice, and Cyprus, and Antioch, <u>preaching the word to none but unto the Jews only.</u> Acts 11:19

Acts 11 clearly shows that "Christian baptism" is a presumptuous terminology imposed by theologians (not the Bible). As mentioned, some theologians still teach that the baptism Peter preached was not the same water baptism of repentance for the remission of sins as John's, and this is due to the words of Jesus in Matthew 28 ("baptizing in the name of the Father, the Son, and the Holy Ghost"). Secondly, in the minds of those Jews who were "scattered abroad," the gospel of the kingdom was the only gospel they knew, and it was being preached to "Jews only" as late as Acts 11, which was over a decade after the time of Pentecost in Acts 2. Acts 11 also clearly teaches that the first "Christians" were "Jews only." Remember, there is no indication that the Jewish believers were preaching to anyone, other than Jews as late as Acts 11. Sure, we have Peter going to the home of Cornelius, a Gentile, but this was a *special* revelation from the Lord to Peter, and Peter was not only fearful of the Jews for having gone to the home of Cornelius (Acts 11), but he was also concerned because it was still "unlawful" for a Jew to be in the home of a Gentile (Acts 10:28).

For the believer today in the Body of Christ, it is the blood of Jesus Christ that cleanses us from all unrighteousness—not water, and there is no indication in Acts 10 that Peter ever preached the gospel of the grace of God to Cornelius and his household. There is no such thing as "Christian baptism" because the "apostle to the Gentiles" was "not sent to baptize, but the preach the gospel" (given to him by direct revelation of Jesus Christ).

It is the "Acts 2 dispensationalists" (those who believe the Church "began at Pentecost") who can't seem to eradicate the

Jewish practice of water baptism during the "dispensation of the grace of God," even though Paul never commanded "repent and be baptized" in his thirteen epistles. The Body of Christ is not promised to be a "kingdom of (royal) priests" like Israel was (Ex.19:6; I Peter 2:6-12), and secondly, Jewish priests were required to perform ceremonial cleansings (Ex. 30:17-21; Num. 19:7). Under Paul's gospel, however, both Jews and Gentiles are one in Christ, and this is only accomplished through us being baptized "*by* one Spirit into one Body." The Body of Christ is "not a royal priesthood"; it is "the one new man" of Paul epistles.

What Does Acts 19 *Really* Teach?

Water baptism is still the major focus of salvation for many denominations, and they believe Acts 19 provides proof:

> *2 He said unto them, <u>Have ye received the Holy Ghost since [once] ye believed?</u> And they said unto him, We have not so much as heard whether there be any Holy Ghost. 3 And he said unto them, Unto what then were ye baptized? And they said, <u>Unto John's baptism</u>. 4 <u>Then said Paul</u>, John verily baptized with the baptism of repentance, <u>saying unto the people</u> [John speaking], that they should <u>believe on him</u> [Jesus] which should come after him, <u>that is, on Christ Jesus</u>. 5 When they [the people John preached to] heard this, they were baptized in the name of the Lord Jesus.*
>
> *Acts 19:2-5 (brackets by the author)*

Was it not John the Baptist who stated that Jesus would "come after him"? Didn't John prepare the way of the Lord? John indeed preached "the baptism of repentance for the remission of sins" (Matt. 3:2; Mark 1:4), so Paul was simply stating to these twelve men (in Acts 19:4-5) what John told the hearers (at the Jordan River) to do, and they (those at the river) were water baptized in the name of Jesus. Acts 19:5 is not about Paul water baptizing these twelve men all over again; it was Paul stating that "they" (those at the Jordan River) were then baptized in the name of Jesus. Is this not the "baptism of John" that the twelve men were already acquainted with in this Acts 19 passage? What these twelve men didn't know was the baptism of the Holy Spirit performed by Jesus in Acts 2.

Please follow this logic: At Pentecost, when the "little flock" was all together "in one place" (which occurred before the Twelve ever preached to the crowd at Jerusalem), did the disciples have to lay hands on one another to receive the Holy Ghost, as Paul did to these men in Acts 19? Not at all, because it was promised that *Jesus* would baptize the "little flock" *with* the Holy Ghost, and no assistance was required from the apostles themselves. So, when the Jews repented and were water baptized, as commanded in Acts 2:38, the Holy Spirit immediately came upon them. There is no indication that the Twelve apostles had to go around and lay hands on the 3,000 new converts for this to have occurred. If Paul had rebaptized (with water) the twelve men in Acts 19, shouldn't they have received the Holy Spirit immediately, just as the believers did at Pentecost (without the laying on of hands)? The twelve men lacked the baptism *with* the Holy Spirit, so

Paul simply laid hands on them, and they received the Spirit. He didn't rebaptize them with water, as some propose; otherwise, the "laying on of hands" wouldn't have been needed. The Acts 19 men did not receive the Holy Ghost at their baptism (John's), so the "laying on of hands" solved this problem for them.

> *6 And when Paul had laid his hands upon them, the Holy Ghost came on them; and they spake with tongues, and prophesied. Acts 19:6*

Again, Paul simply laid hands on them, and they received the Holy Ghost.

Did Peter have to "lay hands" on the uncircumcised Gentiles in the home of Corneilus in Acts 10? Of course not, because the Holy Spirit came upon them even prior to their water baptism. That was something new to Peter, and they (the men with him) were amazed.

> *42 And he commanded us to preach unto the people, and to testify that it is he which was ordained of God to be the Judge of quick and dead. 43 To him give all the prophets witness, that through his name whosoever believeth in him shall receive remission of sins. 44 <u>While Peter yet spake these words, the Holy Ghost fell on all them which heard the word. 45 And they of the circumcision which believed were astonished, as many as came with Peter,</u>*

> *because that on the Gentiles also was poured*
> *out the gift of the Holy Ghost. Acts 10:42-45*

A similar situation occurred in Acts 8 when Peter and John laid hands on the believers who had already been water baptized. The "laying on of hands" gave them the "Holy Ghost," and they were able to do signs and wonders.

> *12 But when they believed Philip preaching the things concerning the kingdom of God, and the name of Jesus Christ, they were baptized, both men and women. 13 Then Simon himself believed also: and when he was baptized, he continued with Philip, and wondered, beholding the miracles and signs which were done. 14 Now when the apostles which were at Jerusalem heard that Samaria had received the word of God, they sent unto them Peter and John: 15 Who, when they were come down, prayed for them, that they might receive the Holy Ghost: 16 (For as yet he was fallen upon none of them: only they were baptized in the name of the Lord Jesus.) 17 Then laid they their hands on them, and they received the Holy Ghost. Acts 8:12-17*

This "laying on of hands" allowed the Holy Ghost to be received by them as well. Peter and John did *not* rebaptize these believers; they only laid hands on them, just as Paul had done in Acts 19. The water baptism had already been accomplished. To teach that the men and women in both Acts 8, and the men in Acts 19, needed to be rebaptized with water is simply a waterlogged tradition promulgated by theologians who refuse to "rightly divide the word of truth."

Did Water Baptism Replace Circumcision?

Many people believe water baptism is a replacement for circumcision, but under the gospel of the kingdom, both were being practiced. Jewish males, and devout proselytes, were commanded to be circumcised, as well as water baptized. Even though Paul water baptized *some* during the transitional period outlined in the Book of Acts, he did not command it in his thirteen epistles. Remember, he declared in I Corinthians 1:17 that he had *not* "been sent to baptize, but to preach the gospel…lest the cross of Christ should be made on none effect." Water baptism was certainly a part of the gospel of the kingdom, so we must wonder what "gospel" Paul is referencing in I Corinthians 1:17. Could any apostle under the gospel of the kingdom (the Great Commission) ever make the statement that "Christ sent me not to baptize"? Not at all, so Paul wasn't under the Great Commission; otherwise, he wouldn't have made such a statement to the Corinthians.

Since we now know that faith in the "blood of Christ" provides the necessary means for "the remission of sins" (Rom. 3:24-26), why then must we water baptize for the same purpose? Aren't sins fully forgiven by "faith in His blood"?

24 Being justified freely by his grace through the redemption that is in Christ Jesus: 25 Whom God hath set forth to be a propitiation <u>through</u>

faith in his blood, to declare his righteousness
for the remission of sins that are past, through
the forbearance of God; 26 To declare, I say, at
this time his righteousness: that he might be
just, and the justifier of him which believeth in
Jesus. Romans 3:24-26

Does the Letter to the Colossians Teach Water Baptism?

Paul, in his letter to the Colossians, wrote the following:

10 And ye are complete in him, which is the
head of all principality and power: 11 In whom
also ye are circumcised with the circumcision
made without hands, in putting off the body of
the sins of the flesh by the circumcision of
Christ: 12 Buried with him in baptism, wherein
also ye are risen with him through the faith of
the operation of God, who hath raised him
from the dead. 13 And you, being dead in your
sins and the uncircumcision of your flesh, hath
he quickened together with him, having
forgiven you all trespasses; 14 Blotting out the
handwriting of ordinances that was against us,
which was contrary to us, and took it out of the
way, nailing it to his cross; 15 And having
spoiled principalities and powers, he made a
shew of them openly, triumphing over them in
it. Colossians 2:10-15

Our circumcision (being cut off from the world) is done spiritually (without hands), and yet, most believers will immediately throw water into the next verse when baptism is mentioned. Why? Since our circumcision is spiritual, why can't our baptism be spiritual as well? After all, Paul clearly taught such a baptism to the Corinthians.

> *13 <u>For by one Spirit are we all baptized into one body</u>, whether we be Jews or Gentiles, whether we be bond or free; and have been all made to drink into one Spirit.*
> *I Corinthians 12:13*

By the end of Paul's ministry, he clearly taught *"one* baptism" (Eph. 4:5), and yet, we see many in the Church preaching and practicing *two* baptisms: one with water, and the other *by* one Spirit (not done through any hands of a pastor or priest). Our circumcision and baptism are both "the operation of God" through the Spirit. Under the Great Commission, there were two baptisms, and since Paul declared that believers in the Body of Christ are "not under the Law, but under grace," we are left with only one baptism that will occur for the believer: the one done *"by* one Spirit."

Water baptism, under the Great Commission, was for the "remission of sins," and it was a commission given under the Law. Remember, Exodus 19:6 declares that Israel will be a "kingdom of priests and a holy nation," and ceremonial cleansings were introduced under the Law in the Old Testament (Lev. 15; Num. 19). We know that John the Baptist preached "the baptism of repentance for the remission of sins" in the "gospels," and the so-called *mikvah* were ceremonial cleansings for the purpose of purification described in the Old Testament, especially considering Exodus 19:6, which promises that Israel will be a "kingdom of priests." Such ceremonial cleansings were required of the Jewish priests in Leviticus, and this should be remembered when studying the context of water baptism in the "gospels." Peter even declared that those in Israel (those scattered abroad) were "a chosen generation, a royal priesthood, a holy nation, a peculiar people" in I Peter 2:9.

Nowhere in the Great Commission did a person have an option when it came to water baptism. Sure, there may be rare exceptions, such as the thief on the cross, but repentance and water baptism were taught as the means for "the remission of sins." There is also no reference in the Bible that water baptism washed away the old Adamic nature, especially when the Jews were still told to "confess their sins" for forgiveness, even after water baptism had been performed on many of them (I John 1:8-9).

Didn't the Jews continue their sacrifices in the temple, even after water baptism had been performed on some of them? Did Passover suddenly cease because water baptism removed the Adamic nature, even for infants? Not at all, because Jesus came to fulfill *all* righteousness for us, especially "the lost sheep of the house of Israel," and this is why He was water baptized "under the Law" (Matt. 3:15; Rom. 10:4). Paul, in Colossians 2, clearly stated that our circumcision is spiritual, and for those who insist the baptism in Colossians 2:12 is done with water, they must then abandon the "one baptism" of Ephesians 4:5, while completely ignoring the baptism of I Corinthians 12:13.

As for being "baptized into His death" and "being buried and risen with him," we clearly see how this is all spiritual. It is "*by* one Spirit" that we have been "baptized into one Body." Besides, Paul clarifies that our spiritual baptism is "through the faith of the operation of God" (Col. 2:12), not a preacher performing some ceremony with water. After also learning that the "handwriting of ordinances" (the Law) was also "nailed to the cross" (Col. 2:14), I'm not sure why water baptism would still be necessary after believers are "quickened and made alive" by the Spirit, and "having been forgiven all trespasses" (Col. 2:13) through the blood of Jesus.

6 To the praise of the glory of his grace,
wherein he hath made us accepted in the
beloved. 7 In whom we have redemption
through his blood, the forgiveness of sins,
according to the riches of his grace; 8 Wherein
he hath abounded toward us in all wisdom and
prudence; 9 Having made known unto us the
mystery of his will, according to his good
pleasure which he hath purposed in himself:
Ephesians 1:6-9

14 In whom we have redemption through his
blood, even the forgiveness of sins: 15 Who is
the image of the invisible God, the firstborn of
every creature: Colossians 1:14-15

I think we can all agree that water baptism was a part of the gospel preached by the Twelve; however, as previously mentioned, Paul taught the Corinthians that "Christ sent me not to baptize." The "preaching of the cross" (I Cor. 1:18) does not include any other means of justification than "faith in His blood...for the remission of sins" (Rom. 3:24-26). Water baptism has certainly contributed to our identity crisis.

Everyone should be clear that the Great Commission instructed water baptism for the remission of sins, but I find it interesting that Paul, in his thirteen letters (epistles) does not demand repentance and water baptism for salvation like the Great Commission commanded it. Why is this? Was Paul confused? If so, how could he declare that his gospel message was given by "revelation of Jesus Christ" (Gal. 1:10-12)? He was clear that "Christ sent me not to baptize, but to preach the gospel," and if we doubt that Paul was speaking the truth, we must also consider what he teaches the Corinthian Church in I Corinthians 14.

> *37 If any man think himself to be a prophet, or spiritual, <u>let him acknowledge that the things that I write unto you are the commandments of the Lord</u>. 38 But if any man be ignorant, let him be ignorant. I Corinthians 14:37-38*

At times, Paul does discuss water baptism, as in I Corinthians 1:17; however, in I Corinthians 12:13, we are told that the Spirit is the Baptizer, placing believers into the Body of Christ. This is the "one baptism" of Ephesians 4:5. We know that John the Baptist was sent to water baptize (preparing Israel to become a "kingdom of priests" (Ex. 19:6)), and the Body of Christ is not a part of this, especially since we are called "the new creature."

Peter and Paul preached the same Christ, but their gospel messages were not identical (Gal. 2:7-9). Peter's commission included repentance and water baptism (this is a work), but Paul's salvation message was by grace, through faith, without works. This is why many pastors do not water baptize, especially since Paul warned that any sacrament could easily make the "cross of Christ…of none effect."

Peter was called to the Great Commission, and that is what he maintained throughout his ministry, even though Paul taught him further revelation about faith in the death and resurrection alone for salvation. The Great Commission was to bring Israel to the Messiah, which would have brought blessings to the whole world. Paul, on the other hand, first introduced the importance of justification by faith, apart from the Law of Moses (Acts 13:38-39), and many Gentiles received it openly at that time, causing jealousy among the Jews (Acts 13:40-46; Rom. 11:11-15). Peter would have never proclaimed what I Corinthians 1:17 taught because water baptism was certainly a part of the gospel of the Great Commission he was commanded to preach, beginning in Jerusalem (Luke 24:47).

To Peter, Jesus was the Baptizer at Pentecost *with* the Holy Spirit, but to Paul, the Holy Spirit Himself was the Baptizer, as Paul recorded in his letter to the Corinthians. At Pentecost, Peter used the cross of Christ as a means of national shame (Acts 2:36-37), but Paul uses the message of the cross as the "power of God unto salvation" (Rom. 1:16). These are not the same gospel messages, and baptism should not be seen in the same manner for both.

The Baptism of Romans 6

We have been spiritually baptized into Christ's death, burial, and resurrection, and as I mentioned already, water had nothing to do with this!

> *What shall we say then? Shall we continue in*
> *sin, that grace may abound? ² God forbid.*
> *How shall we, that are dead to sin, live any*
> *longer therein? ³ Know ye not, that so many of*
> *us as were baptized into Jesus Christ were*
> *baptized into his death? ⁴ Therefore we are*
> *buried with him by baptism into death: that*
> *like as Christ was raised up from the dead by*
> *the glory of the Father, even so we also should*
> *walk in newness of life. ⁵ For if we have been*
> *planted together in the likeness of his death,*
> *we shall be also in the likeness*
> *of his resurrection:*
> *Romans 6:1-5*

Romans 6:4 is likely where the idea came to various theologians and believers that being water baptized shows that we are buried to our old selves and then raised with newness of life, but this is a gross misrepresentation of what Christ is showing us. You are dead to sin, so now you are no longer under its dominion.

> *<u>14 For sin shall not have dominion over you:</u>*
> *<u>for ye are not under the law, but under grace.</u>*
> *15 What then? shall we sin, <u>because we are not</u>*
> *<u>under the law, but under grace</u>? God forbid.*
> *16 Know ye not, that to whom ye yield*
> *yourselves servants to obey, his servants ye are*
> *to whom ye obey; whether of sin unto death, or*
> *of obedience unto righteousness? 17 But God*
> *be thanked, <u>that ye were the servants of sin</u>,*
> *but ye have obeyed from the heart that form of*
> *doctrine which was delivered you.*
> *Romans 6:14-18*

Inserting water baptism into Romans 6 completely undermines the passage. We are buried *with* Christ, not *like* Him. In Luke 12, we read the following:

> *50 But I have a baptism to be baptized with;*
> *and how am I straitened till it be*
> *accomplished. Luke 12:50*

Was Christ referring to water baptism in this passage? If so, it is odd that His water baptism had already taken place by John the Baptist, so what baptism is He referring to for a later time? This baptism from Luke 12 (His death) is the baptism we are associated with in Romans 6 and Colossians 2:12—not water.

Mark 10 also explained:

> *35 And James and John, the sons of Zebedee, come unto him, saying, Master, we would that thou shouldest do for us whatsoever we shall desire. 36 And he said unto them, What would ye that I should do for you? 37 They said unto him, Grant unto us that we may sit, one on thy right hand, and the other on thy left hand, in thy glory. 38 But Jesus said unto them, Ye know not what ye ask: <u>can ye drink of the cup that I drink of? and be baptized with the baptism that I am baptized with?</u> Mark 10:35-38*

Again, is Jesus referring to His water baptism in the Jordan River? Of course not. He is speaking about His impending death at Calvary, and when we were baptized "*by* one Spirit," into the Body of Christ, we were baptized into His death. This is done through "the operation of God" through the Holy Spirit, not water. We were also spiritually buried with Him, and one day we will be resurrected as well (Romans 6:1-4). This is spiritual, not physical. We did not physically die with Christ, nor were we buried with Him physically in a tomb. However, in the future, His resurrection is our resurrection as well. What a day that will be when we, too, are given a new body, incapable of corruption! This is explained to members of the Body of Christ in I Corinthians 15:53-58 and 2 Corinthians 5:1-10.

> *²⁰ I am crucified with Christ: nevertheless I live; yet not I, but Christ liveth in me: and the life which I now live in the flesh I live by the faith of the Son of God, who loved me, and gave himself for me. Galatians 2:20*

Again, were we physically crucified with Christ? Of course not, yet Christ (God) lives in us through the Spirit (Eph. 2:21-22). Romans 6:3, again, is clear that when we were baptized *by* one Spirit, we were baptized into Christ and His death. Just as we are identified with Him in His death, we shall also be raised to walk in "newness of life" (Romans 6:4). At the Rapture, the dead in Christ will rise first, then we who are alive at that time, will be transformed into the reality of an immortal body, fashioned like Christ's. Just as Christ was physically raised from the dead, this, too, is our future hope. Right now, we are "seated in heavenly places in Christ (positionally and spiritually)."

> *⁵ Even when we were dead in sins, hath quickened us together with Christ, (by grace ye are saved;) ⁶ <u>And hath raised us up together, and made us sit together in heavenly places in Christ Jesus:</u> ⁷ That in <u>the ages to come</u> he might shew the exceeding riches of his grace in his kindness toward us through Christ Jesus. ⁸ For by grace are ye saved through faith; and that not of yourselves: it is the gift of God: ⁹ Not of works, lest any man should boast. ¹⁰ For we are his workmanship, created in*

Christ Jesus <u>unto good works</u>, which God hath
before ordained that we should walk in them.
Ephesians 2:5-10

No pastor or priest has the final authority on doctrine, and I have yet to meet anyone (especially myself) who has the final word on all spiritual matters concerning God and His word. We are commanded to "rightly divide" it, not privately interpret it (2 Peter 1:20-21). Water baptism is not a part of the foundation that Paul laid, because two chapters prior to Paul stating how Christ used him as the one who "laid the foundation" (for the Body of Christ) in I Corinthians 3:10, Paul stated in I Corinthians 1:17 that "Christ sent me not to baptize…lest the cross of Christ be made of none effect." Water baptism was a part of the kingdom gospel message, and this is why water baptism is not a part of Paul's "gospel of the grace of God," which had been "kept secret since the world began." The "handwriting of ordinances" (the Law of Moses) were nailed to the cross, as Paul explained in Colossians 2:13-15, so water baptism is not for today, nor is the tradition that is somehow shows the world "an outward sign of an inward change" taking place for the believer. Romans 6 does not include water baptism; we are put to death, buried with, and will rise from the death, and this is done "*by* one Spirit," placing us into the Body of Christ.

Before Paul was sentenced to death, he declared the following to the Ephesians:

⁴ There is one body, and one Spirit, even as ye
are called in one hope of your calling; ⁵ One

*Lord, one faith, <u>one baptism</u>, 6 One God and
Father of all, who is above all, and through
all, and in you all. Ephesians 4:4-6*

The twelve Ephesian men in Acts 19 were disciples of John the Baptist, which certainly made them Jews, but in his letter to the Ephesians, Paul was writing to the members of the Body of Christ. That is a major difference often overlooked for the sake of traditions concerning water baptism.

It is truly sad how so many Christians see the word "baptism" in the Bible and immediately assign water to its meaning and practice. I Corinthians 12:13 is clear that it is *"by* one Spirit that we are baptized," which places us into the Body of Christ. We are spiritually baptized into Christ's death, burial, and resurrection. We are seated in the heavenlies already with Christ where our citizenship is sealed, and our circumcision is spiritual, and our baptism is as well. If repentance and water baptism is still required for the remission of sins today, then Paul, who wrote more books of the New Testament than any other apostle, was certainly deceptive for not sharing this "sacrament" with the Church that Christ called him to establish.

As a remembrance, here are important passages about the foundation Paul was called to lay down for the Body:

*10 According to the grace of God which is
given unto me, as a wise masterbuilder, <u>I have
laid the foundation, and another buildeth
thereon</u>. But let every man take heed how he*

*buildeth thereupon. [11] For other foundation
can no man lay than that is laid, which is
Jesus Christ. I Corinthians 3:10-11*

*[20] This gate of the LORD, into which the
righteous shall enter. [21] I will praise thee: for
thou hast heard me, and art become my
salvation. [22] The stone which the builders
refused is become the head stone of the corner.
[23] This is the LORD's doing; it is marvellous in
our eyes. [24] This is the day which
the LORD hath made; we will rejoice and be
glad in it. Psalm 118:20-24*

*[18] For through him we both have access by one
Spirit unto the Father. [19] Now therefore ye are
no more strangers and foreigners, but
fellowcitizens with the saints, and of the
household of God; [20] And are built upon the
foundation of the apostles and prophets, Jesus
Christ himself being the chief corner stone;
[21] In whom all the building fitly framed
together groweth unto an holy temple in the
Lord: [22] In whom ye also are builded together
for an habitation of God through the Spirit.
Ephesians 2:18-22*

Last Points about Baptism

I have always found it erroneous for Protestants to use the
thief on the cross as an argument for why their denomination

doesn't require water baptism. It's a pointless argument, to say the least. The obvious reason why the thief was not water baptized is because he was on a cross, having also been crucified alongside of Christ. If you believe and preach that we are still under the Great Commission, you should not be using the thief on the cross as a justification for why water baptism is not necessary. On the contrary, you should be water baptizing because that was a command under the Great Commission. All these preachers are doing is trying to reconcile the gospel of the kingdom with the gospel of the grace of God, and they sometimes use the thief on the cross as a poor example to convince believers why they don't need to baptize with water, even though they proclaim the Great Commission, which commands it. They are not "rightly dividing the word of truth," and this has caused nothing but confusion and divisions within and between millions of believers. The reason the thief on the cross was not water baptized was simply because he was a bit preoccupied at the time and was unable to comply. Had he been able to, he would have repented and followed this up with water baptism for the remission of his sins. Thankfully, Jesus is not bound by the silly traditions of men.

The other argument that many believers use to command water baptism is based on their reasoning that since Jesus was water baptized, "...we should be water baptized, too." They are ignorant of the following passages:

> *⁴ But when the fulness of the time was come,*
> *God sent forth his Son, made of a woman,*
> <u>*made under the law, ⁵ To redeem them that*</u>

*were under the law, that we might receive the
adoption of sons. Galatians 4:4-5*

*3 For I could wish that myself were accursed
from Christ for my brethren, my kinsmen
according to the flesh: 4 Who are Israelites; to
whom pertaineth the adoption, and the glory,
and the covenants, and the giving of the law,
and the service of God, and the promises;
5 Whose are the fathers, and of whom as
concerning the flesh Christ came, who is over
all, God blessed for ever. Romans 9:3-5*

*11 Wherefore remember, that ye being in time
past Gentiles in the flesh, who are called
Uncircumcision by that which is called the
Circumcision in the flesh made by hands;
12 That at that time ye were without Christ,
being aliens from the commonwealth of Israel,
and strangers from the covenants of promise,
having no hope, and without God in the world:
Ephesians 2:11-12*

*14 For sin shall not have dominion over you:
for ye are not under the law, but under grace.
Romans 6:14*

Gentiles were not given the Law, nor were they
commanded to place themselves under the Law. Jesus was
baptized because He was sent to fulfill all righteousness,

which included the ceremonial cleansings under the Levitical Law (Lev. 8,14,16).

> *15 And Jesus answering said unto him, Suffer it to be so now: for thus it becometh us <u>to fulfil all righteousness</u>. Then he suffered him.*
> *Matthew 3:15*

Jesus certainly did not have any need for the "remission of sins," so it is clear that He was water baptized because He was "born under the Law...to redeem them that were under the Law." If you insist on being water baptized because Jesus was, then you are now obligated to fulfill all the Law's demands (James 2:10). You might say that Jesus fulfilled the Law already, to which you would be correct, but that was not proclaimed until Paul was converted in Acts 9, and he was, after all, the "apostle to the Gentiles" who proclaimed that there is *now* only "one baptism" for today. You must determine if the one baptism he meant was water or spiritual. You shouldn't practice both at a time when there is only "one baptism" for today.

Concluding Thoughts about Baptism
Water baptism has become one of the major divisions within the Church, not because God has made it a confusing doctrine, but because the Church can't disengage from the nonsensical traditions it has sometime invented because of a refusal to "rightly divide the word of truth." Yes, Christ taught water baptism for the remission of sins, but He also didn't send Paul to water baptize, "but to preach the gospel."

Under Paul's gospel, it is "faith in His blood for the remission of sins."

When we finally "rightly divide the word of truth" and understand "the revelation of the mystery" given to Paul, we will no longer need to argue over such doctrines related to baptism, circumcision, the Law, and salvation by faith alone. The identity crisis we have in Christianity has everything to do with our failure to recognize the unique role of the Apostle Paul to the Gentiles. As I stated, because the Church has failed to "rightly divide the word of truth," we will forever send an ambiguous salvation message to the world, and we will continue to perpetuate the identity crisis we have created. Since God is not the "author of confusion," who is?

> [33] *For God is not the author of confusion, but*
> *of peace, as in all churches of the saints.*
> *I Corinthians 14:33*

CHAPTER 11

Rightly Dividing the End Times: Part One

⁵⁰ Now this I say, brethren, that flesh and blood cannot inherit the kingdom of God; neither doth corruption inherit incorruption.
⁵¹ Behold, I shew you a mystery; We shall not all sleep, but we shall all be changed, ⁵² In a moment, in the twinkling of an eye, at the last trump: for the trumpet shall sound, and the dead shall be raised incorruptible, and we shall be changed. I Corinthians 15:50-52

The Study of the End Times (Eschatology)

The eschatological understanding of the "end times," including the so-called Rapture, has been shortsighted by many Christian denominations around the world. The special revelation, concerning the Rapture (found only in Paul's epistles), is unique to the Body of Christ *only*. It has nothing to do with national Israel (promised an earthly kingdom), nor is there any mention of believers being "caught up to meet the Lord in the air" during the earthly ministry of Jesus Christ. Some theologians have attempted to place the

Rapture into the "gospels," but the "meeting in the air" (described in I Thessalonians 4:13-18) was *never* given to Israel—only individual Jews and Gentiles in the Body of Christ. You will search in vain to find the so-called Rapture in any books outside of Paul's epistles, which makes sense when you reread the quote at the beginning of this chapter from I Corinthians 15:50-52.

It appears Paul was also anticipating this "meeting in the air" to take place within his lifetime, especially when he stated, "Then *we which are alive* and remain shall be *caught up* together…to meet the Lord in the air" (I Thes. 4:17). This "catching away" was revealed as a "mystery" to Paul (by Christ), so it is not found in the Old Testament, "the gospels," early Acts, or even the Book of Revelation; otherwise, Paul couldn't have declared, "Behold, I show you a mystery…" to the Corinthians a couple decades after the so-called Olivet Discourse of Matthew 24. The Book of Revelation is a detailed description of what will occur "in the ages to come."

Just as Paul was expecting this "meeting in the air" to take place in his lifetime, the twelve apostles, and other believing Israelites ("little flock"), were also expecting to see the earthly kingdom that God promised to that nation (long before God had ever revealed "the revelation of the mystery" to Paul). The promised kingdom was *not* a mystery at all; the fact that Gentiles could be fellow heirs with Jesus Christ, apart from Israel, certainly was "the mystery."

Jesus told them what to expect in the following passage:

> *31 And he shall send his angels with a great*
> *sound of a trumpet, and they shall gather*

> *together his elect from the four winds, from*
> *one end of heaven to the other.* *32 Now learn a*
> *parable of the fig tree; When his branch is yet*
> *tender, and putteth forth leaves, <u>ye know that</u>*
> *<u>summer is nigh:</u> 33 So likewise ye, <u>when ye</u>*
> *<u>shall see all these things</u>, know that it is near,*
> *even at the doors.* *34 Verily I say unto you, <u>This</u>*
> *<u>generation shall not pass, till all these things</u>*
> *<u>be fulfilled.</u> Matthew 24:31-34*

Matthew 24:34 has been used by many atheists to assist in their attack on the divinity of Jesus Christ because the Tribulation and Second Coming did not occur as He said it would (within the lifetime of the apostles ("this generation")). These atheists have also failed to "rightly divide the word of truth" by not recognizing "the revelation of the mystery" given to Paul, which caused a pause in the prophetic fulfillment of these events Jesus described in the so-called Olivet Discourse of Matthew 24. Jesus did not reveal any "meeting in the air" during His earthly ministry because it was later revealed as a "mystery" to Paul, the "apostle to the Gentiles." This pause in the prophetic events written in Scripture brought salvation to Gentiles who were supposed to be blessed *through* Israel (Isa. 60:1-3), but Israel's rejection left Gentiles "without hope" (Eph. 2:11-12). No one knew, however, that God already had a "hidden wisdom," which He ordained *before* the world began, and this "revelation of the mystery" would provide salvation to the whole world "by grace, through faith…not of works," and it occurred "because of Israel's fall" (Rom. 11:11).

Why The Body of Christ Was Introduced

Peter, after Acts 2, continued to offer another opportunity for Israel to receive the kingdom promised to Israel. The following passage described the events that took place the day after Pentecost. Note the following:

> *19 <u>Repent ye therefore, and be converted, that your sins may be blotted out, when the times of refreshing shall come from the presence of the Lord.</u> 20 And <u>he shall send Jesus Christ,</u> which before was preached unto you: 21 <u>Whom the heaven must receive until the times of restitution of all things, which God hath spoken by the mouth of all his holy prophets since the world began.</u> Acts 3:19-21*

Did the *nation* of Israel repent of their sins, especially for the death of Jesus, *the* Christ? Not at all, and this is evidenced by their hiring of Saul (Paul) to persecute and destroy the Church that was at Jerusalem (Acts 8:1-2; Gal. 1:13; I Tim. 1:13). In the Old Testament, Israel continually rejected God the Father (killing the prophets He had sent to the nation). They also rejected the God the Son when they cried out for His crucifixion before Pilate. Finally, in Acts 7, they had blasphemed the Holy Ghost and stoned Stephen to death. This is when we are first introduced to Saul (Paul), who was also consenting unto Stephen's death. The Tribulation would have been the next prophetic event to occur at that time, especially when Stephen looked up into heavens and "saw the Son of man standing at the right hand of God" (Acts 7:55-56). In Acts 7:60, Stephen prayed that the Lord would "lay *not* this sin to their charge," and the Lord certainly answered this prayer when He sent the "chief of sinners" (Paul) to preach the greatest gospel ever known to humanity. This was (and is) the "hidden wisdom," which God "ordained before the world unto our glory."

> *7 But we speak the wisdom of God in a mystery, even <u>the hidden wisdom, which God ordained before the world unto our glory</u>: 8 Which none of the princes of this world knew: for had they known it, <u>they would not have crucified the Lord of glory</u>. I Corinthians 2:7-8*

We are told in Luke 9:1-6 that the disciples had gone out to "preach the gospel," which included curing diseases and healing the sick. However, in Luke 18:31-34, we clearly see that the gospel they were preaching in Luke 9 couldn't have been "the preaching of the cross," because the disciples "understood none of these things" about the death and resurrection of Jesus, even as late as Acts 7. The "preaching of the cross" was *not* understood during the earthly ministry of Jesus, and the early chapters in Acts, and we now understand why. Had Satan known about the gospel of the grace of God ("the revelation of the mystery"), he would have made sure that Jesus was never crucified. Israel was, and still is, to be saved through the gospel of the kingdom (Matt. 24:14), but God, before the foundation of the world, also chose to save humanity through the gospel of the grace of

God, which was *first* revealed to Paul "for a *pattern* to them which should hereafter believe on Him to life everlasting" (I Tim. 1:16). This pattern will continue "until the fulness of the Gentiles be come in." The Rapture will conclude God's purpose for the Body of Christ on Earth, but we will still serve an even greater *eternal* purpose through Christ in Glory. Note the following:

> *25 For I would not, brethren, that ye should be ignorant of this mystery, lest ye should be wise in your own conceits; that blindness in part is happened to Israel, until the fulness of the Gentiles be come in.*
> *Romans 11:25*

> *9 Having made known unto us the mystery of his will, according to his good pleasure which he hath purposed in himself: 10 That in the dispensation of the fulness of times he might gather together in one all things in Christ, both which are in heaven, and which are on earth; even in him: 11 In whom also we have obtained an inheritance, being predestinated according to the purpose of him who worketh all things after the counsel of his own will: 12 That we should be to the praise of his glory, who first trusted in Christ.*
> *Ephesians 1:9-12*

The Rapture and Second Coming of Christ

Most believers mistakenly confuse the events associated with the so-called Rapture and the Second Coming of Jesus Christ, not realizing the "mystery" associated with "meeting the Lord in the air" wasn't revealed until long *after* the conversion of Paul. Paul did not preach "the gospel of the kingdom," especially since the Body has a citizenship in Heaven. Yes, he preached to the Jews that Jesus was the Messiah, as the other apostles had declared, but Paul did not teach the so-called Great Commission because he was called to preach "among the Gentiles, the *unsearchable* riches of Christ." The Great Commission (gospel of the kingdom) was already "searchable."

8 Unto me, who am less than the least of all saints, is this grace given, that <u>I should preach among the Gentiles the unsearchable riches of Christ;</u> 9 <u>And to make all men see what is the fellowship of the mystery, which from the beginning of the world hath been hid in God</u>, who created all things by Jesus Christ:
Ephesians 3:8-9

20 For our conversation [citizenship] is in heaven; from whence also we look for the Saviour, the Lord Jesus Christ:
Philippians 3:20 (brackets by author)

13 But he that shall endure unto the end [of the Tribulation], the same shall be saved. 14 And

this gospel of the kingdom shall be preached in
all the world for a witness unto all nations;
and then shall the end come.
Matthew 24:13-14 (brackets by author)

Thankfully, rather than "enduring to the end," the Body of Christ has already "been made conquerors" through Jesus Christ. How can believers read the following verses and still believe we must "endure to the end" to be saved?

31 What shall we then say to these things? If
God be for us, who can be against us? 32 He
that spared not his own Son, but delivered him
up for us all, how shall he not with him also
freely give us all things? 33 Who shall lay any
thing to the charge of God's elect? It is God
that justifieth. 34 Who is he that condemneth? It
is Christ that died, yea rather, that is risen
again, who is even at the right hand of God,
who also maketh intercession for us. 35 Who
shall separate us from the love of Christ? shall
tribulation, or distress, or persecution, or
famine, or nakedness, or peril, or sword? 36 As
it is written, For thy sake we are killed all the
day long; we are accounted as sheep for the
slaughter. 37 Nay, in all these things we are
more than conquerors through him that loved
us. 38 For I am persuaded, that neither death,
nor life, nor angels, nor principalities, nor
powers, nor things present, nor things to come,

*³⁹ Nor height, nor depth, nor any other
creature, shall be able to separate us from the
love of God, which is in Christ Jesus our Lord.
Romans 8:31-39*

Prior to Paul's encounter with Jesus, the "lost sheep of the house of Israel" had already been told that "the kingdom of heaven is *at hand*," but those believers were completely unaware that God would reveal a "mystery" regarding Jews and Gentiles being saved by grace, through faith (in the death and resurrection of Jesus), which baptized them both (*by* one Spirit) into one body with a heavenly citizenship. God had to offer the kingdom to Israel *first*, but with their rejection, God was already prepared to offer salvation to all of humanity through the gospel He sent Paul to proclaim.

*⁴⁵ But when the Jews saw the multitudes, they
were filled with envy, and spake against those
things which were spoken by Paul,
contradicting and blaspheming. ⁴⁶ Then Paul
and Barnabas waxed bold, and said, <u>It was
necessary that the word of God should first
have been spoken to you: but seeing ye put it
from you, and judge yourselves unworthy of
everlasting life, lo, we turn to the Gentiles.</u>
Acts 13:45-46*

They also never knew about a "catching away" of believers "to meet the Lord in the air" until Paul revealed it as a "mystery" much later than Matthew 24 (the so-called Olivet

Discourse). The Jews did, however, anticipate Jesus returning to Earth from where He had ascended. This was following their inquiry into their question about restoring "again the kingdom to Israel" (Acts 1:6). At His ascension, we read:

> *[10] And while they looked stedfastly toward heaven as he went up, behold, two men stood by them in white apparel; [11] Which also said, Ye men of Galilee, why stand ye gazing up into heaven? this same Jesus, which is taken up from you into heaven, <u>shall so come in like manner as ye have seen him go into heaven</u>. [12] Then returned they unto Jerusalem from the mount called Olivet... Acts 1:10-12*

> *Behold, <u>the day of the LORD cometh</u>, and thy spoil shall be divided in the midst of thee. [2] <u>For I will gather all nations against Jerusalem to battle</u>; and the city shall be taken, and the houses rifled, and the women ravished; and half of the city shall go forth into captivity, and the residue of the people shall not be cut off from the city. [3] <u>Then shall the LORD go forth, and fight against those nations, as when he fought in the day of battle.</u> [4] And <u>his feet shall stand in that day upon the mount of Olives</u>... Zechariah 14:1-4*

Has this return happened yet? Has the "day of the Lord" occurred, which is associated with Israel and the Tribulation period, as well as the timing of the Lord's return? The "day of the Lord" is a time of judgment, but since the giving of "the revelation of the mystery," God has dispensed His grace instead of His wrath. We will not experience the prophetic event of the "Day of the Lord," because we have been "saved from wrath" through Jesus Christ.

The following verses describe this "day of the Lord" event:

The word that Isaiah the son of Amoz saw <u>concerning Judah and Jerusalem</u>. 2 And it shall come to pass <u>in the last days</u>, that the mountain of the LORD's house shall be established in the top of the mountains, and shall be exalted above the hills; and all nations shall flow unto it. 3 And many people shall go and say, Come ye, and let us go up to the mountain of the LORD, to the house of the God of Jacob; and he will teach us of his ways, and we will walk in his paths: for out of Zion shall go forth the law, and the word of the LORD from Jerusalem... 12 <u>For the day of the LORD of hosts shall be upon every one that is proud and lofty, and upon every one that is lifted up; and he shall be brought low:</u>
Isaiah 2:1-3 and 12

30 And I will shew wonders in the heavens and in the earth, blood, and fire, and pillars of smoke. 31 The sun shall be turned into darkness, and the moon into blood, <u>before the</u>

great and terrible day of the LORD come.
32 And it shall come to pass, that whosoever
shall call on the name of the LORD shall be
delivered: for in mount Zion and in Jerusalem
shall be deliverance, as the LORD hath said,
and in the remnant whom the LORD shall call.
Joel 2:30-32 (see Acts 2:19-21)

But of the times and the seasons, brethren, ye
have no need that I write unto you. 2 For
yourselves know perfectly that the day of the
Lord so cometh as a thief in the night. 3 For
when they shall say, Peace and safety; then
sudden destruction cometh upon them, as
travail upon a woman with child; and they
shall not escape…9 For God hath not
appointed us to wrath, but to obtain salvation
by our Lord Jesus Christ, 10 Who died for us,
that, whether we wake or sleep,
we should live together with him.
I Thessalonians 5:1-3 and 9-10

8 But God commendeth his love toward us, in
that, while we were yet sinners, Christ died for
us. 9 Much more then, being now justified by
his blood, we shall be saved from wrath
through him. 10 For if, when we were enemies,
we were reconciled to God by the death of his
Son, much more, being reconciled, we shall be
saved by his life. Romans 5:8-11

Paul explained to the Thessalonians that he did not need to write to them about the day of the Lord, with its death and destruction. This is because Paul explained how "God has not appointed us to wrath…" and how we (who believe) "shall be saved from wrath through Him" (I Thes. 5:9; Rom. 5:9). This news should bring great joy to believers, but thanks to the traditions of men, this too has been stolen from the Body by religious doctrines that "spiritualize" these verses in a way Paul never intended.

The seriousness of these "end time" events is such that God would have never allowed the understanding of them to be left up to the allegorical interpretations of humans, especially those who ignore 2 Timothy 2:15. Paul was very clear that the Church is saved from God's wrath, and yet various denominations forbid the preaching of such a truth, and this is done for the "sake of their traditions." Salvation, through the "preaching of the cross," has been provided free to all who believe, but religious traditions have come at a great cost, robbing millions of the precious truths within His word, especially in preparation for the "end times."

Many still believe the Body of Christ must endure the Tribulation, but "to whom" was Jesus speaking when He declared in Matthew 24:13, "…he that shall endure to the end, the same shall be saved"? Was the Body of Christ even known at that time Jesus spoke these words? The "one new man" was not introduced to Paul until after Acts 9. Ignoring these facts has led to an identity crisis, especially regarding the "end times." Some often forget how there will be a sealed remnant in the "ages to come" (Rev. 7:1-4), according to the election of grace (Rom. 11:5-6), and they will endure the

Tribulation, and it was to (and about) them that Jesus was speaking in Matthew 24:13. Revelation speaks of this remnant in the Tribulation.

> *⁴ And I heard the number of them which were* <u>*sealed*</u>*: and there were sealed* <u>*an hundred and forty and four thousand of all the tribes of the children of Israel*</u>*. Revelation 7:4*

Reasons Some Believers Reject the Rapture

Skeptics disregard the Rapture as the unique conclusion to the "time of the Gentiles" (Rom. 11:25) for a variety of reasons. They claim the word "rapture" does not appear in the Bible, but neither do the words Trinity, Christmas, Easter, Incarnation, Immaculate Conception, Purgatory, Second Coming, Transubstantiation and many other words often used to describe both biblical and nonbiblical doctrinal teachings promulgated by various churches. If certain denominations are willing to base entire theological movements on implied teachings not found in the Bible, I would say the absence of the word "rapture" is the least of their worries. The Greek meaning of the Latin "rapture" does appear in the Scripture, but unless you study, you will continue to ignore this blessed truth.

The other reason why some denominations don't believe in a Rapture is due to the tradition that the Church is "spiritual Israel," and God is in the process of fulfilling His prophetic promises to Israel through the Church, *not* the nation to whom these *literal* covenants and promises were made. Again, denominational pastors and priests believe God is fulfilling His prophetic promises to Israel through the Church, and therefore, they often overlook the Rapture.

These same theologians also tend to deny a literal 1000-year reign of Christ in Jerusalem after the Second Coming because they have surmised that the Millennial Kingdom is currently taking place spiritually (or symbolically) in "the hearts of believers" in the Church, so there is no need for a *literal* Millennial Kingdom of 1000 years (according to their claims). This is ridiculous when you consider that Revelation 20 describes how Satan will be bound "a thousand years" during the Millennial reign of Jesus, so if the Millennial Kingdom is currently taking place, it appears Satan is not bound, given all the evil in this world.

This also completely disregards the words of Jesus that "the kingdom of heaven is at hand," which He proclaimed in "the gospels." If it were only a "symbolic" kingdom in the "hearts of believers," then we must ask what the apostles meant in Acts 1:6 when they questioned whether Jesus would, at that time, "restore again the kingdom to Israel." Did Israel not possess, at one time, a literal, physical land prior to Acts 1:6? Were the apostles not asking if this physical kingdom of Israel would be "restored" to them for an "everlasting possession" (Gen. 17:8; 2 Sam. 7:5-13)? Was Abraham mistaken in promising Israel a literal kingdom (land) between the Nile and Euphrates rivers (Gen. 15:18)? Are these rivers symbolic in some way, only meant for the "spiritual Israel" of the future involving the Gentiles as well? This teaching of a "symbolic" kingdom in the "hearts of believers" violates dozens of passages in the Bible that teach otherwise, and I have shared many of them, which refute the "symbolic" views of amillennialism. Again, this is all due to not "rightly dividing the word of truth."

Amillennialists tend to believe the Church has replaced God's promises to Israel, and this somehow permits them to reinterpret the literal fulfillment of past and future prophecies revealed "since the world began." In essence, amillennialists don't fully understand the two-fold purpose of God for Israel and the Body of Christ. By imposing a "symbolic" view upon various prophecies, they are able to completely rewrite eschatology (study of the end times) into whatever doctrine that suits their theology. This allows them to either abandon the teachings of a so-called "Rapture" altogether, or it allows them include elements of it in other passages outside Paul's epistles, especially in verses that discuss "one taken, and one left behind," which has nothing to do with the Body of Christ. Many theologians aren't even sure who is "taken," and who it "left behind."

To accept amillennialism, you must disregard God's *literal* and *unconditional* promises to Israel concerning a kingdom that will be established on Earth in the future. They assume "Israel" means "all the people of God" (from Adam to now), even though there was a "middle wall of partition" between Jews and Gentiles prior to Paul's conversion. Acts 10 introduces the commonality of Jews and Gentiles for salvation, but the "middle wall" was officially "broken down" through the gospel of the grace of God given to Paul (Acts 20:24), especially when Gentiles were brought nigh unto God through the blood of Jesus Christ (Eph. 2:13). Failing to recognize the separation that *did* exist between Israel and the Gentiles (Matt. 10:5-7; 15:21-28; John 4:22), especially during the earthly ministry of Jesus, is one of the reasons some denominations vehemently defend the theology that the Church is "spiritual Israel," which closely resembles the doctrines of Replacement Theology. Once again, these denominations also disregard God's twofold purpose for both "Heaven and Earth." They see only one kingdom where all believers, from all ages, will reside in the New Jerusalem, which will descend from Heaven and exist in "the new heaven and the new earth" (2 Pet. 3:13). They do not regard God's eternal purpose for Israel (Earth), and His eternal purpose for the Body of Christ (Heaven), as two separate destinies—one known "since the world began," and the other "kept secret since the world began."

> *⁹ Having made known unto us <u>the mystery of his will</u> [God's eternal purpose for heaven and earth], according to his good pleasure which he hath purposed in himself: ¹⁰ <u>That in the dispensation of the fulness of times he might gather together in one all things in Christ, both which are in heaven, and which are on earth; even in him:</u> ¹¹ In whom also we have obtained an inheritance, being predestinated according to the purpose of him who worketh all things after the counsel of his own will: ¹² That <u>we</u> should be to the praise of his glory, <u>who first trusted in Christ.</u> ¹³ In whom <u>ye also</u> trusted, <u>after that ye heard the word of truth, the gospel of your salvation: in whom also after that ye believed, ye were sealed with that</u>*

> *holy Spirit of promise, [the seal is the Holy*
> *Spirit] 14 Which is the earnest [guarantee] of*
> *our inheritance until the redemption of the*
> *purchased possession,*
> *unto the praise of his glory.*
> *Ephesians 1:9-14 (brackets by author)*

Is the Kingdom Literal or Symbolic?

Many denominations, which do not "rightly divide" between Paul's "revelation of the mystery," and Israel's prophetic promises, completely omit the Rapture by placing all believers into one eternal kingdom after the return of Jesus Christ, which, as I have stated, means they believe the Body of Christ will endure the Tribulation first. They also completely disregard the "meeting in the air" as nothing more than the Body of Christ being "caught up" quickly to only return immediately with Christ to Earth (as King), which will be followed by the judgment of the (so-called) Great White Throne. Some believe the Judgment Seat of Christ is for all believers (both Old and New Testament), but this judgment is not found anywhere in prophecy—only Paul's epistles to the Church, the Body of Christ. Remember, some denominations teach that there is *no literal* 1000-year reign of Christ in Jerusalem—only symbolically in the "hearts of believers." Again, to them, the Messianic Kingdom is being fulfilled today through the Church, and not according to the past promises of God, which were given only to Israel through covenants that God made specifically with and to them. This fulfillment of God is yet future. There is no "Covenant of Works, Redemption, or Grace" found in the Bible, and these have also been used to conveniently support the Church as being "spiritual Israel."

Those who do not "rightly divide," also believe the final judgment of the saved and unsaved ("just" and "unjust") will take place as *one* end times judgment. Again, they see this as one resurrection in Revelation 20, which I will quote shortly. According to amillennialism, and the churches that defend it, if your name is in the "Book of Life, you will appear before the Judgment Seat of Christ" (2 Cor. 5:10) to receive rewards, or the loss of them. If your name is *not* in the Book of Life, you will appear before the Great White Throne Judgment, only to be cast into eternal damnation, which now some believers doubt even exists as a literal place. I guess Satan is "off the hook" as well.

Again, amillennialists disregard John's 1000-year Millennial reign of Christ on Earth, prior to the final Great White Throne Judgment. They see this millennial reign as nothing more than symbolizing the current "Church age," which has lasted some 2000 years. Interestingly, the denominations that support amillennialism, believe in the Second Coming, but they often, as expected, "spiritualize" the prophecies related to it. Once again, the Body of Christ is not found in prophecy, and neither is its sudden "departure" of the Church. That is why the Body of Christ and the Rapture were both revealed as part of "the mystery, kept secret since the world began." Currently, the nation of Israel is in "blindness," but that will change after the so-called Rapture (Rom. 11:25).

The Judgment Seat of Christ was also given *only* to the Body of Christ, not to the "just" of the Old Testament saints, the "little flock," and those future saints redeemed during the Tribulation. All these saints are associated with Israel, including Gentile proselytes who converted to Judaism. We must remember that the Judgment Seat of Christ only appears in Paul's epistles for the Body, the Church. Paul describes it in three main places in his letters.

8 For whether we live, we live unto the Lord;
and whether we die, we die unto the Lord:
whether we live therefore, or die, we are the
Lord's [eternal security]. 9 For to this end
Christ both died, and rose, and revived, that he
might be Lord both of the dead and living.
10 But why dost thou judge thy brother? or why
dost thou set at nought thy brother? for we
shall all stand before the
judgment seat of Christ.
Romans 14:8-10 (brackets by author)

10 According to the grace of God which is
given unto me, as a wise masterbuilder, I have
laid the foundation, and another buildeth
thereon. But let every man take heed how he
buildeth thereupon. 11 For other foundation
can no man lay than that is laid, which is
Jesus Christ. 12 Now if any man build upon this
foundation gold, silver, precious stones, wood,
hay, stubble; 13 Every man's work shall be
made manifest: for the day shall declare it,
because it shall be revealed by fire; and the

fire shall try every man's work of what sort it is. 14 If any man's work abide which he hath built thereupon, <u>he shall receive a reward</u>. 15 If any man's work shall be burned<u>, he shall suffer loss: but he himself shall be saved; yet so as by fire.</u>
I Corinthians 3:10-15

Catholicism often uses this passage to support the doctrine of "purgatory," because of the use of "fire" (judgment) in this passage; however, this tradition was not formally defined until about 1,000 years after the founding of the Roman Church. There are hints of its earlier belief in oral traditions, but such a tradition only weakens the sufficiency of Christ's atoning sacrifice. Again, believe in what you want, but please understand that it is inherent in many believers to get caught up in "every wind of doctrine" when they don't "rightly divide the word of truth." All the "pomp and circumstance" of religion will likely be burned up at the Judgment Seat of Christ because it is not building upon the foundation establish by Paul for the Body of Christ.

10 For we must all appear before the judgment seat of Christ; that every one may receive the things done in his body, according to that he hath done, whether it be good or bad.
2 Corinthians 5:10

The believer's works (whether good or bad) are judged at once, not according to some prolonged judgment implied by a tradition. Remember, in that same chapter from 2 Corinthians 5, we read the following promise:

> *19 To wit, that God was in Christ, reconciling*
> *the world unto himself, not imputing their*
> *trespasses unto them; and hath committed unto*
> *us the word of reconciliation.*
> *2 Corinthians 5:19*

And to the Body of Christ, we have this promise:

> *13 And you, being dead in your sins and the*
> *uncircumcision of your flesh, hath he*
> *quickened together with him, having forgiven*
> *you all trespasses; 14 Blotting out the*
> *handwriting of ordinances that was against us,*
> *which was contrary to us, and took it out of the*
> *way, nailing it to his cross;*
> *Colossians 2:13-14*

Sin is not judged at the Judgment Seat of Christ, only our works as believers. After all, this is why Paul reminded the Philippians of the following:

> *12 Wherefore, my beloved, as ye have always*
> *obeyed, not as in my presence only, but now*
> *much more in my absence, work out your own*
> *salvation with fear and trembling. 13 For it is*
> *God which worketh in you both to will and to*
> *do of his good pleasure. Philippians 2:12-13*

Please remember this: The Body of Christ is already "reconciled to God" and "declared the righteousness of God in Him" (2 Cor. 5:21), but Paul also shared in Romans 8 that we have not only been "called and justified," but we have already been "glorified" in His sight. Therefore, the Body of Christ will have already been "glorified" by God *when* we appear before the Judgment Seat of Christ. How marvelous is His grace!

What About the Twelve and Israel at Judgment?
On the other hand, Jesus promised the Twelve that they would "sit on twelve thrones, judging the twelve tribes of Israel" during the Millennial reign of Jesus (Matt. 19:28; Rev. 20:4). According to Matthew 24:31, Jesus will send (at His Second Coming) an angel to "gather the elect" of Israel back into their Promised Land where they will be judged, along with the Gentile nations, as described in Matthew 25:31-33 ("sheep from the goats"), and Jude 1:5, which describes the destruction of those from Israel "that believed not." This is when some will remain (in the Millennial Kingdom) and some will be "taken away" and cast into "everlasting punishment." This is quite different than the Rapture when believers will be "taken away" and nonbelievers will be "left behind." Those who are left to enter the Millennial Kingdom will "live and reign with Christ a thousand years" (Rev. 20:4-6). The parable of Luke 19:11-27 pictures how Christ would ascend into Heaven and later return with the Kingdom for Israel, as He promised.

If the amillennialist is correct, and the Millennial reign of Christ is happening now "in the hearts of believers," we are forced to wonder if Satan is bound, as described in Revelation 20, and whether the twelve apostles are reigning on twelve thrones at this time, which is literally promised to occur during the Millennial reign of Christ on Earth (in Jerusalem). I suppose we could somehow "spiritualize" the binding of Satan and the twelve thrones of the twelve apostles, but what do we do about the judgment of the nations in Matthew 25? Has that happened, or is it currently happening at this time? Are the twelve apostles judging at this time, if indeed, the Millennial Kingdom is in the "hearts of believers" today? How is that taking place? Interestingly, when Judas died, Matthias was his replacement, but when James (one of the original apostles) was killed, there was no replacement chosen for him (Acts 12:1-2). Would that not indicate God's shifting from the "twelve tribes of Israel" to the "one body" (the Church) in the Book of Acts?

If you do not "rightly divide the word of truth" concerning these events, you will likely be disregarding the twofold purpose of God described in Ephesians 1:10 and Philippians 2:9-11, which discusses both "heaven and earth" as two different destinies. The Body of Christ is judged at the Judgment Seat of Christ following the "meeting in the air," so we are not judged at the end of the Millennial reign of Jesus, or by the Twelve in Revelation 20. In fact, Paul states this about the Body of Christ:

> *Dare any of you, having a matter against another, go to law before the unjust, and not before the saints? 2 <u>Do ye not know that the saints shall judge the world?</u> and if the world*

shall be judged by you, are ye unworthy to
judge the smallest matters? ³ <u>Know ye not that</u>
<u>we shall judge angels?</u> how much more things
that pertain to this life?
I Corinthians 6:1-3

Why would the Body of Christ need to sit under the judgment of the Twelve, if in fact, we are to "judge the world" and "angels" with Jesus? We will have already been judged at the Judgment Seat of Christ prior to the beginning of the Tribulation. We are not in the prophetic judgment of "the just and the unjust." Our judgment was revealed in "the revelation of the mystery" only, not prophecy.

We should also note the following:

¹⁶ In the day when God shall judge the secrets
of men by Jesus Christ according to <u>my gospel.</u>
Romans 2:16

Through the death of Jesus Christ, God can accept all the prior sacrifices He required before the cross of Calvary. It is upon the basis of *grace, through faith* that salvation was always granted by God, whether it was from Adam until now, but Paul was the *first* apostle chosen to reveal that faith in the death, burial, and resurrection of Jesus Christ, without works, is what "justifies" us today. "In times past," faith required whatever else God commanded, which included: "bring the proper sacrifice," "build an ark," "keep the commandments," "repent and be baptized for the remission of sins," etc. Today, salvation is by grace, through faith, apart from works. This is what we discover when we "rightly divide the word of truth."

Christ is the ultimate sacrifice for sin, as described throughout the Book of Hebrews, and this came through what Paul called "my gospel, and the preaching of Jesus Christ, according to the revelation of the mystery, which was kept secret since the world began." Our salvation and walk do not include "the deeds of the Law" (Rom. 3:28). Paul could make the statement in Romans 2:16 that "God shall judge the secrets of men by Jesus Christ according to *my gospel*," and he could do so because grace and faith have always been the basis of salvation. Therefore, Christ is the Justifier of all those who have placed their faith in what God commanded for them (us) to do for salvation (revealed to and through Paul by Jesus (Gal. 1:11-12)). Any doctrine that violates this truth is clearly teaching the insufficiency of faith in Christ's blood for the "remission of sins." For those who believe their salvation depends upon the sufficiency of their works, their entire walk as believers will always be marked with fear and doubt. We are already "conquerors through Him that loved us" (Rom. 8:37), and we are "complete in Him" (Col. 2:10).

There is a judgment for the Body of Christ (the Judgment Seat of Christ), and there is the prophesied "first resurrection" for the "just" saints, and there is also a "resurrection of the unjust," to which they will appear before the Great White Throne. There will also be judgment involving the nations at the end of the Tribulation (Matt. 25:31-46). We also know there will be judgments and sacrifice during the Millennial reign of Christ after the Second Coming (Zech. 5:1-3; 14:16-21; Isa. 56:6-8; Eze. 43:18-46; Jer. 33:15-18). This is why the Twelve will "sit on twelve thrones, judging the twelve tribes of Israel" (Matt. 19:28). By not "rightly dividing" these judgments, the traditions being taught within the Church have simply made these judgments into one event at the Second Coming, with no Millennial Kingdom reign of Jesus Christ between the "resurrection of the just and the unjust." This calls into question all the Old Testament passages I quoted within this paragraph and book. Many believers forget that the entire earthly ministry of Jesus was to prepare Israel for the Millennial Kingdom, which was "at hand." This is why Jesus sent His disciples to preach the following:

> *5 These twelve Jesus sent forth, and*
> *commanded them, saying, Go not into the way*
> *of the Gentiles, and into any city of the*
> *Samaritans enter ye not: 6 But go rather to the*
> *lost sheep of the house of Israel. 7 And as ye*
> *go, preach, saying, The kingdom of heaven is*
> *at hand. Matthew 10:5-7*

All humans will be judged based on the finished work of Jesus Christ. Before the crucifixion, the saints looked to the day when God would ultimately redeem them from their sins, but to us, who *now* know "the preaching of the cross" through Paul's ministry, we can look back to the cross, knowing that our sins were paid for in full at that time.

> *19 To wit, that God was in Christ, reconciling*
> *the world unto himself, not imputing their*

trespasses unto them; and hath committed unto
us the word of reconciliation.
2 Corinthians 5:19

The gospel Jesus gave to Paul was "the preaching of the cross," which is where and when the sins of the world were atoned for by Christ (Phil. 2:8). Yes, even an atheist's sins have already been atoned for by the shed blood of Christ—along with the sins of the entire world. All nonbelievers must do to be saved is place their faith in the death, burial, and resurrection of Jesus Christ (the "finished work"), as told in I Corinthians 15:3-4. It is on the basis of the cross and resurrection that sins are proven to have been forgiven, and eventually, "the secrets of men will be judged...by my gospel," as Paul taught in the gospel he called "the preaching of the cross."

"The Just" and the "Unjust"
We know Jesus will return to the Mount of Olives (as prophesied (Zech. 14:4)) at His Second Coming. Oddly, as I have stated, there is no "meeting in the air" found *anywhere* in prophecy, especially the nonsensical traditions that describe how believers will meet Christ in the air, only to return immediately with Him to Earth to be a part of the New Jerusalem. There is a prophesied seven-year Tribulation between the Body of Christ being "caught up," and the eventual return of Jesus Christ.

Please note carefully the following passage from Revelation 20 and determine if John meant this passage to be understood as literal or symbolic, and if symbolic, who determines the intent?

And I saw an angel come down from heaven, having the key of the bottomless pit and a great chain in his hand. 2 And he laid hold on the dragon, that old serpent, which is the Devil, and Satan, <u>and bound him a thousand years</u>, 3 And cast him into the bottomless pit, and shut him up, and set a seal upon him, that he should deceive the nations no more, <u>till the thousand years should be fulfilled</u>: and <u>after that</u> he must be loosed a little season. 4 And I saw thrones, and they sat upon them, and judgment was given unto them: and I saw the souls of them that were beheaded for the witness of Jesus, and for the word of God, and which had not worshipped the beast, neither his image, neither had received his mark upon their foreheads, or in their hands; <u>and they lived and reigned with Christ a thousand years</u>. 5 <u>But the rest of the dead lived not again until the thousand years were finished. This is the first resurrection.</u> 6 Blessed and holy is he that hath part in <u>the first resurrection</u>: on such the second death hath no power, but <u>they shall be priests of God and of Christ, and shall reign with him a thousand years.</u> 7 And <u>when the thousand years are expired</u>, Satan shall be loosed out of his prison, Revelation 20:1-6

If this passage is to be understood as a *literal* event, as millions believe it is, there shouldn't be so much confusion over who is raised at the Second Coming of Christ (at the beginning of the Millennial Kingdom reign of Christ). Some theologies believe all people will be raised at the Second Coming; however, John seems quite confident that there is a 1000-year gap between the resurrection of the "just" and the "unjust." He refers to one event as the "first resurrection," which he clearly stipulated another to follow (after 1000 years). We know there will be temple sacrifices during the Millennial reign of Christ (for the sins committed during the Millennial Kingdom), and this is due to the fact that people will be born during that time period, so if John meant this passage (from Revelation 20) to be "symbolic," then we are forced to apply some "symbolic" meaning to the 1000-year reign of Christ, along with the people and the "saints" who will live at that time. Did John lie to the saints who were martyred during the Tribulation? Will they not "live and reign with Christ a thousand years" as Revelation 20 stated?

There is no need to "spiritualize" this passage from Revelation 20 if you simply "rightly divide" and determine "to whom" John was writing. Many assume John was writing to the Body of Christ, but national Israel is the focus throughout the entire Book of Revelation (Rom. 11:25-29). If you "spiritualize" the word "Israel" to mean "all God's people," then the entire book is subject to conjecture by theologians who do not "rightly divide." This has hugely contributed to the identity crisis we are facing in the Church today. The Rapture is the imminent return of Jesus to "meet us in the air," but the prophetic "end time" events include the Tribulation, the Second Coming, the judgment of the "just," the Millennial reign of Christ, and the final judgment (Great White Throne) before the "new heavens and the new earth" (2 Pet. 3:13). Remember, Revelation 20 clearly indicated that there will be a final rebellion at the end of the Millennial Kingdom (Rev. 20:7-10), so are we to somehow apply this into today's times, especially if the amillennialist is correct that no Millennial reign of Christ will take place?

Sadly, as I have mentioned already, many believers are unaware that there is at least 1000 years between the resurrection of the "just" and the "unjust." The resurrection in I Thessalonians 4:13-18 is *not* found in prophecy; it is found as a truth within "the revelation of the mystery" given to Paul. When he introduced the "meeting in the air" as a "mystery," this did not undermine the *prophetic resurrections* already mentioned in the Bible, "since the world began." John identifies these prophetic resurrections as the "first resurrection," and the "second resurrection" for "the rest of the dead," which occurs after the 1000 years have expired, leading ultimately to "the second death." This involves the Great White Throne Judgment for all the "unsaved" (from Adam to the end of the 1000-year reign of Jesus Christ). There is no hope remaining for these individuals.

As I have mentioned, the Judgment Seat of Christ is also *not* found anywhere in Scripture outside of Paul's letters addressing the Body of Christ (Rom. 14:10; 2 Cor. 5:10). According to John 5:22 and 27, we also know that God has given all judgment to Jesus Christ, so whether a person appears before the Judgment Seat of Christ, the *thrones* in

Revelation 20:4, or the so-called Great White Throne, Jesus Christ will be the ultimate Judge. Revelation 20, however, is not addressing the Body of Christ at all because these judgments of the "just and the unjust" are already addressed from *prophetic* passages outside of Paul's epistles. Paul does, however, address the Old Testament passages about the judgment of the "just and the unjust" in Acts 24:15, but the context is associated with his knowledge of what the Law and the prophets wrote about these future resurrections, not the Judgment Seat of Christ, which is not found in prophecy. There will be a resurrection of the "just," and there will be a resurrection of the "unjust," but no Scriptures state how these resurrections will occur at the same time unless you "spiritualize" Scripture to "make it so." Some denominations also "spiritualize" the "first resurrection" in Revelation 20, which I will explain shortly.

Revelation 20 *does* reveal who will be resurrected at the Second Coming of Jesus Christ. Most believe it will be the Church, the Body of Christ, but since this body of believers was "kept secret since the world began," how can the Body appear within the Old Testament, the "gospels" or early Acts before the conversion of Paul? The prophets, long before Paul, spoke of the resurrection of the "just and the unjust," so how the Body of Christ be a part of these prophetic judgments? John is obviously referring to the Old Testament saints, the "little flock," those "scattered abroad" (to whom James, Peter, and John wrote), and the sealed remnant of the Tribulation. Revelation 11:14-19 specifically includes the prophets and "saints" of old who will be "the just" at the "first resurrection." The Body of Christ has no part in the "first resurrection" described within prophecy.

> *4 And I saw <u>thrones</u>, and <u>they sat upon them</u>,*
> *and <u>judgment was given unto them</u>: and I saw*
> *the souls of them that were beheaded for the*
> *witness of Jesus, and for the word of God, and*
> *which <u>had not worshipped the beast, neither</u>*
> *<u>his image, neither had received his mark upon</u>*
> *<u>their foreheads</u>, <u>or in their hands</u>; and <u>they</u>*
> *<u>lived and reigned with Christ a thousand</u>*
> *<u>years</u>. Revelation 20:4*

We can easily recognize these dear saints as "the just," because they will "live and reign with Christ a thousand years." Prior to Paul, however, who were these "just" saints? As I mentioned, *these are they* who are found in the Old Testament, the "gospels," and those to whom James, Peter, and John continued to write, as well as those future Tribulation saints. These are the only saints mentioned in prophecy, so they are "the just" mentioned throughout the Bible. Even Paul mentioned this resurrection in Acts 24:15, but it wasn't in the context of the Body of Christ.

> *14 But this I confess unto thee, that after the*
> *way which they call heresy, so worship I the*
> *God of my fathers, believing all things which*
> *are written in the law and in the prophets:*
> *15 And have hope toward God, which they*
> *themselves also allow, that there shall be a*

> *resurrection of the dead, both of the just and*
> *unjust. Acts 24:14-15*

Paul was defending the resurrection of the dead against the charges of the Jewish high priest who was questioning Paul's claim about the resurrection of Jesus. He reminded them of the prophecies concerning the resurrection of "the just and the unjust." Paul used the Old Testament scriptures to defend himself, which are the only "scriptures" they had available at the time. The high priest should have known about the promises of the resurrection of the just and the unjust.

In addition to this, what did John reveal about the resurrection of the "unjust"?

> *5 But <u>the rest of the dead lived not again until</u>*
> *<u>the thousand years were finished</u>. This is the*
> *first resurrection. 6 <u>Blessed and holy is he that</u>*
> *<u>hath part in the first resurrection</u>: <u>on such the</u>*
> *<u>second death hath no power</u>, but they shall be*
> *priests of God and of Christ, <u>and shall reign</u>*
> *<u>with him a thousand years.</u> Revelation 20:5-6*

If this "Millennial Kingdom" is supposedly being fulfilled today (symbolically) through the Church, the Body of Christ (with Christ reigning on the Throne of David in the hearts of believers), then we must wonder why John places a 1000-year gap between the resurrection of the "just and the unjust." As I have mentioned, if Revelation 20 is written to and for the Body of Christ, then the Body will indeed endure the Tribulation because Revelation 20 addresses the prophetic "first resurrection" of the saints at the Second Coming of Jesus Christ, not some "meeting in the air" (prior to the Second Coming of Christ).

I must explain that some theologians believe this "first resurrection" from Revelation 20 is only *spiritually* associated with the moment someone is converted to Christ, but there are so many passages that teach this "first resurrection" as a *physical* resurrection of the "just," which occurs at the Second Coming of Jesus Christ, when Israel will be "born again." To justify that the "first resurrection" of Revelation 20 only references the "spiritual" conversion of a believer, they will turn to Romans 6 as proof. Oddly, many of these same theologians who treat the "first resurrection" as only *spiritual* are often the same pastors and priests who also add *physical* water baptism to the passage in Romans, forgetting that Paul had already been teaching the baptism "*by one Spirit*" from I Corinthians 12:13 (prior to his epistle to the Romans).

> *What shall we say then? Shall we continue in sin, that grace may abound? 2 God forbid. How shall we, <u>that are dead to sin</u>, live any longer therein? 3 Know ye not, that so many of us as <u>were baptized into Jesus Christ were baptized into his death</u>? 4 Therefore we are <u>buried with him by baptism into death</u>: that like as Christ was raised up from the dead by the glory of the Father, even so <u>we also should walk in newness of life</u>. Romans 6:1-4*

Not one time in this passage does Paul tell the Romans how they are "baptized into water." He teaches clearly that believers are baptized (*by* one Spirit (I Cor. 12:13)) *into Jesus Christ* (not water). Because we are "in Christ," we are then immersed into His death, burial, and resurrection as well. There is *not* one drop of water in this passage, and even though this truly is a *spiritual* immersion into His death, burial, and resurrection, this still does not replace the *physical* resurrection of future saints at the Second Coming of Christ, which John called the "first resurrection." Have believers been *physically* put to death with Christ? Were we *physically* buried with Him? Have we been *physically* resurrected yet? Daniel supports a physical resurrection.

> *And at that time shall Michael stand up, the great prince which standeth for the children of thy people [Israel]: and <u>there shall be a time of trouble [Tribulation], such as never was since there was a nation even to that same time: and at that time thy people shall be delivered [at the Second Coming], every one that shall be found written in the book [Tribulation saints]</u>. [2] <u>And many of them that sleep in the dust of the earth shall awake [resurrected], some to everlasting life [the just], and some to shame and everlasting contempt [the unjust]</u>.*
> *Daniel 12:1-2 (brackets by author)*

John, in Revelation 20, reveals that these resurrections are separated by the 1000-year reign of Christ. Those saints who are raised at the Second Coming, will "live and reign with Christ a thousand years," while Satan is bound.

> *28 Marvel not at this: for the hour is coming, in the which all that are in <u>the graves shall hear his voice, 29 And shall come forth [the first resurrection of prophecy]</u>; they that have done good, <u>unto the resurrection of life [the just]</u>; and they that have done evil, <u>unto the resurrection of damnation [the unjust]</u>.*
> *John 5:28-29 (brackets by author)*

> *25 <u>For I know that my redeemer liveth, and that he shall stand at the latter day upon the earth:</u> 26 And though after my skin worms destroy this body, <u>yet in my flesh [physically] shall I see God</u>: 27 Whom I shall see for myself, and mine eyes shall behold [physically], and not another; though my reins [inner mind/feelings] be consumed within me.*
> *Job 19:25-27 (brackets by author)*

When will Job see his Redeemer? When will he, along with other Old Testament saints, see their Messiah? They will see Him at the Second Coming. When will the "little flock" finally inherit the kingdom promised to them? What about the "strangers scattered abroad…from the twelve tribes of Israel," to whom James, Peter, John, and Jude wrote in their "General

Epistles"? When will they be raised to see the Lord? When will the sealed Tribulation saints be raised? All of this takes place at the Second Coming of Christ, which is when the "first resurrection" of prophecy occurs. These saints, as described in Revelation 20, will "live and reign with Christ a thousand years." Will the Body of Christ take part in this "first resurrection," or will the Body be raised prior to these prophetic events of the Tribulation and Second Coming? After all, Paul never warned believers in the Body of Christ to be prepared for a coming Tribulation when God's wrath is poured out on the world, nor did he ever promise the Body that we would "inherit the earth." Let us recall what faith in the blood of Christ has done for us:

> *8 But God commendeth his love toward us, in that, while we were yet sinners, Christ died for us. 9 Much more then, being now justified by his blood, we shall be saved from wrath through him. 10 For if, when we were enemies, we were reconciled to God by the death of his Son, much more, being reconciled, we shall be saved by his life. Romans 5:8-10*

> *9 For God hath not appointed us to wrath, but to obtain salvation by our Lord Jesus Christ, 10 Who died for us, that, whether we wake or sleep, we should live together with him. 11 Wherefore comfort yourselves together, and edify one another, even as also ye do.*

*Philippians 3:20-21 (conversation is
citizenship) I Thessalonians 5:9-11
20 For our conversation is in heaven; from
whence also we look for the Saviour, the Lord
Jesus Christ: 21 Who shall change our vile
body, that it may be fashioned like unto his
glorious body, according to the working
whereby he is able even to subdue all things
unto himself. Philippians 3:20-21*

"One Taken, and One Left Behind"

In the following passages related to "one taken, and one left behind," the ones taken (just as they were in the Flood) are the wicked, but the righteous in Matthew 24 and 25 remain to enter the Millennial Kingdom to reign with Jesus Christ. Contrary to popular traditions, the following passage is a separation, which takes place on Earth, not the Great White Throne of Revelation 20:11. The Great White Throne is specifically a judgment for all the unsaved ("unjust") throughout all human history.

Matthew 25 describes the separation of the *nations* into "sheep and goats" based upon the treatment of the Jews during the Tribulation. This judgment occurs on Earth prior to the Millennial reign of Jesus Christ. The following section of Scripture is very confusing if you do not "rightly divide" between the prophecies concerning the "end times," and the "mystery" revealed to Paul about the "end times" associated with the Body of Christ.

31 When the Son of man shall come in his glory (the Second Coming), and all the holy angels with him, then shall he sit upon the throne of his glory (on David's Throne in Jerusalem). 32 And before him shall be gathered all nations (at the end of the Tribulation): and he shall separate them one from another, as a shepherd divideth his sheep from the goats: 33 And he shall set the sheep on his right hand, but the goats on the left. 34 Then shall the King say unto them on his right hand, Come, ye blessed of my Father, inherit the kingdom prepared for you from the foundation of the world (The Messianic Kingdom that was "at hand")...

41 Then shall he say also unto them on the left hand, Depart from me, ye cursed, into everlasting fire, prepared for the devil and his angels: 42 For I was an hungred, and ye gave me no meat: I was thirsty, and ye gave me no drink: 43 I was a stranger, and ye took me not in: naked, and ye clothed me not: sick, and in prison, and ye visited me not. 44 Then shall they also answer him, saying, Lord, when saw we thee an hungred, or athirst, or a stranger, or naked, or sick, or in prison, and did not minister unto thee? 45 Then shall he answer them, saying, Verily I say unto you, Inasmuch as ye did it not to one of the least of these, ye did it not to me. 46 And these shall go away

> *into everlasting punishment: but the righteous*
> *into life eternal.*
> *Matthew 25:31-34 and 41-46*
> *(brackets by author)*

Those "taken" in this passage are sent away to await their final judgment at the Great White Throne of Revelation 20. In other words, they "depart," meaning they are taken away. This is obviously not the Rapture because the Body of Christ is not "taken" to the "everlasting fire, prepared for the devil and his angels." Secondly, Jesus revealed these things during His earthly ministry; however, Paul stated a couple decades later to the Corinthians: "Behold, I show you a mystery, we shall not all sleep (die), but we shall be changed." Matthew 25 has nothing to do with the Rapture, even though some theologians insist on using it as such. Remember, Paul didn't reveal "the departure" (of the Body) for another two decades after this description of the separation of the "sheep and goats" by Jesus in Matthew 25.

In another passage (from Matthew 24), Jesus explained the events that will occur during the Tribulation, and He proceeded to explain what it will be like when Jesus returns to Earth at His Second Coming (not the "meeting in the air" of Paul's epistles).

> *40 Then shall two be in the field; the one shall*
> *be taken, and the other left. 41 Two women*
> *shall be grinding at the mill; the one shall be*
> *taken, and the other left. 42 Watch therefore:*
> *for ye know not what hour your Lord doth*

> *come. 43 But know this, that if the goodman of*
> *the house had known in what watch the thief*
> *would come, he would have watched, and*
> *would not have suffered his house to be broken*
> *up. 44 <u>Therefore be ye also ready: for in such</u>*
> *<u>an hour as ye think not the Son of man cometh.</u>*
> *Matthew 24:40-44*

After reading the previous passages, from Matthew 24 and 25, we should understand that "the other left (behind)" will enter the kingdom, along with the saints in the "first resurrection" of the "just." These saints will "live and reign a thousand years" with their Messiah. The "unjust" are those "taken," and they will be cast into "the everlasting fire" (Matt. 25:41). We know from Revelation 20 that the "second death" will be their eternal damnation. In the Rapture, however, the Body of Christ *departs*, while the rest of humanity remains to endure the Tribulation, of which billions of people will sadly not survive this time of the Anti-Christ's deceptions and cruelty, as well as "God's vengeance" (Isaiah 61:1-3). Remember, the Rapture is not found in *any* prophetic writings—only Paul's epistles. If Jesus revealed the Rapture in Matthew 24 and 25, then He revealed something that Paul later declared to be a "mystery." A "mystery" is something kept hidden until it is finally revealed. Please don't forget that the "first resurrection" was known *since the world began*, but the Body of Christ and the Rapture were known only by God *before the world began* (and revealed after the conversion of Paul).

Note the following passages about when the Body of Christ was first known:

> *3 Blessed be the God and Father of our Lord*
> *Jesus Christ, who hath blessed us with all*
> *spiritual blessings in heavenly places in*
> *Christ: 4 According as <u>he hath chosen us in</u>*
> *<u>him before the foundation of the world</u>, that we*
> *should be holy and without blame*
> *before him in love:*
> *Ephesians 1:3-4*

> *8 Be not thou therefore ashamed of the*
> *testimony of our Lord, nor of me his prisoner:*
> *but be thou partaker of the afflictions of the*
> *gospel according to the power of God; 9 Who*
> *hath saved us, and called us with an holy*
> *calling, not according to our works, but*
> *according to his own purpose and grace,*
> *<u>which was given us in Christ Jesus before the</u>*
> *<u>world began</u>, 2 Timothy 1:8-9*

The Body of Christ was still "hid in God" *before* all the prophecies of the Messiah and the Messianic Kingdom (and judgments of the just and unjust) were made known to Israel *since the world began* (concerning the Messianic Kingdom). The Body of Christ will *not* take part in these prophetic events described throughout the Old Testament, the "gospels" and the early chapters of Acts. Our "gathering together" was revealed as a "mystery" (by Paul) to *individual* Jews and

Gentiles in the Body of Christ. Our "gathering together" can't be the "first resurrection" of prophecy because the "resurrection of the just and the unjust" were already known before Paul's conversion, and long before he ever stated, "Behold, I show you a mystery" (I Cor. 15:51-52).

As I have discussed, there are theologians who insist the promises to Israel in the Old Testament (according to prophecy) are already being fulfilled through the Church, even though Jeremiah 30:1-3; 32:37-42; Ezekiel 36:37-42; Zechariah 12:10; Amos 9:14-15; Acts 3:19-21; and Romans 11:25-29 all declare the restoration of *the nation of Israel*, which will still occur at the Second Coming. If these passages listed aren't really to the nation of Israel, then are we (the Church) to wait until the Second Coming to be restored as a Body? Take note of the following passage again:

> *25 For I would not, brethren, that ye should be ignorant of this mystery, lest ye should be wise in your own conceits; <u>that blindness in part is happened to Israel, until the fulness of the Gentiles be come in.</u> 26 <u>And so all Israel shall be saved</u>: as it is written, There shall come out of Sion the Deliverer, and shall turn away ungodliness from Jacob: 27 <u>For this is my covenant unto them, when I shall take away their sins.</u> Romans 11:25-27*

If the Body of Christ, consisting mainly of Gentiles, is "spiritual Israel" in Romans 11, are we then "blind in part... until the fulness of the Gentiles be come in"? If we are "spiritual Israel," why would Paul discuss both the blindness of Israel and the "fulness of the Gentiles" as two separate people? Even though Paul declared in Colossians 2:10 that "We are complete in Him," it seems as though Romans 11:25-27 implies (according to some theologians) that we are *not yet* complete "until the fulness of the Gentiles be come in." We need to "rightly divide."

Conclusion to Part One of the "End Times"
The study of the end times (eschatology) often fascinates many believers, but there are those who avoid discussing it altogether for fear it will cause division. It already has within many churches and denominations. Millions of believers are convinced they will have to endure the Tribulation, and others are gripped with a paralyzing fear over what the Book of Revelation might have in store for them. This is a deeply troubling identity crisis created by those who "spiritualize" passages that should be "rightly divided." Remember, "we are saved from wrath through Him (Jesus Christ)." Don't allow the disturbing traditions of men to rob you of this joy!

As we continue into Part Two of this study, we will examine the importance of knowing when and how the Body of Christ will soon depart this world. It will likely surprise many of you.

CHAPTER 12

Rightly Dividing the End Times: Part Two

13 But I would not have you to be ignorant, brethren, concerning them which are asleep, that ye sorrow not, even as others which have no hope. 14 For if we believe that Jesus died and rose again, even so them also which sleep in Jesus will God bring with him. 15 For this we say unto you by the word of the Lord, that we which are alive and remain unto the coming of the Lord shall not prevent them which are asleep. 16 For the Lord himself shall descend from heaven with a shout, with the voice of the archangel, and with the trump of God: and the dead in Christ shall rise first: 17 Then we which are alive and remain shall be caught up together with them in the clouds, to meet the Lord in the air: and so shall we ever be with the Lord. 18 Wherefore comfort one another with these words.

I Thessalonians 4:13-18

Another "Unsearchable" Truth

As I have written in the previous chapter, the "meeting in the air" (the Rapture) is not found anywhere in the Old Testament or "the gospels," even though many theologians believe it is. However, Acts 17 records Paul's visit to Thessalonica, and in his letters to them, he wrote, "Remember ye not, that, when I was yet with you, I told you these things?" (2 Thes. 2:5). Paul taught the saints at Thessalonica about the hope of their resurrection to "meet the Lord in the air," especially at a time of great adversity. He also had to correct their worry about their loved ones who had died before Christ returned for them. They, too, obviously believed the "meeting in the air" would happen within their lifetime. Again, even though the Rapture is not mentioned in Acts 17, the hope of their resurrection must have been taught to them when Paul visited that region (2 Thes. 2:5) because he reminds them of it in his epistles to them.

Paul explained to the saints at Corinth and Thessalonica that the "meeting in the air," which came "by the word of the Lord" (I Thes. 4:15), was a "mystery" revealed to him (I Cor. 15:51) years after the so-called Olivet Discourse of Matthew 24, which addressed the Tribulation and Second Coming (prophetic events). Since Paul was the *first* to reveal this "meeting in the air," this would exclude it from *ever* being mentioned anywhere during the earthly ministry of Jesus Christ, even though, as I have mentioned, some pastors attempt to quote passages from the "gospels" to justify their theology of a "rapture" prior to its revelation to Paul years later (by Jesus).

As I also mentioned in the previous chapter, many pastors quote passages that state how "one will be taken, and one left behind" (Matt. 24:40-41; Lk. 17:34-36), thinking this is the Rapture Paul described as a "mystery" years *after* Jesus taught these truths in Matthew and Luke. They also quote John 14 as another reference to the Church's resurrection, thinking Jesus went to "prepare a place for them," even though Jesus was speaking to "the lost sheep of the house of Israel," not the Body of Christ, which was still "hid in God" until Paul's conversion. Jesus was referencing His Second Coming in John 14, not the Rapture. We should know by now that the saints, the remnant, are the ones "left behind" at the Second Coming, and they are the ones who will remain and enter the Millennial Kingdom to reign with Christ 1000 years. Again, such references in the "gospels" are in relationship to the Second Coming, not the Rapture (revealed later by Paul as a *mystery* to the Body of Christ).

To review once more, the passages from Matthew 24 and 25, as well as Luke 17, refer to those (at the return of Jesus Christ) who will be *left* to enter the Millennial Kingdom (Matt. 25:31-34), and those *taken* will enter everlasting damnation (Rev. 19:20). The parable of the wheat and tares (Matthew 13) helps illustrate how the tares will be pulled up and burned, but the wheat is left and collected to enter "into my barn" (Israel's promised kingdom). The Body of Christ was still "hid in God" at the time of the "gospels," and the "meeting in the air" was still a "mystery" as well. Any pastor who uses passages outside of Paul's letters to justify the

Rapture will only show their lack of obedience in "rightly dividing the word of truth."   Jesus did not describe the Rapture in His earthly ministry simply because He had not yet given to Paul "the revelation of the mystery, which was kept secret since the world began," which concerned the Body of Christ. James, Peter, and John (and Jude) warn of "false prophets" in the "last days," and this is in relationship to the end times prophecies described in the Old Testament, the "gospels, and, of course, the General Epistles of the four names I just mentioned.

Why Didn't Paul Warn the Body of Christ to Prepare for the Tribulation?
The following two passages reveal this blessed truth for the Body of Christ:

> *13 But I would not have you to be ignorant,*
> *brethren, concerning them which are asleep,*
> *that ye sorrow not, <u>even as others which have</u>*
> *<u>no hope</u>. 14 <u>For if we believe that Jesus died</u>*
> *<u>and rose again</u>, even so them also which sleep*
> *in Jesus will God bring with him. 15 For this*
> *we say unto you <u>by the word of the Lord</u>, that*
> *we which are alive and remain unto the*
> *coming of the Lord shall not prevent them*
> *which are asleep. 16 For the Lord himself shall*
> *descend from heaven with a shout, with the*
> *voice of the archangel, and with the trump of*
> *God: and the dead in Christ shall rise first:*
> *17 Then we which are alive and remain <u>shall be</u>*

*caught up together with them in the clouds, to
meet the Lord in the air: and so shall we ever
be with the Lord. [18] Wherefore comfort one
another with these words.*
I Thessalonians 4:13-18 (circa AD 51)

*[51] Behold, I shew you a mystery; We shall not
all sleep, but we shall all be changed, [52] In a
moment, in the twinkling of an eye, at the last
trump: for the trumpet shall sound, and the
dead shall be raised incorruptible, and we
shall be changed. I Corinthians 15:51-52
(circa AD 57)*

Some theologians attempt to make the "meeting in the air" nothing more than the Body going up to "greet King Jesus," only to return immediately with Him to the earth at the Second Coming. Interestingly, they do admit that Jesus will return to Earth, where He will reign during the Millennial Kingdom. These same theologians also fail to recognize the differences between "the mystery" and the prophecies concerning the "end times."

As a reminder, we are also told the following concerning the coming wrath of God:

*[8] But God commendeth his love toward us, in
that, while we were yet sinners, Christ died for
us. [9] Much more then, being now justified by
his blood, we shall be saved from wrath
through him. [10] For if, when we were enemies,*

> *we were reconciled to God by the death of his*
> *Son, much more, being reconciled, we shall be*
> *saved by his life. Romans 5:8-10*

> *⁹ For God hath not appointed us to wrath, but*
> *to obtain salvation by our Lord Jesus Christ,*
> *¹⁰ Who died for us, that, whether we wake or*
> *sleep, we should live together with him.*
> *¹¹ Wherefore comfort yourselves together, and*
> *edify one another, even as also ye do.*
> *I Thessalonians 5:9-11*

Does this sound as if the Body of Christ will endure the Tribulation? What are we being saved from? Are we *not* saved "from wrath through him," because God has "not appointed us to wrath"? Amillennialism places our "gathering" at the Second Coming, and this is why they vehemently avoid teaching that the Body of Christ will "depart" *prior* to God's wrath being poured out upon this world. The previous passages undermine their entire theology, because Romans 5:9 and I Thessalonians 5:9 no longer places the Church within the time of the Tribulation (involving God's wrath). Remember, at this time, we are "under grace," and we should be thankful God's wrath is not being poured out upon the world today. These previous passages also remove the Church from the focus of Christ's teachings in Matthew 24 and 25, because we are not "left behind" to enter the Millennial Kingdom, and we certainly are not "taken away" to "everlasting damnation."

We should also examine the following passage as well concerning the "day of the Lord":

> *<u>But</u> of the times and the seasons, brethren, ye have no need that I write unto you. [2] For yourselves know perfectly that the day of the Lord so cometh as a thief in the night. [3] For when they shall say, Peace and safety; then sudden destruction cometh upon them, as travail upon a woman with child; and they shall not escape. [4] But ye, brethren, are not in darkness, that that day should overtake you as a thief. I Thessalonians 5:1-4*

Immediately following I Thessalonians 4:18, which states, "Wherefore, comfort one another with these words," we encounter the word "but" in the next chapter (5:1). This indicates a change in content or direction. Paul taught (Chapter 4) a *new* revelation regarding the Church being "caught up...to meet the Lord in the air," and this was to bring great "comfort" to the Church; however, in Chapter 5 of I Thessalonians, Paul reverts to several prophetic terms we would have read about in the Old Testament, "the gospels," and in also Peter's writings. This would include terms such as "times and the seasons" (Dan. 2:21; Acts 1:7); the "day of the Lord" (Isa. 2:12; Amos 5:18-20; Joel 1:15 (Acts 2:16-20); Matt. 12:36; James 5:7-8; 2 Pet. 3:10-13; Jude 1:6; Rev. 1:10); and how Christ will come "as a thief in the night" (Matt. 24:43-44; Luke 12:39; 2 Pet. 3:10). What did Paul say about these prophetic writings? He stated, "...you have no need that I write unto you." Why? The answer lies within I Thessalonians 4:13-18 and I Thessalonians 5:9-10.

Paul was clear that we are "not appointed to wrath, but to obtain salvation by our Lord Jesus Christ." The Rapture is not revealed anywhere prior to Paul's conversion and ministry given to him by Jesus Christ (Gal. 1:11-12). Placing the Rapture of the Church and the Second Coming of Christ into one "resurrection of the just," does a disservice to the entire purpose of "the revelation of the mystery" and the two-fold purpose of God for Heaven and Earth. The Rapture is only revealed during the "dispensation of the grace of God," which was "kept secret" until Paul.

Do we *really* understand that "by grace, through faith," we are now "in Christ," and "Christ lives in us," so why would His Body have to endure the Tribulation, especially since He (and we) have overcome the world?

> [20] *I am crucified with Christ: nevertheless I live; yet not I, but Christ liveth in me: and the life which I now live in the flesh I live by the faith of the Son of God, who loved me, and gave himself for me. Galatians 2:20*

By the "faith of the Son of God," we have been "crucified with Christ," and now, "Christ liveth in me (us)," so to teach that the Body of Christ must endure the Tribulation, according to some theologians, this places Christ under the wrath of God. Was the shed blood of Christ not sufficient enough to save us "from the wrath to come"?

God's justice and wrath must be poured out upon the Christ-rejecting world that preferred "darkness to light," but according to Colossians 2:13, the members of the Body of Christ have already been "forgiven all trespasses." Why must we endure the Tribulation, especially since Christ died for us, and we have been made "the righteousness of God in Him (Christ)"? Remember, the "day of the Lord" will not take us by surprise because we are "not in darkness." If we must endure the Tribulation, as some teach, then I Thessalonians 4:18 seems like a rather cruel hoax, especially since we are told to "comfort one another with these words" (about our gathering to "meet the Lord in the air"), and being "saved from wrath through Him."

Paul does, however, discuss "the day of our Lord Jesus (Christ)" in the context of the Body of Christ, so let us examine what this means (in the following passages):

> *4 I thank my God always on your behalf, for the grace of God which is given you by Jesus Christ; 5 That in every thing ye are enriched by him, in all utterance, and in all knowledge; 6 Even as the testimony of Christ was confirmed in you: 7 <u>So that ye come behind in no gift; waiting for the coming of our Lord Jesus Christ: 8 Who shall also confirm you unto the end, that ye may be blameless in the day of our Lord Jesus Christ.</u> 9 God is faithful, by whom ye were called unto the fellowship of his Son Jesus Christ our Lord.*
> *I Corinthians 1:4-9*

Christ will "confirm you (us) unto the end," especially when we meet Him face-to-face.

> *13 In whom ye also trusted, after that ye heard*
> *the word of truth, the gospel of your salvation:*
> *in whom also <u>after that ye believed, ye were</u>*
> *<u>sealed with that holy Spirit of promise,</u>*
> *14 <u>Which is the earnest of our inheritance until</u>*
> *<u>the redemption of the purchased possession,</u>*
> *unto the praise of his glory.*
> *Ephesians 1:13-14*

> *12 For our <u>rejoicing</u> is this, the testimony of our*
> *conscience, that in simplicity and godly*
> *sincerity, not with fleshly wisdom, but by the*
> *grace of God, we have had our conversation in*
> *the world, and more abundantly to you-ward.*
> *13 For we write none other things unto you,*
> *that what ye read or acknowledge; and I trust*
> *ye shall acknowledge even to the end; 14 <u>As</u>*
> *<u>also ye have acknowledged us in part, that we</u>*
> *<u>are your rejoicing, even as ye also are our's in</u>*
> *<u>the day of the Lord Jesus.</u>*
> *2 Corinthians 1:12-14*

> *6 <u>Being confident of this very thing, that he</u>*
> *<u>which hath begun a good work in you will</u>*
> *<u>perform it until the day of Jesus Christ:</u> 7 Even*
> *as it is meet for me to think this of you all,*
> *because I have you in my heart; inasmuch as*

*both in my bonds, and in the defence and
confirmation of the gospel, ye all are partakers
of my grace. Philippians 1:6-7*

*11 <u>For the grace of God that bringeth salvation
hath appeared to all men</u>, 12 Teaching us that,
denying ungodliness and worldly lusts, we
should live soberly, righteously, and godly, in
this present world; 13 <u>Looking for that blessed
hope, and the glorious appearing of the great
God and our Saviour Jesus Christ; 14 Who
gave himself for us</u>, that he might redeem us
from all iniquity, and purify unto himself a
peculiar people, zealous of good works.
15 These things speak, and exhort, and rebuke
with all authority. Let no man despise thee.
Titus 2:11-15*

Believers are to look forward to the "day of Jesus (Christ)" because it is not the same as the "day of the Lord," which involves destruction before God delivers the remnant of Israel (and proselytized Gentiles from the nations) from the Tribulation. For those who despise the teaching of the Rapture (believing it is a recent "myth"), should they not wonder why Paul informed the Body of Christ to "comfort one another with these words (I Thes. 4:13-18), and why he never warned the Church that it would have to "endure to the end" (of the Tribulation) to be saved?

> *36 As it is written, For thy sake we are killed all*
> *the day long; we are accounted as sheep for*
> *the slaughter. 37 Nay, in all these things <u>we are</u>*
> *<u>more than conquerors through him that loved</u>*
> *us. Romans 8:36-37*

So, Do You *Really* Believe the Body of Christ Must Endure the Tribulation?

It may surprise many believers that the doctrine of so-called Rapture is only found within the letters of Paul, as I have already mentioned. After all, he revealed it as a "mystery," and this means it was (and is) a doctrine unique to his writings from about 2000 years ago. It also means it is not found in the writings of the other apostles and prophets, for no other author in the Old and New Testament books describe the day when believers will be "caught up to meet the Lord in the air." Yes, there are other Scriptures about "one taken, and one left behind," but remember, these are in the context of the Second Coming of Christ to redeem "the lost sheep of the house of Israel." The "nations" will then come to Israel's light from all over the world, as taught in the following passages:

> *19 O LORD, my strength, and my fortress, and*
> *my refuge in the day of affliction, <u>the Gentiles</u>*
> *<u>shall come unto thee from the ends of the</u>*
> *<u>earth</u>, and shall say, Surely our fathers have*
> *inherited lies, vanity, and things wherein there*
> *is no profit. 20 Shall a man make gods unto*
> *himself, and they are no gods? 21 Therefore,*
> *behold, I will this once cause them to know, I*

*will cause them to know mine hand and my might; and they shall know that my name is The L*ORD*. Jeremiah 16:19-21*

*¹⁰ Sing and rejoice, O daughter of Zion: for, lo, I come, and I will dwell in the midst of thee, saith the L*ORD*. ¹¹ <u>And many nations shall be joined to the L</u>ORD <u>in that day, and shall be my people: and I will dwell in the midst of thee, and thou shalt know that the L</u>ORD <u>of hosts hath sent me unto thee.</u> ¹² <u>And the L</u>ORD <u>shall inherit Judah his portion in the holy land, and shall choose Jerusalem again.</u> Zechariah 2:10-12*

In Acts 1:6, the apostles asked when Jesus was going to "restore again the kingdom to Israel," but what they never knew was the future "revelation of the mystery, which was kept secret since the world began." They had no idea that God would pause His prophetic dealings with the nation of Israel for the "dispensation of the grace of God," which was "not made known unto the sons of men..." prior to Paul's conversion (Eph. 3:1-5). The apostles had no idea that God would bring Gentiles nigh unto Himself because of Israel's "fall" (Rom. 11:11), as well as through faith in the "blood of Christ...for the remission of sins" (Rom. 3:19-31). They also did not know that Gentiles would become "fellow (joint) heirs of Jesus Christ," through the "dispensation of the mystery (the grace of God")), as taught in Ephesians 3 (Eph. 3:2-9). They couldn't imagine that Gentiles could be "brought nigh unto God," especially through the blood of Jesus Christ, apart from Israel.

What the apostles *did* know was that Jesus would return "in like manner as you have seen Him go into heaven" (Acts 1:11). He left the earth, and one day, He will return to establish the Millennial Kingdom, which He said was "at hand" during His earthly ministry. However, it is only at the Rapture that the Body of Christ will "meet the Lord *in the air*," but at the Second Coming, Jesus will set His feet on the Mount of Olives. This return of Christ is prophetic, whereas Paul's teachings on the Rapture are associated only with "the mystery."

When we "rightly divide the word of truth," we will recognize that the Church, the Body of Christ, has been saved from God's wrath, and our citizenship is in Heaven, "from whence also we look for the Savior, the Lord Jesus Christ" (Phil. 3:20). We can "comfort one another" because we are "saved from wrath through Him." According to the writings of Paul, as "the apostle to the Gentiles," we will "depart" before God begins the fulfillment of His prophetic promises to the nation of Israel (through the Jewish remnant (Rev. 7:1-8)). Remember, "the gifts and calling of God are without repentance (irrevocable)" (Rom. 11:29). The "mystery" revealed that "God has not appointed us to wrath, but to obtain salvation through our Lord Jesus Christ." Regardless of these blessed truths, millions of believers still embrace the doctrines that refer to the Church as "spiritual Israel," and as the "Bride of Christ," thinking God is fulfilling His promises to Israel through the Church at this time. Replacement

Theology completely ignores the command to "rightly divide," so why follow its teachings?

"The Rapture is Just a Myth"

It has been asserted by many (within various denominations) that the Rapture is a recent doctrine invented in the 1800s; however, research is proving this to be an erroneous assumption on the part of those who do not fully recognize God's purpose in calling Paul. By accepting I Thessalonians 4:13-18 as the word of God, this means they are supporting the teaching of this event by quoting it from writings nearly 2000 years ago (when it was first revealed), not in the 1800s. Secondly, we must remember the limited availability of the word of God to the common people for many centuries, prior to the Reformation. This was by design, thanks to religion. Having the word of God available to common people allowed them to become good Bereans, who "…searched *the scriptures* daily (to see) whether those things (being taught) were so" (Acts 17:11). When Martin Luther "rediscovered" the doctrine of "justification by faith, apart from works," which Paul taught over 1500 years earlier, Luther was not inventing some new doctrine; he was reviving a doctrine that had been buried by the traditions of men, much like today.

When the word of God, "rightly divided," reveals a fallacy in a denomination's doctrine on a particular truth in the Bible, then we have one of two choices: Fix the doctrine to align with the Bible, or continue to practice a tradition that brings about an identity crisis within the faith. The Catholic, Orthodox, and many Protestant churches do not fully acknowledge the dispensational change that took place when

Christ appeared to Paul on the road to Damascus (Acts 9). Instead of adhering to the full teachings of Paul, who was (is) the only "apostle to the Gentiles," religionists tend to ignore Paul's commands, especially when he taught believers to "be ye followers of me, even as I am of Christ" (I Cor. 11:1). Millions of believers are trying to proclaim salvation under the gospel of the kingdom (proclaimed by the Twelve), which preached "repent and be baptized for the remission of sins," not Paul's teachings in I Corinthians 15:1-4.

We should also remember that the earliest Church Fathers quoted from the books (that are now considered the New Testament) thousands of times, which clearly indicates the abundant circulation and affirmation of the letters written by the apostles themselves. Believers did not have to wait for several hundred years (after the death of the apostles) to know the truth related to which books constitute the Bible. In fact, Clement of Rome (before the Bible was compiled into one book) was mentioned by Paul (Phil. 4:3), and history records that some of the earliest writings from the Patristic Church Fathers occurred within decades of the apostles themselves (Polycarp of Smyrna, Ignatius of Antioch, and Justin Martyr). The original writings existed within decades of the life of Christ, not centuries. Several of Paul's letters appear within two decades of the resurrection, and in I Corinthians 15, Paul recorded one of the earliest creeds (15:1-4) that has been established and circulated shortly after the resurrection (within the same decade as the resurrection itself). Paul was converted about one year after Pentecost, and this creed appears quite shortly after the time he began preaching. The so-called Bible is given to us "by inspiration of God," not any denomination that certainly doesn't do its due diligence in "rightly dividing" it.

When Paul was taught (by Christ) to write about our "meeting the Lord in the air" (I Thes. 4:15), I knew this was different from the Second Coming (when the Lord returns to this earth (Zech. 14)). When Paul wrote about the Body being "saved from the wrath to come" and how "God has not appointed us to wrath, but to obtain salvation through Jesus Christ" (Rom. 5:9; I Thes. 5:9), I knew we would be "caught up" *before* God's wrath was to be poured out upon this world. I didn't need the Church Fathers, or any recent theologians from the 1800s, to interpret what the Bible clearly teaches, especially regarding the "dispensation of the grace of God." The Holy Spirit is our Teacher; not some command promulgated by any church's magisterium or theologians, especially those who do not follow 2 Timothy 2:15. The Body of Christ is not found in prophecy, so it makes sense that it will not be found in the coming events of prophecy (such as the Tribulation and Second Coming).

The Church Fathers gave no clear indication they understood the dispensational distinctions between the Twelve apostles and Paul, so I wouldn't expect them to clearly understand a definitive stance of a pre-tribulation doctrine regarding the Rapture. Some Church Fathers clearly taught a "meeting in the air," but they tried to reconcile this with the teachings of Christ during His earthly ministry to the "lost sheep of the house of Israel." We shouldn't boast about any tradition that is not clearly supported by Scripture, especially Scripture not "rightly divided."

In an excellent article written by David Petterson (*Truth & Tidings*) titled "The Rapture: A Pre-Darby Rapture," he cites numerous quotes from some of the early Church Fathers who wrote about the imminent return of Christ and how believers will be "caught up" before the Tribulation. Here are two of those quotes from his article:

> Irenaeus refers to the Church being 'caught up' before the tribulation. *'And therefore, when in the end the Church shall be suddenly caught up from this, it is said, 'There shall be tribulation such as has not been since the beginning, neither shall be'* (Mat 24:21). *For this is the last contest of the righteous, in which, when they overcome they are crowned with incorruption.'* The italicized "this" in his quotation is clearly a reference to the tribulation, which he then introduces."
> *(Against Heresies 5:5)*[1]

> In a sermon entitled 'On the Last Times, the Antichrist, and the End of the World,' Syrian church father Pseudo-Ephraem (fourth to sixth century) wrote, *'For all the saints and elect of God are gathered, prior to the tribulation that is to come, and are taken to the Lord lest they see the confusion that is to overwhelm the*

---

[1] David Petterson, "The Rapture: A Pre-Darby Rapture," *Truth & Tidings*, July 2020, https://truthandtidings.com/2020/07/the-rapture-a-pre-darby-rapture/.

> *world because of our sins.'* The gathering
> Pseudo-Ephraem mentions appears to refer to
> a pre-tribulation Rapture of the Church." (Paul
> J. Alexander, *The Byzantine Apocalyptic
> Tradition* (Berkeley, CA: University of
> California Press, 1985), 210.)[2]

We know the word "rapture" is nothing more than a translation of the Greek word *harpazo*, which simply means a sudden departure (or seizing away). The Latin word *rapturo* is found in The Vulgate, written (circa) AD 400. I will explain this again soon, but for now, we need to examine several more of the teachings found in some of the Church Fathers' writings about the "catching away" of believers, even prior to the Tribulation.

In an intriguing article by James F. Stitzinger, titled "The Rapture in Twenty Centuries of Biblical Interpretation," he explains the various views the early Church Fathers held in relationship to the imminent, literal return of Christ. He quotes Clement of Rome, Ignatius of Antioch, Barnabas, and the Shepherd of Hermas, who each held to the imminent return of Christ. A "post-tribulation" view clearly teaches a seven-year Tribulation *before* Christ's return, so we can hardly refer to this eschatological view that Christ will return for His Church suddenly, especially with a gap in time called the "time of Jacob's (Israel's) trouble." There are signs and wonders that will occur before the return of Christ (Matt. 24:32), but no such signs and wonders are given in Paul's

---

[2] Ibid.

writings that gave us warning to the Tribulation before the Rapture.

Because these Church Fathers did not show clear regard for the "right division" of God's word, which is much easier to do now with the books of the Bible in a more concise order, we can understand the following conclusion from the author of this article: He quotes, "In the end, no one can produce a clear statement of patristic eschatology regarding the rapture. What can be concluded is the following: The early church fathers placed strong emphasis upon imminency. The early church fathers understood a literal coming of Christ, and a literal 1,000-year kingdom to follow. A type of imminent intra-tribulationism (Crutchfield) or imminent post-tribulationism (Walvoord) with occasional pretribulational inferences was believed. The early church fathers understood a kind of 'practical persecution,' due to times of general Roman persecution that they experienced, rather than a specific fulfillment of future tribulational wrath."[3]

Stitzinger also writes the following (regarding Larry V. Crutchfield's conclusion):

> This view of the fathers on imminency, and, in some, references to escaping the time of the Tribulation, constitute what may be termed, to quote Erikson [Millard J. Erikson], 'seeds from which the doctrine of the pretribulational rapture could be developed....' Had it not been

---

[3] James Stitzinger, "The Rapture in Twenty Centuries of Biblical Interpretation," *The Master's Seminary Journal* 13, no. 2 (Fall 2002), https://tyndale.tms.edu/wp-content/uploads/2021/09/tmsj13e.pdf.

> for the drought in sound exegesis, brought on by Alexandrian allegorism and later by Augustine, one wonders what kind of crop these seeds might have yielded—long before J.N. Darby and the nineteenth century (from Crutchfield's "The Blessed Hope" (pg. 103)).[4]

In other words, the Church Fathers were just as confused over the doctrine of the Rapture, the Tribulation, and the Second Coming of Christ as we are today, but they taught foundational truths of "the imminent return of Christ" for the Church, and the "meeting in the air" with Christ and His Church. It's too bad they didn't "rightly divide the word of truth" better because they may have seen the unique "mystery" concerning Paul far better than they did. The Church Fathers obviously retreated to the earthly ministry of Jesus Christ for their "marching orders," rather than His heavenly ministry to Paul for the Body of Christ.

Just as the problem today is a failure to "rightly divide the word of truth," so it was with the early Church Fathers. We *now* have documentation, as I have quoted, which proves some Church Fathers believed the Church would be "caught up, to meet the Lord in the air," before the Tribulation. Nearly 2000 years of traditions have buried the truth Paul revealed in his letters to the Corinthians and Thessalonians, and just because someone revived such truths, this doesn't mean such doctrines weren't already revealed millennia before by the Apostle Paul himself. Paul taught the "dispensation of the grace of God" long before J.N. Darby and others developed it

---

[4] Ibid.

into a theology to differentiate the prophetic promises of God to Israel, and the "revelation of the mystery" God gave to Paul.

The confusion over eschatology has been exacerbated by the "traditions of men," which has resulted from two specific failures: (1) an ignorance in understanding the "revelation of the mystery" given to Paul, and (2) an unwillingness to obey 2 Timothy 2:15, because it might undermine their traditions regarding only one resurrection with the judgment of all to follow. By allegorizing (spiritualizing) the prophecies and promises of God to Israel, rather than accepting the clear and literal fulfillment of them, theologians can infer whatever subjective meaning they choose to confirm their own doctrines. Paul warned Timothy of this.

> *I charge thee therefore before God, and the Lord Jesus Christ, who shall judge the quick and the dead at his appearing and his kingdom; 2 Preach the word; be instant in season, out of season; reprove, rebuke, exhort with all long suffering and doctrine. 3 <u>For the time will come when they will not endure sound doctrine; but after their own lusts shall they heap to themselves teachers, having itching ears; 4 And they shall turn away their ears from the truth, and shall be turned unto fables.</u> 2 Timothy 4:1-4*

> *10 And the brethren immediately sent away Paul and Silas by night unto <u>Berea</u>: who*

coming thither went into the synagogue of the Jews. ¹¹ <u>These were more noble than those in Thessalonica, in that they received the word with all readiness of mind, and searched the scriptures daily, whether those things were so</u>.
Acts 17:10-11

Are you a good Berean? Do you go to the Scriptures to see whether your doctrine aligns with the word of God? Have you obeyed 2 Timothy 2:15? Do you strive, as Paul did, "to make all men see what is the fellowship of the mystery," as he wrote to the Ephesians (Eph. 3:9)? Do you tell people to "be ye reconciled to God" through the blood of Christ and His resurrection, or do you command people to "repent and be baptized for the remission of sins"? Christ taught both doctrines, by are you explaining to people the importance of how to "cut straight" what Christ taught to national Israel ("the lost sheep of the house of Israel"), and what He taught to Paul for the Body of Christ (consisting of individual Jews and Gentiles saved "by grace, through faith, apart from works")?

What about privately interpreting the word of God? Is this encouraged?

¹⁵ Moreover I will endeavour that ye may be able after my decease to have these things always in remembrance. ¹⁶ For we have not followed cunningly devised fables, when we made known unto you the power and coming of our Lord Jesus Christ, but were

eyewitnesses of his majesty. [17] For he received from God the Father honour and glory, when there came such a voice to him from the excellent glory, This is my beloved Son, in whom I am well pleased. [18] And this voice which came from heaven we heard, when we were with him in the holy mount. [19] We have also a more sure word of prophecy; whereunto ye do well that ye take heed, as unto a light that shineth in a dark place, until the day dawn, and the day star arise in your hearts: [20] Knowing this first, that no prophecy of the scripture is of any private interpretation. [21] For the prophecy came not in old time by the will of man: but holy men of God spake as they were moved by the Holy Ghost.
2 Peter 1:15-21 (Peter speaking of his coming departure in death)

Paul also wrote the following to Timothy:

[15] And that from a child thou hast known the holy scriptures, which are able to make thee wise unto salvation through faith which is in Christ Jesus. [16] All scripture is given by inspiration of God, and is profitable for doctrine, for reproof, for correction, for instruction in righteousness: [17] That the man of God may be perfect, thoroughly furnished unto all good works. 2 Timothy 3:15-17

"Our Gathering Together unto Him"
Please carefully note the following passage:

> *2 Now we beseech you, brethren, <u>by the coming of our Lord Jesus Christ, and by our gathering together unto him,</u> 2 That ye <u>be not soon shaken in mind, or be troubled,</u> neither by spirit, nor by word, nor by letter as from us, <u>as that the day of Christ is at hand.</u> 3 Let no man deceive you by any means: <u>for that day shall not come, except there come a falling away first, and that man of sin be revealed, the son of perdition;</u> 4 Who opposeth and exalteth himself above all that is called God, or that is worshipped; so that he as God sitteth in the temple of God, shewing himself that he is God.*
> *2 Thessalonians 2:1-4*

What many refuse to acknowledge is how The Rapture is also outlined in the content of the first three verses of this passage. First, let us remember that these verses were written about two decades *after* Jesus spoke about the end times in Matthew 24 and 25 (involving the Tribulation and Second Coming). After all, Paul specifically mentioned in this passage: "by the coming of our Lord Jesus Christ, and our gathering together unto Him." If we recall from I Thessalonians 4:13-18, we are to "comfort one another with these words," and Paul reiterates this in 2 Thessalonians 2:2 when he informed them not to be "…soon shaken in mind, or be troubled…" over the "day of Christ." Paul did not warn the

Body of Christ of the coming Tribulation because we are "saved from wrath" through Christ Jesus.

The Rapture is something new because it is associated with the Body of Christ ("the one new man"), and the Rapture is related to "our heavenly citizenship," not the Messianic Kingdom associated with Israel. If we do not "rightly divide the word of truth" on this doctrine concerning the Church, and its heavenly citizenship, then we will mix what Christ taught and confirmed about the end time prophecies to Israel, and what Christ taught Paul concerning the mystery, detailing the gathering of believers prior to the "day of the Lord" and the revelation of the "son of perdition" (Antichrist). How can Paul dare to say we should "comfort one another with these words" if we are going to experience the Tribulation, which includes the time of God's wrath and judgment being poured out upon the world?

For those who still argue that the word "rapture" does not occur in the Scriptures, we must remember not to allow our arrogance in the English-speaking world to dominate our complete understanding of God's word, especially since the New Testament was written in Greek. The word *harpazo* is Greek for "caught up" or "caught away suddenly." "Rapture" is the word we use for this. Christ never mentioned (during His earthly ministry to the "lost sheep of the house of Israel") any gathering of believers to "meet the Lord in the air," nor did He proclaim a heavenly citizenship prior to the "revelation of the mystery," which was reserved for "our glory" (I Cor. 2:7). Again, the Greek word for "catching away" or "caught up" is *harpazo*, and this is the word used in the Bible from I Thessalonians 4:17.

*17 Then we which are alive and remain shall
be <u>caught up</u> together with them in the clouds,
to meet the Lord in the air: and so shall we
ever be with the Lord. I Thessalonians 4:17*

At the Second Coming, Jesus will set foot on Earth from where He ascended (the Mount of Olives). Again, this is explained in Zechariah 14:1-4 and Acts 1:11. For those who teach that the Body of Christ will be "caught up," only to return immediately with Christ, this clearly shows their lack of understanding of 2 Timothy 2:15, Romans 5:8-10, and I Thessalonians 5:9-11.

Jesus will return to the Mount of Olives, which means He will set foot on Earth; however, Paul declared *the mystery* concerning a time when believers will "meet the Lord in the air," and this "gathering together" of believers, who are "caught up" to Heaven, was never taught in any prophecy, nor was it revealed by Christ while He was on Earth preaching to Israel "the kingdom of heaven is at hand" (Matt. 4:17). This is the Kingdom that God promised to Israel through Abraham and his seed, and it will be fulfilled in the future—after "the fulness of the Gentiles be come in" (Rom. 11:25). After all, while Israel is experiencing "blindness in part," God is currently focused upon His eternal purpose for the Church (for Heaven), which is predominantly made up of Gentiles. God will, however, remove this blindness from Israel (Zech. 1:3; Hos. 6:1-3; Jer. 24:6-7; 32:37-42; Ezek. 36:24-30). James and John repeat this promise.

⁵ Hearken, my beloved brethren, Hath not
God chosen the poor of this world rich in faith,
and heirs of the kingdom <u>which he hath</u>
<u>promised to them that love him?</u>
James 2:5

And I saw a new heaven and a new earth:
for the first heaven and the first earth were
passed away; and there was no more sea.
² And I John saw the holy city, <u>new Jerusalem,</u>
<u>coming down from God out of heaven,</u>
prepared as a bride adorned for her husband.
Revelation 21:1-2

This is the Kingdom that Jesus said He would go to prepare a place for them (the household of Israel (John 14)). We must understand that the Kingdom, where Christ will reign on the Throne of David in Jerusalem, was promised exclusively to Israel. We should never forget that the Old and New covenant promises were made specifically with the "house of Israel." The "Old covenant" was made with Israel in Exodus 19, and the "New Covenant" (Jeremiah 31) was officially introduced by Jesus in Matthew 26:28 with the words, "This is the new testament in my blood." Paul's gospel is based upon the shed blood of this New Covenant, along with His resurrection. This is why he was declared to be "an able minister of the new testament" in 2 Corinthians 3:6). Peter taught "repent and be baptized for the remission of sins," which was not based doctrinally upon "the preaching of the cross."

Believers today, from the time Paul preached the gospel of the grace of God, have been baptized *by* one Spirit into one body (whether Jew or Gentile), and our citizenship is in Heaven. Remember, Paul stated, "we are seated in heavenly places in Christ" (Eph. 2:6). It is the Rapture that removes the Body of Christ from the world, which ends the "dispensation of the grace of God." That is when the gospel of the kingdom will once again be preached to the "lost sheep of the house of Israel," and the result will bring blessings to the nations, just as prophecy had stated.

> *14 And this <u>gospel of the kingdom shall be preached in all the world</u> for a witness unto all nations; and then shall the end come.*
> *Matthew 24:14*

The Rapture is distinct to Paul's letters for the Body of Christ, specifically in I and II Thessalonians, I Corinthians 15:51; Titus 2:13-15; Romans 13:11-14; and Philippians 1:6-10. Jesus, during His earthly ministry, *did not* reveal anything about the Rapture, so it is assumed that such a doctrine is not biblical, but if you accept Galatians 1:11-12 as truth (Paul taught "by revelation of Jesus Christ"), then you can understand why Paul declared in I Thessalonians 4:15 "by the word of the Lord" about the Church being "caught up, to meet the Lord in the air." Jesus did teach about the Rapture, but He didn't do it under the gospel of the kingdom (expecting an earthly kingdom), but rather He taught it to Paul under "the revelation of the mystery, which was kept secret since the world began." This was revealed *after* Israel fell into spiritual blindness in Acts 7. Again, the Rapture wasn't revealed until some 20-25 years after the Olivet Discourse of Matthew 24, and that generation, to whom Jesus was addressing in Matthew 24, did not see most of the signs that Jesus told them about in the "last days" because God interrupted His prophetic plans concerning the Kingdom when He turned to the Gentiles with the gospel of the grace of God. God knew Israel would reject Christ and the Kingdom, but He also knew "before the world began," that the Body of Christ would be introduced to the world, which has a heavenly citizenship.

The General Epistles and the End Times

In the so-called "General Epistles," many aren't sure to whom the letters of James, Peter, John, and Jude were written, even though those writers address the "twelve tribes scattered abroad." The Body of Christ is "one body," not twelve tribes. Paul was the only "apostle to the Gentiles," and he was given the "gospel of the uncircumcision," whereas Peter (and the other apostles) were to continue their "gospel of the circumcision" to those "scattered abroad." Again, this is taught in Galatians.

> *⁷ But contrariwise, when they saw that the*
> *gospel of the uncircumcision was committed*
> *unto me, as the gospel of the circumcision was*
> *unto Peter; ⁸ (For he that wrought effectually*
> *in Peter to the apostleship of the circumcision,*
> *the same was mighty in me toward the*
> *Gentiles:) ⁹ And when James, Cephas, and*

*John, who seemed to be pillars, perceived the
grace that was given unto me, they gave to me
and Barnabas the right hands of fellowship;
that we should go unto the heathen, and they
unto the circumcision. Galatians 2:7-9*

Paul also declared that he would not tread on another man's ministry in the following verses:

*20 Yea, so have I strived to preach the gospel,
not where Christ was named, lest I should
build upon another man's foundation: 21 But as
it is written, To whom he was not spoken of,
they shall see: and they that have not heard
shall understand. Romans 15:20*

However, Peter stated the following to the Jews scattered abroad in his epistle:

*13 Nevertheless we, according to his promise,
<u>look for new heavens and a new earth, wherein
dwelleth righteousness</u>. 14 Wherefore, beloved,
<u>seeing that ye look for such things</u>, be diligent
that ye may be found of him in peace, without
spot, and blameless. 15 And account that the
longsuffering of our Lord is salvation; <u>even as
our beloved brother Paul also according to the
wisdom given unto him hath written unto you;</u>
16 As also in all his epistles, speaking in them
of these things; in which are some things hard*

to be understood, which they that are
unlearned and unstable wrest, as they do also
the other scriptures, unto their own
destruction. 2 Peter 3:13-16

The "General Epistles" continued to address those Jews who had been saved *already* under the gospel of the kingdom," and they were still anticipating the "new heavens and the new earth," not the "meeting the Lord in the air," which Paul preached as part of the gospel of the grace of God. Again, James, Peter, John, (and Jude) continued to preach to the "circumcision," as they agreed to do, and this does not mean they insisted on the Messianic Jews becoming members of the Body of Christ, even though they learned from Paul that Jesus died and rose again as full payment for their sins. Remember, they were already saved, so why would they need to be saved again under Paul's ministry? In fact, James still insisted (to "the twelve tribes scattered abroad" (James 1:1)) that a man was "justified by works, and not by faith alone" (James 2:24), and John declared it was necessary for a man to "confess your sins" to be forgiven, along with "keep the commandments" (I John 1:8-9; 2:1-5; 3:23-24). Today, however, the only means by which a person can be saved is through faith in the shed blood and resurrection of Jesus Christ (under Paul's ministry). There are glorious truths in the "General Epistles"; however, we must not "frustrate grace" when applying those teachings written specifically to the "scattered tribes of Israel." Many passages in the Bible were certainly written for our understanding, but that does not mean they were written for our obedience. When the General

Epistles speak of the "last days," they are almost always in reference to the "signs and wonders" to occur at the Tribulation and Second Coming of Jesus Christ.

The "Departure"

Let us now examine more closely the importance of 2 Thessalonians 2 for a moment, especially in the context of "the departure." Remember, the Thessalonians feared they had missed this resurrection of the Church, and Paul wrote to them to bring comfort and assurance that it had not yet occurred.

Now we beseech you, brethren, by the coming of our Lord Jesus Christ, and by our gathering together unto him, 2 That ye be not soon shaken in mind, or be troubled, neither by spirit, nor by word, nor by letter as from us, as that the day of Christ is at hand. 3 Let no man deceive you by any means: for that day shall not come, except there come a falling away first, and that man of sin be revealed, the son of perdition; 4 Who opposeth and exalteth himself above all that is called God, or that is worshipped; so that he as God sitteth in the temple of God, shewing himself that he is God. 5 Remember ye not, that, when I was yet with you, I told you these things? 6 And now ye know what withholdeth that he might be revealed in his time. 7 For the mystery of iniquity doth already work: only he who now

letteth will let, <u>until he be taken out of the way</u>.
⁸ <u>And then shall that Wicked be revealed,</u>
whom the Lord shall consume with the spirit of
his mouth, <u>and shall destroy with the</u>
<u>brightness of his coming</u>: ⁹ Even him, whose
coming is after the working of Satan with all
power and <u>signs and lying wonders</u>, ¹⁰ And
with all deceivableness of unrighteousness <u>in</u>
<u>them that perish; because they received not the</u>
<u>love of the truth, that they might be saved</u>.
2 Thessalonians 2:1-10

Even though the King James Version uses the words "falling away" in 2 Thessalonians 2:3, which is the Greek translation from *hee apostasia* (a leaving from a previous standing or to depart), it does not lend itself to meaning "rebellion from the faith" as it is often taught. From Strong's Concordance, the noun *apostasia* (which comes from the root verb *aphistemi*) means "leave or depart." Prior to the King James Version, however, numerous translations used the word "departure," not "falling away." The following is from the 1599 Geneva Bible:

¹ Now [a]we beseech you, brethren, by the
coming of our Lord Jesus Christ, and by
our [b]assembling unto him, ² [c]That ye be not
suddenly moved from your mind, nor troubled
neither by [d]spirit, nor by [e]word, nor
by [f]letter, as it were from us, as though the
day of Christ were at hand. ³ Let no man

deceive you by any means: [g]for that day shall
not come, <u>except there come a departing first</u>,
and that [h]that man of sin be
disclosed, even the son of perdition.
2 Thessalonians 2:1-3

Again, *hee apostasia* (noun for "the departure") comes from the root verb *aphistemi*, which means "to depart." When "depart" is used in the verb form to mean "from the faith," it specifically   states that intended purpose, which occurs in only three instances in the New Testament: "from the faith" (I Tim. 4:1), "from the living God" (Heb. 3:12), and "for a while believed" (Luke 8:13). In all three references, it means "depart from what is to be believed." In all 15 occurrences of *aphistemi*, it means to "depart" from something.

Here are the two passages in the New Testament, which use *apostasia* (simply meaning "departure"):

³ Let no man deceive you by any means: for
that day shall not come, except there come <u>a</u>
<u>falling away first</u>, and that man of sin be
revealed, the son of perdition;
2 Thessalonians 2:3

²¹ And they are informed of thee, <u>that thou</u>
<u>teachest all the Jews which are among the</u>
<u>Gentiles to forsake Moses</u>, saying that they
ought not to circumcise their children, neither
to walk after the customs. Acts 21:21

In the 2 Thessalonians 2 passage, we must determine the context being used as to what the King James Version refers to as the "falling away." If it means rebellion against the faith, as some teach, then the context on Acts 21:21 doesn't make much sense, considering both passages contain the exact same word: *apostasia*. So, 2 Thessalonians 2:3 should state, "except there come 'the departure' first."

In Acts 21, after Paul comes to James in Jerusalem, he explained to James what God was accomplishing through "his ministry among the Gentiles." They praised the Lord, but they also questioned Paul about his message to the Jews (among the Gentiles) about "forsaking Moses." If *apostasia* means "falling away from the faith" or "a rebellion," this would seem odd that Paul somehow told the Jews to "rebel" against Moses rather than simply "depart" from the Law. Paul would not encourage the Jews to "rebel" against Moses, but he did teach Jews and Gentiles in the Body of Christ that they could be "justified from all things, from which they could not be justified by the Law od Moses" (Acts 13:38-39).

In the passage from 2 Thessalonians 2, we must refer to the context of the first two verses to make sense of the third. After Paul wrote his first letter to the Thessalonians, describing how believers will be "caught up to meet the Lord in the air," we see this same mention in 2 Thessalonians 2:1 where Paul stated, "our gathering together unto him." The Greek word *harpazo* simply means to "snatch away" or "rapture" (in English/Latin). When someone is "snatched away," it also means that person has had a "sudden departure." Paul also knew that someday, in the "dispensation of the fulness of times," God was going to gather "all things together, both which are in Heaven and which are on Earth, even in Him" (Eph. 1:10). Either context does not have a negative connotation to it because Paul told them in 2 Thessalonians 3:2 not to "be troubled."

After viewing the following verses, perhaps you can distinguish the differences and see why Paul told believers to "not be troubled" about the "end times." The "day of (Jesus) Christ" is *not* the same as the "day of the Lord," which is associated with the Tribulation.

7 So that ye come behind in no gift; <u>waiting for the coming of our Lord Jesus Christ</u>: 8 Who shall also <u>confirm you unto the end</u>, that <u>ye may be blameless</u> in the <u>day of our Lord Jesus Christ.</u> 9 God is faithful, by whom ye were called unto the fellowship of his Son Jesus Christ our Lord. I Corinthians 1:7-9

4 In the name of our Lord Jesus Christ, <u>when ye are gathered together</u>, and my spirit, with the power of our Lord Jesus Christ, 5 To deliver such an one unto Satan for the destruction of the flesh, <u>that the spirit may be saved in the day of the Lord Jesus</u>. I Corinthians 5:4-5

3 I thank my God upon every remembrance of you, 4 Always in every prayer of mine for you all making request with joy, 5 <u>For your fellowship in the gospel from the first day until</u>

now; 6 Being confident of this very thing, that he which hath begun a good work in you will perform it until the day of Jesus Christ:
Philippians 1:3-6

9 And this I pray, that your love may abound yet more and more in knowledge and in all judgment; 10 That ye may approve things that are excellent; that ye may be sincere and without offence till the day of Christ.
Philippians 1:9-10

13 For it is God which worketh in you both to will and to do of his good pleasure. 14 Do all things without murmurings and disputings: 15 That ye may be blameless and harmless, the sons of God, without rebuke, in the midst of a crooked and perverse nation, among whom ye shine as lights in the world; 16 Holding forth the word of life; that I may rejoice in the day of Christ, that I have not run in vain, neither laboured in vain. Philippians 2:13-16

6 For I am now ready to be offered, and the time of my departure is at hand. 7 I have fought a good fight, I have finished my course, I have kept the faith: 8 Henceforth there is laid up for me a crown of righteousness, which the Lord, the righteous judge, shall give me at that day:

and not to me only, but unto all them also that
love his appearing. 2 Timothy 4:6-8

Now, let us look once more at 2 Thessalonians 2:1-2:

Now we beseech you, brethren, by the
coming of our Lord Jesus Christ, and by our
gathering together unto him. 2 That ye be not
soon shaken in mind, or be troubled, neither
by spirit, nor by word, nor by letter as from us,
as that the day of Christ is at hand.
2 Thessalonians 2:1-2

The "day of Christ" (or "that day") is in reference to the Rapture and the Judgment Seat of Christ to follow, not the wrath of God during the Tribulation.

The "day of the Lord," however, is referenced in the following passages, which are worth exploring again:

Behold, the day of the LORD cometh, and
thy spoil shall be divided in the midst of thee.
2 For I will gather all nations against
Jerusalem to battle; and the city shall be
taken, and the houses rifled, and the women
ravished; and half of the city shall go forth
into captivity, and the residue of the people
shall not be cut off from the city. 3 Then shall
the LORD go forth, and fight against those
nations, as when he fought in the day of battle.

4 <u>And his feet shall stand in that day upon the mount of Olives</u>... Zechariah 14:1-4

30 <u>And I will shew wonders in the heavens and in the earth, blood, and fire, and pillars of smoke. 31 The sun shall be turned into darkness, and the moon into blood, before the great and terrible day of the Lord come.</u>
Joel 2:30-31

9 The Lord is not slack concerning his promise, as some men count slackness; but is longsuffering to us-ward, not willing that any should perish, but that all should come to repentance. 10 <u>But the day of the Lord will come as a thief in the night; in the which the heavens shall pass away with a great noise, and the elements shall melt with fervent heat, the earth also and the works that are therein shall be burned up.</u> 2 Peter 3:9-10

5 They come from a far country, from the end of heaven, even the Lord, <u>and the weapons of his indignation, to destroy the whole land.</u> 6 Howl ye; for the <u>day of the Lord is at hand; it shall come as a destruction from the Almighty</u>...9 Behold, <u>the day of the Lord cometh, cruel both with wrath and fierce anger,</u> to lay the land desolate: and he shall destroy the sinners thereof out of it.

*10 For the stars of heaven and the
constellations thereof shall not give their light:
the sun shall be darkened in his going forth,
and the moon shall not cause her light to
shine. 11 <u>And I will punish the world for their
evil, and the wicked for their iniquity; and I
will cause the arrogancy of the proud to cease,
and will lay low the haughtiness of the
terrible.</u> Isaiah 13:5-6 and 9-11*

*But of the times and the seasons, brethren,
<u>ye have no need that I write unto you</u>. 2 For
yourselves know perfectly <u>that the day of the
Lord so cometh as a thief in the night</u>. 3 For
when they shall say, Peace and safety; <u>then
sudden destruction cometh upon them</u>, as
travail upon a woman with child; and they
shall not escape. I Thessalonians 5:1-3*

It is quite apparent how there is a great contrast between
the "day of Christ," which is anticipated, but occurs suddenly,
and the "day of the Lord," which was prophesied, but is
unexpected ("as a thief in the night"). The "day of Christ" is
for believers who will "depart" from this world (saved from
wrath through Him), and then we will all appear before the
Judgement Seat of Christ (I Cor. 3:1-15). On the other hand,
the "day of the Lord" will include the times of God's wrath
(the Tribulation), which will culminate at the coming of the
Lord to set foot on the Mount of Olives at the Second

Coming. We are to look forward to our "gathering together unto the Lord" because this is our "blessed hope."

We should cautiously remember that the Body of Christ is to appear before the Judgment Seat of Christ, and this is why Paul reminded us that we must "work out our salvation" not "work for it."

> *9 Wherefore God also hath highly exalted him, and given him a name which is above every name: 10 That at the name of Jesus every knee should bow, of things in heaven, and things in earth, and things under the earth; 11 And that every tongue should confess that Jesus Christ is Lord, to the glory of God the Father. 12 Wherefore, my beloved, as ye have always obeyed, not as in my presence only, but now much more in my absence, <u>work out your own salvation with fear and trembling. 13 For it is God which worketh in you both to will and to do of his good pleasure.</u> Philippians 2:9-13*

You can't "work out" something you don't already possess.

> *I beseech you therefore, brethren, by the mercies of God, that ye present your bodies a living sacrifice, holy, acceptable unto God, <u>which is your reasonable service</u>. 2 And be not conformed to this world: but be ye transformed by the renewing of your mind,*

that ye may prove what is that good, and
acceptable, and perfect, will of God.
Romans 12:1-2

8 For by grace are ye saved through faith;
and that not of yourselves: it is the gift of God:
9 Not of works, lest any man should boast.
10 For we are his workmanship, created in
Christ Jesus unto good works, which God hath
before ordained that we should walk in them.
Ephesians 2:8-10

A Final Look at 2 Thessalonians 2
It is vital to understand that the Greek word *apostasia* (departure) was the word found in the translations written prior to the King James Version.

3 Let no man deceive you by any means: for
that day shall not come, except there come a
falling away [hee apostasia: the departure]
first, and that man of sin be revealed,
the son of perdition;
2 Thessalonians 2:3 (brackets by author)

The (*hee*) departure (*apostasia*) mentions nothing about "a falling away *from the faith*," although that has been ongoing since Paul declared "the spirit of iniquity doth already work" (2 Thes. 2:7) some 2000 years ago. We know the Holy Spirit is currently working within the Body of Christ (I Cor. 6:19-20), but when the Body is raptured, the restraining force of the Spirit (within the Church) will not hold back the revelation of the Anti-Christ to the world, and the spirit of lawlessness that has been *somewhat* suppressed by the presence of the Church in this world. Times are certainly changing, though.

For half of the Tribulation, this false Christ will "play along," and many Israelites will be fooled into thinking he is the Messiah; however, during the last half of the Tribulation (the Great Tribulation), this false Christ will set himself up in the temple and declare himself to be God, which will usher in the so-called Great Tribulation. The Tribulation begins with a peace treaty signed in the Middle East between Israel and its neighbors (Dan. 9:27), and it will certainly take a dynamic leader to do this. Such a framework for this treaty is already in place. For now, as long as the Body of Christ is here, God's wrath is held off, and when the Body is "caught up," we will then see God's continuation of the prophetic fulfillments to Israel. For now, our "departure," and this "man of sin" is only anticipated as imminent events to come.

In Paul's second letter to Timothy, he does describe how the "last days" of this "dispensation of the grace of God" will appear before the Rapture of the Church.

This know also, that in the last days
perilous times shall come. 2 For men shall be
lovers of their own selves, covetous, boasters,
proud, blasphemers, disobedient to parents,
unthankful, unholy, 3 Without natural affection,
trucebreakers, false accusers, incontinent,
fierce, despisers of those that are good,

*⁴ Traitors, heady, highminded, lovers of
pleasures more than lovers of God; ⁵ Having a
form of godliness, but denying the power
thereof: from such turn away.
2 Timothy 3:1-5*

Five minutes on social media will confirm that we are certainly in the "last days" of this dispensation. Please trust in the death, burial, and resurrection of Jesus Christ for your personal salvation, and you will be saved from the wrath to come.

Our identity crisis within our faith has left many people scrambling to figure out whether there is a Rapture, and if so, will we "depart" before, during, or after the Tribulation? Most believers today confuse the "appearing of the Lord" at the Second Coming with the Rapture, and this shows their confusion between *prophecy* and *mystery*. When we ignore "the mystery" revealed to the Apostle Paul, we will never have a clear view on these "end time" events.

The Mystery, the Body of Christ, the Rapture, the Judgment Seat of Christ, our citizenship in Heaven, and the Church's specific calling to salvation apart from Israel and the Law is only found within Paul's epistles to and for Gentiles today. Even though Abraham was a Gentile saved "apart from the Law," this does not mean he knew anything about "the revelation of the mystery" given to Paul, nor did he know about faith alone in the death and resurrection of Jesus Christ for salvation. Abraham knew about the inheritance of land to his seed, but he didn't know about the eventual Seed that would form the "one new man," the Body of Christ. This is God's revelation concerning His eternal purpose for Heaven, not the Earth (Eph. 1:10; Phil. 3:20). Our identity crisis has left many wondering how and where the Church fits into these prophetic events, but the only way to determine this is when we "rightly divide the word of truth," which is "the gospel of your salvation" through the "revelation of the mystery, kept secret since the world began." On the other hand, what was foretold by "the mouth of His holy prophets" was known "since the world began."

Leading experts in eschatological studies still mix the Rapture into prophetic events concerning Israel, and they still can't clearly identify the Church today as either the Body of Christ or the Bride of Christ—often making them synonymous. If we are the Bride of Christ (often referred to as "spiritual Israel"), then we will certainly go through the Tribulation. The Body of Christ, however, is promised escape from it. We need to know the differences between the two.

I know the "end times" events outlined in the Scriptures can be confusing, but this is due to the Church refusing to "rightly dividing the word of truth," along with embracing the nonsensical traditions held by those who continue to ignore the distinct calling of the Apostle Paul in Acts 9. I hope, perhaps, you can now understand how mixing the gospel of the grace of God (under Paul), and the prophetic events concerning Israel (which are yet future), has done nothing to clarify our identity as the Body of Christ in these dark and evil days. I hope you can understand that we have no need to be "troubled" concerning the "day of the Lord," but rather, we are to look forward to that "day of Christ" when we will see Him face to face (I Cor. 13:8-13). Simply place your faith in the shed blood of Jesus Christ for the remission of *your* sins, and believe God raised Him from the dead so you could become "the righteousness of God in Him" (Rom. 4:25; 2 Cor. 5:21), and you shall be saved.

CHAPTER 13

Final "Thots"

12 For we wrestle not against flesh and blood, but against principalities, against powers, against the rulers of the darkness of this world, against spiritual wickedness in high places. 13 Wherefore take unto you the whole armour of God, that ye may be able to withstand in the evil day, and having done all, to stand. 14 Stand therefore, having your loins girt about with truth, and having on the breastplate of righteousness; 15 And your feet shod with the preparation of the gospel of peace; 16 Above all, taking the shield of faith, wherewith ye shall be able to quench all the fiery darts of the wicked. 17 And take the helmet of salvation, and the sword of the Spirit, which is the word of God:
Ephesians 6:12-17

Put on the Full Armor of God

I have often said, "One of the greatest destroyers of truth are those who marginalize people who speak it." It is easy for someone to read this book and simply marginalize me as "hyper dispensationalist," thinking I have "gone too deeply" into the interpretation of the Scripture regarding Paul and the "revelation of the mystery." This usually comes from the mouths of those who see no distinctions between what (and why) Jesus Christ taught the twelve apostles and what He taught to Paul.

I also believe I have presented ample evidence for why we have an identity crisis within our faith, and why we should "rightly divide the word of truth." If we are all one Church, one people, and one gospel throughout the entire 66 books of the Bible, then it doesn't seem wise for Paul to tell Timothy (and ultimately us) to "cut straight" what was intended for "the lost sheep of the house of Israel," and what was intended for "the Body of Christ." I maintain that Paul's gospel brings unity, while failing to "rightly divide" only brings chaos to the Church. Failing to obey 2 Timothy 2:15 is the root cause for why we have thousands of denominations around the world, and an identity crisis to match the confusion.

Catholics would call me a confused Protestant, but many Protestants don't really identity with me either, especially with their own systematic, theological ambitions. I do not classify myself with any denomination; I simply identify myself as a member of the Body of Christ, which is not a denomination at all. It consists of many people from various denominations, but in Heaven, there will be no distinctions in such a manner as this.

Back to the Beginning for a Moment

My journey started over forty years ago when I first heard about "the preaching of Jesus Christ, according to the revelation of the mystery, which was kept secret since the world began." Since Paul calls it "my gospel," and he wasn't saved until Acts 9, I began to question what was unique about his gospel message, and why it differed from that of the Twelve. When I also heard how we must "rightly divide the word of truth," again, I started to question the importance of that verse from 2 Timothy 2:15, and I do my best to always consider the advice of Miles Coverdale, a translator of the English Bible. It certainly does help to consider "of whom and to whom" a passage is written, "with what words" and "at what time" it was written. It is also important to "consider what goes before and what follows after" those words in the Bible. I also understand that not everything in the Bible was written to or about me as a Gentile, but I do realize that everything in the Bible is for my edification and growth. We must also live in such a way that people will see Jesus Christ in and through us. Remember that we might be the only Bible some people will ever attempt to read.

I grew up mainly under "Covenant Theology," which is the belief that God has always had "one people," and He operates through *inferred* covenants such as the Covenant of Works, Redemption, and Grace. After *four decades* of studying, I have not found these "covenants" in the Bible. What I *have* found is "the dispensation of the grace of God," but unlike a

Covenant theologian, I do not find a Covenant of Grace, especially from "the apostle to the Gentiles (Paul)." Before Paul's conversion in Acts 9, there wasn't even the "gospel of the grace of God." If Covenant Theology were correct, then God waited over 1500 years before He revealed it, so what did that mean for the believers prior to its invention in the Seventeenth Century? We do have "the dispensation of the grace of God," dating to the time of the Apostle Paul.

Before understanding "the revelation of the mystery," and the need for it, I also found myself struggling to obey God unless I manipulated my way through passages that didn't quite congeal with "rightly dividing" the "gospel of my salvation." I had to often "explain away" the literal meaning of numerous passages from the Bible just to make them fit what I was being taught. I truly believed that if I followed the practices of the churches that I attended, I would find greater favor with God. I didn't realize what 2 Timothy 2:15 stated clearly to me as a believer:

> *15 Study to shew thyself approved unto God, a*
> *workman that needeth not to be ashamed,*
> *rightly dividing the word of truth.*

After hundreds of books and other reference materials over the years, and thousands of hours of studying, I've found numerous answers to lingering questions that no one else would answer without "spiritualizing" nearly every passage that I was questioning. For example, before I heard about 2 Timothy 2:15, I would ask whether I needed to be water baptized, and not one believer or pastor ever mentioned

Ephesians 4:5 (the "one baptism"). I would get a variety of answers and opinions about why I *should* be water baptized, and not a single answer was biblical to me as a Gentile in the Body of Christ. I always assumed that what Jesus taught during His earthly ministry in "the gospels" was for my obedience, but then I couldn't quite figure out the Sermon on the Mount in the context of what Paul was teaching in his letters. "Rightly dividing the word of truth" helped me realize the differences, and why they occurred. Jesus taught the Twelve, and He taught Paul, so I had to "rightly divide" so I could correctly apply what He taught to me.

Like many who also understand the need for the revelation of the "dispensation of the grace of God," I can't unsee what I have learned over the decades, and quite frankly, I don't want to because it has transformed my entire life, along with my understanding of God's word. Honestly, the Bible makes more sense to me as I continue to "rightly divide the word of truth."

If we completely removed Paul and his epistles from the Bible, all we would know as Gentiles is salvation through Israel (becoming proselytes), and a destiny in the Kingdom promised to that nation. We would be under the so-called Great Commission, which means we would need to "repent and be baptized for the remission of sins," show our obedience to the commandments, and we would have to confess our sins to be declared forgiven (I John 1:8-9). In other words, our lives would be consumed with the instructions in the "Sermon on the Mount." We would know that Jesus died and rose again, but there would not be the message of salvation "by grace, through faith in the blood and resurrection, apart from works." That is not found in the so-called Great Commission. We would also expect to have the sign gifts, the likelihood of "enduring to the end," and the anticipation of "the day of the Lord." There would be no escape from entering into the Tribulation (if I were alive at that time as a Gentile), and there would never be a hope for a heavenly citizenship," only an earthly destiny. In essence, we would have never heard about "the Body of Christ." Most of Christianity today is nothing more than a combination of what Jesus taught during His earthly ministry, and what He revealed to Paul after Israel "blasphemed the Holy Spirit" in Acts 7. Acts 9 was a turning point in our faith, but it is often overlooked for the sake of our traditions, which often rob us of vital truths.

Key Takeaways

The confusion we have today is directly related to not "rightly dividing the word of truth, the gospel of our salvation" (2 Tim. 2:15; Eph. 1:13). This has led to so much confusion in our faith, and it has led to thousands of different denominations, causing an identity crisis we are not likely to solve until we all meet in Glory. Right now, it appears many pastors, priests, and congregations spend more time attempting to "please men, rather than God" (Gal. 1:10) with their traditions. It has come at a very high cost to the truth.

The Book of Acts should be "rightly divided" because of its transitional nature from God's focus on the restoration of the kingdom to Israel, and the eventual setting aside of those prophecies to introduce us to the Apostle Paul and the Body of Christ, which was "kept secret since the world began."

Acts begins with Israel anticipating the Messianic Kingdom, but it ended with Paul declaring that the gospel of the grace of God (Acts 20:24) had been "sent to the Gentiles." A failure to understand why this occurred has created part of our identity crisis.

Another key takeaway is understanding the two-fold purpose of God for both Heaven and Earth. We would have never known God's intended purpose for Heaven had it not been for the conversion of Paul and his call to preach "the revelation of the mystery" to a "new creature" never revealed in Scripture until after Acts 9. I believe Scripture is clear that God started the "dispensation of the grace of God" in Acts 9 with the conversion of Paul. As a result, the "one new man" (the Body of Christ) can anticipate "meeting the Lord in the air" where our current citizenship is located. We are now "ambassadors for Christ." God has a purpose for Earth, and He has a purpose for Heaven, and it is our responsibility for knowing the differences.

As far as the notion of the Body of Christ being either "spiritual Israel" or "the Bride of Christ," I presented many passages that refute why such a concept is not needed within Christianity. Regardless of the many theologians who insist these titles are warranted, we know that "rightly dividing the word of truth" greatly diminishes the traditions behind these imposed and inferred titles upon the Body of Christ.

As we still battle over water baptism, I have presented numerous reasons why water baptism has no place, even as a suggestion, in "the dispensation of the grace of God." The only baptism that should be recognized is the "one baptism" of Ephesians 4:5, and this is the spiritual baptism of I

Corinthians 12:13, which is done "by one Spirit." This baptism identifies us with the death, burial, and resurrection of Jesus Christ. Water baptism had its place and time, but the "one baptism" of Paul's "revelation of the mystery" is the only baptism God recognizes today for members of the Body of Christ.

Finally, we must "rightly divide the word of truth" concerning the "end times." As many believers struggle to figure out the differences between the prophetic end times, and the end times of the dispensation of the grace of God, they find themselves worried about the coming wrath of God. Paul is clear that the Body of Christ will "meet the Lord in the air" before that wrath is poured out on this Christ-rejecting world. As we watch our world slip into the "last days," we must do all that we can to "make all men see what is the fellowship of the mystery, which from the beginning of the word has been hid in God, who created all things through Christ Jesus" (Eph. 3:9).

My Closing Desire to My Loved Ones

One of my favorite passages is found in 2 Corinthians 5.

> *18 And all things are of God, who hath reconciled us to himself by Jesus Christ, and hath given to us the ministry of reconciliation; 19 To wit, that God was in Christ, reconciling the world unto himself, not imputing their trespasses unto them; and hath committed unto us the word of reconciliation. 20 Now then we are ambassadors for Christ, as though God*

did beseech you by us: we pray you in Christ's
stead, be ye reconciled to God. 21 For he hath
made him to be sin for us, who knew no sin;
that we might be made the righteousness of
God in him. 2 Corinthians 5:18-21

All of our sins—the whole world's—were placed (imputed) to Christ on the cross. We know that "the wages of sin is death, but the gift of God is eternal life through Jesus Christ" (Rom. 6:23), and because our sins were placed on Christ, He died for them so we can be justified (declared righteous) in the sight of God. God has reconciled Himself to the world, but it isn't until we are reconciled to God that we are justified. The only way to be reconciled is to believe the gospel. If you believe that your sins were paid for by Christ, and that God raised Him from the dead, then you are saved. Religion complicates this simple message, but God can still save people despite what religion teaches and insists upon for believers.

The identity you choose in this world determines your identity with Christ in eternity. You are either "in Adam" or you are "in Christ." When you believe the simplicity of the gospel, you are found to be "in Christ," and you are then granted a "citizenship in Heaven," where you are considered already to be "seated in heavenly places in Christ."

The whole armor of God is needed to combat the corruption of what Satan would desire for your life: to be at odds with God and to never know Him as your Savior. Nothing that this world could ever give you is eternal; only what God can give you "freely by His grace."

As I close this chapter, and this book, I would like to state one final thought to you as the reader. I titled this book *Christian Identity Crisis: Do We Have It All Wrong?* Now, only you can determine whether we have "missed the mark." Let us never assume the final authority of God's word is left to chance and private interpretation, whether it comes from clergy or a denomination. Sure, there are some very consistent doctrines among many churches and denominations, but we have created confusion by not following the advice of people like Miles (Myles) Coverdale. It does greatly help us to know "of whom and to whom" a passage is written, and we certainly must know the intent for why something was said to a particular audience at a specific time. In other words, we must "rightly divide the word of truth," regardless of what our denominations might dictate or enforce in their "statements of faith."

If we do have it all wrong, what must we do to correct it—before it is too late? Millions of souls are depending upon believers to finally "get it right." Unity is still possible when we "rightly divide the word of truth."

May God richly bless you as you strive to obey these words:

I therefore, the prisoner of the Lord,
beseech you that ye walk worthy of the
vocation wherewith ye are called, 2 With all
lowliness and meekness, with longsuffering,
forbearing one another in love;
3 Endeavouring to keep the unity of the Spirit
in the bond of peace. 4 There is one body, and

one Spirit, even as ye are called in one hope of your calling; [5] *One Lord, one faith, one baptism,* [6] *One God and Father of all, who is above all, and through all, and in you all.*
Ephesians 4:1-6

ABOUT THE AUTHOR

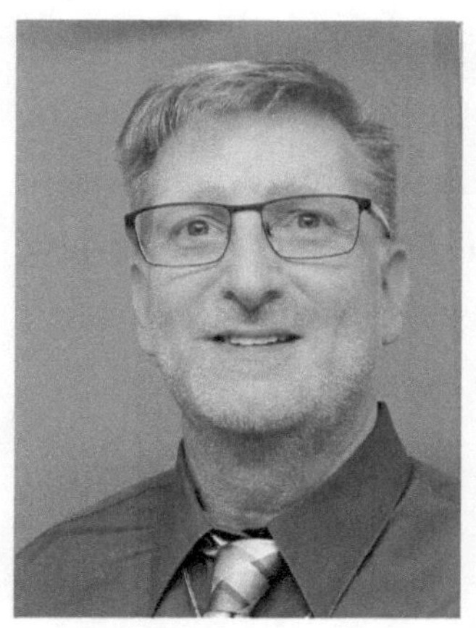 **J**. William Smith is a veteran educator, preacher, award-winning author and film producer, public speaker, screenwriter, as well as an occasional actor. He started his teaching career in 1990, and after earning numerous degrees and awards, he has spent many years as a middle school and junior high teacher, as well as having served several decades as an instructor with the Kent State and Youngstown State universities.

He began his biblical studies as a teenager, and for well over forty years, he has devoted his energy to "rightly dividing the word of truth" and understanding "the preaching of Jesus Christ, according to the revelation of the mystery, which was kept secret since the world began" (Romans 16:25). *Christian Identity Crisis: Do We Have It All Wrong?* has been decades in the making, but after the inspiration of many people, he was able to write a comprehensive guide to assist any believer willing to defend the truth of Scripture.

J. William Smith lives in the historic city of East Liverpool, Ohio, known as "The Point of Beginning" (starting point of the U.S. Public Land Survey System in 1785), and it was once known as "The Pottery Capital of the World." He has been married to his beautiful wife (Connie) since 1998, and they have one daughter (Madison). Of all the "hats" he wears, he knows his calling is to God and family above all things. He and Connie are very proud of their daughter, son-in-law, and several "adopted sons." His greatest desire is to serve Jesus Christ, and guiding others to do the same.